Everyday Law
for Seniors

The Everyday Law Series
Edited by Richard Delgado and Jean Stefancic
University of Pittsburgh Law School

Everyday Law for Individuals with Disabilities
Ruth Colker and Adam Milani (2005)

Everyday Law for Children
David Herring (2006)

Everyday Law for Gays and Lesbians
Anthony C. Infanti (2007)

Everyday Law for Consumers
Michael L. Rustad (2007)

Everyday Law for Latino/as
Steven W. Bender, Raquel Aldana,
Gilbert Paul Carrasco, and Joaquin G. Avila (2008)

Everyday Law for Immigrants
Victor C. Romero (2009)

Everyday Law for Seniors
Lawrence A. Frolik and Linda S. Whitton (2010)

Forthcoming
Everyday Law for Women
April Cherry

Everyday Law for Patients
Alan Scheflin and A. Steven Frankel

Everyday Law for Seniors

Lawrence A. Frolik
and Linda S. Whitton

Paradigm Publishers
Boulder • London

Copyright © 2010 Paradigm Publishers

Published in the United States by Paradigm Publishers, 3360 Mitchell Lane Suite E, Boulder, CO 80301 USA.

Paradigm Publishers is the trade name of Birkenkamp & Company, LLC, Dean Birkenkamp, President and Publisher.

Library of Congress Cataloging-in-Publication Data

Frolik, Lawrence A.
    Everyday law for seniors / Lawrence A. Frolik and Linda S. Whitton.
        p. cm. — (The everyday law series)
    Includes bibliographical references and index.
    ISBN 978-1-59451-701-3 (hardcover : alk. paper)
    ISBN 978-1-59451-702-0 (paperback : alk. paper)
    1. Older people—Legal status, laws, etc.—United States.   I. Whitton, Linda S.
II. Title.
    KF390.A4F7535 2009
    346.7301'3—dc22
                                    2009030848

Printed and bound in the United States of America on acid-free paper that meets the standards of the American National Standard for Permanence of Paper for Printed Library Materials.

Designed and Typeset by Mulberry Tree Enterprises.

14   13   12   11   10   2   3   4   5

Contents

Acknowledgments

I owe a special thanks to my research assistant, Amie E. Schaadt, Pitt Law 2007, for her efforts in the creation of this book. I also wish to thank the staff of the University of Pittsburgh School of Law Document Technology Center—Phyllis Gentille, Karen Knochel, Darleen Mocello, Barbara Salopek, and the director of the center, LuAnn Driscoll—for their assistance in the creation of the manuscript of this book.

—Lawrence A. Frolik

I owe a debt of gratitude to my husband, Dr. John Harris, for cheerfully serving as our critical senior reader. Many thanks also to my research assistant, Meghan Beeler Pridemore, Valpo Law 2008, for the helpful Internet resources she gathered to benefit our readers.

—Linda S. Whitton

1

Law and Seniors

Did You Know?

- Your average life expectancy at age 65 ranges between twenty and twenty-three additional years, depending on your gender.
- Twenty-five percent of those who reach age 65 will live to at least age 90.
- The percentage of the population over age 85 is continuing to increase.
- The likelihood of a person developing a chronic disabling condition or dementia increases significantly after the age of 85.
- If you retire at the normal Social Security retirement age, you may live more than twenty years without earned income.

Who Are "Seniors"?

A book about the law and seniors must necessarily define what is meant by the term "senior." Popular senior discounts are triggered at a variety of ages. For example, you can qualify for AARP membership as early as age 50, but not for a National Parks Senior Pass until age 62. The ages at which movie theaters, restaurants, and other businesses offer special senior discounts often range anywhere from age 55 to age 65.

Although chronological age is certainly one way of determining whether you qualify for senior status, it tells us very little about you as an individual. In reality, no particular chronological age can tell us much about how anyone ages. Indeed, some persons seem old at age 65, whereas others much older seem young in terms of their physical and mental abilities.

Studies confirm that individuals of the same chronological age show great differences in mental and physical abilities. Even within the same individual, physical and mental capabilities often deteriorate at different rates. When a doctor tells a 70-year-old physically fit patient that she has the heart of a 50-year-old, the doctor is focusing on the functional level of her cardiovascular system rather than its chronological age. Not only do individuals age at different rates; so do their bodies. For example, an Alzheimer's patient with severely diminished mental function may still be in sound physical condition.

Determining what senior status means is further complicated by the wide range of ages that fall under this umbrella term. For example, a 65-year-old son and his 87-year-old father may both be described as seniors and yet have very different needs. With the increasing number of individuals who are living to age 100 and beyond, a person could potentially qualify as a senior for more than thirty years!

Given the diverse population to which society applies the label "senior," why make the distinction at all? The answer is that society and the law use chronological age and senior status for practical reasons. Age-based categories are a more cost- and time-efficient way to provide special benefits than are case-by-case individual evaluations.

The use of arbitrary age requirements to trigger benefits eligibility does not, however, always yield just results. For example, federal law provides that those who are age 65 are eligible for Medicare, a federally subsidized health care insurance. Thus, at age 63, Cindy is not eligible for Medicare even though she is unemployed and in poor health, but Bob at age 66 is eligible even though he is a millionaire who has barely been sick a day in his life.

Although basing eligibility for benefits on an arbitrary age requirement may not always produce satisfactory results, experience suggests that the law often performs poorly when eligibility is based on individual case-by-case evaluations. For example, Social Security pays benefits to younger, disabled workers who can substantiate that they are unable to work. Determining who is disabled, however, is not always easy. Often individuals believe they are disabled, but the Social Security Administration disagrees and rejects their claims. The result is excessive delays in benefits to deserving claimants and a disability system clogged with numerous appeals. In contrast, Social Security old-age benefits are paid to all who have reached their full retirement age. There is almost no litigation because either the individual is age 66 (the current eligibility age) or is not. No one can argue with the date on a birth certificate.

Although chronological age—usually age 65 or older—is arbitrarily used by the law to establish eligibility for a number of senior benefits, an important underlying question remains: Why should seniors receive special treatment? The answer to this question is complex and based on a number of demographic and policy considerations.

Even though we all age in different ways and at different rates, in time most of us will suffer a decline in physical strength, flexibility, and endurance, as well as deterioration in hearing and vision. Some will experience serious physical ailments such as congestive heart failure or stroke, and others will experience a decline in mental ability ranging from short-term memory loss to serious dementia. Based on the probability that most seniors will need some degree of help as they age—assistive services, supplementary income, or access to health and long-term care benefits—they receive special treatment under the law. The remainder of this chapter outlines factors that are relevant to why seniors receive this special treatment.

Population Age Trends

The number of seniors in the United States is increasing, as is the percentage of seniors in the total U.S. population. In 2008, about 13 percent of the population was age 65 or older. The percentage of seniors will remain at about 13 percent until the "baby boomers," those born between 1946 and 1964, begin to turn age 65 in 2011. Then the percentage will gradually rise to about 20 percent sometime after 2020.

The actual number of seniors and the percentage of seniors in the total population are increasing both because of declining birthrates and because of longer life expectancies. Not only do more individuals survive until age 65; they also have a longer life expectancy once they reach that age. In 1950, the average life expectancy of a U.S. resident was 68.2 years; by 1985, that figure had increased to 74.9 years. In 2005, it was 77.7 years. More revealing, however, is the life expectancy, not at birth, but at age 65, when women can expect to live twenty-three more years and men about twenty years. In fact, of those who reach age 65, more than 25 percent will live to at least age 90.

Seniors, those age 65 or older, are a diverse population, and it may not make sense to group someone age 65 with someone age 90. In fact, gerontologists subgroup seniors into the "Young Old," those age 65 to 75; the "Old," those age 75 to 85; and the "Old Old," those age 85 and older. Although there may be differences of opinion about where the dividing lines should be drawn for these subgroups, by whatever age someone is considered old, surely those over age 85 qualify.

Today more than 4 million Americans are age 85 or older, with the number growing at an ever-increasing rate. Some are alarmed at this, noting that those over age 85 are more likely to suffer from chronic illnesses, are heavy users of medical care and long-term care, are more dependent and likely to need supportive living arrangements, and have higher levels of poverty. The current legal and social support systems for seniors were created when the number of older individuals was much lower. Some commentators fear that our current programs for assisting seniors, particularly Social Security and Medicare, will become too expensive in the years to come as the number of seniors, and particularly those age 85 and older, continues to climb.

Gender and race are also important elements in understanding the challenge of our increasingly older society. Because women outlive men, there are only seventy-four men age 65 and older for every one hundred women.

The older the population is, the greater is the gender disparity. For example, there are only forty-six men over the age of 85 for every one hundred women. The gender disparity is important because older women on average have lower incomes and fewer savings than men. The health needs of older women differ from those of men, and some would argue that older women have different social needs.

Unfortunately, for a host of economic, health care, and cultural reasons, an African American has a shorter life expectancy than a Caucasian. For example, whereas the average life expectancy of a Caucasian male age 65 is about twenty additional years, the average life expectancy of a 65-year-old African American male is only sixteen additional years. Older African Americans on average have poorer health than Caucasian Americans and suffer higher rates of poverty. Consequently, support from governmental programs—such as Medicare, which provides subsidized health care coverage, and the federal food stamp program, which fights poverty—is critically important to the well-being of many older African Americans.

Physical Effects of Aging and Health Concerns

With advanced age comes an inevitable decline in physical vigor and well-being. Bones gradually lose calcium, become weakened, and may fracture. Joints are likely to become stiff and painful, thus making everyday activities more difficult. Stairs may become an impediment and possibly even a danger. A decline in balance, physical strength, and endurance may also threaten independence. Macular degeneration, or the loss of core vision, affects millions of seniors, preventing them from driving and reading. Loss of hearing, known as presbycusis, is also common and may make it difficult for someone with this condition to talk to others, causing frustration and a sense of isolation.

The incidence of chronic conditions—permanent or long-term ailments such as diabetes, heart disease, arthritis, and congestive heart failure—rises with age, as does the severity of such conditions. Someone who lives past age 80 is very likely to suffer from a chronic condition, at least in the last few months of life. For some seniors, severe chronic conditions signal the end of life, but other elderly live for years with chronic, disabling conditions that make them dependent on others for care and assistance.

Mental decline also afflicts many, but not all, seniors. Most older persons experience mild short-term memory losses, such as trouble remembering a new phone number. Fortunately, there are simple coping strategies to deal with mild "senior moments." These include the use of lists and electronic storage of important information. For example, cell phones and computers can be programmed to store frequently used addresses and phone numbers.

Far more serious is the loss of memory caused by dementia. Most seniors do not have dementia, though the chances of developing it rise rapidly after age 85. It is estimated that from one-quarter to one-half of those age 85 or older suffer from some form of dementia. Particularly devastating is Alzheimer's disease. During the early stages, the individual suffers episodes of disorientation as to time and place. Failing memory produces confusion and uncertainty. As the disease progresses, mental and physical skills decline until the victim loses the capability of self-care. In time, speech and all meaningful awareness are lost, and the individual may fall into a coma if death does not come first.

Because elderly seniors as a whole are not as healthy as the rest of the population, they are more likely to be hospitalized and have longer hospital stays. For most Americans, the cost of health care is paid by medical insurance. Given that most medical insurance is acquired as a benefit of employment, retirement often means the loss of, or a significant reduction in, medical insurance. As a result, there is significant subsidized governmental health care assistance for seniors in the form of Medicare and Medicaid. These programs raise the issue of how much health care assistance society can afford for seniors and how to allocate it. An even more fundamental question is whether advancing age reduces an individual's moral right to medical aid. Other questions include who should make the allocation decisions, whether some lives are more valuable than others, and whether the maintenance of life is always the highest priority. Our society has not formally answered these difficult questions. As with other puzzling questions of public policy, the answers are never clearly articulated, but public programs do provide a sort of answer because they reflect society's prioritization of generational rights and obligations.

Economic Vulnerability

Because of the loss of physical and mental vigor, seniors are less likely to be employed and more likely to have lower incomes. Many are economically very vulnerable, with low incomes and little or no savings. In response, America has created programs for seniors such as Social Security and Medicare. Although these financial assistance programs are open to almost all elderly, other programs, such as Medicaid, are designed to assist poor seniors or seniors made poor because of the expense of paying for their health care needs or the cost of a nursing home.

Although these programs and others have been very successful in reducing poverty among seniors, such programs are very costly. There is constant pressure on government to reduce costs (or raise more revenue) and to require seniors to pay for more of their own care. Unfortunately, there is no easy way to reduce the cost of these programs without reducing benefits.

With the increase in the senior population and the growing strain on federal and state budgets, the national debate over how much assistance should be provided to seniors has intensified. This debate brings into question whether we can expect the same level of benefits in our old age as was enjoyed by our parents and grandparents.

At present, most seniors who need financial help do receive some assistance. Consequently, in terms of percentages, fewer seniors are officially poor than are younger persons. However, that statistic underplays poverty among seniors because many have incomes just above the poverty line. They are able to survive financially only with the income they receive from Social Security and the subsidized medical care provided by Medicare. Even though not officially poor, they are impoverished and dependent upon governmental assistance.

Notwithstanding that some seniors are poor, alone, and isolated, most are married, are not poor, and are in good health. For example, at any one time only 5 percent of seniors—about 1.5 million—live in a nursing home, and most of those live there for less than a year. Most younger seniors enjoy relatively good health, have adequate though modest incomes, and live in the community, many with a spouse or life partner. Of course, that picture changes with age. The older a person is, the more likely she or he is to be poor, to be in bad health, and to live alone. In short, generalizations about the economic state of seniors are not of much use because of the wide discrepancies in individual well-being.

Social and Family Support

Due to the infirmities of old age, many seniors need support and assistance that can range from occasional help with household chores or a ride to the grocery store to daily personal assistance with dressing and bathing. If you are old and in need of help, it is likely to be provided by your spouse, family, and friends or possibly by volunteers from your church or community.

As long as you live with your spouse or a partner, the two of you can usually care for each other as needed. For example, one of you may shop for groceries, and the other one cooks. One may pay the bills, and the other takes responsibility for keeping the two of you in touch with family and friends.

Those who live alone often replicate the advantages of having a spouse by calling on friends or relatives for help. For example, if you live alone, you may have an arrangement with a family member or a neighbor who checks on you daily and assists as needed. Perhaps a grandchild or niece will move in with you to help take care of the house and provide transportation.

If your needs are great or you have no one to help, you may have to hire professional assistance. In some communities, you may qualify for local, county, or state governmental free or low-cost assistance, such as visiting nurses or homemaker services. You might also obtain help from community volunteers or find assistance at a federally funded senior citizens center.

Most seniors obtain assistance from informal networks comprising spouses, relatives, and friends. Most elderly men are married and so find support and assistance from their wives. Because women live longer and because wives on average are four years younger than husbands, most married women can expect a period of widowhood. In fact, about 70 percent of women over age 75 are widows. Lacking a spouse, these older widows must turn to others for help.

The first choice is usually an adult child, although the tendency to rely upon a child depends upon the child's proximity, the family's cultural background, and the elderly individual's financial resources. Proximity has become an increasing problem because of a tendency for both children and parents to move from their home communities to pursue work or more attractive retirement communities. Even children who live nearby may not be of much assistance—perhaps because of work responsibilities or challenges in their own families, such as a disabled child, economic pressures, or personal health issues. Some children of divorced parents may not feel that they owe much assistance to the noncustodial parent or to a parent who remarried and had a child with a new spouse.

The number of seniors who rely upon a child for assistance has been undercut as well by other demographic and social trends. For example, the shrinking size of the family coupled with an increasing rate of life expectancy results in some parents outliving their children. Women are increasingly in the workforce and so are unable to devote as much time to caring for their parents as they might have in times past. Even though many seniors receive some assistance from friends and neighbors, typically they lack the support that formerly might have been provided by children.

If a child does help, usually the child is female. Despite the increased participation of women in the workforce, one study found that women constitute more than 70 percent of all the adult children identified by their parents as primary caregivers. Women are often the primary caregivers because of cultural practices that identify caregiving as more appropriate for women, particularly if it consists of personal care such as dressing or bathing. Also for some women, who on average have lower earnings than men, giving up a job or working only part time in order to care for an elderly parent represents less of an income sacrifice than it might for some men. Of course, as women rise in status and pay in the workforce, this is less likely to continue to be the case.

In the absence of spouses or children, seniors rely on friends, neighbors, and social organizations. The longer the elderly individual has lived in the neighborhood, the more reliance the individual will place on friends and neighbors. Just as important is the attitude of the individual. Many seniors are fiercely independent and self-reliant. They abhor turning to a stranger or government for help. Others live in a culture that expects them to turn to friends for assistance. Elderly Asian Americans, for example, are more likely to seek help from friends than from governmental support systems. Hispanic elders with no relatives to assist them are less likely than any other ethnic group to seek outside help in times of need.

Many seniors seek support and assistance from social or religious organizations. If you are a woman, you are more likely than a man to seek such help. Even though many seniors get assistance from a church, synagogue, or mosque, reliance on religiously affiliated groups declines as wealth increases. Well-to-do seniors can afford to buy assistance that is unavailable to poorer seniors, who must rely on volunteers or government-subsidized services.

Conflicting Values

Autonomy versus Protection

The legal problems of seniors are made more complicated by an inherent conflict in public policy goals. One goal is to maintain a senior's autonomy—the right to act independently and to make choices for oneself. The other goal is to protect vulnerable seniors from the harm that may result from self-neglect or abuse at the hands of others. This conflict raises profound questions that have no easy answers.

Consider the following example. Imagine that you are a poor, elderly person who is unable to purchase healthy and nutritious meals. How would you prefer that the government help you? A cash subsidy might seem ideal, but that would burden you with buying food and preparing it, something your health might not permit. Being poor, you do not own a car, and public transportation may be unreliable, or you may lack the strength to tote groceries home on a bus or on foot. Also, carrying cash exposes you to theft or fraud.

Instead of cash, should the government provide food stamps, or is that too paternalistic because it denies you the choice of whether to purchase groceries or to buy a restaurant meal? In many communities, the Meals-on-Wheels program provides home-delivered meals. This is very helpful to shut-ins and those who prefer not to leave home, and it also assures a nutritious meal. Yet it also denies the recipient any choice. Because you have no say as to the menu, you must eat what they deliver to you. The Meals-on-Wheels program thus offers protection against malnutrition, but at the expense of individual choice. The question is whether the goal of protection—assuring that you have enough nutritious food to eat—has been properly balanced against your right to autonomy and the dignity of choosing what you think is best for yourself.

As protection increases, autonomy necessarily decreases, and vice versa. A cash subsidy gives you the greatest range of autonomy, but the least amount of protection against malnutrition. After all, you might not be physically able to shop, or you might choose to buy lottery tickets rather than food. Food stamps offer more protection than cash, but greater autonomy than Meals-on-Wheels. You can decide what food to purchase rather than eating a preprepared meal. However, although food stamps offer more autonomy in food choice, there is also the risk that you might choose to buy junk food rather than nutritious food. Thus, food stamps provide more au-tonomy than Meals-on-Wheels, but that increase in autonomy comes at the price of less protection.

In the designing of governmental programs to assist seniors, there is al-ways the tension between efficient solutions and the right of the individual to freedom and dignity. Few would disagree that independent choice is preferable to control by others, but autonomy also means the power to make bad choices. Too often governmental aid for seniors does not strike the balance between choice and protection that is accomplished by our food stamp example—providing needed assistance, but with only modest limits on individual choice. Governments and other institutions often err on the side of protecting seniors at the expense of their right to choose for them-selves. Because of the perceived vulnerability of some seniors, it is tempting to focus only on their need for protection and to overlook their equally compelling right to autonomy.

Generational Justice

Not only must society determine whether to favor autonomy or protection in meeting the needs of seniors; it must also determine how much help to give seniors in light of the public assistance that may be needed by other segments of the population. Many point out that money directed to seniors has to come from somewhere, and that usually means from the young—those under age 65. The notion of generational justice raises the question, How much do the young owe the old? What is a just allocation of govern-mental aid? For example, is it just to increase spending on Medicare, or should those dollars be used to improve the health care of children without health care insurance? Is it fair to raise bus rates for the young, while giving reduced or even free fares for seniors?

Whether in the form of greater federal benefits, such as Social Security or Medicare, or more assistance from state and local governments, such as property tax relief or subsidized housing, seniors benefit greatly from gov-ernmental assistance. Some question whether the government is providing too much assistance to seniors. The burden on the young to subsidize se-niors, it is asserted, is becoming too great, particularly as the ratio of the old to the young increases so that there are proportionately fewer young to pay the benefits granted to the old.

Even though seniors have serious needs, the question of whether seniors are receiving too much assistance relative to other needy segments of soci-ety is a legitimate one. Of course, there is no "right" answer. It only raises the fundamental and unanswerable questions of what do the young owe to the old, what is a good society, and what is justice?

Much of the impetus for the generational justice argument comes from the sense that seniors are reasonably well off and do not deserve the amount of assistance they receive. Some note that the measurement of senior poverty looks only at their income and not at other benefits, such as subsidized medical care (Medicare), free or reduced cost public transportation, property tax rebates, subsidized housing, and even lower fees for public recreation.

A few contend that seniors receive more than their fair share because of their political power. They argue that because a high percentage of seniors vote, politicians approve benefits for seniors in order to get reelected. Proponents of this argument conclude that the elderly should give up some of their benefits either to increase assistance for younger, needier individuals or to lower taxes for the younger population.

Others argue that intragenerational injustice exists between poor seniors and more-well-to-do seniors. The two most expensive benefit programs for seniors, Social Security and Medicare, are available without regard to need. The rich and poor alike receive the same benefits. What is the fairness, some contend, of assisting well-to-do seniors while allowing other elderly individuals to remain below or only modestly above the poverty line? Instead, the argument goes, federal and state assistance programs should be based on economic need or at least poor seniors should receive more benefits relative to rich seniors. To date, this position has not gained much support.

Age Discrimination versus Justice

Although discrimination is usually thought of as a bad thing and harmful to society, that is not always the case. The dictionary definition of the word "discriminate" is the act of making or perceiving differences. In the case of age discrimination, it can be either bad or good. Most would agree that discrimination is bad when used to harm seniors, but good when used to single out seniors for assistance.

That society should condemn discrimination against seniors may be self-evident, but it is less apparent why society should condone discrimination in favor of seniors. For example, why should Medicare be available only for those who are age 65 or older and available without regard to their financial need? The simple answer is that seniors are selected as the favored group because old age, at least historically if not currently, is associated with financial need. Seniors are also perceived as a sympathetic group who deserve our assistance. Old age is seen as something to be feared because it is perceived as a lonely, depressing time of life fraught with illness and impending death. Consequently, society tries to ease the problems of old age by providing benefits to seniors.

Sympathy aside, an objective case can be made for using only chronological age as a basis for governmental assistance because it is an efficient method of identifying those who are likely in need while avoiding the demeaning aspects of need-based eligibility criteria. For example, suppose you had to prove that you were poor in order to qualify for Social Security benefits. How would you feel filling out a form that in essence declared your life a financial failure? To avoid that indignity, many programs for seniors are available to all without the need to demonstrate financial need. All are eligible and all benefit.

The counterargument to age-based benefit eligibility is that individuals ought to prepare for their old age by saving for the loss of income that accompanies retirement. Most poverty among seniors, so the argument goes, is largely the result of a personal failure to plan. The tension between these conflicting images of the deserving old person versus someone who failed to plan for the future will never be resolved, but it does underlie much of the public debate about the proper treatment of seniors.

For More Information

Administration on Aging (202-619-0724)
(http://www.aoa.gov)

Find comprehensive information from the U.S. Administration on Aging about programs and services for seniors.

AARP (202-434-AARP)
(http://www.aarp.org)

Find discussions about timely topics of interest to seniors.

DisabilityInfo.gov (800-333-4636)
(http://www.disabilityinfo.gov)

Find information about government resources for disabled individuals and their families.

Eldercare Locator (800-677-1116)
(http://www.eldercare.gov)

Find resources for seniors in any U.S. community. Links are provided to state and local area agencies on aging and community-based services.

FDA for Older People (888-463-6332)
(http://www.fda.gov/oc/seniors)

Find information for seniors on a wide range of health issues.

GovBenefits.gov (800-333-4636)
(http://www.govbenefits.gov)

Find information on more than one thousand government benefit and assistance programs.

Healthfinder
(http://www.healthfinder.gov)

Find reliable health information from the U.S. Department of Health and Human Services Office of Disease Prevention and Health Promotion.

Medicare (800-MEDICARE)
(http://www.medicare.gov)

Find information about all aspects of Medicare coverage and benefits, including enrollment, choice of plans, costs, and appeals. Links are provided to state-specific resources.

National Indian Council on Aging (NICOA) (505-292-2001)
(http://www.nicoa.org)

Find information about services and advocacy for American Indian and Alaskan Native seniors.

NIH Senior Health
(http://www.NIHSeniorHealth.gov)

Find reliable health and wellness information on a variety of medical conditions that are of particular concern to seniors.

Senior Corps (800-424-8867)
(http://www.seniorcorps.org)

Find information about volunteer programs in local communities where seniors can share their life experiences and skills. Examples include Foster Grandparents, Senior Companions, and RSVP (Retired and Senior Volunteer Program).

Social Security Administration (800-772-1213)
(http://www.ssa.gov)

Find information about retirement benefits, disability benefits, and the location of local Social Security offices. The site also includes tools for estimating benefits and deciding when to begin receiving retirement benefits.

2

Age Discrimination in Employment

Did You Know?

- If you are over age 40, you may be protected against being fired or passed over for promotion because of your age.
- Showing that you were replaced by someone younger is not enough, by itself, to prove age discrimination.
- If you are the victim of age discrimination, you should save all employer communication that reflects a negative age bias and also make note of any negative comments about age or older workers.
- Not all employment policies that adversely affect older workers more than younger workers violate the law.
- Partners, business owners, and consultants are not protected against age discrimination in employment.

Most seniors are protected against age discrimination in employment by federal law. Some are also protected by state law. If you were passed over for a job or promotion that was given to a much younger worker, or terminated from a job while other, younger workers were retained, you may have a legal claim for age discrimination in employment. The following discussion outlines what situations may give rise to a valid age discrimination claim and what situations do not.

The Age Discrimination in Employment Act

In 1967 Congress passed the Age Discrimination in Employment Act (ADEA) (29 U.S.C. §§621 *et seq.*) to protect older Americans from age discrimination in the workplace. With a few exceptions, the ADEA prohibits employers from discriminating against older workers with respect to hiring, firing, compensation, and conditions of employment (29 U.S.C. §623[a]). The goal of the ADEA is to promote the employment of older Americans, to ban the arbitrary firing of older workers, and to encourage employers to create age-neutral employment practices. Mandatory retirement on account of age, excluding a few narrow exceptions, is also prohibited by the ADEA. Many states have enacted anti–age discrimination statutes that are similar to the ADEA; some state statutes offer age discrimination protection to employees who are not protected by the ADEA.

Who Is Protected?

Not every employee is protected by the ADEA. The act applies only to individuals age 40 and older (29 U.S.C. §631[a]) who work for employers that have twenty or more employees (29 U.S.C. §630[b]). The ADEA also covers labor unions and employment agencies (29 U.S.C. §630). To fall within the "twenty or more employees" category of covered employment, an employer must have twenty or more employees for each working day for at least twenty weeks. Thus, some part-time employees may not count in a determination of whether the employer meets the requirement (29 U.S.C. §630[b]). However, if the employer does fall under the ADEA, then all employees, including part time, are protected.

Given that the ADEA protects only employees who are age 40 and older, younger employees may be fired or not hired because of their age. For example, suppose an employer with one hundred employees is not happy with the performance of an employee, Sarah, who is age 35. The older employees are covered by the ADEA, but 35-year-old Sarah is not protected. Her employer tells Sarah, "I am firing you because you are just too young and lack the experience necessary to do your job." Sarah is not protected by the ADEA even though she was fired because of her age. The ADEA was enacted to address age bias against older workers, not to bar age discrimination against the young.

Even though the ADEA does not prohibit "reverse" age discrimination in favor of older workers (*General Dynamics Land Systems, Inc. v. Cline*, 540 U.S. 581 [2004]), it also does not require affirmative action for the benefit of older, protected workers. For example, it was not an ADEA violation when a university did not hire an applicant even though a hiring committee recommended that he be hired because of his age and experience (*Bryan v. East Stroudsburg Univ.*, 101 F.3d 689 [3d Cir. 1996]). If, however, an older worker is not hired or promoted and the position or promotion is given to a younger person with similar qualifications, an age discrimination claim may exist even if the younger worker is also over age 40. So long as the age difference is significant, it may be used as evidence of age discrimination by the employer (*O'Connor v. Consolidated Coin Caterers Corp.*, 517 U.S. 308 [1996]). For example, if the employer fires Laura, age 60, and replaces her with Lydia, age 44, it may have violated the ADEA.

Much ADEA litigation focuses on whether a person is an employee. The act does not protect partners, directors, business owners, consultants, or independent contractors (29 U.S.C. §630[f]; *Kennel v. Dover Garage, Inc.*, 816 F. Supp.178 [D.D.N.Y. 1993]; *Caruso v. Peat, Marwick, Mitchell & Co.*, 664 F. Supp. 144 [S.D.N.Y. 1987]). For example, Ken is a partner in a law firm that has thirty partners and eighty staff personnel. The firm has a rule that partners must retire at age 65. Because Ken is a partner, he is not protected by the ADEA, and so his firm can force him to retire. The firm, however, cannot force the nonpartners to retire at age 65 because they are protected employees.

Whether an individual is a partner or an employee turns on more than just the individual's job title. Courts look to the job description rather than the job title. If the relationship to the firm of those labeled partners is in reality one of an employee, courts will find that they are protected by the ADEA. For example, an accountant who was called a partner was found in actuality to be an employee because he had no management authority, did not participate in the firm's profits or losses, and had no ownership interest in the firm (*Simpson v. Ernst & Young*, 100 F.3d 436 [6th Cir. 1996]).

Even though a company that is subject to the ADEA cannot mandatorily retire or fire employees based on age, it is free to do so with respect to consultants and members of its board of directors. Consider the following example of Kelly, age 60, hired as a consultant by Acme Co. to provide marketing advice. If the company fires her and indicates that it did so because some of the company's officers thought she was too old to do a good job, she has no protection under the ADEA. Likewise, Acme Co. can legally require members of its board of directors to retire at age 70 (or any age) because directors are not protected by the ADEA.

Sometimes when an older individual sues under the ADEA, the alleged "employer" will claim that the individual was not an employee, but was an independent contractor and thus not protected by the ADEA. In response, the individual will argue that he or she was a protected employee. To resolve the issue, courts consider the facts and circumstances surrounding the job in question. Even if the individual was hired with the title "consultant" or "independent contractor," a court will consider the actual relationship of the individual to the employer rather than merely the title of the job. Generally, an individual will be considered an employee if the employer can dictate the time, place, and manner of employment; furnishes tools and equipment; or controls the individual's job performance (Rev. Rul. 87-41, 1987-1 C.B. 296).

Exceptions to the ADEA

Firefighters, Police, and Prison Guards

The ADEA exempts selected employees from its protection. The exemptions recognize that in some situations age may be a relevant indicator of the ability to perform job functions. Consequently, the ADEA grants government employers the right to use age as a reason to refuse to hire or to mandatorily retire police, firefighters, and prison guards (29 U.S.C. §623[j]). If the mandatory retirement policy was adopted after September 30, 1996, the age of required retirement cannot be less than age 55 (*id.*).

The exemption recognizes that if older individuals cannot adequately perform the strenuous duties required by these jobs, they might put others at risk. Absent mandatory retirement, the government would have to individually test all police, firefighters, and prison guards to see if they were fit to perform their jobs. Unfortunately, even such a test would not uncover all employees who might fail at their jobs. For example, the risk of a heart attack rises with age, but no test can reveal with certainty which employee is likely to have a heart attack. Yet if a firefighter suffers a heart attack on the job, his collapse could put fire victims or other firefighters at risk, not to mention that a firefighter who has a heart attack while on the job would be at risk of additional injury.

Executive Policymaker Exceptions

The ADEA does not protect those individuals who are employed in a bona fide executive or a high policymaking position if they are entitled to an immediate and nonforfeitable annual retirement benefit of at least $44,000 (29 U.S.C. §631[c][1]). This exception applies only to a few top-level employees and never to individuals in middle management, even if they meet the retirement income requirement. A bona fide executive is usually a manager who has the power to hire, fire, and direct the work of other employees. Whether an employee qualifies as holding a high-policy position is determined by the nature of the employee's responsibilities with respect to the direction of the company and the company's operations (*Colby v. Graniteville Co.*, 635 F. Supp. 381 [S.D.N.Y. 1986]). These are employees, such as a chief economist or chief research scientist, who lack the power of an executive but play a significant role in determining company policy.

The ADEA exclusion of high-ranking executives and policymaking individuals recognizes that companies often benefit from new leadership. Companies generally require very-high-ranking employees, such as the president or chief financial officer, to retire at a designated age. By setting a retirement age, the company avoids a debate about whether the company would be better off with new management. A designated retirement age also permits the company to plan for replacing high-ranking employees who reach the mandatory retirement age. For example, Jennifer, age 64, is president of Beta

Co., which has a mandatory retirement age of 65 for its president. Beta Co. knows that Jennifer will be retiring in one year and so can make appropriate plans to replace her.

Federal, State, and Local Government Immunity

Because of a U.S. Supreme Court decision, the ADEA does not apply to state and local governments (*Kimel v. Florida Bd. of Regents*, 528 U.S. 62 [2000]). However, state and local employees may still be protected from age discrimination under state anti–age discrimination statutes. Although federal employees are protected by the ADEA (29 U.S.C. §633[a]), specific provisions of other statutes permit mandatory retirement of selected employees such as federal air traffic controllers (5 U.S.C. §8335[a]).

Proving Illegal Discrimination

In Hiring

Only about 10 percent of ADEA complaints claim age discrimination in hiring. In most cases, individuals do not know why their employment applications were rejected and thus are unaware of any discriminatory reasons. Even if the rejected applicant has reason to believe that employment was denied because of age discrimination, proving discrimination in hiring is not easy. It is never enough to show only that a younger applicant was hired. Rather, the rejected applicant must prove that his or her age was the main reason for the employer's decision not to hire. This is very difficult to prove, though sometimes it can be shown. For example, an employer was held to have engaged in age discrimination when an applicant for a federal job was told during the hiring process, "You old timer, you've been around here. You know what this is all about" (*Lucas v. Paige*, 435 F. Supp. 2d 165 [D.D.C. 2006]).

In Termination of Employment

Most complaints filed under the ADEA arise when an employee who was fired claims that the firing took place because of his or her age. Naturally, the employer will not have announced that the employee is being fired because he or she is "too old." However, if the employee believes that whatever the employer's stated reason, the real reason for termination was age, the employee will have the burden of proving that claim.

An illegal termination because of age can be proved in any of three ways. First, the discharged employee may provide direct proof of discrimination, such as an internal employer memo, if such evidence exists. Second, age discrimination can be shown through circumstantial evidence, such as statements that show an age prejudice on the part of the employer. And third, the discharged employee may demonstrate an ADEA violation through the use of employment statistics that show a "disparate impact" on older employees—

that is, the statistics must show that the employer's policies and practices are not age neutral; they produce a greater negative effect on older employees than on younger ones. The following is an overview of each of these methods for proving age discrimination in the termination of employment.

Direct Proof. Direct proof of age discrimination requires offering explicit evidence that age was the motivation for the termination. For example, the employer may have created a paper trail such as an internal letter or memorandum to the human resources department. The memo might be employee specific—"We need to fire Smith because he is over the hill. Hire someone younger with some energy."—or it might relate to all employees over a certain age—"Terminate all marginal employees age 55 or older in order to reduce operating costs." Even a metaphorical statement about age as a reason for termination might be sufficient. In one case, a statement by a supervisor that it was necessary to cut down "old, big trees so the little trees underneath can grow" qualified as direct evidence of age discrimination (*Wichmann v. Bd. of Trustees of S. Ill. Univ.*, 180 F.3d 791, 801 [7th Cir. 1999]). An admission that age was one of several factors used to determine which employees would be terminated was also held to be direct evidence of illegal age discrimination (*Febres v. Challenger Caribbean Corp.*, 214 F.3d 57 [1st Cir. 2000]).

Because today most employers are better educated about age discrimination, few create documents like those just described. Usually, an employee who believes that he or she was a victim of age discrimination must find another way to prove the case. One alternative way to directly demonstrate illegal age discrimination is by producing evidence of an employer's negative remarks about old age and older employees. It is not necessary that such remarks were made specifically about the discharged employee. These statements are offered to prove that the employer had a bias against older workers and that this bias accounted for why the employee was fired.

An employer's remarks are considered relevant if they were age related, made in the same general time period as the termination by an individual with authority over the employment decision in question, and related to the employee's termination (*Cooley v. Carmike Cinemas, Inc.*, 25 F.3d 1325 [6th Cir. 1994]). Statements that an office needed to get rid of "old heads" and that "younger employees were running circles around the older employees" were found to be evidence of age discrimination in the termination of an employee even though the statements were not made to him at the time of his termination (*Denesha v. Farmers Ins. Exch.*, 161 F.3d 491, 498 [5th Cir. 1999]).

Circumstantial Evidence. Because most employers are careful not to leave a paper trial or to make age disparaging comments, a claimant is also permitted to prove age discrimination through circumstantial evidence. Known as a "prima facie" case, this method applies the ruling of the *McDonnell Douglas* case (*McDonnell Douglas Corp. v. Green*, 411 U.S. 792 [1973]). To prove a prima facie case, the claimant must first show that (1) he or she is age 40 or over, applied for or was employed in a job that he or she was qualified for, and was rejected despite those qualifications; and (2) after the rejection, the position remained open and the employer sought applications from persons with similar qualifications or hired a younger individual for the position who had comparable qualifications (*id.*). The younger person need not be below age 40. An ADEA violation can occur, for example, if a 60-year-old is replaced by a 45-year-old (*O'Connor v. Consolidated Coin Caterers Corp.*, 517 U.S. 308 [1996]).

If a claimant can show all the necessary circumstantial elements, the employer will typically offer alternative nondiscriminatory reasons for the dismissal, such as claiming the discharged employee was not performing well enough. If the employer is able to successfully prove a nondiscriminatory reason for the discharge, the employer will win the lawsuit. Therefore, in response to the employer's arguments, the claimant must argue that the reasons offered by the employer were merely a pretext to cover the true reason for the discharge, which was the claimant's age.

In order to successfully rebut the employer's nondiscriminatory reasons for the discharge, the claimant will have to offer proof that the employer's reasons were not the real motivating reasons for the discharge or that the reasons given, such as poor performance, were not true. Typically, the claimant will offer proof that the alleged reasons were implausible, inconsistent, or not supported by the evidence (*Brewer v. Quaker State Oil Ref. Corp.*, 72 F.3d 326 [3d Cir. 1995]). It will not be enough for the claimant to show that the reasons were bad business decisions. The ADEA is not meant to interfere with nondiscriminatory business decisions, even when the employer's business practices are unwise or the managers are mistaken about the ability of the terminated employee.

If the claimant produces enough evidence that the employer's reasons were a mere pretext for the termination, the court can find that the employer violated the ADEA (*Reeves v. Sanderson Plumbing Products, Inc.*, 530 U.S. 133 [2000]). Courts, however, are increasingly less likely to reject an employer's reasons for the discharge despite stray age-related remarks by company officials. For example, a claim of age discrimination was dismissed when the evidence indicated that the claimant's job performance was substandard despite the employer referring to the claimant as an "old man" (*Trahant v. Royal Indemnity Co.*, 121 F.3d 1094 [7th Cir. 1997]).

Winning a prima facie case is not easy. There are many reported cases in which the employee alleges that the reasons given for his or her termination were a mere pretext and that age discrimination was the real reason. Very few of these claims succeed at trial. Without direct proof of discrimination or a statistical showing of a pattern of age discrimination, most employees lose their claim for illegal age discrimination.

Statistical Pattern of Disparate Impact. The third method for proving age discrimination is by the use of statistics to show that the employer's behavior had a "disparate" (much greater) impact on older employees (*Smith v. City of Jackson, Miss.*, 544 U.S. 228 [2005]). The claimant must identify the specific employer practice or policy being challenged, show that it had a disproportionate impact on older workers, and prove that the practice caused the harm to the older, protected employees. To win a claim based on statistical evidence, the claimant must also prove that he or she was replaced by a younger worker. In response, the employer must either discredit the statistics or concede the statistics and offer a legitimate business reason for the use of a policy that disproportionately affects older workers.

Employer Defenses

There are certain lawful reasons for adverse employment decisions that can serve as employer defenses to an ADEA action. These include terminations that are part of a reduction in force, situations where reasonable factors other than age exist for the termination, jobs for which an employee's chronological age is considered a bona fide qualification, and circumstances in which the employer learns after the termination that legitimate grounds existed for the termination apart from the employee's age.

Reduction in Force
An employer may reduce its workforce in order to terminate surplus employees. When reducing the workforce, many employers terminate the highest-paid employees, who are usually the older employees. Most courts have held that it is not a violation of the ADEA to reduce the workforce by terminating only the higher-paid employees provided their positions are terminated along with the employees (*Bilas v. Greyhound Lines, Inc.*, 59 F.3d 759 [8th Cir. 1995]). For example, Acme Co. needs to cut its payroll expense by 25 percent. Rather than firing 25 percent of its employees, however, it decides to fire 15 percent of the highest-paid workers, who collectively account for 25 percent of Acme's payroll expense. Of the 15 percent fired, all but one were age 40 or older and thus protected by the ADEA. Acme Co. has not violated the ADEA. It did not fire anyone because of age, but because of high salary, and it did not replace ADEA-protected workers with younger employees.

Reasonable Factors Other Than Age Defense
When an employer fires an ADEA protected worker, the employer must be prepared to offer an explanation other than the worker's age. Almost any

reason is acceptable if the practice or policy is age neutral (*E.E.O.C. v. Johnson & Higgin, Inc.*, 887 F. Supp. 682 [S.D.N.Y. 1995]). Lawful reasons for termination include inability to perform the job, personality conflicts, insubordination, absenteeism, uncooperativeness, and low quality of production. Termination of an employee for a legally valid reason is known as the "reasonable factors other than age" defense, or RFOA. Termination may even be based on factors that are often associated with advancing age, such as an inability to work as fast or carry heavy objects, provided the termination was not based merely on chronological age.

Bona Fide Occupational Qualification Exception

Employers can also discriminate against older employees if only a younger employee is generally capable of performing the job. This is known as the bona fide occupational qualification exception, or BFOQ. This exception is limited to a few cases of physically demanding jobs or jobs that involve public safety, such as airplane pilots. The Federal Aviation Administration's regulation prohibiting commercial airline pilots from flying after age 60 was approved as a BFOQ in the 1980s (*E.E.O.C. v. Boeing Co.*, 843 F.2d 1213 [9th Cir. 1988]). Congress recently raised the mandatory retirement age to 65 (Fair Treatment for Experienced Pilots Act, 49 U.S.C. §40101).

The BFOQ exception is very narrow, and for it to apply, the employer must show that there is a sound factual basis for believing that all or nearly all persons over the age limit would be unable to perform the job or that it would be impractical or impossible to individually test such persons to see if they are qualified for the job. An employee may challenge a BFOQ defense by arguing that the employer should have relied on individual testing to evaluate job performance rather than using an arbitrary age as the reason for terminating or not hiring an older employee.

After-Acquired Evidence of Wrongdoing

If an employer violates the ADEA by firing an employee because of age, but later finds there were independent, legal reasons for termination that would have justified it, such as employee misconduct, the employer will not be liable to the employee. However, the employer must prove that the employee's misconduct was severe enough to warrant termination. For example, suppose that Beta Inc. fired Jessica, age 67, and replaced her with Ashley, age 37, for the express reason that Jessica is "too old." Jessica sues under the ADEA. Just before the trial, Beta learns that Jessica, while an employee, stole a computer worth $2,000 from Beta. In light of Jessica's theft, Beta would have been justified in firing her. Thus, although Jessica can show that Beta violated the ADEA, Beta does not have to rehire her or pay her money damages because Beta would have been justified in firing Jessica once it learned of the theft.

Enforcement of the ADEA

If you believe that your rights under the ADEA have been violated, either because you were not hired, were not promoted, were demoted, did not receive a pay raise, or were fired because of your age, you can sue your employer. Before a lawsuit may be filed, however, the law requires that you exhaust all other remedies (29 U.S.C. §626[d]). If the state in which you live has a law that prohibits age discrimination, and many do, you must first file a complaint with the proper state agency (29 U.S.C. §633[b]). Within 300 days of that filing, you must also file a complaint with the federal Equal Employment Opportunity Commission (EEOC) (29 U.S.C. §626[d]). If the state where you live has no law prohibiting age discrimination, you must file a complaint with the EEOC within 180 days of the alleged discrimination (29 U.S.C. §633[b]). After that filing, you must wait 60 days before filing a private lawsuit. If the EEOC brings a lawsuit based on your complaint, you may not initiate a private suit. You cannot sue in federal court until after you have received notice from the EEOC that it has terminated its proceedings (29 U.S.C. §626[e]). If the EEOC has not sued after 60 days, you may file suit. In the event that the EEOC later sues, your lawsuit may nevertheless continue (see generally 29 U.S.C. §626). If you are seeking unpaid wages or other monetary damages, you may request a jury trial; many claimants do so because they believe a jury will be more sympathetic than a judge (Fair Labor Standards Act §16, 29 U.S.C. §§201 *et seq.*).

Voluntary Early Retirement Plans

With the elimination of mandatory retirement, many employers rely on incentives to encourage voluntary retirement. Employer-provided benefits that serve as an incentive to retire are lawful if the employee retirements are genuinely voluntary and if the benefits are offered in a nondiscriminatory manner (29 U.S.C. §623[f][2][B][ii]). Offering a bonus of $20,000 to all workers who voluntarily retire in the next sixty days is legal. However, an early retirement plan may violate the ADEA if it favors younger employees. For example, a plan that gives early retirement benefits for each year that an employee worked for the company but grants fewer benefits for each year after twenty-five years of work is illegal.

Employers may also legally offer employees a choice of a voluntary retirement plan with extra benefits as an alternative to possible involuntary termination (*Vega v. Kodak Caribbean, Ltd.*, 3 F.3d 476 [1st Cir. 1993]). For example, the employer could announce a planned 10 percent reduction in the number of employees and provide that if enough employees volunteer to retire early, with a 20 percent increase in their retirement benefits, no one will be fired. Given such a choice, many older employees may decide it is safer to retire with the 20 percent bonus rather than risk being fired.

The employer can also require employees who select the voluntary retirement plan to sign a waiver of rights that releases the employer from liability under the ADEA (29 U.S.C. §626[f][1]). Even if the employee chooses the voluntary retirement plan, the employer may have violated the ADEA if the employee was not given adequate time and opportunity to decide whether to accept the offer. Under the ADEA, a waiver is only valid if the employee was advised in writing to consult a lawyer, given twenty-one days to consider the agreement, and given seven days after signing to revoke the agreement. Furthermore, the waiver must clearly state the rights and claims being waived by the employee. It must have been signed voluntarily and with knowledge of the rights (*id.*). Duress or mistake will make the waiver ineffective.

Older Workers Benefit Protection Act

Employers sometimes find that the cost of employee benefits, such as health care insurance, is much higher for older employees than for younger employees. The Older Workers Benefit Protection Act amended the ADEA so that an employer cannot use the existence or cost of an employee benefit plan as a justification for failing to hire or for involuntarily retiring older workers (29 U.S.C. §623[f][2]). Employers may not refuse to hire older employees in an attempt to reduce their employee benefits cost, and an employer cannot selectively reduce or terminate employee fringe benefits because of the employee's age. However, the employer can legally spend the same amount on benefits for each worker even if that amount buys fewer benefits for the older workers.

Remedies

A number of remedies are available to the employee who successfully proves an age discrimination case, including injunctive and monetary relief (29 U.S.C. §626[b]). Injunctive relief is in the form of a court order that requires the employer to do something, such as reinstate the employee, or to refrain from doing something, such as not continuing the discriminatory practice. For example, the injunction might prohibit an employer from firing the older employee.

A winning claimant can ask for reinstatement (or to be hired) (*Philipp v. ANR Freight Sys.*, 61 F.3d 669 [8th Cir. 1995]), which is the judicially preferred remedy over the granting of front pay—damages for the loss of future pay (*Woodhouse v. Magnolia Hosp.*, 92 F.3d 248 [5th Cir. 1996]). Employees who were fired are entitled to back pay from the time they were fired, and that can include loss of pay, overtime, sick leave, vacation pay, pension benefits, and other fringe benefits lost because of the age discrimination (*E.E.O.C. v. Kentucky State Police Dep't.*, 80 F.3d 1086 [6th Cir. 1996]).

A successful claimant is usually awarded attorney's fees (29 U.S.C. §§216[b], 626[b]). If the employer's violation was willful, liquidated damages equal to double the amount of the claimant's losses are awarded. An employee has a duty to lessen his or her damages (called mitigation) by seeking other employment, including the duty to accept a reasonable offer for reinstatement from the employer. Both front pay and back pay awards must be reduced by the amount the claimant could have earned using reasonable efforts during the time period in question (*Cassino v. Reichhold Chems., Inc.*, 817 F.2d 1338 [9th Cir. 1987]). The burden is on the employer to prove that an employee did not take reasonable steps to lessen damages (*Coleman v. Omaha*, 714 F.2d 804 [8th Cir. 1983]). All damages awarded under the ADEA, including back pay and liquidated damages, are considered to be a part of the claimant's federal gross income and as such are taxable (I.R.C. §104[a]; *Comm. of Internal Revenue v. Schleier*, 515 U.S. 323 [1995] [interpreting I.R.C. §104[a]]).

For More Information

Equal Employment Opportunity Commission (EEOC) (800-669-4000) (http://www.eeoc.gov)

Find information about how to file an age discrimination charge and where to find the closest EEOC field office.

3

Social Security and Supplemental Security Income

Did You Know?

- Social Security is the only source of retirement income for nearly one-half of all retirees.
- Social Security benefits are based on your work record and age (or on your relationship to a qualified Social Security beneficiary).
- A portion of your Social Security benefits may be taxed depending on the amount of your other income.
- If you are divorced, you may be entitled to Social Security benefits based on your ex-spouse's work record.
- If you are a senior with limited income and resources, you may be entitled to Supplemental Security Income even if you do not qualify for Social Security benefits.

When Social Security was created, it was intended to be one leg of a "three-legged stool" for income security in retirement, with pensions and personal savings forming the other two legs. However, today nearly three out of five retirees receive at least one-half of their retirement income from Social Security. For almost one-half of all retirees, it is their only source of income.

You must earn eligibility for Social Security retirement benefits through wage taxes paid while you are employed. Family members of workers with qualifying employment records may also be entitled to derivative and survivors benefits. In addition to retirement benefits, the Social Security Administration (SSA) oversees benefits for disabled workers and their families.

Disability benefits, like retirement benefits, are based on the disabled worker's employment record.

The official name for Social Security retirement and disability benefits is Old-Age, Survivors, and Disability Insurance, or OASDI. Although there is an "earned" aspect to both retirement and disability benefits under OASDI, there is a third type of government income benefit—known as Supplemental Security Income (SSI)—that is based not on work record, but on the recipient's status as poor and either aged, blind, or disabled. This chapter provides a general overview of the qualifications for retirement, disability, and SSI benefits. The Social Security regulations are quite complex. If you have questions about your individual entitlements, you should consult your local Social Security Administration office.

Social Security Eligibility

Only employment that is subject to wage taxes under the Federal Insurance Contributions Act (FICA) (26 U.S.C. §§3101 *et seq.*) qualifies as covered employment for Social Security purposes. An application for retirement, survivors, or disability benefits must be based on a work record during which FICA taxes were paid for the required number of "covered quarters." The required number of quarters differs depending on the type of benefit claimed. The following discussion explains FICA taxes, what constitutes a quarter of coverage, and what it means to have insured status for retirement, survivors, and disability benefits.

FICA Wage Taxes
Social Security benefits are available to workers who have paid FICA wage taxes for the required number of covered quarters of employment. Today, almost all workers, regardless of the form of employment, participate in the program. Employees must pay a 6.20 percent wage tax on earnings up to a maximum amount, which is adjusted annually for inflation ($106,800 in 2010) (26 U.S.C. §3101[a]). Employers also pay a 6.20 percent FICA tax on the employee's wages, but the employer-provided portion of the FICA tax is not considered taxable income to the employee (26 U.S.C. §3111[a]).

Whereas employees and employers share the responsibility for paying the FICA tax, self-employed individuals must pay the entire amount. To equalize the tax impact of this difference, self-employed individuals are permitted to deduct from taxable income one-half of the amount they pay in FICA taxes. Self-employment earnings of less than $400 per year are not subject to the FICA tax.

Quarters of Coverage
A quarter of coverage is the basic unit for determining whether a worker is insured (42 U.S.C. §413).[1] Although a quarter of coverage is based on a calen-

dar quarter of three months, in actuality income need not be earned in a specific calendar quarter to satisfy the requirement. An employee's quarters of coverage for the year are computed by dividing the worker's yearly before-tax earnings by the minimum required earnings amount per quarter ($1,120 in 2010). Fringe benefits are usually not included in calculating earnings.

Even if you earn well over the minimum, you cannot receive credit for more than four quarters of coverage in any calendar year. If, however, you earn under the minimum, you can receive credit only for whole quarters. For example, consider Susan, who works only during the summer months. She earns $4,000 for the summer. Her yearly earnings of $4,000 divided by $1,120 equals 3.6 credits. Her quarters of coverage will be rounded down to the next whole number, which in this example is 3. If Susan has another job, the earnings from that job can be added to her summer earnings for the purpose of calculating her quarters of coverage.

Only wages and salaries earned in "covered employment" count toward quarters of coverage. Even independent contractors are generally subject to Social Security tax as self-employed persons. However, a few jobs are not covered by Social Security, such as federal government workers who were hired before January 1, 1984, some state and local government workers, railroad workers who are covered under the Railroad Retirement Act, most students who work for their school or college, and children under the age of 18 who are employed by their parents or who perform domestic services.

Insured Status

The number of quarters of coverage determines if a person has reached insured status and is eligible for benefits (42 U.S.C. §414). Insured status is computed based on the record of wages or self-employment income that the SSA maintains. A Personal Earnings and Benefit Estimate Statement can be requested from the SSA to determine how many quarters a person has completed. If the form contains omissions, generally tax returns and wage reports on Form W-2 can be used to supply missing earnings figures. There is an assumption that an earnings record is correct after the passage of three years, three months, and fifteen days.

Fully Insured Status. The maximum number of quarters of coverage required for any type of Social Security benefit is forty (42 U.S.C. §414[a][2]). If you have accumulated forty quarters of coverage, you are considered permanently and fully insured.

Currently Insured Status. You can claim benefits as the mother or father of a deceased worker's child if the deceased was "currently insured," meaning that the worker was credited with quarters of coverage in at least six of the previous thirteen quarters, including the quarter in which death occurred (42 U.S.C. §414[b]). Other qualifications apply to this benefit, including

- you were married to the worker,
- you have remained unmarried since the worker's death, and
- the child must be under age 16 or disabled.

Disability Insured Status. To be eligible for disability benefits, you must have worked twenty quarters out of the previous forty-quarter period, which includes the quarter in which you become disabled. Or if you became disabled before age 31, an alternative calculation requires one quarter of coverage for every two calendar quarters between age 21 and the onset of the disability. If the period of time is less than twelve quarters, then you must have at least six quarters of credit. No quarters of coverage are required to receive benefits on the basis of blindness (42 U.S.C. §423[c]).

Worker's Retirement Benefits

If you have forty quarters of coverage, you are entitled to a monthly benefit when you reach early or full retirement age. Full retirement age—also called normal retirement age—is based solely on your year of birth and has nothing to do with retirement (42 U.S.C. §416[l]). If you were born before 1938, your full retirement age is 65. If you were born after 1959, your full retirement age is 67. See Table 3.1 for full retirement ages for the intervening years.[2] Once you reach full retirement age, you can collect your full Social Security retirement benefits even if you are still employed.

Early and Deferred Retirement Options

You can choose to begin receiving retirement benefits as early as age 62 (42 U.S.C. §416[l][2]), but at the cost of reduced monthly benefits for life (42

Table 3.1   Full Retirement Age by Year of Birth

Year of Birth	Full Retirement Age
1938	65 years and 2 months
1939	65 years and 4 months
1940	65 years and 6 months
1941	65 years and 8 months
1942	65 years and 10 months
1943–1954	66 years
1955	66 years and 2 months
1956	66 years and 4 months
1957	66 years and 6 months
1958	66 years and 8 months
1959	66 years and 10 months
After 1959	67 years

U.S.C. §402[q]). Because taking benefits early means potentially more monthly benefit payments than if you waited until your full retirement age, the benefit amount is reduced proportionately. Thus, if you live what Social Security calculates to be an average life expectancy, the total benefits you receive will be the same whether you began receiving the lesser monthly amount at age 62 or the larger benefit at your normal retirement age.

If you defer receipt of Social Security benefits beyond your full retirement age, you will get a bonus in the form of higher monthly benefits to compensate for the shorter payout term (42 U.S.C. §402[w]). The amount that delayed retirement will increase your monthly benefit is based on your year of birth (see Table 3.2).

The annual increases apply for each year that you delay taking retirement benefits, up until age 70. After that point, further delay produces no further increase in benefit amounts.

The Primary Insurance Amount

The Primary Insurance Amount (PIA) is the monthly benefit paid by Social Security to a retired or disabled worker (42 U.S.C. §415). It is calculated using the average monthly earnings of the covered person while working, with inflation taken into account (called the Average Indexed Monthly Earnings, or AIME). Only wages subject to Social Security taxes are used in this calculation. For example, wages subject to FICA tax in 2010 were capped at $106,800. Any earnings above this amount are disregarded for purposes of calculating AIME.

The AIME is calculated on a thirty-five-year work record even if a person does not have thirty-five years of earnings. If, for example, an individual worked for only twenty-eight years, total earnings are still divided by thirty-five years to find the AIME. Thus, individuals who work less than thirty-five years have a significantly lower AIME than their actual average wage. For workers with more than thirty-five years of earnings, only the thirty-five years of highest earnings are considered.

Table 3.2   Delayed Retirement Benefit Credit by Year of Birth

Year of Birth	Percentage Increase for Each Year of Delay
1931–1932	5
1933–1934	5.5
1935–1936	6
1937–1938	6.5
1939–1940	7
1941–1942	7.5
After 1942	8

Although the formula results in a higher PIA for higher-income workers, it is also designed to provide a proportionately higher percentage of replacement income for lower-income workers. Lower-income retirees have about 40 percent of their wages replaced by Social Security benefits, whereas higher-income workers receive approximately 25 percent replacement of those wages that were subject to the FICA wage tax. The PIA formula is intended to be redistributive; higher-income workers' wage taxes actually pay for part of the benefits enjoyed by lower-income workers.

Derivative Benefits

Social Security benefits can be paid simultaneously to a retiree, the retiree's current spouse, the retiree's ex-spouse in some situations, and the retiree's qualified children. Benefits paid to individuals other than the retiree do not affect the amount paid to the retiree. The following explains eligibility for derivative benefits.

Spousal Benefits

Current Spouse. If you are a spouse of a retired worker, you are entitled to receive the greater of either the benefit based on your own earnings record or a benefit equal to one-half of your spouse's benefit (42 U.S.C. §402[b]-[c]). For example, Adam, age 66, is retired and receives $1,600 a month from Social Security. His wife, Alice, age 66, would receive $500 a month based on her earnings record. Instead, she receives $800 a month, or one-half of what her husband, Adam, receives. Social Security automatically pays a spouse the higher amount.

To be eligible for spousal benefits, you must have been married to the insured worker for at least one year and be at least 62 years old or have in your care a child of the insured worker who is under age 16 or who is disabled. You may receive spousal benefits only if the worker is receiving retirement benefits. Even an invalid marriage can be the basis for spousal benefits if under the Social Security regulations it is "deemed valid." For a marriage to be deemed valid, you must establish that you entered into the marriage in good faith.

If you elect to take spousal benefits before reaching full retirement age, you will receive a permanently reduced amount. However, if the insured worker collects benefits early, the reduction in the worker's benefits will not affect your derivative benefits. Likewise, if the insured worker delays receipt of benefits and is entitled to delayed retirement credits, those credits will not be included in your derivative benefits.

Consider the example of Eve, who took reduced Social Security benefits at age 62 (her full retirement age was 65). Her husband, Eli, claimed his spousal benefits at age 66, his full retirement age. Although Eve only receives $1,000 a month, Eli receives $570 a month, or one-half of $1,140, the monthly amount Eve would have received had she waited to claim benefits at her full retirement age of 65.

Divorced Spouse. If you are divorced, you may be entitled to a monthly benefit equal to one-half of your ex-spouse's monthly benefit (or a reduced portion of this amount if you claim the benefit before your full retirement age) (42 U.S.C. §402[b]-[c]). You are eligible if you are at least 62, the marriage lasted a minimum of ten years, the divorce has been final for at least two years, you are unmarried, and you are not entitled to a larger benefit on your own earnings record. Unlike a spouse, a divorced spouse can receive Social Security benefits even though the worker from whom the benefit is derived has not begun to receive benefits. Receipt of benefits by a divorced spouse does not affect the right of the ex-spouse's current spouse to also claim benefits based on the worker's record.

If you are divorced and your ex-spouse has died, you may be entitled to a benefit equal to your ex-spouse's full retirement benefit if you are at your full retirement age or are disabled and age 50 or older. The full benefit is also available at any age if you are caring for the deceased worker's child who is younger than 16 or disabled (42 U.S.C. §402[g]). You may also choose to begin receiving permanently reduced benefits as early as age 60.

Widows and Widowers. When retirees die, their spouses are eligible for an amount equal to the greater of their own benefit based on their own earnings record or 100 percent of the deceased worker's benefit (42 U.S.C. §402[e]-[f]). For example, Carlos, age 70, receives $1,000 a month in retiree benefits. His spouse, Rosa, receives $700 a month. After Carlos dies, Rosa will receive $1,000 a month. If the retiree had chosen an early retirement, the spouse would receive 100 percent of the reduced amount. If the surviving spouse has not yet reached full retirement age, the benefits are reduced based on the number of months left until full retirement age.

A surviving spouse is eligible for survivor benefits starting as early as age 60 (or age 50 if the surviving spouse is totally disabled). Surviving spouse benefits are payable only if the surviving spouse was married to the worker for at least nine months before the worker's death. Furthermore, benefits to the surviving spouse are generally paid only if that person is not currently married, unless he or she did not remarry until after age 60.

A surviving spouse who is not yet 60 years old may be entitled to a mother's or father's benefit if he or she is caring for a child of the deceased worker who is either under age 16 or disabled (42 U.S.C. §402[g]). The benefit amount is equal to 75 percent of the deceased worker's benefit. A father or mother's benefit terminates if he or she remarries, when the surviving spouse becomes entitled to survivor benefits at age 60, or when the surviving spouse is eligible for Social Security retiree benefits.

Finally, there is a one-time payment of $255 to a surviving spouse. If the worker dies without a surviving spouse, the payment goes to any dependent children (42 U.S.C. §402[i]).

Children's Benefits

Children of a retiree can receive benefits if they are under 18 years of age, under 19 years of age and still attending elementary or high school, or over 18 years of age and disabled if the disability began before age 22 (42 U.S.C. §402[d]). A child includes natural children, adopted children, stepchildren, children born out of wedlock, and grandchildren. The legal definition of child can be expanded by claims of dependency. If the alleged parent claimed the child as a dependent on an income tax return, the child is entitled to child's benefits. To receive benefits, children must be unmarried and dependent upon the retiree for support.

A child's benefit is generally one-half of the retired worker's monthly benefit, but there is a family limit that caps the amount that Social Security will pay on any one worker's account. The family maximum does not affect the retired worker's own benefit, only the derivative benefits for spouse and children. Thus, the more children a retiree has, the smaller the benefit each child and his or her spouse will receive.

On the death of the retired worker, the benefits for any child who still qualifies rise to 75 percent of the retiree's benefit until the child outgrows age-based eligibility. Disabled children remain eligible so long as their disability continues.

Parental Benefits

Parents age 62 or older of a deceased worker are eligible for benefits based on the worker's earnings record if the parent receives at least one-half of his or her support from the worker (42 U.S.C. §402[h]). A "parent" includes natural parents and adoptive parents or stepparents who became such before the child reached age 16. Support means food, shelter, routine medical care, and other necessities.

Effect of Earnings after Retirement

Since 2000, a worker who reaches full retirement age can continue to work and receive the full amount of his or her retirement benefits. If you elect to take benefits before your full retirement age, an income test limits the amount of earnings you can receive before your Social Security benefits are reduced. This test includes only income from employment or self-employment and excludes income from other sources such as interest, dividends, or pensions.

Scope of Earnings

Income that triggers a reduction in your benefit includes any form of wages, salaries, bonuses, commissions, and net earnings from self-employment. Annuities, investment income, interest, pensions, and veterans or other government or military retirement benefits do not reduce Social Security benefits.

Applicable Thresholds

Once you reach full retirement age, your earnings have no effect on retirement benefits. Workers who claim benefits before reaching full retirement age have their benefits reduced $1 for every $2 earned above an earnings threshold ($14,160 in 2010) (42 U.S.C. §403[b]). This exempt earnings amount is adjusted annually for inflation. For example, Doris claims benefits at age 62. She works part time and earns $20,480, or $6,320 above the 2010 earnings limit. Her Social Security benefits will be reduced by $3,160.

In the year a worker reaches full retirement age, $1 in benefits will be deducted for each $3 earned above a higher earnings threshold ($37,680 in 2010). This exempt earnings threshold is also adjusted annually for inflation. Only earnings before the month when the worker reaches full retirement age are counted.

Effect on Derivative Benefits

The Social Security retirement earnings test is applied on an individual basis; a spouse's earnings are not considered in applying the earnings test to the retiree. However, if the benefits to the retiree are reduced due to excess earnings, any derivative benefits paid to a spouse or to any children will be reduced as well. The exception is for benefits to a divorced spouse, whose benefits are not affected by the reduction.

Taxation of Benefits

For most recipients, Social Security benefits are not taxed. However, approximately 25 percent of recipients are subject to a two-tiered federal income tax on benefits, based on the recipient's overall income (see 26 U.S.C. §86). This tax is triggered by income from any source, unlike the retirement earnings test, which considers only earned income. Individuals who do not have any earned income may still owe federal income tax on their Social Security benefits if their income from other sources is more than a certain amount. Income is calculated as the sum of

- adjusted gross income,
- tax-free interest income, and
- one-half of the recipient's Social Security benefits.

The tax on Social Security benefits is broken into two tiers. To be subject to the first tier of the tax, you must have income greater than $25,000 if single and $32,000 if married and filing a joint return. The amount in excess of the threshold is taxable, but under the first tier, no more than one-half of the recipient's Social Security benefits are taxed. To be subject to the second tier of the tax, a recipient must have income greater than $34,000 if single and $44,000 if married and filing a joint return. Eighty-five percent of the amount exceeding the threshold is added to the result from the first tier. This total amount is then taxable. At a maximum, no more than 85 percent of a recipient's Social Security benefits will be subject to taxation.

Disability Benefits

Disability benefits are payable to disabled workers as young as 21 years old. To qualify as disabled, the individual must be unable to perform any substantial gainful activity by reason of a medically established physical or mental impairment (42 U.S.C. §423[d]). The disability is determined by medical examinations, as well as vocational tests that assess whether a worker can be retrained for another type of employment. A disabled person can receive benefits up to full retirement age when the individual then begins receiving old-age benefits.

A disabled worker who receives workers compensation benefits may have his or her Social Security disability benefits reduced (42 U.S.C. §424a). This is known as the 80 percent rule because combined benefits cannot exceed 80 percent of the highest average monthly earnings in the five years preceding the onset of disability. If the combined benefits exceed 80 percent of the highest average monthly earnings, the Social Security benefits will be reduced so that total benefits will meet the 80 percent rule.

Application and Appeals Procedures

You can complete a Social Security benefit application online or at any of the SSA's local field offices. In general, you must provide proof of eligibility, such as proof of age, for the specific benefit sought. If your application is denied, SSA has a four-step process for contesting the determination (20 C.F.R. pt. 404, subpt. J). The field office handles the first step, in which it reconsiders initial determinations. The reconsideration is done by an employee of SSA who was not previously involved with the application. You may submit new evidence at this stage. The second step is a hearing before an administrative law judge within the SSA. The third step is a review of the administrative law judge's decision by the Appeals Council of the SSA. The Appeals Council can deny hearing on a case, remand the case back to the administrative law judge for further review, or hear the case and render a decision itself. Finally, you can seek judicial review in a federal district court.

Throughout the appeals process, you may have someone represent your interests. This person can be an attorney, but need not be. Other advocates, such as a union official, can represent a claimant.

Supplemental Security Income

If you are age 65 or older, blind, or disabled, and have very limited income and resources, you may be eligible for a federal cash assistance program known as Supplemental Security Income (SSI) (42 U.S.C. §1381a). Eligibility for SSI is very important because in most states it automatically qualifies you for Medicaid, the federal/state program of subsidized medical care (see Chapter 6 for a discussion of Medicaid eligibility), as well as for food stamps. Although SSI is funded and operated through the Social Security Administration, SSI eligibility differs from Social Security because it is based on financial need rather than your work record or the work record of your spouse. The following describes SSI benefits and eligibility requirements.

Benefits

SSI pays monthly cash benefits to qualified individuals and couples. The maximum benefit for an individual in 2010 was $674 per month, and the maximum benefit for a couple was $1,011 per month. Benefit amounts are adjusted annually for inflation. If you live in a nursing home or another institution with more than sixteen residents, your SSI benefit will be limited to a $30 per month personal needs allowance. Couples living in institutions can receive up to $60 per month.

If you live in someone else's household (for example, you live with an adult child), the benefit is reduced by one-third (20 C.F.R. §416.1131). This reduction is based on the presumption that you are receiving free food and shelter. The actual value of the items received is irrelevant. However, additional in-kind support will not cause a further reduction in benefits.

The one-third reduction will not apply if you pay your pro rata share of the cost of the room and food (20 C.F.R. §416.1133). The pro rata share is determined by dividing the average monthly household expenses, such as food, rent, property taxes, and utilities, by the number of persons in the household, regardless of age. For individuals who cannot pay their share of the expenses until they receive benefits, no reduction will be made if the person in charge of the household is only loaning the value of food and shelter with the expectation of repayment.

Another exception to the one-third reduction rule applies when the SSI recipient is a tenant in the house rather than merely living in someone else's household (20 C.F.R. §416.1132). This arrangement is viewed for SSI purposes as two separate households. Factors that establish separate household status include that the SSI recipient is not

- participating in household expenditure decisions,
- pooling money with others to meet expenses, and
- responsible for specific household bills.

All but five states supplement SSI benefits by providing additional monthly benefits.[3] Each state has its own criteria for determining who qualifies for such benefits and how much the state will pay. A number of states have the Social Security Administration administer payment of their state supplement.[4] If you live in one of these states, your state supplement will be included as a part of the SSI payment. No separate application for the state supplement is necessary.

In states that administer their own supplemental payment, you must apply for the supplement with the appropriate state agency. Some states pay supplements that depend on where the recipient is housed. Usually the objective of the state supplement is to help the recipient afford room and board in a setting such as a board and care home.

If you have an immediate need for either income or health care coverage, SSA may give emergency advance payments of SSI benefits. A onetime emergency advance payment may be made to address a financial emergency, which is defined as an immediate threat to health or safety, such as the inability to obtain food, clothing, shelter, or medical care. The amount of the emergency advance payment cannot exceed the federal benefit rate plus any available state supplement. Emergency advance payment amounts are recovered by SSA through proportionate reductions in SSI benefits over a period up to six months.

Eligibility for SSI Benefits

To be eligible for SSI, you must be a resident citizen of the United States or a qualified alien.[5] Illegal aliens are not eligible for SSI. If an SSI beneficiary is out of the country for more than thirty days, benefits are suspended until the beneficiary returns to the country (42 U.S.C. §1382[f]).

To receive SSI, you must file an application at a Social Security office or other authorized federal or state office (20 C.F.R. §416.305). Applicants are required to provide detailed information, including proof of income and resources, written authorization for the SSA to investigate their bank accounts, and proof of their living arrangements such as receipts and utility bills.

Applicants must also prove that they meet the SSI eligibility requirements as to age, blindness, or disability. To qualify based on age, you must prove that you are at least 65 years of age, verified by a public record such as a birth certificate, a religious birth record documented before age 5, or Immigration and Naturalization Service documents. If you are blind or disabled, you must submit to medical and vocational evaluations to substantiate those conditions. Applicants who knowingly provide false information or omit material information may have benefits suspended up to sixth months for the first offense, twelve months for the second offense, and twenty-four months for subsequent offenses.

Income Eligibility Requirements

Because SSI eligibility is based on financial need, there are strict income and asset rules that determine who is eligible (20 C.F.R. pt. 416, subpt. B). To receive benefits, your monthly income and assets must be below amounts set by the federal government. These amounts are adjusted annually for inflation.

Income eligibility is determined on a monthly basis. In 2010, to qualify for SSI an individual must have less than $674 in "countable income" per month, and a couple must have less than $1,011 (20 C.F.R. pt. 416, subpt. K).

Countable Income. Countable income is anything a person receives in cash or in-kind support that can be used to meet the need for food or shelter. It includes earned income, such as wages, and unearned income, such as pensions, Social Security, dividends, and interest (42 U.S.C. §1382a). Countable income even includes gifts. In-kind income may be earned, such as rent-free housing provided by an employer, or unearned, such as a gift of food. Whatever the form, all in-kind income that meets the need for food and shelter is countable income in determining eligibility for SSI. In-kind support that is not food or shelter, however, is not income and so does not count for determining SSI eligibility. For example, free medical or dental care is not considered income for SSI purposes, nor are gifts of a television or clothing.

SSI eligibility is determined monthly based on the countable income received two months previously. For example, SSI eligibility for March is determined by January's countable income. For initial eligibility, however, the countable income for the month in which SSI benefits are requested is used to determine SSI eligibility for that month and the next two months.

Not all income is countable income. The following are examples of some of the income that is not countable:

- value of food stamps
- home energy assistance
- state assistance
- disaster assistance
- loans that you have to repay
- income tax refunds
- food or shelter provided by nonprofit agencies

There are also exclusions from earned and unearned income used to arrive at the countable income figure for SSI eligibility. The monthly exclusion from unearned income is $20 and the monthly exclusion from earned income is $65. First, the $20 exclusion is subtracted from an applicant's unearned income, which is income other than wages, salary, or other employment compensation. For example, if you receive $70 per month in pension income, only $50 a month would be countable unearned income.

If you have less than $20 a month in unearned income, the $20 is subtracted from whatever unearned income you have, and the remainder is subtracted from your earned income. For example, if you have $15 a month in dividends and $125 a month in wages, the $20 is first subtracted from the unearned income of $15 ($15 − $20 = −$5), which leaves $5 to be deducted from the $125 of wages ($125 − $5 = $120). Then the $65 exclusion from earned income is subtracted from the $120 figure ($120 − $65 = $55), leaving $55 in earned income.

Once you have determined your earned income by this formula, one-half of whatever is left in earned income is then excluded. After the exclusions are taken out, the remaining earned income and unearned income figures are added together. If the sum is less than the maximum amount of the applicable monthly SSI benefit ($674 for individuals and $1,011 for couples in 2010), the individual or couple qualifies for SSI.

Consider the following example. Abby is single, age 67, and has no resources. She receives $200 a month from Social Security and has a part-time job that pays her $475 a month. The following calculations will be used to determine Abby's countable income:

Unearned income:	$200
Exclusion:	−20
	$180
Total countable unearned income = $180	
Earned income:	$475
Exclusion:	−65
	$410
	$410
Less one-half of earned income:	−205
	$205
Total countable earned income = $205	
Total countable income:	
Unearned	$180
Earned	+$205
	$385

Because the maximum monthly benefit in 2010 was $674, each $1 of countable income reduces Abby's SSI benefit by $1, yielding a monthly SSI benefit of $289 ($674 − $385 = $289) (20 C.F.R. §416.410).

Couples. The basic calculation of countable income for couples is the same but may be complicated by changing circumstances. For example, if an eligible individual becomes a couple with an ineligible spouse, the ineligible spouse's income is deemed to be available to the eligible spouse and is included in determining countable income. If both individuals are eligible and they separate, each will be paid at the individual rate (20 C.F.R. §416.432). If only one is eligible before separation, the income of the ineligible spouse will not be considered when determining benefits for the eligible spouse after separation. Couples need not be legally married under state law, but are considered married for SSI purposes if they live together and hold themselves out to the community as being married (42 U.S.C. §1382c[d][2]).

Resource Eligibility Requirements

Resources are cash, or liquid assets, and any real or personal property that an applicant could convert to cash for food and shelter. Individual applicants are ineligible for SSI if they have more than $2,000 in countable resources (20 C.F.R. §416.1205). Couples are excluded if they have more than $3,000 in countable resources (*id.*). Unlike income, however, resources that exceed the limits can be converted into exempt resources or spent down in order to make the applicant eligible, subject to the resource transfer rules to be discussed later in this chapter (20 C.F.R. pt. 416, subpt. L).

Some assets are partially or totally excluded from the eligibility test (42 U.S.C. §1382b). They include the following:

- the value of your home and the land on which it is located
- proceeds from the sale of the home if used to purchase another home within three months
- household goods and personal effects (but not investment property such as gems or collectibles)
- medical equipment
- the value of one vehicle if used for your transportation or that of your household members
- real or personal property necessary for self-support up to a value of $6,000 or items for self-support, such as a vegetable garden
- the value of burial plots for you and your immediate family
- up to $1,500 specifically set aside for burial expenses
- life insurance with a death value up to $1,500 (life insurance with a death value greater than $1,500 is a countable resource in the amount of its cash surrender value)
- cash received to be used to replace lost, damaged, or stolen excluded property if it is so used within nine months of receipt

The receipt of a lump sum such as an inheritance or lawsuit settlement is considered income in the month received. Any portion retained into the next month is considered a countable resource. A condition for receiving SSI benefits is the agreement to pursue all available sources of food and shelter. Therefore, an individual cannot renounce an inheritance to acquire or maintain eligibility for SSI.

If the individual has resources that exceed the limit, he or she may still begin to receive SSI benefits immediately if the following conditions exist:

- Total excess liquid resources, such as cash, do not exceed one-fourth of the dollar amount of the basic federal benefit.
- The applicant agrees to dispose of the excess nonliquid resources within nine months if real property and within three months if personal property (the three-month period can be extended another three months for good cause) (20 C.F.R. §416.1245).

The individual will not be forced to sell a jointly owned house if its sale would cause an undue hardship because the other owner lives in the house or if attempts to sell the house have been unsuccessful. An undue hardship means that no other housing is readily available.

Resource Transfer Rules. An individual or couple who gives away countable resources may be ineligible for SSI. On application for SSI, you must account for any transfer that was for less than fair market value during the thirty-six months preceding the application (42 U.S.C. §1382b[c]). You will not be eligible for a period of time equal to the value of the transferred resources divided by the federal SSI payment rate and the state supplement, if any, up to a maximum of thirty-six months. The penalty period begins to run in the month of the transfer.

For example, Mel, age 68, gave $3,100 to his daughter on May 1, 2009. The period for which he is ineligible for SSI is five months ($3,100 ÷ $674 = 4.6 months [the period is rounded to the nearest whole number]). If a married applicant makes a transfer that results in a period of ineligibility, and then the spouse becomes eligible for benefits, the penalty is divided between the applicant and the spouse.

SSA presumes that transfer or disposal of assets for less than fair market value was made to establish initial or continued eligibility for SSI benefits. An individual can challenge that presumption by presenting evidence that the transfer was for a purpose other than creating eligibility. Transfers that were not made with the intent of qualifying for benefits can be reversed and the penalty avoided if the resources are returned. Where a transfer penalty would impose a hardship, the SSA can waive the penalty.

Certain transfers are exempt from the transfer penalties. Transfers to or for the sole benefit of the spouse do not create a period of ineligibility. Other exempt transfers include the transfer of a home to a spouse, a child under age 21, a child who is blind or disabled, a sibling with an interest in the house who has resided there for more than one year prior to the applicant entering an institution, or a child who resided in the home for a period of at least two years immediately prior to the applicant entering an institution and who provided care to the applicant that delayed the applicant's entry into an institution (42 U.S.C. §1382b[c][1][C][i]).

Notes

1. For more information on calculating quarters of coverage, see 20 C.F.R. §404.140-146.

2. Social Security Amendments of 1983, Pub. L. No. 98-21, 97 Stat. 65 (1983) (codified as amended in scattered sections of 42 U.S.C.).

3. Arkansas, Kansas, Mississippi, Tennessee, and West Virginia do not provide additional benefits.

4. These states are California, Delaware, District of Columbia, Hawaii, Iowa, Massachusetts, Michigan, Montana, Nevada, New Jersey, New York, Pennsylvania, Rhode Island, Utah, and Vermont.

5. There are seven categories of noncitizens who are qualified aliens as determined by the Department of Homeland Security. Qualified aliens must meet additional requirements for SSI eligibility beyond being aged, blind, or disabled and having limited income and resources (8 U.S.C. §1612[a]).

For More Information

Social Security Administration (800-772-1213)
(http://www.ssa.gov)

Find information about retirement, disability, and SSI benefits. The site provides guidance concerning online applications as well as the location of local Social Security offices. There are also tools to help you estimate benefits and make decisions about when to begin receiving retirement benefits.

4

Employer-Provided Retirement Benefits and IRAs

Did You Know?

- You could owe a 10 percent penalty tax if you withdraw retirement benefits before age 59½.
- You can receive early distributions from your individual retirement account (IRA) without penalty if the money is for the higher education expenses of yourself, your spouse, your child, or your grandchild.
- You could owe a penalty if you *fail* to begin taking benefits from your retirement plan and IRAs after you reach age 70½.
- Distributions from most retirement plans are taxable to the recipient, even when the recipient is the spouse or beneficiary of a retiree who dies.
- If you leave your job after you are vested in the retirement plan, you may be able to roll over your benefits into an individual IRA without tax consequences.

Most Americans look forward to a time when they can retire. After a lifetime of work, they hope to enjoy their later years without the burden of a daily job. Of course, retirement means the loss of a steady paycheck, and so seniors must have another source of income. Social Security benefits are a start, and many seniors will save for their retirement. Most seniors expect to receive retirement benefits from their former employer. In reality, only about one-half of retirees enjoy retirement benefits other than Social Security benefits.

This chapter discusses the laws that govern retiree pensions and retirement benefits such as 401(k) plans. All private employer–sponsored retirement benefit plans are exclusively governed by federal law, the Employee Retirement Insurance Security Act enacted in 1974, commonly referred to as ERISA (29 U.S.C. §§1001 *et seq.*). Federal law preempts any state law in this area, meaning that states cannot attempt to regulate employee pension, retirement, or welfare benefit plans in a way that is inconsistent with federal law. ERISA, however, does not govern pension plans sponsored by public entities such as states and cities.

ERISA defines two basic types of employee benefit plans: (1) "employee pension benefit plans" or "pension plans" and (2) "employee welfare benefit plans" or "welfare plans" (29 U.S.C. §1002[1], [2], [3]). Employer-offered benefit plans, both pension and welfare, are also regulated under the Internal Revenue Code (IRC), which grants very favorable tax treatment to those plans that meet a number of detailed requirements. Plans that receive favorable tax treatment are called "qualified" plans because they meet the qualifications required by the IRC.

Pension plans are created by employers to provide employees with retirement income after the employee reaches a certain age and ends employment with the employer. In contrast, welfare plans provide employees, and sometimes retirees, with a variety of benefits, the most important of which are health, disability, and life insurance. Health care insurance is by far the most important and valuable benefit offered by employer-provided welfare plans.

Pension and Retirement Plans

Employee pension benefit plans are further defined by ERISA as either "defined benefit plans" or "defined contribution plans"(29 U.S.C. §1002[34], [35]). For the purposes of this book, the term "pension plan" is used interchangeably with the term "defined benefit plan" to refer to plans that provide lifetime benefits, usually a fixed monthly payment for life. The term "retirement plan" is used interchangeably with "defined contribution plan" to refer to plans that provide a lump-sum dollar amount to the employee upon retirement. Employers can offer both pension and retirement plans. The following examples illustrate the difference.

Jill worked for Alpha Inc., which provides its retired employees with a *pension plan* equal to 60 percent of their last year's earnings. Jill earned $50,000 her last year before she retired, and so she will be paid $30,000 a year for life (60% x $50,000 = $30,000). In contrast, Jason worked for Beta Inc., a company with a *retirement plan* to which it contributes an amount equal to 5 percent of the employee's wages. The funds in this account are payable to that employee upon retirement. Jason has worked for Beta Inc. for thirty years, during which time each pay period Beta contributed 5 percent of his wages to his retirement account. Upon Jason's retirement at age 65, he is entitled to his retirement account worth $472,300.

This chapter discusses the important differences between pension and retirement plans and provides information on related topics such as normal retirement age (NRA), vesting requirements, 401(k) plans, and the role of IRAs.

Defined Benefit or Pension Plans

Defined benefit plans are pension plans that promise participating employees a specified monthly pension benefit at retirement. Most defined benefit plans do not promise a particular dollar amount; rather, they promise a benefit determined by a formula. This formula is based on the employee's number of years of employment and his or her rate of pay.

Consider the following example. John works for Chi Company, which offers a plan that will pay a pension for life. The formula used by Chi to determine the benefit amount for its retirees is the employee's average pay for the last three years of employment multiplied by a percentage based on the number of years of employment. Chi Company uses a factor of 1.5 to determine this percentage. At age 65 John retires. He has worked for Chi Company for thirty years, and his average pay for the last three years of employment was $60,000. His pension is computed as follows: 30 years x 1.5 = 45%; 45% x $60,000 = $27,000. After his retirement at age 65, John will receive a yearly pension of $27,000 for life.

Some employees, such as construction workers, work for a variety of firms over their careers. In industries where employees work for various employers, the employers may contribute to a common defined benefit plan known as a "multiemployer" pension plan (29 U.S.C. §1002[37][A]). Typically this is available when the employees are members of a union that bargains for a pension plan on behalf of its members. A multiemployer plan operates like any defined benefit plan. Over the working life of the employee, the various employers contribute to a single defined benefit pension plan. The plan pays benefits based upon a formula that treats the employees as if they had worked for a single employer during their careers.

Regardless of how a defined benefit pension is calculated, payments are made for the life of the employee and, if the employee is married, until both the employee and the spouse have died (unless the spouse has waived his or her rights under the pension) (29 U.S.C. §1055). For married retirees, the amount of the monthly payment is often reduced because the benefit will likely be paid for more years. For example, Hank and Tom have both been employed by Sigma Inc. for thirty years and have identical pay histories. They share the same birthday and retire on the same date. Hank is single. According to the formula used to determine pensions, he is entitled to $25,000 a year for life. If Tom were single, he, too, would receive $25,000 a year for life. Tom, however, is married to Tina and so will receive a joint life annuity, meaning that the annuity will be paid until the last of the two dies. As a result, Tom's pension is reduced to $18,000 a year because, taken together, Tom and Tina have a longer life expectancy than does Hank. Although employers are not required to reduce the benefit paid to a husband and wife, they typically do.

In a defined benefit plan, the employer each year contributes the amount that is estimated as necessary to ensure enough plan assets to pay the benefits promised to employees. The employer contributions are held in a trust fund and invested, usually in stocks and bonds. The investment earnings are added to the fund and help pay for the promised pensions.

Actuaries, using estimates of how many years employees can be expected to work, their estimated average compensation when they retire, and the expected rate of investment return on the plan assets determine how much the employer must contribute each year. The rate of return on the investments is a critical component in determining how much the employer must contribute to the pension fund. Because the fund invests its assets and earns income, the employer does not have to contribute every dollar that will eventually be paid in benefits.

The greater the earnings are by a defined benefit plan fund, the fewer are the dollars the employer will need to contribute to the fund. In some years, the employer will not need to pay any money to the fund because the earnings on the fund will have exceeded what the actuary estimated is needed. In other years, the investments of the fund will not have produced as much income as expected. This means that the employer will have to contribute more to make up for the shortfall. Because employer contributions vary based upon the fund's investment earnings, defined benefit plans place the risk of how well the plan investments perform upon the employer. Regardless of how well the plan investments perform, the employee benefits do not vary. The employer contributions to the plan cannot be returned to the employer unless the plan is terminated and there is more money in the plan than is needed to pay off all the promised employee pensions (29 U.S.C. §1344).

A defined benefit plan can be "integrated" with Social Security, meaning that benefits paid by the plan to an employee are reduced to reflect in part the benefits that the employee receives from Social Security (I.R.C. §401[a][5][D]). Integration, which lowers the cost of plans for the employer, is complicated and subject to complex statutory and regulatory requirements, but the bottom line is that integrated plans pay fewer benefits than do nonintegrated plans.

Another form of defined benefit pension plan that is growing in popularity with employers is the "cash balance plan." In a cash balance plan, the employer makes an annual contribution to a pension account for the employee based upon a formula, typically a percentage of the employee's compensation. The employer also announces an investment rate of return. This rate is not the actual investment return on the plan fund, but rather the rate that will determine the annual amount credited to the fund. For example, the plan may announce that it will credit employees' accounts with an annual compounded rate of return of 6 percent. Even though each account will be credited with the announced rate of return, in reality the rate of investment return on the collective fund could be higher or lower. If the actual rate of return is higher than the announced rate of return, the excess investment income does not benefit the employees but rather reduces the employer's required annual contribution. If the actual return is lower, the employer must make up the difference.

Employers that offer a cash balance pension plan try to select an announced rate of return that they are confident the plan investments can earn. For example, they might select the interest rate on U.S. Treasury bonds. Upon retirement, the employee is paid a lump sum equal to the contributions made by the employer plus the announced rate of return.

Defined Contribution or Retirement Plans

Retirement plans are quite different from pension plans. Called defined contribution plans, they do not promise any set amount of benefits. Rather, the employer promises to place a set amount aside in an account for the benefit of the employee. Each year of employment that the plan is in effect, the employer adds an additional amount to the employee's retirement account. The account is invested in stocks, bonds, and other investments, and the earnings are added to the account of the employee. On the date the employee retires (leaves the employment of the employer) and has reached the designated retirement age, the employee is given access to his or her retirement account.

Payment options under retirement plans vary from employer to employer. Depending on the plan rules, the employee will either be able to withdraw all the money in the retirement account or use that money to purchase a lifetime annuity. For example, Betty has worked for Delta Inc. for the last thirty years. Each year, pursuant to the company's retirement plan, Delta placed an amount equal to 3 percent of Betty's annual wages into her retirement account. It invested the account, and the earnings from that investment were added to the account. When Betty left the company at age 62 (the earliest year in which she could access her account), her account had a total value of $210,000. Under the terms of the plan, Betty could either withdraw the entire $210,000 or she could purchase a lifetime annuity that would pay her $15,000 a year for life.

Under a traditional defined contribution plan, the employer names a plan administrator or trustee who has the responsibility for managing the plan, which includes investing the employee accounts and distributing the benefits to the retired employees. The defined contribution plan combines all the funds for the employees into a single investment account. The employees have no control as to how the fund is invested; that is the duty of the plan administrator. Employer contributions to the plan cannot be returned to the employer.

A defined contribution plan places the risk of success of the plan's investment upon the employees. The employer only promises to contribute a set amount and makes no promises as to how rapidly the amount will grow. The amount the employee will eventually receive depends heavily on how well the investments of the defined contribution plan perform. The greater the earnings are, the greater is the employee's retirement benefit. For example, Kathy works for Delta Inc. and Kent works for Epsilon Inc. Both are paid the same wage, and both companies contribute an amount equal to 5 percent of their wages to a defined contribution plan. Kathy's account, managed by the Delta fund over her twenty-five-year work history, has an average investment return of 7 percent. During Kent's twenty-five-year work history, the Epsilon plan has an average rate of return of only 5 percent. As a result, when Kathy and Kent retire at the same time, Kathy's lump-sum distribution is $500,000, whereas Kent's is only $400,000.

Employee stock ownership plans (ESOPs) are a particular type of defined contribution plan. An ESOP creates individual accounts for each participant that are funded primarily with the employer's stock, and the benefits are generally paid in the form of employer stock. For example, Lisa works for Alpha Company, which operates an ESOP. The ESOP fund consists of 85 percent Alpha Company stock and 15 percent U.S. Treasury bonds. When Lisa retires, she will receive a distribution that will consist almost exclusively of Alpha Company stock, which she can then sell or continue to hold.

Because ERISA is supposed to promote fairness and greater employee participation in pension and retirement plans, it limits an employer's ability to exclude certain employees from pension and retirement plans and restricts the employer's authority to discriminate against lower-paid employees with respect to benefits. For example, a company cannot operate a qualified pension or retirement plan—a plan that enjoys the federal income tax advantages of a qualified plan—if the plan covers only the higher-paid management employees. The act contains complex nondiscrimination rules that generally require a plan to benefit at least 70 percent of non–highly compensated employees so that the plan does not disproportionately benefit highly compensated employees such as the company officers (I.R.C. §401[a][4]).

Normal Retirement Age

If you participate in an employer-sponsored pension or retirement plan, you cannot receive retirement benefits from it until you have reached the normal retirement age stated in the plan. An NRA cannot be later than either age 65 or ten years after you start work. For example, Alpha Inc. has an NRA of age 65, but Tom begins to work for Alpha at age 58. Alpha can use age 68 (ten years after Tom's start date) as Tom's NRA. When you reach the NRA, you may, but are not required to, retire and collect your retirement benefits.

To retire means only that you quit your job with your employer. It does not mean that you have to stop working altogether. You can quit, collect retirement benefits, and find a new job. For example, Carol works for Beta Inc., which has a defined benefit pension plan with an NRA of age 62. Carol turns age 62 and retires from Beta Inc. and begins to collect her defined benefit pension. She then goes to work for Kappa Company. Her employment with Kappa Company will not affect her right to collect her monthly pension from Beta Inc.

If you quit before you reach the NRA, you cannot collect any benefits until you reach the NRA. For example, Dale also works for Beta Inc. After thirty years of working for Beta Inc., Dale quits at age 60 and does not take another job. He must wait until he turns age 62 to begin to collect his pension from Beta Inc. The same is true for Emily, who quits at age 42 after working for Beta Inc. for ten years. She has earned a pension by virtue of her ten years of employment, but she must wait twenty years, until she turns 62, to collect it.

If you continue to work past the NRA, you will continue to earn additional pension benefits, subject to any plan limits. The plan, for example, may cap the number of years of employment used to determine the size of your pension. For example, Ed, age 68, has worked thirty-seven years for Kappa Company, which has a pension plan with an NRA of age 65 and a thirty-five-year limit on the number of countable years used to calculate the defined benefit pension. No matter how many years above thirty-five Ed actually works at Kappa, his pension will be calculated as if he had worked there for only thirty-five years.

Defined benefit plans sometimes have an NRA of 65 and an alternative trigger for benefits based on a combination of the employee's age and years of employment. For example, the plan might permit employees to qualify for their pension whenever the combination of their age and number of years of employment totals a designated number, such as ninety. Fred is age 60 and has worked for the employer for thirty years. He can retire and begin his pension payments because the total of his age plus the number of years worked adds up to ninety.

Plans may offer survivor's benefits to family members of employees who die before they have retired or reached the NRA. Some plans pay a lump-sum death benefit to surviving spouses or heirs of a deceased employee. Plans may also pay a disability pension to a disabled employee until he or she reaches the normal retirement age and is eligible for the retirement pension.

Vesting

Under ERISA, employees must become "vested" to receive retirement benefits. Vesting means that an employee's retirement benefits cannot be lost or forfeited once he or she has participated in the plan for a prescribed number of years—typically five years or on a graduated basis over seven years (29

U.S.C. §1053). After an employee is vested, termination of employment will not mean the loss of the pension. For example, Garth worked for Beta Inc. from 1990 to 2000 and quit before he reached the plan NRA of 62. When Garth turns age 62, he will be eligible for whatever retirement benefits he earned while employed with Beta.

Note that Garth could have vested pension benefit plans from more than one employer. Suppose that after he left Beta Inc. he went to work for Rho Company for ten years and earned a vested pension payable at the NRA of age 62. When Garth turns age 62, he can begin to collect pensions from both Beta Inc. and Rho Company.

Like defined benefit plans, defined contribution plans also provide for vesting after a minimum number of years of participation, usually five, but as long as seven. If you terminate employment after being vested, the value of your retirement account will continue to grow according to the success of the plan's investments until you withdraw the value of the account. You can withdraw money from a defined contribution account operated by a former employer at any age, but because of income tax advantages (discussed later in the chapter), you would be wise not to withdraw funds until you have reached at least age 59½.

In the past, defined benefit plans were the most commonly offered form of pension or retirement plan, but they have lost favor in recent years and now represent fewer than 20 percent of all plans. The greatest attraction of a defined benefit for employees is the knowledge that the longer they work for the employer, the larger will be their pensions. Employees also like that at any time they can calculate their future benefits. For example, if you expect to retire at age 62 under a defined benefit pension plan, at age 60 you could estimate pretty closely what your monthly benefit is likely to be by plugging numbers into the pension formula. Many employers with defined benefit plans provide their workers with annual estimates of individual employee projected pension benefits.

Employees who change employers frequently or who are not sure how long they will stay with their present employer are less attracted to defined benefit plans. Suppose, for example, that during your work career you work for three companies, Alpha, Beta, and Chi, each for ten years. You are vested in each company's defined benefit plan, and each uses the same formula to determine your retirement pension. The formula is (2% × the number of years employed) × (your average wage for the last two years of employment). In other words, based on ten years of employment, you will receive a 20 percent replacement (2% × 10 yrs.) of your average ending wage. Suppose that your average wage during the last two years of employment at Alpha was $40,000; at Beta, $50,000; and at Chi, $70,000. Your Alpha pension will be $8,000, your Beta pension will be $10,000, and your Chi pension will be $14,000, for a total of $32,000.

Now assume that you had spent all thirty years of your career with the same employer, Alpha, and had averaged $70,000 a year for the last two years of employment. You would have been credited with thirty years of employment multiplied by 2 percent for a multiplier of 60 percent (instead of 20 percent). At 60 percent of your $70,000 average wage, your pension would be $42,000 a year, or $10,000 more than it was when you worked for three employers.

The defined benefit plan pension is clearly most beneficial to employees who have only one or two employers in their lifetime of work. That employment pattern, however, is much less common today than in the past. Today's employees frequently change jobs, with the result that fewer employees are able to earn a substantial defined benefit pension. Consider the different outcome in our example if Alpha, Beta, and Chi all had defined contribution, rather than defined benefit, plans. Assuming that each had contributed the same percentage of your wages to a defined contribution plan, you would have the same amount in your account (provided that each had the same investment return) as if you had worked for just one of them for the entire thirty years.

Employers have also come to prefer defined contribution plans, both because they are less costly to administer and because today's employer does not expect that most employees will stay with one employer for the majority of their careers. The decline of unions, which often insisted on defined benefit plans, has also contributed to the decline of such plans. The main reason, however, that employers have turned to defined contribution plans is that such plans shift the risk of the plan investments to the employee. If a defined benefit plan has poor investment returns, the employer will have to make additional contributions to the plan in order to meet its pension obligations. In contrast, if a defined contribution plan has poor investment returns, only the employees suffer.

401(k) Plans

The fastest growing form of retirement plan is the 401(k) plan, which is a form of defined contribution plan named after the Internal Revenue Code section that authorizes it. More than one-half of all retirement plans and an overwhelming majority of new plans are 401(k) plans. The plans are very popular because the employee, rather than the employer, directs how the employee's retirement account is invested.

A 401(k) plan is a "cash or deferred arrangement" (CODA) that gives employees the choice whether to receive all of their wages now as cash wages or to have a portion of their wages contributed to a retirement plan account. If the employee elects to receive all of his or her wages now, the amount received is taxable income. However, if the employee elects to have part of his or her wages contributed to a retirement account, the retirement account contribution is not currently taxed. This tax advantage is designed to encourage employees to contribute to their retirement accounts. The employer can either make the contribution to the retirement account automatic, though reversible by the employee, or the default can be that the employees receive the cash unless they authorize it to be paid to the retirement 401(k) account (I.R.C. §401[k][2][A]). Contribution rates to 401(k) accounts are much higher if employees are automatically enrolled and contributions made on their behalf unless they choose not to contribute.

The amount that an employee can contribute each year to a 401(k) account is limited, with the limit adjusted annually for inflation. In 2010 the amount was $16,500. 401(k) plans are also subject to limitations on contributions by what the statute refers to as "highly compensated employees," typically the company executives, so that the rate of participation by these employees is not excessive compared to the rates of participation by the non–highly compensated employees (I.R.C. §401[k][3]). Employee contributions to 401(k) plans are immediately vested (I.R.C. §401[a][3]). That is, the employee will not lose his or her contributions even if the employee does not remain with the company long enough to become vested in matching amounts contributed by the employer.

Typically, a 401(k) plan permits employees to contribute up to some percentage of their wages. For example, the plan might permit a 3 percent contribution (up to the annual limit). In addition, many employers offer matching contributions. For example, suppose the plan provides for a 50 percent employer match of the employee's contribution. If you contribute 3 percent of your wages to your 401(k), a 50 percent employer match means that your employer will contribute another 1.5 percent. Neither the amounts contributed by the employer nor the amounts contributed by you are taxed until you later take distributions from your account.

When you take money out of your 401(k) account, it will be taxable income. If you take it out too soon, it will be taxed and also subject to an additional 10 percent penalty tax (I.R.C. §72[t]). Withdrawals of money are not subject to the penalty if the withdrawal does not occur until after the earliest of

- termination of employment from the employer that sponsors the plan after age 55 in conjunction with an early retirement plan,
- reaching of age 59½,
- death or disability,
- the occurrence of an immediate and pressing financial hardship, or
- reaching of the plan's NRA, which cannot be later than age 65 (29 U.S.C. §1002[24]).

Most withdrawals occur after the employee has reached age 59½ and is no longer working for the employer. Once you have reached the NRA, you can begin to take money out of the plan without the penalty tax even if you are still working for the employer who sponsored the plan. Your employer may have an early retirement plan that would permit you to withdraw funds from your 401(k) plan without the 10 percent penalty as early as age 55.

If you terminate employment with the plan sponsor before age 59½ or the normal retirement age, and you do not want to be taxed on a distribution from the 401(k), you can do either of the following:

- Leave the 401(k) account with that employer's 401(k) plan, and begin withdrawing funds from it when you reach age 59½ or the normal retirement age of the plan (subject to federal income taxation on the distributions at that time).
- Roll over the 401(k) account to an IRA that you manage (although you cannot receive money from the IRA without penalty until you reach age 59½) (I.R.C. §402[c]).

If you have a 401(k) account, you can participate in decisions about how the funds are invested, but your employer is permitted to limit your investment choices. The plan as created by the employer must offer a choice of at least three different, diversified investment options, and the plan must permit participants to transfer their assets among the three options at least every three months (29 U.S.C. §1104[c]; 29 C.F.R. §2550.404c-1[b]). Very commonly, 401(k) plans permit employees to choose among investing in bank certificates of deposit, bonds, the stock of the employer, and one or more designated mutual funds. Some plans simply permit the employee to invest in a "family" of diversified funds offered by an investment firm. Whatever the permitted choices, your employer is not liable if the investments that you choose decline in value or fail to perform as you had hoped.

Unfortunately, many 401(k) participants are not very knowledgeable about how to invest. They tend to be too conservative in their investments, investing too much in bank certificates of deposit and bonds and not enough in stocks, and so they earn a relatively low rate of return. Commonly, the employee will fail to reallocate investments and just stay with the original investment choices.

Another potential problem with 401(k) plans is that employees are permitted to borrow funds from their accounts (29 U.S.C. §1108[b][1]). While the money is out on loan, it is not growing as an investment. In some cases, the employee will never pay back the loan, with the result that the loan becomes taxable income and may be subject to the additional 10 percent penalty tax. Thus, mediocre investment results, unpaid loans from 401(k) accounts, and a failure of some employees to fully participate in the plan are some of the reasons that many employees are going to retire with only modest retirement accounts and without the economic security they will need in their later years.

Another practice that can result in poor retirement plan performance is the employer contribution of company stock, rather than cash, to match employee contributions. Employees may also be encouraged to purchase employer stock with their 401(k) contributions. As a result, many employee retirement accounts are much too concentrated in the stock of the employer. Any long-term investment should be well diversified. Investing too much in your employer's stock carries a double risk. If your employer gets into financial difficulty, not only is your job at risk, but also the value of your 401(k) account will fall. It is simply common sense not to bet both your job and your retirement investment account on the same employer.

A factor that can add to the risk of investment in employer stock is the employer practice of setting time limits on when employees can sell employer stock. For example, some employers prohibit the sale of contributed stock for five or even ten years. In the severe stock market decline of the early 2000s, many employees were unable to sell a significant proportion of their 401(k) assets because of employer time limits on the selling of the employer-contributed company stock. As a result, employees were helpless to divest or sell off stock that was rapidly losing value, some even to the point of having to retain the stock while the employer went bankrupt. The result was devastating losses of 401(k) retirement funds for many employees. Nonetheless, ERISA generally does not prohibit employers from restricting participants in the sale of company stock.

Despite some of the potential problems with 401(k) plans, they have the great advantage of being portable. Because all of your contributions to your 401(k) are immediately vested, the account belongs to you no matter what happens. Even if you are fired or quit, you continue to own the account and direct the investments until you finally take distributions from it. If you stop working for the employer who sponsored your 401(k), you have the option to leave it alone, to transfer it to a new 401(k) account offered by your new employer, or to "roll over" your 401(k) investments into an IRA that you own and whose investments are directed by you (I.R.C. §408[d][3]). If you roll over the account within sixty days of termination of your employment, the transfer is not subject to federal income tax. The returns on the investments by the IRA continue to be free of income tax until finally distributed to you. Over your work career, you could roll over several 401(k) accounts to an IRA as you move from job to job.

Some employers permit employees to convert their 401(k) accounts to "Roth" accounts. Even though the amounts placed in a Roth 401(k) are taxed as income, all future distributions from the account are tax free, including all the investment income earned by the account. For taxation purposes, you can think of a Roth 401(k) as just the opposite of the traditional 401(k). In a traditional 401(k) the contributions are excluded from income taxation, but the distributions (including any earnings) are eventually taxed.

With a Roth account, the contributions are subject to income taxation, but the earnings and distributions are not.

Qualified Plans

Qualified plans are retirement plans that receive favorable federal income tax treatment because they meet the complex requirements of the Internal Revenue Code. This favorable tax treatment is meant to promote employer-provided pension and retirement plans. Nonqualified plans are those plans that do not meet these requirements and do not receive favorable tax treatment.

Qualified plans enjoy three significant income tax advantages:

1. The employer may deduct from its taxable income contributions made to the plan (I.R.C. §404[a][1],[2], [3]).
2. Though the employer takes a tax deduction for contributions, the employees do not report any income or pay any tax until distributions are actually paid to them (I.R.C. §402[a]).
3. Investment earnings on the retirement account funds are not taxed until paid out to the employee (I.R.C. §501[a]).

How Pension and Retirement Plans Operate

Employers are not required to create or operate pension or retirement plans, and about one-half of all employers do not. Moreover, the employer has the right to change or terminate the plan at any time. An employer that has decided to create a pension or retirement plan is a "plan sponsor" and decides whether the plan will be a defined benefit, cash balance, or defined contribution plan. The employer also decides which employees will be included in the plan. Absent a collective bargaining agreement with a union, employers are granted by federal law a fair amount of discretion as to whom to include in the plan. A qualified retirement plan may exclude employees under age 21 and may also require an employee to complete one year of employment before becoming eligible to join the plan (29 U.S.C. §1052). The plan can also exclude classes of employees. Often an employer will exclude union members because the union members may have collectively bargained for a separate pension plan. Some employers exclude a particular job classification. A law firm, for example, might exclude messengers from participating in its plan, which is otherwise open to all the other staff and all the attorneys.

If the plan is a defined benefit plan, the employer must determine the benefit formula. For a defined contribution plan, it must decide on the amount of the employer contribution or whether to adopt a 401(k) plan. The employer must also determine the kind of distributions the plan will pay, such as lump-sum distributions or annuities.

The employer, as plan sponsor, must name a plan administrator, who may be a single individual or several persons. The plan administrator will be responsible for managing the plan, including identifying who is eligible, overseeing the investments, paying the benefits, filing required governmental reports, and maintaining the plan records. The plan sponsor can name itself as the plan administrator, and many do. Others name banks or other institutions as the plan administrator. Some name corporate officers, such as the vice president for finance.

ERISA requires that retirement benefits become vested no later than seven years after the employee started employment. Employees must be allowed to join the retirement plan at least by the time they reach age 21 or have been employed for one year, whichever comes later. However, a pension plan may require three years of employment for eligibility if at the end of those three years the employee also immediately becomes 100 percent vested (29 U.S.C. §1052).

Spousal Benefits

ERISA requires that qualified plans offer joint and survivor annuities for married employees. A joint and survivor annuity pays a retirement benefit until both spouses have died, unless that right was specifically waived in writing by the employee and the spouse (29 U.S.C. §1055). To reject the survivor option, both the employee and the spouse must sign a written waiver that is witnessed by a plan representative or notary public. The employee has ninety days to change his or her mind and revoke the waiver of spousal rights.

Normally qualified plan benefits cannot be assigned for payment to creditors or other third parties. The only exception is that the benefits can be subject to a state qualified domestic relations order (QDRO) (29 U.S.C. §1056[d][3]). Under a QDRO, pension rights can be altered and reassigned. For example, the QDRO could provide that the divorced spouse of the plan participant, rather than the current spouse, will be treated as the surviving spouse for purposes of receiving the survivor's annuity after the death of the plan participant. Or the benefits under the plan might be made payable to the former spouse, rather than to the employee.

Payment of Benefits

When you qualify and apply for benefits under a pension or retirement plan, you will either receive a lump-sum amount or a lifetime annuity. If you are married, the plan must pay an annuity until both you and your spouse have died, unless your spouse waived the right to the annuity. Plans often purchase annuities for retired employees from an insurance company, which in turn pays the lifetime annuity to the retired employee.

In the case of a 401(k) plan, upon your retirement you have the right to withdraw the entire value of the account, but of course any amounts withdrawn are subject to federal income taxation. In many cases, it would be much wiser to roll the 401(k) funds over into an IRA and then take annual distributions from the IRA. Once you reach age 70½, the Internal Revenue Code requires that you take a minimum distribution from your retirement plan or IRA to ensure that tax-deferred funds do not go untaxed indefinitely.

If you have a defined benefit plan, the amount of the monthly payment under the annuity contract will depend on the formula adopted by the employer when it created the plan. If the actuarial value of an employee's benefits at the date of termination is worth $5,000 or less, the plan can pay the employee the actuarial value of the vested pension rather than an annuity (I.R.C. §417[e][1]).

If you participate in a defined contribution plan, upon retirement you will either receive a lump sum that represents the value of your account or the plan may permit the lump sum to be converted into a lifetime annuity, much as if it were a defined benefit plan. The lump sum will be used to purchase an annuity that will pay a monthly benefit in an amount that is determined by your life expectancy (without regard to sex) or, if you are married, by the combined life expectancy of you and your spouse and the value of your defined contribution account. The older you are and the greater the value of your defined contribution account is, the larger will be your monthly annuity benefit. Employees who participate in a defined contribution plan and who terminate employment before their retirement date eventually receive their vested retirement benefits when they reach the plan's normal retirement age.

Under the Internal Revenue Code, the employer may permit employees who have reached the age of 55 to take early retirement and receive their retirement benefits without imposition of the 10 percent penalty tax. Employers often use early retirement as a way to reduce the number of employees and thereby reduce their payroll because doing so encourages older, more highly paid employees to voluntarily leave. For example, Beta Inc.'s normal retirement age for its defined benefit plan is 62. Beta Inc. needs to reduce its workforce by 10 percent. To do so, it permits employees age 55 or older to take early retirement and begin to collect their pension. Even though the amount of the pension is less than if they continued to work until age 62, many prefer to retire. Others elect to take early retirement because they fear that if they do not, the company will fire many employees and they might be one of those fired. Employees who are involuntarily terminated would not be able to collect their pension until they reach the NRA of age 62.

Absent the exclusion for early retirement, if an employee receives benefits before age 59½, the benefits are subject to the federal income tax plus a penalty tax equal to 10 percent of the amount withdrawn. The penalty tax does not apply to benefits paid to

- a beneficiary or an estate of a deceased employee,
- a disabled employee, or
- an alternate payee pursuant to a QDRO, or to
- payments that are part of a series of substantially equal periodic payments made for the life of the employee, such as an annuity (I.R.C. §72[t][2]).

Nonqualified Employer-Provided Plans

Nonqualified employer-provided plans do not enjoy the federal income tax advantages of qualified plans. In essence, a nonqualified plan is merely a deferred income arrangement. Employees sometimes want deferred income because they anticipate that after they retire, they will be taxed at a lower rate. Employers may offer a nonqualified plan along with qualified plans when the employer wishes to provide additional deferred compensation to a limited number of employees, such as highly paid executives. Nonqualified plans permit an employer to supplement an employee's benefit package without violating the nondiscrimination rules of qualified plans or being bound by the funding limits imposed on qualified plans.

If the nonqualified plan is not funded and is merely a promise to pay benefits to the employee at a later date, the employees are not taxed until they actually receive the benefits. Of course, the employee takes the risk that the employer will not be able to pay the benefits in the future. To minimize that risk, employees often insist that the employer place the value of the deferred compensation into a "rabbi" trust, so named because the Internal Revenue Service ruled favorably on a deferred compensation arrangement created for a rabbi by his congregation (I.R.S. Priv. Ltr. Rul. 81-13-107 [December 31, 1980]). Using a rabbi trust, the employer funds a trust for the benefit of an employee, who will receive the funds on retirement at a designated age. The employer is taxed on any earnings in the trust prior to it being paid to the employee, and the assets of the trust must be available to satisfy the claims of the employer's general creditors before the deferred compensation due the employee is paid.

Welfare Benefit Plans

Employers often offer benefits such as health insurance, postretirement health insurance, life insurance, and other forms of noncash compensation. Known as welfare benefit plans, they are governed by ERISA and are a tax-free benefit for the employees (29 U.S.C. §1002[1]). Employers are not required to offer welfare benefits and can reserve the right to cancel them at any time (absent a collective bargaining agreement). As a result, employees and retirees are not assured that in the future they will receive welfare benefits currently provided by the plan.

One common welfare benefit provided by employers for older, retired employees is health care insurance. Many plans provide supplemental retiree health care benefits for those age 65 or older to cover co-pays, deductibles, and exclusions not covered by Medicare. The plan may also pay the monthly Medicare Part B premium. Unless prohibited by a collective bargaining agreement, the employer will almost certainly have reserved the right in the plan to amend or terminate such retiree health care benefits.

In light of the sharp increase in health care costs, many employers have reduced health care benefits for future retirees and in some cases even for those already retired. Retirement benefits based on a contractual obligation may not be unilaterally discontinued by the former employer. If, for example, Chi Company promised its employees that if they retired early, they would receive lifetime health care benefits, Chi Company will not be able to reduce benefits to those early retirees. It could, however, reduce benefits for future retirees.

Self-Employed Pension Plans (Keoghs)

Self-employed individuals can establish qualified pension plans, commonly known as Keogh or HR-10 plans (I.R.C. §401[c][1]). As with any qualified plan, contributions are tax deductible and distributions from the plan are included in the recipient's income. The earnings on the plan funds are not taxed until distributed.

Under the Internal Revenue Code, you are a self-employed individual if you earn income other than as an employee. You can be both an employee and a self-employed person. For example, Meredith is a lawyer employed by Gamma Inc. In her spare time she is self-employed as a dog breeder. With her earnings from the part-time self-employment, she can fund a Keogh retirement plan even if she also participates in the Gamma Inc. retirement plan.

Also available is the SEP, or simplified employee pension, which can be used by employers or self-employed persons to put up to15 percent of compensation into an IRA (I.R.C. §408[k]). The contribution to the SEP IRA is deductible, but all distributions from the account are taxable. An employee is fully vested in the SEP at all times.

Individual Retirement Accounts

To encourage individuals to save for their retirement, Congress created IRAs (I.R.C. §408). Some can be funded with tax-deductible dollars, but the distributions are subject to income tax; others are not deductible when funded, but the earnings on the account are never taxed; and still others are nondeductible when funded, and the investment earnings are taxed only when distributed (I.R.C. §2190).[1]

Some individuals are eligible to contribute and deduct up to $5,000 for contributions to an IRA if they are not an active participant in a qualified pension plan. Even individuals who are active participants in a qualified plan, or whose spouse is an active participant, may still qualify for deductible contributions to an IRA if their adjusted gross income falls below limits set by the Internal Revenue Code. No deductible contributions can be made to an IRA by an individual who reached age 70½ before the end of the taxable year. Individuals who are participants in retirement plans and whose income exceeds the limits for making deductible contributions may make nondeductible IRA contributions up to $3,000 annually.

The earnings on the IRA accumulate tax free until distribution and can be invested in many ways, including stocks, saving accounts, mutual funds, and bonds. However, the IRA cannot be invested in life insurance or collectibles such as stamps or art. All distributions from a deductible IRA are taxable on receipt. Distributions before age 59½ are subject to an additional 10 percent penalty tax except in the case of death, disability, or the distribution being paid subject to a divorce decree. The penalty also is not applicable if the distribution reimburses the participant, or the participant's spouse, child, or grandchild, for higher education expenses. Likewise, the penalty does not apply to distributions up to $10,000 per year for the expenses of a first-time home buyer, including the participant, his or her spouse, child, grandchild, or ancestor.

In contrast with the traditional IRA, a Roth IRA offers tax-free distributions, but the contributions to the IRA are not deductible from income. Because all distributions from a Roth IRA are tax free, the income earned on the Roth IRA account is never taxed (I.R.C. §408A). Individuals who do not participate in a qualified retirement plan are eligible to contribute to a Roth IRA without regard to their income. Individuals who do participate in a qualified retirement plan must have adjusted taxable income below certain phaseout amounts in order to participate.

The maximum annual contribution to a Roth IRA is the *lesser* of the amount of the individual's compensation reduced by any other IRA contribution or $5,000 in 2008. This amount will be increased annually for the cost of living. Individuals who are age 50 or older can contribute $6,000 (increased annually for the cost of living).

In addition to the annual contributions, individuals who have terminated employment with an employer who operates a defined contribution plan or 401(k) plan may roll over amounts from those accounts into an existing or new IRA. Such rollovers, if done according to Internal Revenue Code requirements, are not taxable. Individuals may also convert non-Roth IRAs into Roth IRAs subject to certain limits based on their adjusted taxable income. The conversion must be made within sixty days of receipt of any lump-sum distribution from the previous employer's plan.

Distributions from an IRA can be made any time after the contributor reaches age 59½ without regard to whether the individual recipient is retired. Except in the case of a Roth IRA, distributions must begin no later than April 1 following the calendar year in which the contributor reaches age 70½. The amount of the minimum mandatory distribution is determined using tables published by the Internal Revenue Service. If all of the amounts contributed to the IRA were deductible from income, all the distributions are taxable. Amounts that were not deducted when placed in the IRA are not taxable when distributed. The recipient is responsible for paying any income taxes due on distribution. This is true whether the recipient is the original contributor or the IRA beneficiary of a contributor who has died. For a Roth IRA, no distributions are taxed if made after the contributor turns age 59½ and no earlier than five years after the first day of the year in which a contribution was first made to a Roth IRA.

If the creator of an IRA dies before retiring or withdrawing all of the funds in the IRA account, the account passes to a named beneficiary. An IRA is not governed by the contributor's will, but by the beneficiary designation in the IRA agreement. It is therefore very important to select an IRA beneficiary when the account is established and to keep the beneficiary designation current in the event of changing circumstances such as divorce or death of a named beneficiary.

An IRA can be used to defer distributions for a considerable number of years. If the IRA recipient delays taking funds until age 70½ (the latest age to which distributions can be deferred), it is possible that the recipient will die before depleting the account. A spouse who is an IRA beneficiary can roll over the remaining IRA balance into the spouse's own IRA and distribute the funds over a lengthy payout period. If any other individual is designated as the beneficiary, that individual's life expectancy may be used to calculate the minimum distribution period. Even if a trust is named the beneficiary of the IRA, an extended payout will be permitted if the beneficiaries of the trust can be identified. They, in turn, will be treated as the designated beneficiaries who are eligible for extended payout treatment.

If the original IRA recipient dies before age 70½, all of the account must be paid out within five years unless the designated beneficiary is the spouse. A spousal beneficiary has the right to take minimum distributions calculated with reference to his or her life expectancy. Distributions to the surviving spouse need not begin until the date that the original IRA recipient would have turned age 70½.

Note

1. See IRS Publication 590 for detailed information about the operation and tax treatment of IRAs as well as current dollar amounts.

For More Information

U.S. Department of Labor
(http://www.dol.gov)

Follow the links for "frequently asked questions" to learn more about retirement plans and benefits.

5
Medicare

Did You Know?

- You are not eligible for Medicare until age 65 even if you receive Social Security retirement benefits earlier.
- Your Medicare Part A deductible is based on a "spell of illness" rather than on the calendar year.
- If you fail to enroll in Medicare Part B or Part D when you are first eligible, you may have to pay higher premiums.
- You cannot be denied a Medigap policy so long as you apply during the first six months after enrollment in Medicare.
- If you have health insurance through your employer or that of your spouse, you can delay Medicare Part B enrollment without penalty.
- If you have adequate prescription drug coverage through your employer or that of your spouse, you can delay enrollment in Part D without penalty.

A common misconception among the young is that Medicare is free government health insurance for seniors. Even though it is true that Medicare is available to individuals age 65 or older without regard to health status or financial resources, Medicare is not free. Medicare is part of the Social Security system and is funded through a combination of payroll taxes and general tax revenues, as well as the premiums, deductibles, and co-payments paid by participants.

This chapter discusses Medicare coverage, eligibility requirements, the costs, and participant rights. The discussion is organized according to the four parts of Medicare: Part A, which pays for hospitalization and other institutionalized care; Part B, which pays for physician charges and outpatient services; Medicare Advantage, or MA (formerly known as Part C or Medicare +

Choice), which provides health care through managed care companies; and Part D, which pays for prescription drugs. Medigap insurance, which is additional insurance that can be purchased to pay for costs not fully covered by Medicare, is also discussed.

Medicare Part A

Financing
A special federal wage tax funds most of Medicare Part A. Employees and employers each pay a 1.45 percent tax on employees' wages. Unlike the Social Security wage tax, there is no limit on the amount of wages subject to the Medicare wage tax. For example, Alice is employed by Acme Co. and earns $200,000 a year. Both Alice and Acme Co. will pay a Medicare wage tax of $2,900, or a combined tax of $5,800. Medicare Part A is also funded by the deductibles and co-payments paid by those who receive Medicare-covered services.

Eligibility and Enrollment
You are eligible for Medicare Part A without charge if you are age 65 or older and also eligible for Social Security old-age benefits or Railroad Retirement benefits, though you need not actually be collecting those benefits to enroll in Medicare (42 C.F.R. §406.10). Because there is no premium for Part A if you satisfy the work record eligibility requirements, you should enroll at age 65 even if you have other insurance. If you choose to receive Social Security old-age benefits before age 65, keep in mind that Medicare eligibility still does not begin until age 65.

Spouses, widows, or widowers of someone eligible for Social Security benefits are also entitled to Medicare Part A coverage when they reach age 65 (42 C.F.R. §406.10; 20 C.F.R. §§404.330, 404.335). A divorced spouse who has not remarried may be eligible for Medicare at age 65 based on the former spouse's eligibility if the marriage lasted at least ten years (42 C.F.R. §406.10; 20 C.F.R. §404.331).

Certain workers who meet the age 65 requirement are entitled to Medicare even though their employment was not covered by Social Security. This group includes federal, state, and local government employees hired after March 31, 1986, who did not participate in Social Security but paid the Medicare wage tax (42 C.F.R. §406.15).

If you are age 65 or older and receive Social Security (or Railroad Retirement) benefits, you are automatically enrolled in Medicare Part A. No separate application procedure is required. Individuals who are not receiving Social Security or Railroad Retirement benefits, but who are eligible for Medicare coverage, must apply for coverage to begin. You should file your application for Medicare during your initial enrollment period, which runs for seven months beginning three months before the month you turn age 65.

If you are over the age of 65 but do not qualify for Medicare Part A based on your work record (or that of your spouse), you can choose to enroll and pay a monthly premium (42 U.S.C. §1395i-2). To be eligible for voluntary enrollment, you must reside in the United States as a U.S. citizen or as a resident alien who has lived in the United States for the preceding five years. The amount of your premium will depend on how many work quarters you have paid Medicare wage tax, if any. In 2010 the maximum monthly premium amount was $461. The amount of the premium is adjusted annually.

Individuals who must pay the monthly Part A premium but who do not enroll during the initial enrollment period may do so during the general enrollment period from January 1 to March 31 each year. However, they will have to pay a 10 percent surcharge on the monthly premium for failure to enroll during the initial enrollment period. The surcharge lasts two years for every twelve months that enrollment was delayed (42 U.S.C. §1395i-2[c][6]).

If you are eligible for Medicare but have group health coverage through your employer or that of your spouse, you are entitled to a delayed eight-month enrollment period that begins on the first day of the month you are no longer covered by the employer-provided insurance (42 U.S.C. §1395i-2[c][7]). Thus, when your employer-provided insurance ends, you do not have to wait for a general enrollment period to enroll in Part A and Part B, and you will not be penalized for having delayed your enrollment past age 65.

In limited circumstances, individuals who are younger than age 65 may qualify for Medicare. Early eligibility is available for disabled individuals who have received Social Security disability payments for at least twenty-four months as well as for individuals with end-stage renal disease, which means irreversible kidney impairment that requires dialysis or kidney transplantation (42 C.F.R. §§406.12, 406.13).

Coverage

Medicare Part A reimburses the costs of hospital care, short-term skilled nursing facility care, part-time home health care after a stay in a hospital or nursing home, and most hospice care (42 U.S.C. §1395d). Medicare will reimburse the cost of only those services that are considered "reasonable and necessary" for the diagnosis or treatment of illness or injury. Procedures considered experimental and medically unproven are not covered by Medicare (42 U.S.C. §1395y[a]).

Hospitalization Benefits. Hospital inpatient benefits under Medicare Part A include reimbursement for daily hospital bed and board charges, nursing services, intern or residents-in-training services, medical social services, drugs, equipment, supplies, certain diagnostic and therapeutic services, and the cost of ambulance transportation to and from the hospital (42 C.F.R. §409.10[a]). Medicare will only pay the cost of a semiprivate hospital room.

If the beneficiary insists upon a private room, the hospital can charge the beneficiary the prevailing rate for the additional cost of a private room. If only private rooms are available, or a private room is medically necessary, the beneficiary will not be charged the extra cost. Part A does not pay for physicians (who are covered by Part B), nurse practitioners, private duty nurses or attendants (unless required by the beneficiary's condition), phones, televisions, or posthospitalization drugs, supplies, and equipment.

Part A beneficiaries must pay a deductible for the first sixty days of hospitalization in each spell of illness. This deductible, which was $1,100 in 2010, is adjusted annually. A spell of illness begins with admission to the hospital and ends when the patient has been out of the facility for a period of sixty consecutive days (42 U.S.C. §1395x[a]). If a patient is readmitted within the sixty days, even if for a different ailment, it will be considered within the same spell of illness. For example, Heather has a stroke and enters the hospital on May 1 but is discharged on May 21. She must pay the deductible. On June 15 Heather is readmitted to the hospital with pneumonia. Because she is within the same spell of illness, she does not have to pay the annual deductible upon her readmission to the hospital. Other than the deductible, Medicare Part A pays for all relevant services (excluding television and telephone expenses) during the first sixty days of a single spell of illness.

After the first sixty days of care in a single spell of illness, the beneficiary is responsible for a daily co-pay. In 2010, the co-pay was $275 a day. This co-pay continues for days sixty-one to ninety. After ninety days of coverage, the basic Medicare hospitalization insurance for that spell of illness ends. However, each Medicare Part A beneficiary has sixty lifetime reserve days of coverage. These sixty days are the maximum that each beneficiary receives and are not reset for subsequent spells of illness. Lifetime reserve days are also subject to a daily co-pay requirement, which was $550 in 2010. An individual can choose not to use his or her lifetime reserve by notifying the hospital in writing during the stay or within ninety days after discharge. For example, Julian has cancer and is admitted to the hospital on June 1. He remains in the hospital until September 10. The first ninety days (June 1 through August 29) are covered by Part A, though Julian has to pay the deductible and the daily co-pay. After August 29, he uses twelve of his sixty lifetime reserve days to cover the additional stay.

Medicare Part A has less generous benefits for inpatient psychiatric hospital care. Such care is subject to a lifetime maximum limit of 190 days. Once the beneficiary has been reimbursed for 190 days of care, no further reimbursement for inpatient care is available (42 U.S.C. §1395d[b][3]).

Skilled Nursing Facility Care. Medicare benefits for care in a skilled nursing facility (SNF), better known as a nursing home, are very limited. Part A reimburses only skilled nursing services, not custodial care, and will pay for only one hundred days of care for each spell of illness (42 U.S.C. §1395d[a][2]).

Four requirements must be met for SNF coverage under Part A. First, the facility must be Medicare approved, meet all federal and state standards, and have a transfer agreement with at least one hospital that participates in Medicare. Second, admission into a SNF must occur within thirty days after a discharge from a hospital; individuals who go directly from their homes to a SNF do not satisfy this requirement. Third, the preceding hospital stay must have lasted at least three days, not counting the day of discharge. Fourth, a medical professional must certify that the individual requires skilled nursing or skilled rehabilitative services that can be provided only in a SNF. This certification must show that the patient is receiving skilled care daily and that the care is for a condition that was treated in the hospital or related to that condition. In general, skilled nursing care involves services that require the skills of technical or professional personnel, including intravenous feedings, catheters, and injections (42 C.F.R. §409.33).

If all of the foregoing requirements are satisfied, Medicare Part A will pay the full cost of the first twenty days of SNF care for each spell of illness. The beneficiary must pay a daily co-pay for days twenty-one through one hundred, which was $137.50 in 2010. After the first one hundred days, Medicare pays no further costs for skilled nursing home care.

Home Health Care. Part A provides a limited range of home health services for individuals confined to their homes (42 U.S.C. §1395f[a][2][C]). To qualify, a beneficiary must be under a physician's care plan and confined to the home or to another residential living arrangement that is not a hospital or SNF (42 C.F.R. §409.42). The individual must need one or more of the following:

- intermittent skilled nursing care
- physical therapy
- speech-language pathology services
- continuing occupational therapy

This care must be furnished by a Medicare-certified home health care provider.

Medicare Part A home care is sometimes referred to as "postinstitutional care" because when an individual is enrolled in both Part A and Part B, Part A home care is available only after a three-consecutive-day hospital stay or posthospitalization extended care services in a SNF. Furthermore, the home health services must begin within fourteen days after the individual was discharged from the hospital or SNF (42 U.S.C. §1395x[tt][1]). Medicare Part A pays for home health care for one hundred visits within a "home health spell of illness" (42 U.S.C. §1395d[a][3]), which begins on the first day that the individual receives home health services and ends sixty days after the last day the individual receives home health services or was not a patient in a hospital or SNF (42 U.S.C. §1395x[tt][2]). If the foregoing requirements for home health services under Part A are not met, the individual may be eligible for home health services under Medicare Part B. Part B generally provides limited home care benefits when a homebound beneficiary has exhausted the maximum one hundred visits under Part A, does not meet the prior institutional care requirement, or has only Part B coverage.

Only Medicare beneficiaries who are confined to the home, or are "homebound," are eligible for Medicare home health care. An individual is homebound if leaving home takes a considerable or taxing effort. Examples include individuals confined to a wheelchair or who require the aid of crutches to walk, those who have lost the use of upper extremities and require assistance to open doors or use stairways, and individuals who, because of dementia or blindness, require the assistance of another to leave the house. An individual who meets the definition of homebound but does in fact leave home infrequently for nonmedical reasons (such as a trip for religious services) still qualifies for home health services. In addition, individuals who attend adult day care are eligible for home health care if they are otherwise homebound (42 U.S.C. §1395f[a]).

Covered services include physical, occupational, and speech therapy; medical supplies; and durable medical equipment. The nursing care must be reasonable and necessary as well as part time or intermittent, which is defined as care provided less than seven days each week or less than eight hours a day over a period of not more than twenty-one days. The total care each week cannot exceed twenty-eight hours, though it can be as much as thirty-five hours if determined to be necessary on a case-by-case basis (42 U.S.C. §1395x[m]).

Care may be provided by more than one provider. For example, a nurse might provide care for one hour a day, five days a week, and a physical therapist might visit three days a week for one hour. The hour and day limits may be extended in exceptional circumstances if the attending physician can predict when the need for such care will end. In other words, home health care will not provide assistance for an indefinite period.

Part A does not cover drugs, delivered meals, and homemaker services. However, for the services covered, Medicare will pay 100 percent of the cost, except for durable medical equipment for which the patient must pay 20 percent. Supplemental medical insurance may cover this portion of the cost.

Hospice Care. Hospice care is a combination of home care, occasional inpatient institutionalization, and palliative care (care for pain control and comfort) (42 U.S.C. §1395x[dd][1]). To qualify for Part A hospice care, a patient must be certified as not likely to live more than six months. Hospice care is meant to provide pain relief and symptom control, rather than curative treatment for the patient's condition. The goal of hospice care is to improve the quality of the patient's remaining life by reducing pain, stress, and anxiety. Hospice care is usually delivered in the patient's home or a homelike setting and generally consists of nursing and attendant care that supplements family caregiving.

Patients must elect to receive hospice care instead of other Medicare services. In other words, the patient must be willing to discontinue attempts to cure the medical condition. The patient is initially entitled to ninety days of hospice care but can continue to receive services if the hospice medical director or the patient's physician certifies continued eligibility. At any time, the patient can revoke hospice care and return to full Part A benefits (43 C.F.R. §418.28[a]).

Generally, Part A will pay for all costs associated with hospice care, including registered nursing care, therapy, homemaker services, and counseling. The two exceptions to full coverage are prescription drugs and respite care. Patients in hospice care must pay the lesser of 5 percent of the cost of outpatient drugs or $5 per prescription. They must also pay 5 percent of the Medicare reimbursement rate for respite care, which is short-term institutionalization of a patient in order to give the regular caregiver a break from his or her duties.

Payment Procedures

Medicare does not directly pay hospitals, doctors, or other health care providers. Instead, Medicare contracts with large, private insurance companies that reimburse providers for covered services. Medicare in turn reimburses the insurance companies. The provider generally takes care of the paperwork and bills the patient for the deductible or co-pay. The provider may also appeal a decision of Medicare not to reimburse certain treatment for a patient.

If a Medicare beneficiary has been admitted to the hospital, but the attending physician and the hospital agree that the stay will not be reimbursed by Medicare, they must promptly notify the patient of their opinion. Having notified the patient of noncoverage, the hospital can begin to charge the patient for the customary cost of care beginning on the third day after the notification. The patient has the option of paying for the care or appealing the decision.

Appeals from Denial of Coverage

Medicare Part A will pay only for medical care that is "medically reasonable and necessary." This vague term sometimes is misinterpreted by providers that mistakenly believe Medicare will pay for the care provided. Patients are not financially responsible for such care if the patient did not know or could not have been expected to know that Medicare would refuse to pay for the services. The provider will usually be responsible for the cost of care if the patient was not notified in advance of Medicare noncoverage.

If the provider properly informs the patient that Medicare will not pay for medical care and Medicare refuses to pay, the patient can request a reconsideration of the denied coverage within sixty days of receiving the original decision. Further appeal is allowed within sixty days of receiving the reconsideration decision if the amount in question is at least $100. This appeal takes place before an administrative law judge. Finally, the decision of the administrative law judge can be appealed to a federal court if the case involves more than $1,000 (42 U.S.C. §1395ff[b]; 42 C.F.R. §478). If the initial denial was made by a state quality improvement organization (QIO), the dollar amounts are $200 and $2000, respectively (42 C.F.R. §§478.40, 478.46).

Typically, it is the provider that appeals a denied coverage decision because it is the provider that is at financial risk if the cost of care is not paid. To avoid coverage disputes, hospitals rely on utilization review committees to determine for what and how much Medicare will pay. If the patient's physician who requested the treatment disagrees with the utilization review committee, the hospital can appeal to the state QIO. The QIO will determine if the proposed care is medically necessary and eligible for Medicare coverage.

Patients can appeal Medicare coverage decisions to the QIO as well. For example, a patient who does not believe he or she should be discharged from the hospital can appeal to the QIO and will not be charged until the appeal is approved or denied. If the patient wishes to contest the bill, an administrative appeal can be made within 120 days if the claim exceeds $200 (42 C.F.R.§478.46). A patient can appeal to a federal court if the claim exceeds $2,000 (42 U.S.C. §1395ff).

Many patient appeals arise when a hospital wishes to discharge the patient to a SNF, but the patient objects because either there is no Medicare skilled nursing home bed available or no bed is available in a facility acceptable to the patient. A hospital cannot discharge a patient in need of skilled nursing care unless there is an available Medicare skilled nursing home bed. If a skilled nursing home bed is available, Medicare will not pay for additional days in the hospital even though the patient refuses to transfer. Although the law does not provide a right to refuse a transfer to a Medicare skilled nursing home bed, a patient who appeals the discharge decision to the state QIO may gain a few extra covered days in which to arrange more satisfactory posthospitalization care.

Medicare Part B

Financing

Medicare Part B, Supplemental Medical Insurance, is voluntary medical insurance that helps pay the costs of physician and outpatient services (42

U.S.C. §1395j). Participants in Medicare Part B must pay monthly premiums that vary according to the participant's income—the higher the income, the higher the premium. Premiums are set at a level so that in the aggregate they cover approximately 25 percent of the cost of Part B, with general federal revenues paying the rest. The premium is deducted from the beneficiary's monthly Social Security payment or other government benefit payment. If a beneficiary receives no government benefit payments, the premium is billed monthly.

The basic monthly premium in 2010 was $96.40 for individuals with a modified adjusted gross income (AGI) of $85,000 or less and for couples with a modified AGI of $170,000 or less.[1] For purposes of this computation, your modified AGI is your adjusted gross (taxable) income plus tax-exempt interest income. Table 5.1 shows the respective premium levels for individuals and couples who had modified AGI above the standard premium levels in 2010. Medicare Part B premium rates are adjusted annually.

Eligibility and Enrollment

Eligibility for Part B is the same as for Part A, although all participants in Part B must pay a premium (see the Eligibility and Enrollment discussion for Medicare Part A). Individuals who receive Social Security or Railroad Retirement benefits and who are at least 65 years old are enrolled automatically. However, automatically enrolled beneficiaries are notified of their right to decline Part B.

Individuals who are not entitled to premium-free Part A and who choose not to enroll in Part A may still enroll in Part B. The enrollment period begins three months before the month that the individual turns age 65 and continues for seven months. An individual who delays enrollment beyond this initial enrollment period may enroll during the general enrollment period from January 1 to March 31 each year, but he or she will have to pay a 10 percent surcharge on the monthly premium.

Table 5.1   2010 Medicare Part B Premium Rates

	Modified AGI	Monthly Premium
Individuals	$85,001–107,000	$154.70
Couple	$170,001–214,000	$154.70
Individuals	$107,001–160,000	$221.00
Couples	$214,001–320,000	$221.00
Individuals	$160,001–214,000	$287.30
Couples	$320,001–428,000	$287.30
Individuals	Above $214,000	$353.60
Couples	Above $428,000	$353.60

Like the surcharge for delayed premium-paid Part A enrollment, the surcharge for delayed Part B enrollment lasts two years for every twelve months that enrollment is delayed (42 U.S.C. §1395i-2[c][6]; 42 C.R.F. §408.22). However, this increase does not apply to those who delay enrollment because they have employer-provided health insurance from their own employment or that of a spouse. These individuals have a special eight-month enrollment period that begins when their employer-provided health insurance ends (42 U.S.C. §1395i-2[c][7]).

Coverage

Medicare Part B reimburses physicians' services, including those provided in a hospital (42 U.S.C. §1395k[a]; 42 C.F.R. §410.10). Part B also covers diagnostic services, outpatient therapy, durable medical equipment, ambulance services, medical supplies, dialysis, pacemakers, blood transfusions, and pneumococcal and hepatitis B vaccines. There are limitations, however, on these covered services. For example, covered ambulance service is limited to transportation from home to a hospital or SNF and only if it is medically necessary because any other form of transportation could harm the patient. Outpatient therapy is subject to a billing cap and is covered only if prescribed by a physician. A doctor's prescription is also required for durable medical equipment.

Among the services that Part B does *not* cover are routine physical examinations, dental care, custodial care, routine foot care (unless necessary for an underlying condition), cosmetic surgery, and eye examinations. Also, Part B does not cover eyeglasses and contact lenses (except for postsurgical devices), hearing aids, orthopedic shoes (unless they are a part of leg braces), and personal comfort items in a hospital.

Payment Procedures

The beneficiary must pay an annual deductible for Part B, which in 2010 was $155. The beneficiary is also responsible for a 20 percent co-pay for most doctor services, outpatient therapy, preventive services, and durable medical equipment. Medicare Part B reimbursement is limited to what are known as approved charges. For each service, Medicare establishes an approved charge, which is the amount that Medicare believes appropriate for that procedure. Medicare then pays for 80 percent of the approved charge, regardless of the amount charged by the physician (42 U.S.C.§1395l[a]). The other 20 percent is paid by the patient.

Physicians often find collecting patient payments costly and sometimes impossible. To assist physicians, Medicare permits them to "participate" in Part B. This is sometimes known as "taking assignment" and means that the physician agrees not to charge the patient more than the Medicare-approved charge. In return, Medicare directly reimburses the physician for its 80 percent obligation. In some states, physicians are required by law to participate in Medicare as a condition of their licensure. In most states, physicians need not participate. Physicians who do not participate must collect the entire 100 percent from the patient, who in turn is reimbursed by Medicare for its 80 percent payment obligation.

A physician who does not participate in Medicare is allowed to charge the patient up to 15 percent more than the Medicare-approved charge. The patient is responsible for the 20 percent co-payment, plus the extra 15 percent of the Medicare-approved charge. For example, Dr. Jones does not participate in Medicare Part B. Andy visits Dr. Jones and receives care for which Medicare Part B has established an approved charge of $1,000. Dr. Jones can charge Andy $1,150. Medicare is obligated to pay $800 (80% × $1,000, which is the approved charge). Andy will pay $1,150, which includes the 20 percent co-pay of the approved charge ($200), the additional 15 percent ($150), and the $800 that will be reimbursed eventually by Medicare.

Medicare Part B pays 100 percent of certain clinical laboratory services, vaccines, and home health services. However, Part B pays only 50 percent of the approved physician's charges for outpatient treatment for mental, psychoneurotic, and personality disorders (42 C.F.R. §410.152).

Appeals from Denial of Coverage

Part B claims are handled on Medicare's behalf by private insurance companies called "carriers." The patient can request that a denied claim be reconsidered by the carrier within six months of the date of the denial. If not satisfied, a patient can appeal to the carrier's hearing officer within six months of the reconsidered decision. This option is available only if the dispute is for more than $100, though claims can be combined to meet the minimum amount (42 C.F.R. §405.815). Appeals from the hearing officer go before an administrative law judge if filed within sixty days of the hearing officer's decision and worth at least $500, either alone or in combination with other claims. Cases involving more than $1,000 can be appealed to the federal court system.

Medicare Advantage

Medicare Advantage (formerly known as Medicare Part C or Medicare + Choice) is a managed care alternative to the original fee-for-service Medicare (42 U.S.C. §1395w-22). Seniors may elect to enroll in MA instead of participating in Medicare Parts A and B. Although MA plans must provide all Part A and Part B covered services, most provide additional coverage as an incentive for seniors to join.

MA plans vary, so if you are considering MA, you should read the plan materials carefully. Often MA plans charge a single monthly premium that covers Part A and Part B services, Medicare Part D prescription drugs, and sometimes extra services, such as vision, hearing, and dental, that are not covered by original Medicare. However, with some MA plans, you must still pay all or part of your Part B premium. Co-payments and deductibles also vary by plan.

If you choose to enroll in MA, you will not need a Medigap supplemental insurance policy. In fact, Medigap insurance does not cover MA plan deductibles and co-payments. One risk of enrolling in MA and dropping your Medigap policy is that you may not be able to obtain another Medigap policy if you later decide to return to original Medicare. However, there are protections for individuals who join MA for the first time and who decide to return to original Medicare within the first twelve months. Generally, these individuals are entitled to be reinstated under their former Medigap policy provided that the company still offers it.

MA plans appear in several forms, including health maintenance organizations (HMOs), preferred provider organizations (PPOs), provider-sponsored organizations (PSOs), medical savings account plans (MSAs), private fee-for-service plans (PFFSs), and special needs plans (SNPs). The rules for each type of MA plan differ significantly. For example, whether you need to choose a primary care doctor or must obtain a referral to see a specialist depends on the plan. Under some plans, if you use out-of-network providers, you may have to pay a higher cost, or, in some cases, the full cost of services received. Before you enroll in an MA plan, be sure you understand what it provides and how it operates.

Eligibility and Enrollment

If you are eligible for Medicare Part A or Part B, you are eligible to enroll in an MA plan. You can elect to enroll during an initial eligibility period that runs from three months before you turn age 65 and continues for seven months. You can also enroll in, change, or drop your MA plan each year between November 15 and December 31, with your new coverage beginning on January 1 of the following year. Changes during the general Medicare enrollment period between January 1 and March 31 are prohibited if the MA plan is an MSA or involves prescription drug coverage.

Generally, MA participants must stay enrolled for the calendar year in which MA coverage begins. You may be able to join, change, or drop an MA plan at times other than the usual enrollment periods if you live in an institution, qualify for a subsidy to help pay Medicare prescription drug costs, are qualified for both Medicare and Medicaid, or move out of your plan's service area.

Coverage

MA plans must offer the same benefits as Part A and Part B, but to encourage enrollment, they typically offer additional benefits, such as routine physical examinations, eyeglasses, hearing aids, and dental care (42 U.S.C.

§1395mm[c]). Many offer better prescription drug subsidies than Medicare Part D. The extent and value of the benefits offered depend primarily on the amount of the reimbursement provided to the plans by Medicare. Therefore, the greater the payment by Medicare is to the plan for each Medicare enrollee, the more generous the plan can be in the provision of benefits. Because Congress periodically changes the amount of the MA plan subsidies, the number of such plans and the benefits also periodically change.

Appeals from Denial of Coverage

MA plans are required to provide dispute resolution procedures. The plan must also provide written notice of denial of services or termination of hospitalization and must offer beneficiaries a form of internal review. The beneficiary must be given sixty days to request a review of a contested care decision as well as an expedited form of review.

Medicare Part D

The Medicare Prescription Drug Improvement and Modernization Act of 2003 added prescription drug coverage known as Medicare Part D (42 U.S.C. §1395w-101). Part D subsidizes prescription drug costs by providing financial assistance to private drug plans (PDPs) that sell prescription drug insurance to individuals eligible for or enrolled in Medicare Part A or Part B. Individuals enrolled in Medicare Advantage generally receive prescription drug assistance though their MA plan.

Eligibility and Enrollment

Anyone eligible for or enrolled in either Part A or Part B is eligible to enroll in Part D. Enrollment is voluntary. Beneficiaries enroll by joining one of the federally subsidized prescription drug plans offered by private insurance companies. The beneficiary pays a monthly insurance premium to the plan insurer. The plans vary greatly in coverage as well as in the specific drugs that are available on the plan drug list known as the "formulary." The formulary may contain different tiers or categories of drugs that have different costs.

The monthly premiums in 2010 averaged a little less than $39 and ranged nationally from $8.80 to $120.20, depending on the amount of coverage and the formulary. Although plans cannot refuse to enroll Medicare beneficiaries, they can and do charge higher premiums in geographical areas where residents have higher drug expenses. Low-income enrollees, as well as those eligible for both Medicare and Medicaid, or SSI, are eligible for a reduction in cost or a complete subsidy.

Enrollment in Part D occurs during the coordinated annual enrollment election period that runs each year from November 15 through December

31. Beneficiaries who move or have other reasons for a special enrollment period are accommodated as necessary. Individuals eligible for both Medicare and Medicaid are automatically enrolled as soon as their eligibility for Part D is determined. After enrollment, those beneficiaries have the right to opt out.

An individual who fails to enroll when first eligible is subject to a late enrollment penalty in the form of increased premiums unless the individual has comparable prescription drug coverage (known as "creditable coverage") and is not without such coverage for more than sixty-three days prior to enrollment (42 C.F.R. §423.46). Typically, this includes individuals whose employer provides them with health insurance. Those who do not enroll in the program when they initially become eligible must pay a penalty of 1 percent of the national average premium for *each* month that they delay enrollment unless they had creditable coverage. This penalty applies as long as the beneficiary is enrolled in Medicare Part D.

In lieu of enrolling in a PDP, beneficiaries can join a Medicare Advantage plan that offers prescription drug coverage. MA plan prescription drug coverage is comparable to or better than the coverage required by Medicare Part D. Beneficiaries do not have to enroll in any form of Part D if they choose not to participate.

Coverage

Participating plans cannot require Part D beneficiaries to pay more than federally established deductibles. Most offer more generous terms. In 2010, a plan could not require an annual deductible of more than $310. The deductible is adjusted each year to reflect the annual growth in the spending by beneficiaries on Part D drugs. After the deductible is met, in 2010 the beneficiary could be required to pay 25 percent of the drug costs incurred between $310 and $2,830. The beneficiary could then be required to pay 100 percent of prescription drug costs from $2,830 to $6,440. This amount is known as the "donut hole" in the plan coverage. Once the beneficiary has reached the other side of the donut hole ($6,440 in 2010), he or she is eligible for catastrophic coverage under which the beneficiary pays the greater of 5 percent of the cost of the prescription or $2.50 for generic drugs and $6.30 for brand name drugs. Institutionalized beneficiaries, such as those in a nursing home, have no such co-pay.

As a result of the foregoing drug coverage structure, a Part D beneficiary in 2010 could be required to pay as much as $4,550 in drug costs before achieving catastrophic coverage. For example, Lucas enrolls in a prescription drug plan that uses the maximum deductible and co-pays allowed by law. Table 5.2 lists the costs he will incur. If Lucas has any additional drug costs in the plan year, he will qualify for catastrophic coverage.

Note that Lucas may elect to join a plan that does not require him to pay all of the deductible, the 25 percent co-pay, or even all of the costs of the donut hole (the uncovered costs between $2,830 and $6,440). Most plans

Table 5.2   2010 Medicare Part D Out-of-Pocket Costs

Deductible	$310
25% of costs between $310 deductible and $2,830	$630
100% of costs between $2,830 and $6,440	$3,610
Total out-of-pocket cost	$4,550

provide some relief from the maximum participation amounts that can be charged to beneficiaries, but many do not provide any coverage of the donut hole. However, beneficiaries can expect higher premiums the greater the plan coverage and the lower the costs-per-prescription paid by the beneficiary.

Part D covers only prescription drugs and only those that are considered reasonable and necessary. Vaccines not covered by Part B are covered by Part D. Otherwise, Part D will not pay for a drug if either Part A or Part B will pay for it. Plans may also exclude drugs that are excluded under Medicaid, such as vitamins, barbiturates, and those for weight loss, fertility, cosmetic results, and cough or cold relief.

PDPs may limit drug coverage to a set list of drugs created by the secretary of the Department of Health and Human Services (HHS) or may design other lists subject to approval by the secretary of HHS. PDPs are prohibited, however, from designing lists with the purpose of excluding beneficiary groups with certain drug needs. PDPs may change their lists of covered drugs annually, but they must provide notice to the plan beneficiaries.

MA plans may offer coverage as an alternative to Part D if the coverage has an equal value to Part D plans and is approved by the secretary of HHS. As of January 1, 2006, companies offering Medigap insurance could no longer sell new policies with prescription drug coverage.

Appeals from Denial of Coverage

PDPs are required to establish a process for handling beneficiary grievances. Although PDP coverage is defined by set lists of prescription drugs, the plans must provide access at a favorable price to all medically necessary drugs not on the list. If unsatisfied with the coverage, a beneficiary can appeal a denial of coverage determination. Appeals under Part D are first subject to internal review by the PDP. An unfavorable decision for the beneficiary can be appealed to an independent review entity for reconsideration. The appeal next goes to a hearing before an administrative law judge. A beneficiary can appeal further to the Medicare Appeals Council and finally to a federal district court.

Medigap Insurance Policies

Medicare does not provide complete coverage to its beneficiaries, who must pay deductibles, co-pays, coinsurance, and the cost of noncovered services.

The out-of-pocket amount that any beneficiary will have to pay is difficult to estimate in advance, but it can be considerable. As a result, many individuals purchase supplemental Medicare health care insurance known as Medigap because it fills in the coverage "gaps" left by Medicare. These insurance policies are sold by private insurance companies and are entirely optional.

As of 2009, federal standards for Medigap policies limited all policies to one of twelve standard packages of coverage identified in most states by the letters A through L, with A being the least comprehensive (42 U.S.C. §1395ss). As of June 1, 2010, plans E, H, I, and J will be phased out and two new plans—M and N—will be available. In some states, another Medigap alternative called Medicare SELECT will be offered. Medicare SELECT policies require participants to use designated hospitals and doctors to get full coverage. All packages with the same letter designation are identical across all insurance companies, although the premium may vary from company to company.

Insurance companies do not have to offer all Medigap packages and can restrict availability of plans to certain groups based on factors such as age or medical conditions. Because companies set their own premiums for the various packages, different companies charge different premiums for identical coverage. If you are thinking of buying a Medigap policy, consider the financial strength of the insurance company, the customer service offered, and how willing the company is to pay benefits.

Consumer Protection Provisions

Federal law provides several consumer protections for those who purchase Medigap insurance (42 U.S.C. §1395ss[o]). First, you may not be denied a policy because of a preexisting condition if you apply during the first six months after enrollment in Medicare. Second, your Medigap policy must be guaranteed renewable unless the premium is not paid or there was a material misrepresentation in the application. Third, insurance companies are prohibited from selling more than one Medigap policy to any one buyer. A company that violates this prohibition may face criminal penalties and the buyer will be refunded any premiums paid on the second plan. Every state has a State Health Insurance Assistance Program (SHIP) that provides free counseling about Medicare, Medigap, and PDPs.

Benefits

All Medigap plans within the A through J plan categories contain the following basic benefits:

- Medicare Part A daily hospitalization co-payment for days 61–90
- Medicare Part A daily lifetime reserve days co-payment
- an additional 365 days of hospitalization without any co-payment

- Medicare Part B 20 percent co-payment for medical services and durable medical equipment (after the annual deductible is met)
- the first three pints of blood not covered by Medicare

In addition, a hospice care co-insurance benefit will be added to all new Medigap policies beginning June 1, 2010.

The foregoing basic benefits are the only benefits included in a Medigap plan A policy. Plans B through J offer these benefits as well as some combination of the following benefits:

- Part A hospital inpatient deductible
- Part B deductible
- SNF co-insurance for days twenty-one to one hundred
- foreign travel emergency costs (subject to limit)
- some percentage of Part B excess charges

Prescription drug benefits are not available under new Medigap policies because of the availability of prescription drug coverage under Part D.

Medigap plans K and L differ from plans A through J in two primary ways—they have lower monthly premiums, and they have higher out-of-pocket costs. After the beneficiary meets the out-of-pocket limit and Part B deductible, these plans pay 100 percent of covered services for the rest of the year.

Medigap plans M and N also offer lower premiums in exchange for higher cost sharing. For example, participants in plan M must pay their own Part B deductible and half of the Part A deductible. Plan N participants cost share through co-payments rather than deductibles.

Costs

The cost of a Medigap policy depends not only on the coverage offered, but also on the way the policy is "rated." Policies are rated in three different ways: (1) based on the age of the beneficiary when the policy is issued, (2) adjusted annually based on the beneficiary's current age, or (3) set without regard to the beneficiary's age. Other factors that may affect the policy's cost include gender-based or smoking-status discounts, as well as a high-deductible option if available.

The Best Medicare Plan for You

Choices about original Medicare, Medicare Advantage, Medicare Part D, and Medigap insurance are complex and depend on your personal situation and preferences. Fortunately, many resources are available to help you make these decisions. SHIPs provide free one-on-one counseling about these choices. Medicare also makes available to all eligible beneficiaries a publication called *Medicare and You*, tailored for your state. This publication is available in print and online. It contains the phone number for your state's SHIP program as well as state-specific information about Medicare Advantage and Part D drug plans.

Note

1. Some persons will pay a slightly higher Part B basic premium of $110.50 if they are new enrollees or do not pay their premium through a deduction from Social Security benefits.

For More Information

Center for Medicare Advocacy (860-456-7790)
(http://www.medicareadvocacy.org)

Find specific information by topic about all aspects of Medicare coverage, proposed Medicare changes, and guidance for asserting your rights under Medicare.

Medicare (800-MEDICARE)
(http://www.medicare.gov)

Find information about all aspects of Medicare coverage and benefits including enrollment, choice of plans, costs, and appeals. Links are provided to state-specific resources.

National SHIP Resource Center
(http://www.shiptalk.org)

Find information about free one-on-one counseling to help you make decisions about Medicare and other health insurance matters.

6

Medicaid and Long-Term Care Insurance

Did You Know?

- Medicaid eligibility criteria vary from state to state.
- Medicaid may be available to pay for long-term care services in your home.
- Even if your spouse needs Medicaid nursing home benefits, you can maintain your lifestyle at home with careful advance planning.
- Gifts you make today could disqualify you or your spouse from Medicaid later.
- Special long-term care insurance may make it possible for you to keep your assets and still qualify for Medicaid.

Perhaps what seniors fear most is that someday they will need long-term care. Second to this fear is the worry about how they will pay for it. Although Medicaid is the single largest source of funding for nursing home care, not all seniors qualify for Medicaid.

If you do not meet Medicaid's financial eligibility requirements, you must rely on your own private funds or insurance to pay for your long-term care. Whether received in a nursing home, an assisted living facility, or at home, long-term care is expensive. This chapter discusses Medicaid long-term care benefits, eligibility requirements, and special planning considerations for married persons. Asset transfers that may cause you to lose Medicaid eligibility are also discussed.

In addition to Medicaid, long-term care insurance is explained. Long-term care insurance may be a good alternative if you cannot qualify for

Medicaid. It may also be beneficial if you could meet the Medicaid income requirements but have assets that exceed what Medicaid allows. Many states now permit qualified persons to both shelter assets and receive Medicaid if they first exhaust benefits from a state-approved long-term care insurance policy.

Medicaid Benefits

Medicaid is a federal program, but it is administered by the states. Medicaid pays the medical expenses of defined categories of persons who also meet financial eligibility requirements (42 U.S.C. §1396a). Medicaid categories of coverage include low-income children, pregnant women, adults in families with dependent children, and the aged, blind, and disabled. This chapter looks at Medicaid eligibility for persons who qualify because they are aged—that is, age 65 or older.

Every state as well as the District of Columbia participates in Medicaid. The federal government pays for about one-half of the cost of Medicaid-covered services, with the states paying the rest. In some states, the program is referred to as Medical Assistance (California labels it Medi-Cal). Regardless of the title, Medicaid pays almost one-half of all long-term care spending in the United States. One-third of Medicaid dollars are spent on health care for seniors.

Even though states must follow federal Medicaid standards, they may offer more liberal benefits than those required by federal law (42 U.S.C. §§1396a[a][10][A], 1396d[a]). The mandatory services that all states must provide include the following:

- inpatient and outpatient services
- laboratory and x-ray services
- physicians' services
- nursing facility services
- home health services for individuals who qualify for nursing facility care

Optional services include these services:

- care provided by licensed practitioners other than physicians
- diagnostic, screening, and preventive services
- physical, speech, occupational, and audiology therapies
- dentures, prosthetic devices, and eyeglasses
- case management
- durable medical equipment
- inpatient and nursing facility services in an institution for mental diseases

- hospice services
- transportation services
- home and community-based waiver services
- PACE services (Programs of All-Inclusive Care for the Elderly)

Although prescription drug coverage is an optional service, all states include some level of prescription drug coverage in their Medicaid plan.[1]

More than one-half of the total optional state Medicaid spending is for long-term care.[2] Of the Medicaid spending on long-term care, approximately two-thirds pays for institutional care, with the remaining one-third paying for home and community-based waiver services.[3] Unlike Medicare, which pays for only skilled nursing care on a limited basis, Medicaid covers both skilled and custodial nursing home care.

Given that the most costly aspect of Medicaid reimbursement is nursing home care, federal waivers permit states to cover less expensive long-term care provided in the home or community (42 U.S.C. §1396n[c]; 42 C.F.R. §440.180). Home and community-based services can include case management, homemaker services, home health aides, personal care services, adult day health services, respite care, and habilitation services (42 C.F.R. §440.180[b]). Although home care and community-based care are less expensive than nursing home care, the availability of waiver services usually results in an increased number of Medicaid applications. This is because home care is more attractive to most seniors than nursing home care.

Thus, even though the cost per Medicaid applicant may be less for home and community-based care than for nursing home care, the widespread availability of waiver services could substantially raise a state's Medicaid budget. Therefore, the federal government permits states to limit the number of waiver participants. In most states, there is a long waiting list for home and community-based services.

Medicaid Eligibility

Although federal law sets the basic parameters for Medicaid eligibility, state interpretations of the federal standards differ, resulting in eligibility standards that are not completely consistent from state to state. Another source of inconsistency among the states is something known as the 209(b) option. In 1972, Congress replaced other joint federal/state welfare programs with the Supplemental Security Income (SSI) program (see Chapter 3 for a discussion of SSI). Under SSI eligibility guidelines, an increased number of persons would have qualified for Medicaid. Fearing that states would exit the program, Congress allowed states to retain their pre-SSI Medicaid eligibility standards (Pub. L. No. 92-603, §209[b]; 42 U.S.C. §1396a[f]). Currently, eleven states utilize the 209(b) option to require tougher financial limits for

Medicaid eligibility. They are Connecticut, Hawaii, Illinois, Indiana, Minnesota, Missouri, New Hampshire, North Dakota, Ohio, Oklahoma, and Virginia.

Most seniors who qualify for Medicaid do so because they are considered "categorically needy"—in other words, they fall within the federal definition of aged (age 65 or older), blind, or disabled, and are eligible for SSI (42 U.S.C. §1396a). Although 209(b) states can use more restrictive Medicaid eligibility requirements than the SSI criteria, they must allow applicants who would otherwise qualify for Medicaid to "spend down" excess income. Applicants may deduct their medical expenses from their income to accomplish this spend-down (Pub. L. No. 92-603, §209[b]; 42 U.S.C. §1396a[f]).

States also have the option of extending Medicaid eligibility to individuals who are "medically needy" (42 U.S.C. §1396a[a][10][C]). More than two-thirds of states grant Medicaid to medically needy individuals. The definition of medically needy varies from state to state, as do the available benefits. In general, you are considered medically needy if you cannot afford the cost of your nursing home care, your assets are within SSI eligibility limits, but your income exceeds the SSI eligibility threshold. Medicaid will make up the shortfall when a medically needy applicant's monthly income is inadequate to cover the monthly nursing home bill.

All U.S. citizens and certain legal immigrants can qualify for Medicaid. Because Medicaid is administered at the state level, an applicant must also be considered a resident of that state. You are considered a resident of the state in which you live and intend to stay, permanently or indefinitely (42 C.F.R. §435.403[i][1][i]). Individuals over age 21 who are unable to express their intent are considered residents of the state where they are physically present (42 C.F.R. §435.403[i][3]). States cannot impose minimum residency requirements for Medicaid eligibility, such as a waiting period for persons moving into the state (42 C.F.R. §435.403[j]).

Consider the example of Sam, age 77, who lives in Arizona but has a stroke while visiting his daughter in Ohio. Due to the effects of the stroke, Sam moves into a nursing home in Ohio. Because he is physically present in Ohio, Sam will be entitled to Ohio Medicaid to help cover the costs of his nursing home care if he otherwise meets the eligibility requirements.

Resource and Income Requirements

At the heart of Medicaid eligibility are the resource and income requirements. These requirements vary depending on the state, the applicant's marital status, and, if married, whether one or both members of the couple are seeking Medicaid services in a nursing home. The following discussion is a general overview of Medicaid resource and income requirements. Special considerations for married persons are addressed in a subsequent section.

Resources

To qualify for Medicaid as categorically needy or medically needy, you must also meet the state's resource eligibility test. Most states use the SSI resource standard, but 209(b) states are permitted to use more restrictive standards (42 C.F.R. §435.840). If you live in a state that uses SSI resource limits and you are unmarried, you cannot have more than $2,000 in countable resources. If you are married, the countable resource limit is $3,000. Some states use slightly higher dollar amounts. By comparison, in Indiana (a 209[b] state) an individual may have only $1,500 in countable resources and a couple may have only $2,250.

Countable Resources. Most states use the SSI resource rules to define countable resources. Countable resources are any assets you own that count toward the Medicaid resource limit. The following are examples of assets that are generally considered countable:

- cash on hand (other than current income)
- financial accounts (such as bank accounts, certificates of deposit, individual retirement accounts, and Keogh plans)
- stocks and bonds
- assets in trust (but only to the extent the assets are available to you)

Like assets in trust, pension plan assets and annuities are countable resources only if you can access them. For example, if you have the ability to make lump-sum withdrawals from a pension plan or annuity, the assets are deemed available and countable, even if the withdrawal will trigger fees or penalties. Countable resources are valued at their fair market value, adjusted for any early withdrawal penalties or other legitimate fees.

Assets that were transferred for less than fair market value within sixty months of the date an applicant would otherwise be eligible for Medicaid are also treated as a countable resource.[4] Such transfers result in a penalty period of ineligibility (see the asset transfers discussion in this chapter). Real estate, household goods, personal effects, motor vehicles, and insurance may be completely or partially excluded from countable resources depending on their value and the applicant's circumstances.

Noncountable Assets. Of particular importance for Medicaid planning is an understanding of what assets are excluded from the resource calculation (42 U.S.C. §1382b[a]). Provided that the equity in your principal residence does not exceed $500,000, it is excluded from countable resources if you live there or intend to return home after institutional care or if your spouse or other qualified family member lives there (42 U.S.C. §1396p[f][1][A]).[5] If the house is sold, the proceeds are exempt if used to purchase another house within three months.

Household goods and personal effects are excluded, as well as one car of any value provided it is used to transport you or a member of your household. Other cars are considered countable resources. If you have property used in a trade or business that is essential for self-support, such property is not counted.

Your life insurance is excludable to the extent that the combined face value does not exceed $1,500. If the value exceeds $1,500, all cash surrender value is a countable resource. Burial spaces for yourself or your immediate family are also exempt. Likewise, prepaid burial expenses or a burial fund up to a value of $1,500 for an individual and $3,000 for a couple is excluded.

Resource Spend-Down. If your countable resources exceed the limit, you may still be able to qualify for Medicaid by spending down those resources on your medical care. For example, Jean enters a nursing home when she has savings of $20,000. After she spends $18,000 for the cost of her nursing home care, she will have only $2,000 and will meet the resource eligibility requirement. Individuals may also spend down by converting a countable resource into an exempt asset or by paying for their own support needs or those of their spouse. For example, Rachael and Ralph are married. Ralph has to enter a nursing home. In order to meet the resource eligibility limits, they buy a new car for Rachael. Because it is the only car they own, it is an excludable resource.

Income

The income limits for Medicaid applicants depend on the size of the applicant's household. In 2010 the income standard for a household of one was $674 per month and $1,011 for a household of two. For applicants seeking home and community-based waiver services, the income limit is usually more generous. There are also special rules for married couples when one spouse plans to reside in a nursing home and the other will remain in the community. These rules, known as the spousal impoverishment protections, are discussed in the next section.

If an applicant's income exceeds the income limit, the applicant can deduct incurred medical expenses to achieve eligibility. For example, Tina, age 68, lives in an apartment and has a monthly countable income of $800. Tina has medical bills of $150 a month. After deducting the $150, Tina has countable income of $650 and so is eligible for Medicaid.

In determining income eligibility for medically needy individuals who reside in nursing homes, states have a choice between two methods—the spend-down method or the income-cap method. The spend-down method requires the applicant to spend all of his or her income on medical care except for a personal needs allowance. The monthly amount of the personal needs allowance varies by state, but a single individual may keep at least $30 and a married couple may keep at least $60. Provided the applicant also meets the resource test, Medicaid will pay the portion of the nursing home expenses not covered by the applicant's income.

Consider the example of Janet, who resides in a nursing home and has no resources. Her income is $2,030 per month, which exceeds the $674 income limit to qualify her as categorically needy under Medicaid. Because her nursing home monthly cost is $5,500, Janet qualifies as medically needy. Janet can retain $30 as a personal needs allowance, but she must apply the remaining $2,000 to her monthly nursing home bill. Medicaid will pay the additional cost of her nursing home care.

Income-cap states have a more restrictive income standard for eligibility. These states set a fixed cap on an applicant's monthly income—usually at 300 percent of the SSI income benefit. In 2010, this cap in most states was $2,022 (3 x $674). An applicant whose income exceeds this limit by even $1 is not eligible for Medicaid. The income-cap states are Alabama, Alaska, Colorado, Connecticut (uses income cap only for those receiving home health care services), Delaware, Idaho, Mississippi, Nevada, New Mexico, Oregon, South Carolina, South Dakota, and Wyoming. Several other states—Arizona, Arkansas, Florida, Iowa, Louisiana, and Oklahoma—do not permit the cost of nursing home expenses to be used to spend down excess income and so as a practical matter are income-cap states. Texas is also an income-cap state with respect to seniors because it excludes the aged from its spend-down, medically needy program.

In income-cap states, you can still obtain Medicaid eligibility by assigning your excess income to what is known as a Miller trust (42 U.S.C. §1396p[d]). Under a Miller trust, a trustee collects and holds all of your income and has authority to distribute monthly income to you only up to the income-cap amount. At your death, the state has a claim on the trust assets for all amounts paid by Medicaid on your behalf.

Special Considerations for Married Individuals

When a married individual enters a nursing home (the institutionalized spouse), the costs of his or her care can place a significant financial strain on the other spouse (the community spouse). Medicaid rules for a married, institutionalized applicant are designed to help the community spouse have adequate income and resources. The rules allow a married individual to become medically eligible for Medicaid without requiring the noninstitutionalized spouse to become destitute. The noninstitutionalized spouse is known as the "community spouse" regardless of where he or she lives so long as it is not in a nursing home.

Only the income of the institutionalized spouse is counted in determining eligibility for Medicaid (42 U.S.C. §1396r-5[b][1]). None of the income of the community spouse is counted. This is known as the "name on the check rule" because it is the name on the check that determines whether the income is considered to be that of the institutionalized or the community spouse. If the institutionalized spouse and the community spouse receive joint income, such as interest payments from jointly held investments, each is considered to be the owner of one-half of the income (42 U.S.C. §1396r-5[b][2][A] and [C]).The community spouse does not have to spend any of his or her income on the cost of the nursing home for the institutionalized spouse.

If the couple lives in an income-cap state and the institutionalized spouse has income that exceeds the income limit, it may be possible to go to court for an order of separate maintenance. Under this order, the institutionalized spouse signs a qualified domestic relations order that assigns part of his or her pension income to the community spouse and thereby reduces the income of the institutionalized spouse to an amount that is below the income cap.

Resources

Whereas the income test considers only the income of the institutionalized spouse, the resource test considers all resources of the married couple (42 U.S.C. §1396r-5[c]). All countable resources owned by the couple, regardless of how owned or titled, are considered available resources that must be spent down before either spouse is eligible for Medicaid. The resources are valued as of the first day of the month of continuous nursing home residency that is expected to last thirty days (42 U.S.C. §1396r-5[c][1][A]). This determination of value is known as the snapshot; it has important consequences for the community spouse.

On the snapshot date, only countable resources are considered, and each is valued at its fair market value. What qualifies as a countable resource is determined by the SSI rules. Once the couple's countable resources have been established, the amount of those resources that may be retained by the community spouse can be determined. Resources that cannot be retained by the community spouse must be spent down until the institutionalized spouse meets the eligibility requirement.

Community Spouse Resource and Income Rights

Community Spouse Resource Allowance. To avoid reducing the community spouse to poverty while the institutionalized spouse spends down income and assets, Medicaid allows the community spouse to retain all of his or her income and some resources, known as the Community Spouse Resource Allowance (42 U.S.C. §1396r-5[f]). The amount of the retained resources is adjusted annually for inflation. In 2010, federal law permitted states to award the community spouse a resource allowance between $21,912 and $109,560. A few states grant the community spouse the lesser of the maximum amount ($109,560) or all of the couple's countable resources. Most states, however, grant the community spouse one-half of the countable resources, up to the maximum amount of $109,560.

Consider the following examples. If a couple had $120,000 of countable resources in 2010, some states would permit the community spouse to retain the maximum of $109,560, but most states would permit a resource allowance of only $60,000 (half of the countable resources). If the couple had $250,000 in countable resources, the community spouse could retain $109,560. If the couple had only $25,000 in countable resources, the community spouse could retain the minimum of $21,912 and, in a few states, $25,000. If the couple had only $10,000 in countable assets, the community spouse would keep all $10,000 in all states.

Minimum Monthly Maintenance Needs Allowance. In addition to the Community Spouse Resource Allowance, the community spouse is permitted to have a minimum income. If his or her own income is below that allowed amount, known as the Minimum Monthly Maintenance Needs Allowance (MMMNA), the community spouse can claim income from the institutionalized spouse (42 U.S.C. §1396r-5[d]). The MMMNA is equal to 150 percent of the federal poverty level for a two-person household ($1,821.25 as of July 1, 2009) plus an excess shelter allowance that together cannot exceed the annual cap of $2,739 per month in 2010 (adjusted annually).[6] The excess shelter allowance is the sum of the spouse's expenses for rent or mortgage payments, taxes, insurance, condominium or cooperative maintenance charges, and either a standard utility allowance or the spouse's actual utility expense. If that sum exceeds 30 percent of the MMMNA, the community spouse may be permitted to keep an increased allowance up to the annual cap.

For example, Lucy, the community spouse, has a monthly income of $1,000. She is permitted to claim at least $821.25 of monthly income from her institutionalized spouse. If she could demonstrate excess shelter costs, she could further increase her MMMNA up to a maximum in 2010 of $2,739. A few states have adopted the maximum dollar amount as the MMMNA for every community spouse.

If the institutionalized spouse is under a court order to provide support to the community spouse, the income must be diverted from the institutionalized spouse to the community spouse even if the amount exceeds the MMMNA. Therefore, a community spouse who is dissatisfied with the amount of the MMMNA can seek more support by suing the institutionalized spouse. The community spouse may also request a hearing from a state Medicaid agency if not satisfied with the MMMNA and can ask for additional income based on exceptional circumstances such as costly medical expenses.

Income First Rules. If the community spouse's income is below the MMMNA amount, states must allow the community spouse to keep that portion of the institutionalized spouse's income necessary to bring the community spouse's monthly income up to the MMMNA amount (42 U.S.C.

§1396r-5[d]). For example, George, the community spouse, has a monthly income of $1,500 and is entitled to an MMMNA of $2,000. He is entitled to $500 a month from the income of his institutionalized spouse. If his institutionalized spouse's income is less than the amount needed to meet the MMMNA, for example, the institutionalized spouse has only $400 a month income, George will be given all of his spouse's income minus the $30 personal needs allowance, or $370. George, however, is still short $130. The shortfall will be made up by an increase in George's Community Spouse Resource Allowance. He will be allowed to keep additional resources equal to an amount that if invested or used to purchase an annuity would create the necessary additional income of $130.

Planning Techniques for Married Couples

Married couples will want to consider methods of creating eligibility for Medicaid while preserving assets for use by the community spouse. The following are some of the planning techniques to help couples retain income and resources.

Repayment of Debts by Institutionalized Spouse. The snapshot calculation of a couple's total, countable resources is made on the first day of entry into a nursing home. After the calculation of the community spouse's resource allowance has been made, the institutionalized spouse must spend down the remaining resources before becoming eligible for Medicaid. Fortunately, there is no requirement that the institutionalized spouse spend his or her allocation solely on medical care. Institutionalized spouses may spend down their resources on items that will benefit the community spouse. For example, any outstanding debts of the couple should be paid for by the institutionalized spouse. This could include a mortgage, car loan, and credit card debt. Couples can even accumulate debt before the entry into a nursing home with the intent that it will be paid off by the institutionalized spouse.

Conversion of Countable Resources into Exempt Assets. If the couple owns their residence, a number of techniques to preserve assets for the community spouse exist. After the snapshot, the institutionalized spouse should pay all real estate taxes. By paying the taxes, the institutionalized spouse is spending down countable resources while simultaneously benefiting the community spouse and preserving the community spouse's portion of the assets. The institutionalized spouse can purchase a reasonable amount of household goods and pay for any repairs or improvements to the home. Because the value of one car is an excluded asset, the institutionalized spouse may want to purchase a new car for the community spouse soon after the day of the snapshot. A couple can even purchase a new home as a means of spending down the resources of the institutionalized spouse.

Changing Beneficiaries. Many couples have life insurance that names the partner as the beneficiary. A community spouse who owns life insurance should remove the institutionalized spouse as the beneficiary in order to protect the death benefit in the event that the community spouse dies first. The name of the institutionalized spouse should be removed because any funds paid to him or her would be spent on nursing home care. For the same reason, no bank accounts of the community spouse should name the institutionalized spouse as a beneficiary, and the will of the community spouse should leave only the statutorily required minimum to the institutionalized spouse.

Asset Transfers

Look-Back Period and Period of Ineligibility

Many older Americans would like to create Medicaid eligibility by giving away assets to their family members rather than spending them down on their own care. Unfortunately, gifts by Medicaid applicants or their spouses may trigger a period of ineligibility for Medicaid benefits (42 U.S.C. §1396p). The Medicaid application for nursing home benefits requires that the applicant disclose any gifts made within sixty months prior to the application. For gifts made before February 8, 2006, the disclosure period is thirty-six months. These sixty (or thirty-six) months are known as the look-back period, and all assets transferred for less than fair market value during this period must be reported on the Medicaid application.

If an applicant made a gift during the look-back period, the length of Medicaid ineligibility will depend on the gift's value. The period of ineligibility is determined by dividing the gift's value by the average monthly cost of nursing home care in the applicant's state. The result (rounded up if not a whole number) is the number of months of Medicaid ineligibility. For example, if Tom gives $40,000 to his daughter, and the state average monthly cost of nursing home care is $5,000, he will be ineligible for Medicaid for eight months.

The period of ineligibility begins the month the individual is in a nursing home or is medically eligible for nursing home care and, except for the penalty period, would "otherwise" be eligible for Medicaid. For example, on June 1, 2007, Ben gives away $50,000 to his son. The average monthly nursing home cost in Ben's state is $5,000. On June 1, 2009, two years after he made the gift, Ben moves into a nursing home with $4,000 of countable resources and a monthly income of $2,500. The nursing home charges $6,500 per month. By July 1, 2009, Ben has exhausted his savings and his income is less than his monthly cost of care. Ben's state is an income spend-down state, and so he is now "otherwise" eligible for Medicaid. His gift on June 1, 2007, within the sixty-month look-back period, causes ten months of ineligibility, which begins to run on July 1, 2009, the date when he is otherwise eligible for Medicaid. As a result of the penalty period, Ben will not be eligible for Medicaid until May 1, 2010.

If an individual gives away assets but does not apply for Medicaid until after the look-back period, the gift will not affect eligibility. When the individual eventually submits an application, the gift does not have to be revealed on the Medicaid application. If a couple have made gifts and both later apply for Medicaid nursing benefits, the state must apportion the period of ineligibility between them. The state may not create a single period of ineligibility and apply it to both individuals.

Provided an individual can show that assets were transferred for a reason other than to qualify for Medicaid, no period of ineligibility will accrue. However, this argument is rarely successful. The applicant must provide convincing evidence about the specific purpose for which the assets were transferred in order to qualify for the exception. States can grant hardship waivers that permit eligibility even though the applicant made disqualifying transfers, but states are very reluctant to grant such waivers.

Depending on the state, community spouses may or may not be permitted to give away resources. Some states allow the community spouse to give away assets after the institutionalized spouse has become eligible; others maintain that any gifts by the community spouse after eligibility trigger a period of ineligibility for the institutionalized spouse.

Exempt Gifts

Some gifts do not trigger a period of ineligibility. These include gifts to the applicant's spouse or to another for the sole benefit of the applicant's spouse. Also included are gifts to a blind or disabled child of the applicant or to a trust solely for the benefit of that child.

Transfer of Home

The home is an exempt resource if the equity value does not exceed $500,000 (or up to $750,000 if the state so elects) and the community spouse is living in it at the time available resources are calculated. In the case of a single individual, the home is also an exempt resource as long as the individual expects to return to it (even if that expectation is unreasonable). A few states deem the home a countable resource for a single individual after a set period of time, such as a year.

Though the home is normally exempt, gifts of a home will typically trigger a period of ineligibility, because the home will lose its exempt status once transferred. However, certain transfers will not trigger a penalty period. If the house is given to a spouse, a child under the age of 21, or a child who is blind or permanently and totally disabled, the gift will not cause a period of ineligibility for the applicant. Furthermore, if the house is given to the applicant's sibling who has an equity interest in the home and who resided in it for at least a year prior to the application, the gift will not cause ineligibility. Neither will a penalty period be triggered if the house is given to a child who resided in it for at least two years immediately before the applicant was institutionalized and who provided care that permitted the applicant to reside at home.

The state may forgo the penalty period if it determines that denying eligibility would be an undue hardship on the applicant. Undue hardship is interpreted as meaning that the transfer penalty would endanger the applicant's life by depriving him or her of medical care.

If the house is titled in the name of the institutionalized spouse or is jointly owned, the standard practice is to retitle the house in the name of the community spouse. Retitling the house protects its value in the event that the community spouse predeceases the institutionalized spouse. If the house were left to the institutionalized spouse, it would likely become an available resource and as such would disqualify the institutionalized spouse for Medicaid. In many states, after the institutionalized spouse has become eligible for Medicaid, the community spouse may transfer the home to a third party, such as a child, without affecting the institutionalized spouse's eligibility.

Gifts in Trust

Revocable trusts do not shield assets from counting as available resources to the Medicaid applicant (42 U.S.C. §1396p[d]). Because the creator of the revocable trust can revoke it and reclaim the trust assets, all the trust income and assets are considered available resources. The effects of an irrevocable trust are more complicated. If the applicant or the applicant's spouse transfers assets to an irrevocable trust that cannot distribute principal for the benefit of the applicant or spouse (i.e., the trust can make distributions only to a third party), the assets may trigger a penalty period. The look-back period for trusts is sixty months. If the trust can make distributions to the applicant or to his or her spouse, the trust is considered an available resource for the applicant. If a trust makes distributions of principal or income to a third party, the distributions are considered gifts.

Estate Recovery

The federal Medicaid statute requires states to attempt recovery of Medicaid payments from the estates of those who were provided benefits (42 U.S.C. §1396p[b][1][B]). The state has the right to recover from the beneficiary's estate or to enforce a Medicaid lien when the Medicaid beneficiary's property is sold. The beneficiary's estate is all real and personal property included in the state's definition of a probate estate. The state may also include other assets in which the beneficiary had a legal interest, such as jointly titled assets or assets in trust.

A lien on the house cannot be enforced so long as the house is occupied by certain individuals. For example, a lien cannot be enforced while a surviving spouse or a minor, blind, or disabled child is living in the house. The same is true while a sibling is living there, provided the sibling has an equity interest in the house and resided there for at least one year prior to the beneficiary's institutionalization. If the house sharer is a child who is not a minor or is not blind or disabled, the child must have resided in the house for at least two years prior to institutionalization and must prove that he or she provided care to the Medicaid beneficiary that permitted the beneficiary to live at home. A state may waive recovery if it would cause an undue hardship, such as where the property is the sole source of income for survivors. A few states have ignored the rule and do not enforce estate recovery.

Long-Term Care Insurance

Seniors who wish to pass on their assets or avoid burdening their children often purchase long-term care insurance. Long-term care insurance policies are sold by private insurance companies, not by the federal government. The policies guarantee a fixed monthly cash payment in the event the insured individual enters a nursing home or assisted living facility or requires long-term care at home.

Reasons to Purchase Long-Term Care Insurance

Three reasons exist for purchasing long-term care insurance. First, you may want to protect the value of your estate against the potentially high costs of long-term care. Second, you may want to protect your spouse or yourself against a lower standard of living if one of you needs nursing home care. And third, you may fear relying on Medicaid.

If your concern is maintaining the size of your estate, you should consider whether preservation of the estate is worth the cost of paying long-term care insurance premiums for potentially twenty or thirty years. You should consider how much you would be willing to spend from your estate on long-term care and then purchase only enough insurance to cover the additional risk. For example, Alison and Art, both age 66, own a house worth $250,000 and have savings of $300,000. Each has income from a pension and Social Security of $40,000 a year, for a total income of $80,000. They buy long-term care insurance that will pay $200 a day for up to three years for each of them. In other words, the maximum benefits from the policy are approximately $219,000 per person or $438,000 for both. They buy the policy because they are willing to spend some of their income and resources on their long-term care but do not want to exhaust all of their savings on their care. They have three children and four grandchildren and hope to pass some money to them when they die.

One alternative to long-term care insurance is life insurance if your concern is depletion of your estate. Life insurance is typically less expensive, particularly second-to-die policies that do not pay death benefits until the last of the two spouses dies. Although life insurance will not help pay for long-term care needs, it can be viewed as replacement money for the money spent on long-term care. If the estate is depleted because of nursing home expenses, the life insurance will ensure the heirs an estate of a meaningful size.

If your concern is protecting the quality of your life or that of your spouse in the event one of you needs expensive nursing home care, you should consider whether you would likely qualify for Medicaid under the spousal impoverishment protections and calculate what the community spouse would be able to retain under those rules versus the cost of maintaining long-term care insurance. Even though Medicaid does allow the community spouse to retain some assets and income, long-term care insurance can reduce the risk of having to divest assets to that level.

For example, Caitlin and Curtis buy a policy with a ninety-day elimination period that pays $200 a day for five years. Curtis develops dementia. As the disease progresses, he moves to an assisted living facility at a cost of $150 a day. After ninety days, the couple has spent $13,500 on his care, which they paid from their savings. Curtis's condition has worsened, and so he moves to a nursing home that costs $250 a day. Their long-term care policy begins to pay $200 a day. After three years in the nursing home, Curtis dies. The nursing home cost to the couple was $50 a day for three years or $54,750. In total, the couple's cost of care for Curtis in assisted living and in the nursing home was $68,250. Although they had only $250,000 in savings, thanks to the long-term care insurance, the couple was able to meet the cost without resorting to Medicaid and its spend-down requirements.

If you want long-term care insurance because you are reluctant to rely on Medicaid, it is important to look realistically at the trade-offs. If you fear that Medicaid will not be available in the future, that fear is probably unfounded. Public subsidy of long-term care is not going away so long as so many cannot afford the cost of long-term care. And if you would presently qualify for Medicaid, then long-term care insurance is not cost-justified for you.

If you fear that the quality of care in Medicaid-reimbursed nursing homes will decline, there is no doubt that individuals with long-term care insurance who can privately pay for nursing home care will have a greater choice of nursing homes. With that said, more than 90 percent of nursing homes accept Medicare and Medicaid reimbursement, and there is typically no difference in care between residents on Medicaid and those who are paying for their care with private funds and long-term care insurance.

Probably more realistic are concerns that Medicaid waiver services in your home or in the community (such as adult day care) might not be available when you need them because of long waiting lists or the possibility that your assets or income would disqualify you for such services. Long-term care insurance that includes a home care benefit can help alleviate those concerns.

Choosing a Long-Term Care Policy

More than one hundred companies offer long-term care insurance, though many that once sold such policies have retreated from the market because it is so difficult to estimate the cost of future benefit payouts. The most important aspect of choosing a policy is its coverage, including the scope— what it will pay and for what type of care (e.g., nursing home, assisted living facility, in your own home) and the terms under which coverage will begin, including the length of any elimination period before benefits are payable and the triggers for the onset of coverage. You will also want to consider whether the policy is "tax qualified" and whether the policy qualifies as a "partnership policy" under your state's Medicaid law.

Coverage. Because there is no standard long-term care coverage, you should examine each policy carefully. Most policies provide coverage for care in nursing homes, but you should consider whether home care and coverage for an assisted living facility are also important to you. The scope of coverage will impact the cost of the premiums.

Most long-term care insurance policies are pure indemnity, that is, they pay a fixed dollar amount for each day that you are in a nursing home or assisted living facility or are receiving home care. Other policies pay only for the actual daily cost of care up to a fixed amount. Some policies also have an inflation-adjustment rider that will increase the daily benefit by a set percentage, typically 5 percent per year. Given the rising cost of long-term care, you should consider purchasing the inflation-adjustment rider to assure that the benefit amount will keep pace with the actual cost of care.

Long-term care insurance generally pays benefits if you are certified by a physician as having cognitive deficits, such as those caused by dementia, or are unable to do two of the five activities of daily living:

- bathing
- toileting
- eating
- dressing
- transferring (getting out of a bed or chair without assistance)

Many policies pay benefits for home care as well as nursing home care. Often home care benefits are one-half as generous as benefits paid if you are in a nursing home or assisted living facility. For example, the policy might pay $150 per day for nursing home care or care in an assisted living facility, but only $75 a day for care received at home. Because nursing home care is usually more than $200 a day, long-term care insurance will generally not meet the entire cost. It may cover most of the cost of care in an assisted living facility.

A long-term care insurance policy may limit how long it will pay benefits. Though it is possible to buy a policy that will pay benefits for the life of the insured, many pay benefits for two, three, or five years. The longer the policy pays benefits, the higher the premiums are. Time limits on benefit payments apply without regard to whether you are at home or in an institution, although some policies have separate time limits for home and institutionalized benefits. For example, Jack owns a long-term care insurance policy that pays home care benefits for two years and institutional care benefits for five. Jack receives eighteen months of home care benefits and then moves into a nursing home. Under the terms of the policy, he will still have five years worth of institutionalized care benefits.

Some policies have an "elimination" period of thirty, sixty, or ninety days, meaning the benefits are not paid until after you first meet the qualifications for receiving benefits for the length of the elimination period. For example, Pauline enters an assisted living facility because she cannot perform two activities of daily living. She qualifies for the daily benefit under her long-term care insurance policy, but the policy has a sixty-day elimination period. She must wait sixty days before she will begin to receive benefits.

Choosing a longer elimination period can reduce your premium costs. Some policies do not require the elimination period to be consecutive days. These policies have an accumulation period during which the total number of elimination days may be met. For example, if a policy has a ninety-day elimination period and a nine-month accumulation period, you will begin receiving benefits as soon as you spend ninety days in a nursing facility, even if they are not consecutive, provided they occur during a nine-month period.

Long-term care policies may exclude coverage for mental illness other than Alzheimer's disease or other forms of dementia. Often policies will not cover treatment for alcoholism, drug addiction, illness related to wartime injuries or sickness, and treatment necessitated by attempted suicide. Preexisting conditions may not be covered or may be excluded from coverage for the first six months that the policy is in effect. You generally must submit to a physical examination to qualify for long-term care insurance. Based on the physical or other factors, many applicants are denied. An estimated 25 to 50 percent of applicants are turned down by at least one insurance company.

Age, at least until age 84, will not exclude an individual from purchasing a policy, as policies are generally sold to individuals between ages 50 and 84. The annual premium rises with the age at which the policy is purchased. Premiums are much lower when the policy is purchased at age 60 than at age 75. Plus the likelihood of being denied insurance increases with age. Once you purchase a policy, the premium will not be raised unless the company raises premiums for all similar policies; unfortunately, that is very likely to occur.

Long-term care insurance is costly because you will need to keep the policy in effect for the rest of your life. A 65-year-old buyer, for example, can expect to pay premiums for twenty to thirty years. Although many purchasers find the annual cost of the insurance to be very burdensome, once purchased it makes no sense to let a policy lapse because the likelihood of needing the benefits increases with age.

Almost all long-term care insurance policies are indefinitely renewable unless the company withdraws coverage from the state in which the insured resides. The policy can be terminated, however, if the insured does not pay the premium, but there are usually antilapse protections if the failure to pay the premium is due to a condition over which the insured has no control, such as mental incapacity. Most policies will waive the premium when the insured begins to collect benefits. This provision is usually standard in policies, but you should check the particular policy. If you voluntarily terminate a policy, generally the coverage is terminated with no credit for prior premiums paid.

Federal Tax Benefits. The benefits paid by a long-term care insurance policy are not taxable as income if the policy is "tax qualified" (I.R.C. §7702B[a][1]). Most, but not all, policies are tax qualified, which means that the policy is guaranteed renewable, does not require prior hospitalization to trigger the payment of benefits, and complies with the Long-Term Care Insurance Model Regulation and the Long-Term Care Insurance Model Act developed by the National Association of Insurance Commissioners (NAIC) (I.R.C. §7702B[b]). The premiums for such insurance can be deducted as a medical expense, though the amount that can be deducted is capped and increases with the age of the taxpayer (I.R.C. §213[d][1][C]). In 2010 a taxpayer age 70 or older could deduct up to $4,110 in premiums. This amount is adjusted annually for inflation. Only taxpayers who itemize deductions (rather than claiming the standard deduction) may take this deduction and then only if all medical expenses, including the allowable portion of the long-term care insurance premium, exceed 7½ percent of adjusted gross income.

Medicaid Long-Term Care Insurance Partnerships. In order to encourage more private payment of long-term care and less reliance on Medicaid, Congress enacted legislation promoting state long-term care insurance partnership plans (42 U.S.C. §1396p[b][1][C]). An individual who has received benefits under a long-term care partnership insurance policy will be permitted to retain assets up to the amount of those benefits. For example, if Joan owned a long-term care insurance policy that paid her $150,000 in benefits and she then applied for Medicaid, Joan would be permitted to own $150,000 in countable resources and still be eligible for Medicaid. Of course, Joan would still have to meet the state income requirements. To be eligible for partnership policy status, the long-term care insurance policy must meet the specifications of the Long-Term Care Insurance Model Act and offer inflation protection by increasing the benefits over the life of the policy. About one-half the states have adopted partnership plans.

Tips for Purchasing Long-Term Care Insurance

The National Association of Insurance Commissioners provides suggestions on shopping for and purchasing long-term care insurance. It suggests that you check with several companies and agents and compare premiums against similar benefits. If the company cannot or will not explain the terms of the policy, you should not purchase a policy from the company. You should purchase only one good policy instead of stacking multiple policies. NAIC also urges that you disclose your entire medical history. If you do not disclose everything, the company may be permitted to refuse to pay benefits or even cancel the policy. Although most states require insurance companies to provide purchasers with a thirty-day cancellation period in which they can obtain a full refund, you should always check how much time you have to cancel with full refund rights.

Notes

1. Kaiser Commission on Medicaid and the Uninsured, *Medicaid: An Overview of Spending on "Mandatory" vs. "Optional" Populations and Services*, Issue Paper No. 7331 (Menlo Park, CA: Kaiser Family Foundation, June 2005), 8, available at http://www.kff.org/medicaid/upload/Medicaid-An-Overview-of-Spending-on.pdf.

2. *Id*. at 7.

3. *Id*. at 8.

4. This rule applies to transfers on or after February 8, 2006. Prior to this date, the look-back for asset transfers other than to a trust was thirty-six months and sixty months for transfers to a trust (42 U.S.C. §1396p[c][B][i]).

5. States may elect a higher equity cap not to exceed $750,000 (42 U.S.C. §1396p[f][1][B]).

6. The MMMNA amounts may vary slightly by state.

For More Information

Centers for Medicare and Medicaid Services
(http://www.cms.hhs.gov)

Follow the links for Medicaid to find information about many Medicaid-related topics.

National Association of Insurance Commissioners
(http://www.naic.org)

Follow the consumer links to find educational information tailored to the insurance needs of seniors. Also find complaint and financial information about specific insurance companies.

National SHIP Resource Center
(http://www.shiptalk.org)

Find information about free one-on-one counseling to help you make decisions about your insurance needs, including long-term care insurance.

7

Housing

Did You Know?

- Hiring regular help at home may be less costly than moving to assisted living.
- Medicaid-funded help may be available at home as well as in a nursing home.
- Age-restricted housing may prohibit children not only as residents, but also as overnight guests.
- An owners association may have the right to change the rules after you buy your condominium or house in a planned community.
- An assisted living facility may have the right to terminate your contract even if your heath crisis, such as a stroke, is temporary.
- Nursing Home Compare is a federal website that provides information about the quality of all nursing homes that receive Medicare or Medicaid funding.

Where you live has a significant impact on your overall quality of life. The need to choose a new place to live usually results from a change in circumstances such as marriage, divorce, different employment, children leaving home, retirement, or a health crisis. Physical changes that come with advanced age are also common reasons that seniors move.

If you are a young senior thinking about a move at retirement or when the children leave home, you are likely to want a place that will meet your present interests as well as your future needs. You may want a quiet community that includes easy access to favorite activities such as golf, tennis, fishing, or cultural events. If you are an older senior, you may want housing options that also offer supportive services. These can range from limited assistance, such as light housekeeping, laundry services, and group meals, to more extensive assistance, such as help with dressing and bathing and skilled nursing care.

Just as seniors are a very diverse group in terms of age, health, and needs, so are senior housing options diverse in terms of services offered, eligibility requirements, and cost. Often the housing options that are most widely promoted are those that produce income for someone else—the developers of retirement communities or the service providers associated with assisted living facilities. This is why retirement communities and assisted living facilities are so aggressively marketed to seniors.

Equally adequate, or perhaps even better, options may exist for "aging in place" in your own house, condominium, or apartment. Information about these options, however, may be more difficult to find. The senior who wants to age in place may have to spend more effort to locate and coordinate needed services than would be required if he or she moved to a retirement community or assisted living facility. There is almost always a cost and convenience trade-off when choosing among senior housing options.

The remainder of this chapter provides an overview of senior housing options as well as important factors to be considered with each. First, the option of aging in place is explored, followed by a discussion of special age-restricted housing alternatives. Next, different types of independent living retirement housing are described, followed by an examination of supportive housing options that offer some degree of assistive services. Finally, residence in a nursing home is discussed for seniors with greater care and medical needs.

Aging in Place

For many seniors, the best housing is the house, condominium, or apartment where they presently live. Memories, friends, and familiar neighborhood places are some of the reasons that seniors want to age in place. Even though you may want to stay connected to the home, people, and places that are familiar, you may also fear what will happen if your health or that of your spouse deteriorates. The main challenge of aging in place is how to get help if your needs become greater than your ability to meet them.

Although aging in place presents challenges, the advantages go beyond the mere comfort of staying in a familiar situation. A move to a new residence has real downsides. It not only costs money to move; it also takes a great deal of physical and psychological energy. Preparing one residence for sale while finding a new place to live can be very stressful.

Yet aging in place also has disadvantages. You may have too much money tied up in a house that is too big and expensive to maintain. As you age, so does your house, and you may be less capable of maintaining it. What were routine tasks in the past may now require hired help to accomplish. Regular chores, such as cutting the lawn, raking leaves, cleaning gutters, and even taking out the garbage, may become difficult or impossible because of chronic health conditions or loss of stamina.

Sometimes changes take place in a neighborhood or community that make it less safe or appropriate for senior living. If you live in a city, essential services may have relocated from a central to a suburban location. If you live in the suburbs, necessary services may be accessible only if you can drive. The following discussion examines other important factors to consider if you want to age in place.

Practical Responses

Seniors who want to age in place can do so, but it takes planning. You must determine how to adapt your home to the realities of old age and do so with little or no assistance from the government. Unfortunately, there is little public money or support available for seniors trying to age in place. However, private solutions are available for seniors who are flexible and imaginative.

Paying the Bills. You must first calculate current monthly housing expenses. This calculation should include converting annual expenses (such as property taxes and insurance) and extraordinary expenses (such as periodic roof repair) into estimated monthly amounts. If you have enough income to meet those expenses (as well as the other costs of living), the next step is to consider what improvements would make your home more "senior friendly."

Examples of senior-friendly improvements include the installation of grab bars in the bathroom or the addition of a bathroom on the first floor. Moving a washer and dryer from the basement to the first floor is another. Some seniors who have difficulty climbing stairs convert an underused first floor dining room into their bedroom. Of course, using capital to modify the house should only be done if you can afford to spend part of your savings. When the house is eventually sold, the improvements may not increase the value of the home because many younger purchasers will either not care about the modifications or may even have to pay to reverse them, such as reconverting the bedroom into a dining room.

House Sharing with a Relative. If you cannot afford the cost of aging in place, there are alternatives. One is to invite someone to share the house. Many seniors ask a relative, typically an adult child or grandchild, to live with them. Some only ask the relative to share expenses, whereas others ask for at least some rent. Local zoning laws probably do not prohibit house sharing as long as no rent is paid because zoning laws do not prohibit two unmarried or even unrelated persons from living together.

House sharing can benefit both participants, but problems can arise, even when the house sharer is a relative. You should clearly define what you expect from the relationship. For example, in return for not requiring rent, do you expect the house sharer to take care of upkeep and minor repairs? Or do you expect the house sharer to provide your transportation to doctor's appointments, church, and the grocery store? Are you going to share meals, and, if so, who pays for the groceries, who cooks, and who cleans up? Seemingly minor points such as these, if not clearly answered, can lead to friction and possibly end the arrangement. It is far better to discuss possible problem areas upfront.

Another potential problem is the possibility that the person sharing your house will take advantage of you if you later become dependent because of declining physical or mental health. Exploitation of older persons takes many forms. It may be financial, such as using your money in ways that do not benefit you, or physical, such as neglecting to provide you with needed food and care. If you choose to participate in a house sharing arrangement and think that you may eventually become dependent on the house sharer, it is a good idea to have another relative or friend visit regularly to monitor your well-being.

Even though dependency on the house sharer may be unavoidable, you should not unnecessarily increase it by choosing the house sharer to serve as your agent under a power of attorney. A power of attorney is a legal document that gives the agent control over your property and finances (see Chapter 9 for general information about a power of attorney). Although appointing the house sharer to handle your financial affairs seems convenient, it creates big risks. If you are already physically dependent on the house sharing relative, that individual has a great deal of control over your person. Giving that same individual control over your property further increases the opportunity for financial exploitation. The solution is either to name someone other than the house sharer as agent under a power of attorney or to name another person as a co-agent with the house sharer to serve as a check-and-balance.

House Sharing with a Stranger. Some seniors are willing to share their house with a stranger. If rent is involved, the local zoning law may prohibit the arrangement. Such laws, however, are rarely enforced unless someone complains. Some homeowners do not charge rent but expect the house sharer to "pay" his or her way by handling certain chores, such as taking out the garbage or shoveling snow and doing basic repairs and maintenance.

Unfortunately, inviting a stranger into your house creates serious risks. Some churches, community service organizations, and senior citizen centers help screen potential house sharers. These organizations act as brokers and match interested older homeowners with trustworthy house sharers. If no organization is willing to do so, the necessary background search must be performed by the homeowner, but this is not very practical. It is difficult for an individual to undertake a background check that includes a search of criminal and civil court records, credit records, and employment records, as well as interviews with the prospective house sharer's past and current neighbors.

If you choose to enter into a house sharing arrangement with a relative or someone else, you should check with your insurance agent to see if your homeowner's insurance covers the new house sharer, both for injury to property and person caused by the house sharer and for injury to the house sharer and his or her property.

Reverse Mortgage. If you want to remain in your own home but would rather not enter into a house sharing arrangement to cover expenses, another option to consider is a reverse mortgage. A reverse mortgage is merely a fancy term for taking out a loan and pledging your house as security. What makes a reverse mortgage different from traditional home loans is that repayment is delayed until a triggering event occurs. Common repayment triggers include the homeowner selling the house, no longer living in it, failing to properly maintain or pay the property taxes on it, or dying. Reverse mortgages are not for everyone, but they can provide needed financial resources to seniors who are "house rich and cash poor."

Seniors should carefully consider the costs associated with a reverse mortgage. These costs are substantial and can include onetime charges, such as origination fees and closing costs, as well as fees that accumulate over the length of the loan, such as loan servicing fees and monthly mortgage insurance premiums. A senior borrower may not fully appreciate how sizable these fees may become because they are usually financed as a part of the total loan rather than paid upfront. When the borrower's house is eventually sold, these fees will be deducted from the sale proceeds along with the sums necessary to repay the loan principal and accrued interest.

Consider the example of Ann, age 75, who owns a home worth $150,000. She decides to borrow $60,000 from a bank in the form of a reverse mortgage because her monthly income is not adequate to cover her living expenses. Under the terms of the reverse mortgage, Ann agrees to pay 6 percent annual interest on the unpaid balance of the loan. She will not have to make any payment of principal and interest until she dies, sells the house, or no longer lives in it. If Ann dies at age 80 and her estate sells the house for $165,000, the estate will owe the bank $80,000 as a repayment of the principal and interest as well as accrued loan fees, which will likely total more than $10,000. The remaining sum of approximately $75,000 will go to her estate. By taking out the reverse mortgage, Ann was able to both stay in her home and meet her living expenses. However, to obtain the use of $60,000, Ann in actuality paid approximately $30,000 in interest and fees.

Not all older individuals who take out a reverse mortgage receive a lump sum. Instead, they may choose to establish a line of credit, such as the right to borrow up to $60,000, which they can take in set dollar amounts each month or on an as-needed basis. For example, Bart, age 80, has a house worth $200,000. He arranges with a bank to borrow $400 a month or $4,800 a year for the next twelve years at a rate of 7 percent annual interest. If Bart actually does borrow $400 a month for twelve years, he will owe $57,600 in principal plus interest of approximately $13,400, or a total debt of $71,000. Bart would then be age 92. Assume that Bart continues to live in his house until age 95, when he moves into a nursing home. That move triggers the repayment obligation on the loan. The debt of $71,000 will have grown by the annual interest of 7 percent per year to an additional $15,000. Bart would owe the bank approximately $86,000 to cover the principal and interest on the loan plus accumulated fees, which could total more than $20,000. If he is able to sell his house for $256,000, the bank would receive approximately $106,000 and Bart would keep $150,000.

Although the most common trigger for repayment of a reverse mortgage is the borrower's death or the sale of the house, declining health and the need for assisted living or nursing home care are also significant repayment events. Given the large origination fees and closing costs often associated with reverse mortgages, seniors should think carefully about whether a triggering event is likely to occur sooner rather than later. The proportionate impact of large onetime fees is less the longer the mortgage repayment is delayed. One way in which repayment can be delayed is by a couple taking out a reverse mortgage that conditions repayment when the last of the borrowers dies or when neither borrower is able to live in the house.

One advantage of reverse mortgages is that they are typically nonrecourse, which means that the borrower is not personally liable for the debt. In other words, the lender can look only to the house sale proceeds for repayment of the loan. For example, Carol, age 77, owned a house worth $120,000 in 1997. She took out a reverse mortgage and by age 88 owed the lending bank $90,000. Due to the onset of dementia, she moved into an assisted living facility. In 2008, when her house was sold, the value had fallen to $85,000, so the sale proceeds were insufficient to pay off the entire $90,000 debt. Because the reverse mortgage was nonrecourse, Carol does not owe the bank the $5,000.

Lenders limit the amount of home equity that can be borrowed under a reverse mortgage in order to ensure that there will be sufficient sale proceeds to cover the loan when a triggering event occurs. For example, a lender might limit the amount of a reverse mortgage to no more than 70 percent of the estimated fair market value of the house. The amount of the loan or the limit on the line of credit is also affected by the age of the borrower. The younger the borrower is, the less the lender will loan. Because the loan will not be repaid until the house is sold or the borrower dies (or one of the other triggering events occurs), interest on the debt continues to rise. The lender wants the assurance that the total debt owed—principal, interest, and fees—will not exceed the value of the house when it is finally sold. The younger the borrower is, the greater is the amount of interest that is likely to accrue.

To qualify for a reverse mortgage, a homeowner must usually own the house free and clear of any mortgages or liens. In order to postpone repayment until death or the sale of the house, the homeowner will need to take out an insured reverse mortgage. The Federal Housing Administration (FHA) insures reverse mortgages, as do private lenders.[1] An FHA-insured loan is usually less expensive because it has lower upfront fees and may carry a lower rate of interest. However, an FHA-insured loan is available only if the borrower is at least age 62 (24 C.F.R. §206.33), the borrower holds title to the property (24 C.F.R. §206.35), and the house (or condominium) is his or her principal residence (24 C.F.R. §206.39).

The lender must explain to the borrower how a reverse mortgage works and must also provide the names of third parties who can counsel the borrower about the financial realities and consequences of the loan (24 C.F.R. §206.41). Counseling is mandatory and can cost up to $125 for the hour it typically takes. The lender must also disclose to the borrower all costs of obtaining the mortgage and which charges are not required to obtain the mortgage (24 C.F.R. §206.43). The allowable charges and fees are listed in the federal regulations (24 C.F.R. §206.31). The Housing and Economic Recovery Act of 2008 (Pub. L. No. 110-289) limits fees to a maximum of 2 percent on the first $200,000 borrowed and 1 percent of the balance, subject to a cap of $6,000 (Pub. L. No. 110-289, §2122). The law also prevents lenders from requiring borrowers to purchase additional insurance products, such as an annuity, as a precondition for getting a reverse mortgage.

The amount that can be obtained in the form of an insured reverse mortgage loan is a factor of the borrower's age, the interest rate, and the value of the house. There are limits on the loan amounts that can be insured, but the amounts vary throughout the nation and change over time. You can learn the estimated dollar limits for an insured reverse mortgage in your area by using the reverse mortgage calculator available on the AARP website.[2] Remember, even though a reverse mortgage may provide you with cash to cover living expenses so that you can remain in your home, it is not right for everyone. Before committing to a reverse mortgage, think carefully about all of the costs, the events that could trigger your repayment obligation, and your other options and future needs.

Medicare- and Medicaid-Financed Home Health Care

For some, aging in place requires onsite health care assistance. Medicare provides part-time and intermittent home health care for homebound seniors who need skilled nursing care, home health aides, or physical, speech, or occupational therapy (see Chapter 5 for general information about Medicare eligibility). Medicare home health care, however, is not designed to provide long-term care for a chronic condition. Although Medicare home health care can help you return home after hospitalization or remain home while recovering from a medical incident, such as a stroke, it is not a solution if you need long-term care.

Medicaid, the primary public payer of long-term care in nursing homes, has established a "waiver" program by which states can obtain a federal waiver of the Medicaid requirement that it only reimburse institutionalized care (see Chapter 6 for general information about Medicaid eligibility). A waiver permits the state to apply federal Medicaid dollars to pay for long-term care services delivered in your home. The number of waivers and the type and extent of home health care vary from state to state, as do financial eligibility requirements, such as resource and income limits.

Medicaid waiver care is often combined with other home care assistance programs operated by the state or county or by the local Area Agency on Aging. Every state has Area Agencies on Aging, often called by other names, which operate with federal and state funding to coordinate services for seniors. For example, the state Medicaid waiver program might provide a home health aide for twenty hours a week, which might be supplemented by county-provided homemaker services, Meals-on-Wheels meals, and a visiting nurse. The nature and extent of other home assistance vary considerably depending on the policy of the state and the availability of the services. The regional Area Agencies on Aging can provide information to you about home assistance programs available in your area.

The goal of the waiver program, known in some states as Home and Community-Based Services, is to permit you to live in your own home or community for as long as possible at a cost less than that of living in a nursing home. Some waivers provide help to seniors in residential situations other than a private home. Examples include board and care homes, where the waivers make possible the receipt of medical care that the facility is otherwise not licensed to provide, and domiciliary care homes, usually defined under state law as a home for two to four residents where the homeowner is the caregiver.

Another option for seniors who want to age in place but who need both skilled health care and long-term care is known as the Program of All-Inclusive Care for the Elderly (PACE). PACE relies on an interdisciplinary team and often uses adult day care supplemented by in-home care. Individuals age 55 or older may be eligible for PACE if they need nursing home care but would be able to live in the community if provided with the right help. They must meet state Medicaid income and resource eligibility requirements and must sign an agreement to accept PACE as the sole provider of services. The individual's care needs are reviewed twice a year, and eligibility for PACE is reviewed annually. Participants who are dissatisfied with the quality or level of care may submit a formal grievance as described in the program's grievance procedures.

Adult Day Care

Adult day care provides daily care for seniors who either should not or prefer not to be alone during the day. It is often the critical service that makes aging in place possible for an older adult who can no longer manage all alone. Such individuals usually have a family-member caregiver available in the evening, but adult day care makes it possible for that caregiver to go to work or take care of other responsibilities during the day.

Located throughout the community, adult day care centers are usually open from early in the morning until late afternoon five days a week to accommodate those with whom the older adult lives. A few centers are open on the weekends to provide respite care for families who care for the older adult during the week but seek relief on the weekend.

All adult day care centers feature supervised care, meals, and, usually, exercise classes, music, crafts and, sometimes, field trips. Participants typically arrive in the morning and stay all day. For example, an adult child will leave the older adult at the center in the morning and pick her up at the end of the workday. Some centers provide door-to-door transportation, whereas a few communities provide free or subsidized transportation to and from adult day care centers.

The typical client of an adult day care center is an older senior, usually age 80 or older, frail, and possibly suffering a mild loss of mental capacity. Those who attend adult day care cannot be in need of supervised medical care because adult day care centers are not licensed to provide such care. Many who attend, however, do have some degree of dementia.

Adult day care charges by the day, and the daily cost varies greatly based upon labor costs, but it is usually only 25 to 35 percent of the cost of a nursing home. The centers are often operated by nonprofit institutions, but many of the more than three thousand centers are for-profit businesses. Some Area Agencies on Aging offer subsidized adult day care, and some states have programs that offer assistance to low-income individuals in adult day care. Most long-term care insurance will pay benefits for an individual in adult day care if that individual otherwise meets the criteria for the receipt of benefits.

Age-Restricted Housing

Many seniors prefer to live with other older residents in housing that is open only to persons of a minimum age. Such housing includes apartment houses, condominiums, mobile home parks, subdivisions, villages, and even entire towns. Age-restricted housing is not necessarily designed to meet long-term care needs, but it does promise a safe and secure environment that caters to the needs and interests of older persons.

Age-restricted senior housing often provides special recreational, social, or community activities. The larger communities feature clubs, political activities, educational opportunities, charitable and religious activities, and recreational facilities designed for older residents. For many, just living with other seniors is attractive enough to make age-restricted housing a desirable choice.

Critics complain that it is unnatural to remove seniors from the community, and indeed age-restricted housing does not appeal to all older persons. Nevertheless, age-restricted housing is popular enough that it is exempt from the federal fair housing statute that otherwise bars discrimination based on "familial status" (e.g., no discrimination against families with children under age 18) (42 U.S.C. §3607[b][2]). State fair housing laws and even local ordinances also commonly permit housing that accepts only older residents.

Housing for Older Persons Defined

The federal fair housing law defines housing for older persons as housing that is limited to residents age 55 or older and has at least 80 percent of its units occupied by at least one person age 55 or older (42 U.S.C. §3607[b][2][C]). The alternative is to require all units to be occupied by residents age 62 or older (42 U.S.C. §3607[b][2][B]). The requirement that all residents are age 62 or older is a fixed rule that allows no exceptions. For example, a couple is disqualified if only one is age 62 or older. Imagine that Andy and Ann, when both are age 63, move into a retirement village restricted to those age 62 or older. Ann dies at age 64. A year later, Andy, now age 65, marries Katy, age 60. She will not be permitted to move into the retirement village because she is too young.

The age 55 or older test is more flexible. For example, at age 70, Ben and Betty move into an apartment complex that insists that at least 80 percent of the residents be age 55 or older. Ben dies at age 75. Betty, age 75, and in need of daily assistance, wants her 50-year-old daughter, Dora, to move in with her. The apartment complex permits Dora to move in because at the time 90 percent of the occupants are age 55 or older.

You may notice a number of formalities associated with age-restricted housing. Under the law, such communities must demonstrate an intent to meet the requirement that 80 percent of the residents are at least age 55 or older by publishing and following policies that

- describe the housing as age restricted,
- use advertising directed at those age 55 and older,
- use procedures to verify residents' ages, and
- have and enforce written rules, regulations, and lease provisions that ensure compliance with the law (24 C.F.R. §100.306).

The owner or manager of the facility is responsible for enforcing the age limitations.

Many states have laws that are similar to the federal exception for age-restricted senior housing. California, for example, has the Mobile Home Residency Law, which exempts mobile home parks from the state's general law against age discrimination. In California, mobile home parks may discriminate against those under age 55.

Sometimes underage would-be buyers or renters sue age-restricted housing facilities alleging that they violate the federal Fair Housing Act. Such claims may also be brought by a unit owner in the facility who wants to sell to an underage buyer. Despite exceptions under the act for age-restricted housing, a claim may be successful if the facility has failed to consistently enforce the age restrictions (*Massaro v. Mainlands Section 1 & 2 Civic Ass'n, Inc.,* 3 F.3d 1472 [11th Cir. 1993]).

Types of Age-Restricted Housing

When choosing age-restricted housing, you should consider which type is likely to be most appropriate as you age and perhaps require supportive services. Most age-restricted condominium or apartment houses are not likely to provide much in-unit help. If your ability to care for yourself declines, you may have to move to housing that provides in-unit assistance. For many seniors, the better choice is a retirement community or age-restricted subdivision or planned development. Such communities are more likely to offer supportive services as an option.

There are many self-contained small cities or towns designed exclusively for older residents. They include, for example, Leisure World in Southern California, with more than twenty thousand residents, and Sun City in Arizona, with more than forty-five thousand residents; both feature detached single-family houses and townhouses. Large retirement communities typically have extensive recreational facilities, including golf courses, tennis courts, swimming pools, shuffleboard courts, game rooms, libraries, and studios for arts and crafts, woodworking, and other leisure activities. Residents of these communities can find clubs that cater to almost every interest. To attract less financially secure elderly, some retirement towns feature less expensive manufactured housing or mobile homes.

Although individuals with chronic ailments may find it difficult to take advantage of many of the social or recreational attractions of these communities, other conveniences may still make residence in a retirement community worthwhile. Services such as stores, banks, restaurants, and religious facilities may be close enough to your residence to permit easy access on foot or with the use of a golf cart or personal scooter.

Smaller age-segregated villages typically are not self-contained. Residents must be able to drive to obtain services outside the residential area. If you require supportive assistance, such a community may not be a wise choice. Smaller, gated communities are even more isolated and require the resident to be able to drive out of the community to obtain almost any service. They offer few advantages over nonage-restricted housing for those older persons who need supportive assistance.

Age-restricted housing that only requires 80 percent or more of the units to have at least one resident age 55 or older promises a much greater mix of ages, but the facility may be less aimed at the interests of seniors. For example, it may include some recreational facilities that in general do not appeal to or benefit seniors. Also keep in mind that a facility that meets the age 55 and older exemption to the federal Fair Housing Act may legally exclude children, but not all do. Conversely, some facilities not only bar children under age 19 as residents but also do not permit them even as overnight guests.

If it is important to you to live in a community where property ownership or occupancy is limited to older persons, you should inspect the deed or condominium declaration and bylaws to ensure that the age restrictions exist and are enforceable. If supportive services are important, you should be aware that there is rarely any guarantee that such services will continue to be provided in the future. Even the current recreational facilities may not be maintained or provided in the future.

If the age-restricted property is rented, the landlord can choose the nature of the age restrictions. Unless it is part of the written lease, a landlord's promise to operate an age-restricted facility is not enforceable. Under the Statute of Frauds, oral promises regarding property are normally not enforceable, although applicability of the Statute of Frauds varies according to state law. The general rule, however, is that oral promises or representations regarding rental property are not enforceable. The provisions of the written lease determine the obligations of the landlord.

Also keep in mind that the landlord of age-restricted housing has no legal obligation to provide services or facilities that serve the needs of older persons. Consequently, you should note carefully what services, if any, are provided and whether the landlord has promised in writing to continue to provide those services. Also pay close attention to the physical nature of the building. For example, a few stairs leading up to an apartment may prove difficult or impossible for a resident suffering from arthritis. If you wish to leave before the end of the lease term, even for medical reasons, you may be financially responsible for the remaining term of the lease. The lease provisions will determine whether you can sublease your unit to someone else for the remainder of the lease. Even if subleasing is permitted, you will have to rent to someone who meets the facility's age restrictions.

Varieties of Retirement Housing

Planned Communities

Many seniors are attracted to planned communities, which are collections of houses or townhouses controlled by a homeowners association. The primary purpose of the homeowners association is to enforce the community's uniform standards and to assess fees for the upkeep and maintenance of the common areas, including recreational facilities such as tennis courts, exercise facilities, and swimming pools. There are usually strict rules about the appearance and use of properties in the community. Planned communities generally appeal to those who value uniformity of appearance, quality of design and construction, and standards for use and maintenance. They are often gated and limit access to provide increased security for their residents.

The uniformity of design and maintenance and the right to impose fees result from legal land use controls known as easements and covenants. These restrictions are said to "run with the land," meaning that they are enforceable against the original owner and also against subsequent purchasers. Easements usually establish rights-of-way for access, common area use, parking, and utilities. Covenants are restrictions that typically govern design features and the type of structures that can be built. They are also used to prevent certain actions, such as subdividing lots, and even may prohibit what the community considers to be eyesores, such as satellite dishes, fences, and utility sheds. Covenants also subject properties to control by the homeowners association and to certain payment obligations, such as maintenance fees.

If you are considering the purchase of a house or condominium in a planned community, you should ask to examine the community's Declaration of Restrictive Covenants. All easements and covenants that benefit or restrict use of the property either will appear directly in the property's deed or the deed will likely reference another document where the easements and covenants are described. At the time you purchase the property, you are also considered to be "on notice" of any easements and restrictions that have been properly recorded in the property's "chain of title" regardless of whether those restrictions appear in your individual deed. The chain of title is made up of all of the recorded deeds and agreements that affect the property.

It is generally too late when you accept a deed at closing to decide that you no longer want the property because of certain easements or covenants. You should carefully consider such restrictions before you sign the purchase agreement or include in the purchase agreement a contingency that allows you a reasonable amount of time to review the restrictions and change your mind about the purchase. If you request a title report, it will identify all of the important documents that affect the property's chain of title, but you must still read the contents of those documents to learn about the restrictions. Before you sign anything, you should consider having a lawyer review these documents and the terms of the proposed purchase agreement if you are uncertain about your rights and responsibilities.

Covenants in planned communities can generally be enforced by any other property owner in the community or by the homeowners association. Most covenants can be eliminated only upon the agreement of all of the parties who have a right to enforce the covenant, typically all landowners in the development. For example, suppose all the lots are subject to a covenant that requires houses to be two stories tall. Several years after the opening of the development, the final vacant lot is sold. The new owner wishes to build a one-story house, which would not be permitted by the covenant. If all the other property owners agree to waive their right to enforce the covenant, the new lot owner will be able to build a one-story house. But if only one other property owner objects, the new lot owner will have to build a two-story house.

In some communities, the initial covenants create authority in the homeowners association, or in a certain percentage of the property owners, to make decisions that will bind all property owners in the development. This authority may include the power to terminate existing covenants or to create new ones. It is therefore important that you consider whether this method of decisionmaking is acceptable to you and whether your opinions are likely to be shared by a majority of your neighbors.

In addition to easements and covenants that directly affect the use of individual properties in a planned community, residents are usually subject to other rules created by the homeowners association. Although most of the rules center on the use of the common areas, the association may have authority to regulate use of individual properties or units. For example, the association may be able to limit who may enter the grounds of the community. This in turn might potentially limit the kind and frequency of services that can be brought to your home. If you might require in-home assistance, it is best to learn whether the association has any rules that might prohibit access to that type of service provider. Even if the association has no rules at present that would cause a conflict, does the association have the power to enact such rules in the future?

Condominiums. Many seniors move to condominiums where they still have the economic advantages of home ownership but are spared most maintenance and repair problems. Although condominiums do have many advantages, they represent a form of property ownership with unique rights and responsibilities.

Ownership. The basis of a condominium is a registered corporation that is operated by the condominium unit owners, who own an individual interest in an apartment or a townhouse and a shared interest in the common areas, such as the land, parking areas, elevators, stairways, and recreational areas. The unit owners own and are responsible for everything within their units, but the common, shared ownership areas, including central furnaces or other mechanical equipment, are supported by a monthly maintenance fee paid by each unit owner.

The condominium is operated under a master deed, called the Declaration of Condominium, that contains a description of the land and the other common elements, a list of the individual units, and a description of how the corporation or association is governed. The unit owners each have a deed that shows ownership of their individual units and joint ownership of the common areas and that subjects them to the provisions of the declaration, the rules of the unit owners association, and all restrictions, covenants, and easements contained in the master deed. Ongoing governance of the condominium is by a unit owners association, whose leadership is selected by the unit owners.

Condominium Governance. Initially, the developer of the condominium owns all the units and the common areas. But after a certain number of the units are sold, the unit owners organize a unit owners association that elects a board of directors, which in turn manages the property, assesses the monthly common area maintenance fee, and adopts rules and regulations for the operation of the condominium. The rights and duties of the board of directors are stated in the Declaration of the Condominium and include operating the commonly owned property, such as the common entry and the elevator or stairs leading to the units.

The declaration states the voting power of each unit (which is usually one vote for each unit); the percentage of unit owners required to approve amendments to the declaration (subject to state law requirements); the rules for electing a board of directors and officers; and what kinds of bylaws may be adopted by the board and what bylaws must be approved by the unit owners. Although the votes of a majority or supermajority of unit owners is usually all that is needed to govern, some decisions, such as increasing the number of units or selling common property, may be subject to state laws that require unanimous consent of the unit owners.

If you are considering the purchase of a condominium, you should carefully examine the declaration and the condominium bylaws to see whether you can live with the various restrictions. Special attention should be paid to any rights of the board of directors to limit or regulate the use of individual units. For example, you should be sure that nothing in the condominium rules will prohibit in-home care if it is eventually needed.

The unit owners association assesses a monthly fee upon all unit owners for the repair, maintenance, and property taxes on the common areas. Unit owners are responsible for their share of the assessment even if they do not use the common area. For example, even if you never use a commonly owned tennis court, you will still be responsible for helping to pay for the court maintenance and repair. In addition to paying for normal maintenance, members can be assessed by the board of directors for special repairs such as fixing the roof or replacing the furnace. The condominium declaration may require a vote by a supermajority to authorize a special assessment to pay for unusual or major repairs.

Failure to pay an assessment will result in a lien against the unit, which is a legal obligation to pay the assessment from the sale proceeds if the unit is sold. A lien may become attached to the property despite valid claims by the unit owner that the condominium association did not provide the level of service called for in the declaration or bylaws. If the unit is sold without payment of the assessment and release of the lien, the new purchaser's interest in the unit will be subject to the lien. Consequently, when purchasing a condominium unit, you should examine the title report to identify any outstanding liens and obtain an agreement from the seller that such liens will be satisfied on or before closing of the sale.

Architectural control restrictions are common with condominiums. These generally restrict external changes to the unit. Internal changes rarely need approval. Some modifications, such as satellite dishes or changes to the windows, may be prohibited. In contrast, modest changes may be permitted, but only with the approval of the board of directors. Some larger condominiums have an architectural review board that must approve significant modifications of the individual units that are visible from the street. Even some internal modifications may need approval, particularly if they result in a change to the exterior of the unit. You should not purchase a condominium expecting to change its appearance without first obtaining the assurance of the board of directors that it will not interfere with the proposed alteration.

If a unit owner's request to modify the exterior is refused, the unit owner can sue, but she or he will probably lose because courts are reluctant to overrule subjective decisions about the appearance of property. If the board does not consistently enforce its rules, however, the unit owner may win.

Pets. The issue of pets can be very controversial in a condominium setting. Some condominiums have no policy; residents are free to own pets as they see fit. More commonly, condominiums restrict the number of pets per unit and sometimes the kind of pet, such as prohibiting cats or dogs but permitting birds and fish. Other condominiums limit the size of dogs by pounds or height. Some only forbid "dangerous" animals, such as snakes.

Before buying a condominium, you should ask about the rule on pets. Even if you have no pets, it is important to know whether the other unit owners are permitted to own them. Seeing dogs or cats on the premises does not necessarily mean that the condominium permits them. Such pets may have been grandfathered in when the condominium adopted restrictions prohibiting new dogs or cats. Also consider that if the condominium forbids all pets, or all cats and dogs, such a prohibition might make the condominium less attractive to buyers when the time comes to sell it. Condominium pet restrictions are frequently litigated, but usually courts uphold the restrictions so long as they are consistently applied.

Liability Issues. State law determines the potential liability of condominium owners. Condominium owners, if negligent, are liable for injuries to guests that occur in their unit. They may also be liable for injuries to individuals that happen in the common areas. Because of the potential for liability, a unit owner should buy adequate liability insurance and insist that the condominium association carry high-limit liability insurance for the common areas as well as liability insurance to protect board members, officers, and others against claims arising from their acts on behalf of the association.

Limits on Lease or Sale. Some condominiums have restrictions on the sale of a unit, but that is unusual. More common are limits on leasing a unit. Some even prohibit altogether the renting of units. If you are purchasing a unit for seasonal residence, it may be important to you to rent the unit when you are not using it. Or if you need to sell the unit, but the real estate market is slow, you may wish to rent the unit until the market improves. Consequently, it is a good idea to inquire about leasing policies before purchasing a condominium unit.

Cooperatives. Cooperatives, although seemingly similar to condominiums, are in fact quite different. The most significant difference is that a condominium unit owner actually owns the unit but the occupant of a cooperative unit does not. Rather, a resident in a cooperative development owns shares in the cooperative, which in turn owns all the units. Ownership of the shares gives the shareholder exclusive possession of a particular apartment unit, but that possession is subject to all of the rules in the cooperative shareholders agreement.

A board of directors makes most of the important decisions for the cooperative, including decisions about who may purchase shares of the cooperative. Thus, if you live in a cooperative and want to move, you can sell your shares only with the approval of the board of directors. The board can withhold consent to transfer shares for any reason it chooses so long as it is not a legally prohibited reason such as race, religion, or sex. For example, boards have rejected potential shareholders on reasonable bases, such as a poor credit rating, as well as on bases that some would view as unreasonable, such as the potential shareholder's political affiliation or profession. Most cooperatives insist that the buyer pay cash for shares and will not approve the sale of shares financed by a mortgage. As a result, a cooperative member may find that it takes longer to dispose of a cooperative unit than other forms of housing.

Mobile and Manufactured Homes. Many seniors live in mobile and manufactured homes because of the cost savings. By lowering the cost of their housing, the owners have more disposable income to spend on other needs. Thanks to the federal Manufactured Home Construction and Safety Standards (42 U.S.C. §§5401 *et seq.*), which mandate specifications for strength, durability, fire and wind resistance, and energy efficiency, today's manufactured houses are competitive in construction with traditional houses. Despite improvements in quality, mobile and manufactured homes may not be available in all areas due to restrictive zoning laws.

There are some significant differences between manufactured and mobile homes. A manufactured house looks very much like a traditional house, though it costs less to build because it features walls built offsite and may have metal where a traditional house would have wood. The owner of a manufactured home, like the owner of a traditional home, generally owns the land on which the house is located. In contrast, mobile home owners, whose homes are located in a mobile home park, usually do not own the land upon which their homes are located. Rather, they rent the lot, which can create a problem if they want to relocate.

The high cost of moving a mobile home generally means that if the owner wants to move, he or she must sell the mobile home to someone who will take over the lease of the lot on which it is located. Some landlords try to restrict such sales with lease clauses that either force removal of the mobile home or result in its sale at a bargain price to the landlord. To protect mobile home owners, many states have laws overriding such restrictions. State laws may also limit the grounds on which a landlord can evict a mobile home park tenant as a check-and-balance on landlords using eviction to force a sale of the mobile home.

Although mobile homes are generally less costly than traditional or other manufactured houses, financing a mobile home can be difficult because mortgages are usually shorter in duration and carry a higher interest rate. Casualty insurance may also be more costly in relation to the value of the home, typically 25 to 30 percent higher. However, in many jurisdictions, a mobile home is classified as personal property and so is not subject to local property taxes. Despite some of these issues, the overall cost savings make mobile homes an attractive option for low-income seniors.

Supportive Housing

Many older seniors find that they need daily assistance. Fortunately, supportive housing—that is, housing that offers assistance inside the home—is available in a variety of forms and at a range of prices.

Congregate Housing

"Congregate housing" is a term used to describe a variety of housing that combines age restrictions with some nonmedical services. Usually constructed in the form of apartments or condominiums, it is designed for individuals capable of independent living. The individual units are supplemented with some common areas, such as a library, card rooms, and, perhaps, a dining room. Whether a condominium or rental facility, the monthly fee will include the cost of providing limited in-unit housekeeping services. Even though the facility may have a dining room, it may not serve three meals a day. Even the evening meal may be optional, although some congregate housing facilities mandate the evening meal to support the cost of a dining facility.

A monthly fee pays for all repair and maintenance of both the common areas and the individual units. Housekeeping, including a change of bed linens and cleaning of the unit, is usually also provided. The facility will not provide medical monitoring or assistance, nor will the facility provide personal in-unit care. Congregate housing is not a viable option if you need daily, in-unit care.

For some seniors, congregate housing is attractive because it is age restricted; it offers housekeeping, some recreational facilities, and a sense of community; and it does not have the costs of additional supportive services. They assume that if personal care or medical services are later needed, they will move to a facility that will meet that need. In particular, congregate housing developments attract many seniors who do not want to move into "elderly housing" before they need the kind of personal and limited medical care offered in an assisted living facility. If you are considering congregate housing, you should investigate its financial stability. Competitive pressures have resulted in some of these facilities going into bankruptcy.

Assisted Living Facilities

An assisted living facility (ALF), as opposed to congregate living, is for individuals who need personal assistance in addition to the conveniences of congregate living. The need for personal assistance may result from physical infirmities, memory difficulties, or both. Separately or combined, mental and physical problems are the reason that millions of older seniors live in housing that provides supportive personal care and some medical assistance. Whereas some seniors are ill enough to need nursing home care, most do not. Today, more than 80 percent of ALF residents are women with an average age near 80.

In the past, assisted living was more commonly known as board and care homes, personal care homes, or retirement homes. In some states, assisted living is merely a board and care home with a new name. Other states, however, have adopted regulations that distinguish ALFs from board and care homes, with ALFs being licensed to care for individuals who need personal care and modest medical supervision. ALFs can also serve as temporary posthospitalization residences or provide short-term respite care for families who care for an older person at home.

ALFs vary from state to state in response to state regulations. Generally, however, they feature individual or shared studio apartments and provide three meals a day served in a common dining area, as well as housekeeping services, in-unit personal care as needed, and medication management. The facility provides round-the-clock staff and supervision, in-room emergency call systems, and, usually, some limited social and recreational activities. Some ALFs also provide transportation services for shopping and medical appointments.

The goal of assisted living is to provide a level of care that will delay the need to move to a more institutionalized and expensive nursing home. For many frail elderly, or those who have dementia but are otherwise healthy, assisted living is a safe, affordable alternative to living alone. Those with mild to moderate dementia often live in a special section of an assisted living facility so that they can be monitored and prevented from wandering away from the facility.

Although assisted living is designed for seniors with personal care needs, the distinction between personal care and medical care is an important one. An ALF is a personal care provider, not a medical provider. Residents must be able to get out of bed and to the dining room. State assisted living regulations usually prevent ALFs from admitting bedfast individuals because they require a degree of health care that can be provided only in a licensed nursing home. Some state laws permit an assisted living facility to continue to house residents who become bedfast if a physician will certify that they are not in need of skilled nursing care.

Most ALF residents are unable to perform some activities of daily living (ADLs). Although there is no formal, legal definition of ADLs, the term is usually meant to refer to

- bathing
- toileting
- eating
- dressing
- ambulating (getting out of a chair or bed without assistance)

An individual who cannot perform one of these tasks without assistance is said to have an ADL deficit and is in need of custodial care as opposed to skilled nursing, which provides medical care.

Another measure of a person's capabilities for self care are the instrumental activities of daily living (IADLs), which include going grocery shopping, using a telephone, cleaning a house, and paying bills. Some assisted living residents have no ADL deficits but move into the facility because they cannot perform IADLs. For example, they may have very poor vision and so are unable to navigate in the larger world.

The goal of an assisted living facility is to provide a safe and supportive environment that includes meals and assistance with bathing, grooming, and dressing. The facility monitors the individual's health and will likely have a nurse on its staff. It will have procedures to ensure that residents regularly take their medications. Some facilities also provide or contract for Medicare-reimbursed home health or rehabilitative care.

Residents of assisted living sign an admission contract. The resident agrees to pay the daily or monthly cost of care in exchange for the facility agreeing to provide room and board and specified personal care. Prior to entering the facility, the individual may be required to submit to a physical examination. Individuals who are too sick or who have more advanced dementia will not be admitted because the facility is not licensed to provide the level of care that they need. Some ALFs also charge an "entrance fee" that is often equivalent to two months rent and nonrefundable. Admission contracts vary but generally contain the following:

- date of initial occupancy
- identification of the unit to be occupied
- specification of who provides the room furnishings (usually the resident)
- a list of the services that the facility will provide (it may also list additional services that can be purchased)
- the monthly fee and any security deposit (including the right of the ALF to raise the fee)
- the right of the resident to return to the room after a period of hospitalization
- the conditions under which the facility can move (such as to a dementia ward) or evict the resident

Because state regulation of assisted living facilities is minimal, it is important that you carefully review the admission contract. Many contracts give the ALF management broad discretion to determine whether you meet the requirements for continued residence in the facility. Consider, for example, a situation in which you have suffered a moderate stroke. Your doctor believes that with speech and physical therapy you will have a full recovery; however, that may take three to four months to achieve. During that period, will the ALF allow caregivers to assist you in your room or apartment? If not, do you have the right to pay to keep your apartment available while you recover somewhere else? Could you afford to do this? Some ALFs are associated with nursing homes and require residents to move to the nursing home when they no longer meet the standards for semi-independent living in the ALF.

The lack of protection against the ALF management terminating your right to remain in the facility, or to return after a hospital stay, is one of the disadvantages of assisted living. A few states have laws that give ALF residents some of the same protections as other tenants of rental housing have, but most do not. You should also keep in mind that a number of the in-home services that are available to seniors aging in place in their own residence (such as services provided through Medicaid waivers or the Area Agency on Aging) are not permitted in ALFs.

Residents of assisted living usually pay their own way. There is almost no public reimbursement of the cost of assisted living. A few states provide limited Medicaid waivers to help with the cost of assisted living. Most residents who run out of money must leave the facility. Many who do so move to a nursing home where they can qualify for Medicaid reimbursement. Most long-term care insurance pays benefits to residents of assisted living provided that they have difficulty performing at least two ADLs or they are cognitively impaired, such as having dementia.

Because seniors who live in assisted living often spend down a considerable amount of their assets doing so, they may have few financial options left if a temporary health crisis occurs. Often rehabilitation in a nursing home after a hospitalization event turns into permanent residence because of the lack of funds to reenter assisted living or obtain other independent or retirement housing. Therefore, before you leave your own residence to move to assisted living, ask yourself the following questions:

- How much help do I need?
- Can my home be modified to make living there easier?
- Can I hire the additional help that I need?
- How much would services in my home cost?
- If I move to assisted living, how long will I be able to afford to live there?

You should compare the costs of living in your own residence with the costs of living in an assisted living facility. Most seniors can purchase considerable services in their own home before the cost approaches the cost of assisted living.

Board and Care Homes

Board and care homes, also known as personal care or retirement homes, provide care for many seniors, particularly those with lower incomes. Even though such facilities vary greatly, they provide room, board, and some degree of personal care. A few house hundreds of residents. Others are merely older houses converted into a board and care home and have as few as three or four residents. It is estimated that there are fifty thousand licensed homes across the nation, with six hundred thousand or more residents.

Even though such homes are supposed to be licensed by the state and subject to periodic inspection, many smaller ones operate without a license. For example, a couple may merely take in older persons without bothering to obtain a state license. Typically, board and care homes are much less costly and provide fewer amenities than ALFs. In some states, board and care homes are licensed to care for individuals who require less personal care or assistance than do the residents of assisted living. Such board and care homes function more as boarding houses than as care facilities.

Some board and care homes are sponsored by nonprofit organizations or churches, but most are privately run, profit-seeking businesses. Most residents are private pay, but many states subsidize the cost of the very poor residents' care, sometimes augmenting the individual's monthly Supplemental Security Income (SSI) benefit (see Chapter 3 for general information about SSI eligibility).

Board and care homes are regulated by the state governments. If they house a significant number of SSI recipients, they are subject to federal requirements that the state establish and enforce minimum standards. However, because the penalty for failing to maintain these standards is reduction in the SSI payment to the resident, rather than a penalty on the noncompliant facility, the law is rarely enforced.

Continuing Care Retirement Communities

Continuing care retirement communities (CCRCs) provide three levels of housing: independent living, assisted living, and nursing home care. They advertise that once admitted, you will never have to leave to find appropriate care.

CCRCs are found in cities, suburbs, and rural areas. Some feature single-story townhouses, whereas others are high rises. Most have a central facility that contains the shared amenities, such as a dining room and recreational facilities. Usually, the assisted living units and the nursing home beds are also located there. A few CCRCs lack nursing home beds and contract for that care at offsite locations. CCRCs are operated by both for-profit and nonprofit entities. The nonprofit CCRCs are often affiliated with a religious organization. These facilities sometimes solicit charitable funds to help subsidize the monthly fee of lower-income residents or to pay for those who have run out of money.

Residents of CCRCs pay both a monthly residence fee, which can run from $3,000 to $6,000 per month, and an initial admission fee, which is usually $100,000 to $500,000. The initial admission fee may be refundable in diminishing amounts the longer the individual resides in the facility, or the resident may have the option of a smaller, nonrefundable admission fee. Obviously, CCRCs are not for the poor. To be admitted, you must provide financial proof that you will be able to afford the monthly fee now and as it rises in the future.

Most residents raise the money for the admission fee by the sale of their houses. A few CCRCs sell the independent living units to the residents, who in turn resell the unit when they leave it. The admission fee is a form of long-term care insurance that is purchased at the time of admission to the CCRC. It represents, in part, prepayment for health care that may be needed later. Generally, the monthly fee will not rise merely because the resident requires more assistance; however, some CCRCs do charge a somewhat higher fee if the resident requires skilled nursing care. The part of the admission fee that is prepayment for health care is deductible on the resident's federal income tax as a Section 213 medical deduction (I.R.C. §213[d]).

CCRCs only admit individuals capable of independent living and require a physical examination as proof of their ability to live in an independent living unit. The unit will be an unfurnished studio or one, two, or even three bedroom unit, which contains a small kitchen. The CCRC provides one meal a day in the common dining room as well as recreational and social opportunities. Most residents will own a car and experience the CCRC much as if they were living in an age-restricted apartment. But as they age, they will receive more supportive services. The individual will reside in the independent living unit until unable to do so because of mental or physical problems. At that time, the resident will move to an assisted living unit, which will be smaller, have no cooking facilities, and be located in the central building or part of the facility. Because residents are reluctant to move to the assisted living units, CCRCs often provide custodial care, such as help with dressing, in the independent living units, but they charge a daily service fee for doing so.

The monthly fee pays for the meal (or three meals if the resident is in assisted living or in the nursing home), all utilities, recreational facilities such as an indoor swimming pool, and the various services provided by the facility. Many CCRCs offer breakfast and lunch on a per-meal payment to those living independently.

CCRCs are regulated only by states except for their nursing homes, which must comply with federal regulations if they receive Medicare and Medicaid reimbursement. State regulation varies considerably. From a resident's standpoint, the market is the best regulator because a CCRC must appeal to individuals who have enough resources and income to have a choice as to where they seek long-term care. The biggest fear is that the CCRC will run into financial difficulties and not be able to provide the promised care. States try to protect residents by requiring CCRCs to place a portion of the admission fee into an escrow or other protected account. Before signing the contract of admission to a CCRC, you should insist on reviewing a financial statement for the CCRC to assess its financial stability. A CCRC may also be subject to state laws that govern providers of assisted living at least as to the CCRC's assisted living units.

Problems often arise when the CCRC wants to move the resident from an independent living unit to assisted living. Residents are naturally resistant to such a move because they will be moved into a smaller unit, have less privacy, and lose their kitchen. The resident may suspect that part of the motive for the move is the desire of the CCRC to release or sell the vacated independent living unit. Unfortunately for the resident, the contract of admission will permit the CCRC to move the resident to assisted living or to the nursing home without the resident's consent.

The real protection for the resident is the CCRC's fear of bad publicity should the resident create a fuss about the move. Usually, the CCRC will negotiate with a reluctant resident and gradually convince the resident and the resident's family that a move is necessary because of the resident's declining health. Occasionally, a resident will become so difficult to deal with—possibly because of dementia—that the CCRC will evict him or her. The contract of admission usually permits this. The resident's only recourse is to claim that the illness is not severe enough to trigger the eviction conditions as specified in the admission contract. The resident can also claim that eviction would violate the federal Fair Housing Act (42 U.S.C. §§3601 *et seq.*) or the federal Rehabilitation Act (29 U.S.C. §§701 *et seq.*), which prohibits a federally funded state program from discriminating against a handicapped individual solely by reason of the handicap.

Nursing Homes

More than 1.6 million, or about 4.5 percent of Americans age 65 or older live in a nursing home. Of those age 85 or older, about 12 percent of the men and 21 percent of the women live in a nursing home. The length of stay in nursing homes varies considerably. Some residents stay only a short time while they recover from a temporary health crisis for which they were hospitalized. Some, the very ill, die soon after they enter the facility. For other seniors, particularly those with dementia, the stay in a nursing home can extend for years until finally ended by death. In the past twenty years, however, both the percentage of seniors in a nursing home and the length of the average stay have dropped. In part this is a reflection of the popularity of assisted living, and in part the lower numbers reflect the relatively improved health of seniors.

Federal law defines "nursing home" as an institution that provides skilled nursing care or rehabilitation services for injured, disabled, or sick persons as well as custodial care, which is defined as health-related care and services above the level of room and board. Such care is expensive. The average monthly cost of a nursing home runs from $5,000 to more than $8,000 a month. The cost of labor is usually the main reason for the extreme differences in cost.

Nursing homes, while necessary, are usually viewed negatively as institutions that take away an individual's autonomy, privacy, and independence. Residents usually share a room and have a set schedule for meals, showers, and activities. Many residents are bedridden, vulnerable, and very dependent on the staff. Nevertheless, for many, only a nursing home offers the needed combination of custodial and skilled nursing care. In response to complaints about their institutional nature, some nursing homes are making renovations to be more homelike, such as replacing long hospital-like corridors with clusters of rooms.

Because almost all nursing homes participate in Medicare and Medicaid, they are subject to federal laws and regulations, the result of which is that most nursing home operations are fairly similar. Medicare, the federal program of subsidized health care for those age 65 and older, reimburses only skilled nursing care. The Medicare skilled nursing benefit is available only for nursing home care immediately following a hospital stay of at least three continuous days (not counting the day of discharge) and if recommended by a physician. When these conditions are met, Medicare will pay for the following:

- physician's services
- twenty-four-hour nursing services
- room and board, including specialized dietary services
- rehabilitative services such as speech, physical, or occupational therapy
- drugs supervised by a pharmacist and delivered by a nurse
- laboratory and diagnostic services
- medically related social services
- appropriate resident activities

Medicare pays for nursing home care as a means of encouraging patients to leave very expensive hospitals and move into relatively affordable nursing homes. The program was not intended to reimburse long-term care and so pays for only one hundred days of skilled nursing home care. After the first twenty days, the resident has a co-pay, which in 2010 was $137.50 per day. The amount is adjusted annually.

More than one-half of all nursing home costs are paid for by Medicaid, a federal-state program based on financial need that will pay for the cost of a nursing home for as long as it is needed (see Chapter 6 for general information on Medicaid eligibility). Although Medicaid has no co-pay, in essence it requires nursing home residents to exhaust nearly all of their assets and to apply all of their income to the cost of the nursing home care before Medicaid will begin to reimburse the cost of care. Medicaid pays for both skilled and custodial care. Like Medicare, Medicaid also requires a physician's order for care, but unlike Medicare, it does not require any period of prior hospitalization.

Regulation

Nursing homes are heavily regulated by both the federal and state governments. Every nursing home needs a state-issued license to operate. The federal government does not license nursing homes, but nursing homes must take care to comply with federal requirements under the Medicaid and Medicare programs or risk loss of funding. Federal regulations give residents detailed rights that must be observed by nursing homes that participate in Medicare or Medicaid. (Residents' rights are found in the Code of Federal Regulations, 42 C.F.R. §483.10.) A few nursing homes do not accept Medicare or Medicaid and so are not subject to federal law, but state licensing requirements generally mirror the federal rules so that all nursing homes are essentially subject to the same requirements. In addition, nursing homes are also subject to federal and state civil rights laws, consumer protection statutes, and state common-law tort and contract remedies.

The nursing home medical supervisor is responsible for the coordination, adequacy, and appropriateness of resident care. Federal law requires that a physician must see each resident in a nursing home at least once every thirty days during the first ninety days of residence and at least once every sixty days thereafter (42 C.F.R. §483.40[c][1]). New residents must be given a comprehensive assessment fourteen days after admission, which must be updated once a year to ensure that the nursing home is appropriate for their needs (42 C.F.R. §483.20[b][2]).

Nursing homes must also assess residents at least every three months by using a state-approved review procedure (42 C.F.R. §483.20[c]). The initial assessment is used to create an individual, written care plan that details the necessary treatment and rehabilitation efforts to be provided to the resident. If the resident's condition changes significantly, there must be a new comprehensive assessment within fourteen days (42 C.F.R. §483.20[b][2]). The assessments, signed by a registered nurse, are to be used to monitor, develop, review, and revise the resident's care plan. Families of new residents should insist upon obtaining a copy of the assessments and the care plan so that they can monitor whether the facility is carrying out its obligations under the plan.

Contracts of Admission. A new resident of a nursing home is required to sign a contract of admission. If the resident is mentally incapacitated, the individual's guardian or family member will sign the agreement. Depending on state law, a nursing home may have some discretion about whom it admits. Most prefer not to admit mentally ill or mentally retarded individuals and so use a preadmission screening to identify individuals whom they are not legally required to admit. Note that dementia is not grounds for an admission refusal.

Many nursing homes prefer private pay residents as opposed to those who are paid for by Medicaid because the nursing home typically charges a higher private pay daily rate than Medicaid is willing to pay. Medicaid is notorious for paying a low daily rate—so low that a nursing home cannot operate if every resident is Medicaid reimbursed. Whether a nursing home can refuse a Medicaid patient, or one who is likely to become a Medicaid patient, depends upon state law.

As a practical matter, most nursing homes probably give admission preference to private pay residents. Some state laws prevent the nursing home from giving preference to private pay patients in its admissions policy, and some states require that a certain percentage of the patients admitted be Medicaid patients. Once admitted, however, no resident can be prevented from seeking and accepting Medicaid reimbursement (42 C.F.R. §483.12[d][1][i] and [ii]).

Federal law also prohibits Medicare- or Medicaid-reimbursed nursing homes from requiring a third party to guarantee payment as a condition of admission (42 C.F.R. §483.12[d][2]). Nevertheless, many nursing homes do attempt to induce family members to sign the admission contract as a responsible party who agrees to pay the nursing home in the event that the resident cannot and is not eligible for Medicaid. These so-called responsible party agreements may not be enforceable, although state law differs. The best advice is to refuse to sign such an agreement.

Transfers and Discharges. Residents are protected under federal and state laws against unwarranted transfers and discharges. These laws apply even when there are contrary terms in the nursing home admission contract. Before any transfer or discharge, the facility must notify the resident, a family member, or guardian at least thirty days in advance and explain the reasons for the move (42 C.F.R. §483.12[a][5][i]). Under federal law, a resident can be transferred only for medical reasons, for the welfare of the resident, for the welfare of other residents, for nonpayment, or because the facility is ceasing to operate (42 C.F.R. §483.12[a][2]). The advance notice of thirty days is inapplicable if one of the following conditions applies:

- The transfer is necessary for the health or safety of residents.
- The resident's health has improved enough that the resident no longer qualifies for nursing home care.
- The resident's urgent medical needs require a more immediate transfer (42 C.F.R. §483.12[a][5][ii]).

Before discharging a resident, the nursing home must create a postdischarge plan of care (42 C.F.R. §483.20[l][3]). If a resident goes to a hospital, the nursing home must explain its bed-hold policy, that is, the resident's right to return (42 C.F.R. §483.12[b]). When transferring or discharging residents, a nursing home must treat all of them alike regardless of whether they pay for their own care or their care is paid for by Medicare or Medicaid (42 C.F.R. §483.12[c]).

Federal Nursing Home Reform Act. The most important source of resident rights is the federal Nursing Home Reform Act, which applies to all nursing homes that accept Medicare or Medicaid (42 U.S.C. §1395i-3 [Medicare]; 42 U.S.C. §1396r [Medicaid]). The act, part of the Omnibus Budget Reconciliation Act of 1987 (Pub. L. No. 100-203, 101 Stat. 1330), requires that nursing homes must "promote maintenance or enhancement of the quality of life of each resident" (42 U.S.C. §1395i-3[b][1][A] [Medicare]; 42 U.S.C. §1396r[b][1][A] [Medicaid]). Unfortunately, an individual resident cannot sue to enforce the act, which is enforceable only by the state or federal government. Nevertheless, the act can be used to define the quality-of-care standard that should be expected of nursing homes.

The act's requirements are explained in the Code of Federal Regulations beginning at 42 C.F.R. §483. These regulations require that at the time of admission to the facility, the nursing home must tell a resident about the resident's rights and also provide the resident with a written copy of those rights (42 C.F.R. §483.10[b]). These rights include the following:

- *Freedom of choice*: Residents have a right to choose their own doctor and to help plan their care and treatment decisions.
- *Freedom from restraints and abuse*: Residents have a right to be free of chemical and physical restraints except to ensure their physical safety or that of other residents, and then only upon a physician's written order specifying the duration and circumstances of the restraint.
- *Privacy*: Residents have a right to privacy as to their medical treatment, written and telephonic communications, visits, and meetings with their families.
- *Confidentiality*: All personal and clinical records of residents must be kept confidential. A resident or a resident's legal representative has a right to access current records within twenty-four hours of making such a request.
- *Accommodation of individual needs*: Residents have a right to care that meets their individual needs.
- *Personal items*: Residents have a right to personal items, including furniture, clothing, and decorations.
- *Grievances*: Residents have a right to voice grievances about their treatment or care without fear of retaliation.
- *Participation in groups and other activities*: Residents have a right to participate in resident groups and social, religious, and community activities. Families of residents have the right to meet together in the facility.
- *Examination of survey results*: Residents have a right to the official survey results of a nursing home. The facility must post a notice of the availability of the survey.
- *Access and visitation rights*: Residents have a right to see governmental representatives, their individual physicians, the state's long-term care ombudsman, and anyone who provides health, social, legal, or other services to residents.

Nursing homes cannot charge residents for items that are paid for by Medicare or Medicaid, including routine personal hygiene items such as soap, razors, toothbrushes, tissues, deodorants, dental care items, incontinence care supplies, and over-the-counter drugs (42 C.F.R. §483.10[c][8][i]). The nursing home, however, can charge for in-room telephones, televisions, and radios; cosmetic and grooming items not paid for by Medicare or Medicaid; flowers and plants; and special food even if required by dietary or medical needs (42 C.F.R. §483.10[c][8][ii]). Medicare and Medicaid pay only for a shared room unless a private room is needed for a therapeutic reason such as isolation for infection control. A resident who wants a private room must pay the additional daily fee.

Theft and loss of residents' personal property and money are common problems. Federal law requires nursing homes to safeguard and account for residents' funds and maintain a written record of all financial transactions involving the personal funds of a resident that were deposited with the facility (42 C.F.R. §483.10[c]). Any resident funds in excess of $50 must be deposited into an interest-bearing account. Within thirty days of the resident's death, the facility must give the resident's personal funds to the administrator of the resident's estate and provide a final accounting.

State Ombudsman

Federal funding is provided to each state for the purpose of operating a Long-Term Care Ombudsman Office, the duty of which is to identify, investigate, and resolve complaints made by nursing home residents or others on their behalf (42 U.S.C. §3058g). The ombudsman investigates nursing homes to assure that they are providing proper care for their residents and may investigate other providers of long-term care services, as well as public health and social service agencies. If necessary, the ombudsman can represent residents before governmental agencies and is also expected to help develop citizen organizations that promote residents' rights. Anyone can contact the state Long-Term Care Ombudsman to register complaints or concern about the care provided by a nursing home.

Nursing Home Liability

Nursing home residents and their families are increasingly suing nursing homes and their staffs when the resident receives inadequate care, is injured, or dies due to a lack of proper care. Whereas in some instances the harm suffered by the resident may subject the nursing home or its employees to criminal liability, more common are civil lawsuits. These suits may be brought by the resident or the resident's family based on breach of the nursing home admission contract or on wrongful conduct known under the law as a "tort." Torts are categorized either as "intentional" or as "negligence." Nursing homes may be liable for intentional torts such as assault, battery, and false imprisonment or for the negligence of their staff. Absent contrary state law, the employer is liable for the personal injury or property damage, loss, or theft, whether intentional or negligent, caused by its employees.

Intentional Torts. Residents often sue claiming that they were the victims of harmful threats or contact that are known under the law as the intentional torts of assault and battery. Assault is defined as intentionally acting in a manner designed to cause a harmful or offensive contact or to create the fear of such contact. For example, throwing a tray toward a resident but missing her is an assault. Even a mere threat, such as "Eat or I'll slap you," can be an assault if it puts the victim in reasonable fear of imminent harmful or offensive contact.

Battery is an intentional harmful or offensive contact. It includes hitting, kissing, or striking the resident with an object. A battery occurs whenever the contact would be offensive to a reasonable person, though the victim does not need to be aware of the offensive touching. For example, fondling a sleeping resident is a battery.

There is also the tort of intentional infliction of emotional distress, defined as intentional or reckless acts of extreme or outrageous conduct that cause severe mental distress. One family member successfully sued for the intentional infliction of emotional distress when her 98-year-old mother was intentionally and maliciously hidden from her on three separate occasions when she came to visit her at the nursing home (*Miller v. Currie*, 50 F.3d 373 [6th Cir. 1995]).

Negligence. Negligence consists of failing to provide reasonable care to a resident. To bring a successful negligence case, the person claiming negligence must show that there was a duty of care, that the nursing home breached that duty, that the resident was injured, and that the injury was caused by the breach of duty. Most residents who claim that a nursing home acted negligently will have to prove that the facility failed to meet the proper standard of care and that this failure led to the resident's injuries. For example, when a resident suffers injuries from a fall, which is the most common basis for a negligence claim, liability is not established merely because the resident fell and was injured. The plaintiff must prove that the fall was the result of negligent care such as the failure of the nursing home to provide adequate supervision, failure to respond promptly to a call button, or failure to instruct the staff on how to prevent falls.

There are some exceptions to the need to provide proof of causation. Sometimes the existence of the injury itself is sufficient to prove negligence. For example, severe, infected bedsores or burns may be enough to establish what is known as a "prima facie" case of negligence by the nursing home. A prima facie case simply means that the facts are enough "on first appearance" to establish the elements. When the court finds that the severity of the injuries constitute a prima facie case, the burden shifts to the nursing home to bring forward contradictory evidence that it did not breach its duty of care.

Another exception to the need to produce proof of causation is the doctrine of *res ipsa loquitur* ("The thing speaks for itself"). Under this doctrine, the causation requirement is met by showing that when the resident was injured, the nursing home had exclusive control over the person or thing that injured the plaintiff and that the injury could not have occurred unless the nursing home was negligent. For example, the doctrine was applied in a case where a resident died when the respirator that was keeping her alive inexplicably stopped functioning (*Redfield v. Beverly Health & Rehabilitation Services, Inc.*, 42 S.W.3d 703 [Mo. Ct. App. 2001]). The respirator was under the exclusive control of the nursing home, and its stoppage was not something that would have occurred if the nursing home had exercised due care. Consequently, the court held that a jury could find that the nursing home had been negligent without specific proof of how the nursing home was negligent.

Even apart from what might be specified in the admission contract, every nursing home owes its residents a professional standard of care—typically defined as the level of care and skill used by other facilities in the community. The care must meet the needs of the resident in light of the resident's condition. What makes nursing home litigation difficult is that most residents are already suffering some type of serious physical ailment when they are admitted to the nursing home. Nursing homes often argue in defense of a negligence action that the resident's poor health upon admission was the cause of the resident's subsequent injury or poor condition rather than negligent care by the nursing home. For example, if a resident falls and breaks a hip, the nursing home may claim that despite its adequate supervision of the resident, his poor health led to his fall.

In some states, a lawsuit against a nursing home is considered a claim for medical malpractice, and so testimony by an expert witness is required. Also, there is usually a relatively short statute of limitations—the period of time in which to bring a claim after the harm has occurred—for malpractice actions. To avoid having the claim classified as a medical malpractice action, some residents have successfully sued under state consumer protection laws such as unfair trade practices laws.

Contract of Admission. Nursing home residents may also recover by claiming that the nursing home failed to provide the level of care promised in the contract of admission. Breach of contract, misrepresentation, fraud, and breach of implied warranties are all legitimate grounds for a lawsuit. However, most contract claims against nursing homes fail because the nursing home is careful to write the contract in a manner that favors the facility.

Mandatory Arbitration. Increasingly, nursing home contracts of admission require the resident to submit any potential lawsuit to mandatory arbitration and to agree to limits on possible damage awards. Although a few state courts have held such clauses to be unenforceable (*Bruner v. Timberlane Manor Ltd. P'ship*, 155 P.3d 16 [Okla. 2006]), the trend is to uphold them.[3]

As a result, an injured resident will not be able to sue in civil court but will have to submit the claim to arbitration and be content with limits on available damages, such as caps on awards for pain and suffering, and no punitive damages.

Choosing a Nursing Home

Although the operating standards for nursing homes are very similar community to community and state to state, the actual quality of life within a nursing home may vary greatly among facilities. This is due in large part to the philosophy of the nursing home management and the quantity and quality of its staff. So how can you make a good choice when it comes to a nursing home for yourself or someone else?

Making an informed decision about a nursing home involves doing some background investigation as well as spending time visiting facilities and asking questions. The federal government has a website called Nursing Home Compare, which provides detailed information about the quality of all nursing homes that are certified to receive Medicare and Medicaid funds. You can search nursing homes by state, county, or closeness to your location using your city name or zip code. If you know the name of a particular nursing home, you can also use the name as a way to access information. On this website there is also a link to a list of nursing homes that have a record of persistently poor performances and thus have been selected for more frequent inspections and monitoring.

Keep in mind that all Medicare- and Medicaid-certified nursing homes are subject to an annual review process called a "survey." Because the regulations for nursing homes are very strict and detailed, nearly all nursing homes receive some "tags" or citations for violations. Thus, just because a nursing home has been cited does not necessarily mean it is a "bad" nursing home. Try to collect as much information as possible to assess the seriousness of any past violations.

Once you have checked the quality record of a nursing home, you should visit the facility. It is a good idea to make both a scheduled visit and at least one unscheduled visit. During the scheduled appointment, you can ask questions of the director of nursing, the facility social worker, or the facility administrator. The unscheduled visit will allow you to judge the typical atmosphere of the home. It is a good idea to pick a time that is typically busy in order to see whether the staffing levels are adequate and how well the staff handles resident requests for assistance. For example, morning is usually a busy time because residents are being assisted with showers and dressing, breakfast, and morning medications. An evening visit may help you assess how the nursing home functions when the administrator and director of nursing have gone home for the day.

A benchmark for evaluating nursing homes that is easy to remember is the "three C's"—compassionate care, cleanliness, and choice. Appearances can be deceiving. An elegantly furnished nursing home may be understaffed or staffed with indifferent personnel. For someone who must now live in a nursing home, compassionate staff will mean much more than color-coordinated furnishings. Likewise, the cleanliness of the facility is more important than fancy furniture. Most seniors would also prefer some flexibility and choice about daily routines, meals, and room furnishings. For example, does the nursing home always offer a few alternative food items in addition to the set menu for the day? Is there choice about shower schedules? May residents watch television late in the evening, or is there a curfew? Respecting and encouraging residents to make choices about what to wear, what to do, and what to eat go a long way toward softening the otherwise institutional atmosphere of a nursing home.

Notes

1. Known officially as a "home equity conversion mortgage," an FHA-insured reverse mortgage is subject to rules found at 24 C.F.R. §§206 *et seq*. The regulations provide that the borrower must pay an initial mortgage insurance premium equal to 2 percent of the maximum amount of the claim and a monthly mortgage insurance premium equal to 0.5 percent per annum on the unpaid balance of the loan (24 C.F.R. §206.105).

2. http://www.aarp.org/money/revmort.

3. See Lawrence A. Frolik and Melissa C. Brown, *Advising the Elderly or Disabled Client* (2008 Supp.), chap. 15: 9.

For More Information

AARP (202-434-AARP)
(http://www.aarp.org)

Find timely discussions about senior housing topics, such as aging in place, house sharing, reverse mortgages, adult day care, age-restricted housing, planned communities, assisted living, CCRCs, and nursing homes, by entering these individual topic phrases into the search engine on the AARP home page.

Eldercare Locator (800-677-1116)
(http://www.eldercare.gov)

Find resources for aging in place in any U.S. community. Links are provided to state and local Area Agencies on Aging and community-based services.

National Hospice Foundation (800-658-8898)
(http://www.hospiceinfo.org)

Find information about hospice care and support services for seniors and their families.

National Long-Term Care Ombudsman Resource Center
(202-332-2275)
(http://www.ltcombudsman.org)

Find state and regional ombudsmen by using the locator search link, as well as general information about residents' rights and current issues in long-term care.

NCCNHR: The National Consumer Voice for Quality Long-Term Care (202-332-2275)
(http://www.nccnhr.org)

Find helpful links, information, and consumer support for improving long-term care practices, programs, and service delivery.

Nursing Home Compare
(http://www.medicare.gov/NHcompare)

Find detailed information about the quality of all nursing homes that are certified to receive Medicare and Medicaid funds.

U.S. Department of Housing and Urban Development (HUD)
(800-333-4636)
(http://www.hud.gov/groups/seniors.cfm)

Find resources for aging in place in your own home or apartment, as well as housing options for seniors who need assistive services.

8

Mental Incapacity, Guardianship, and Conservatorship

Did You Know?

- Without a power of attorney, you may need a guardianship if you lose the ability to make decisions for yourself.
- Guardianship terminates many legal rights and privileges, such as the ability to vote, sign a contract, and make a will.
- A guardian may have the power to make medical decisions, including whether to terminate life support for a mentally incapacitated person.
- With advance planning, no one should need a guardianship.

You may know someone—an elderly parent or relative or perhaps a neighbor—who is no longer able to make decisions about his or her own personal care and finances. This inability to make decisions is likely the result of illness or injury—either dementia resulting from a disease such as Alzheimer's or Parkinson's or a mental impairment caused by a stroke or head injury. If this person has not planned ahead for a substitute decision-maker, there may be no alternative but to seek a guardianship.

This chapter explains what it means to have a guardian appointed for an incapacitated person and what the consequences are for that person's legal rights and privileges. The different types of guardianship are discussed, as are the standards the court uses to decide whether a guardianship is needed and who should serve as the guardian. Finally, the chapter provides an overview of how to obtain a guardianship.

Mental Capacity

The law presumes that every adult has the mental ability, or mental capacity as it is commonly known, to make rational decisions about his or her property and person. Note that the law assumes only that an adult has the ability to make rational decisions; the law does not require a person to make sensible or "good" decisions. Individuals who have the ability to make rational decisions are free to make eccentric, foolish, or even "bad" choices; that is the right of all adults who have mental capacity.

Although the law assumes that all adults have mental capacity, not all do. Some adults suffer from developmental disabilities that cause them to be mentally incapacitated. Other adults who once had mental capacity lose it as a result of injury or illness. These incapacitated persons are in a form of legal limbo, unable to make their own decisions but with no one else who has authority to act for them. Not surprisingly, the law provides a solution for incapacitated individuals.

When an individual lacks the mental capacity to make rational choices, the law permits another person, a substitute decisionmaker, to make legally binding decisions for the incapacitated individual. In the eyes of the law, it is as if the substitute decisionmaker "stands in the shoes" of the mentally incapacitated individual because the decisions of the substitute decisionmaker are treated as if the mentally incapacitated individual made them.

There are two methods of creating a substitute decisionmaker. If a person has planned ahead, then the substitute decisionmakers named in that individual's durable power of attorney and health care advance directives can act if the person later loses capacity (see Chapter 9 for a discussion of durable powers of attorney and health care advance directives). If a person has failed to plan ahead, or the named substitute decisionmakers are not available to act, then a court will have to appoint a guardian.[1]

Guardianship

A state's authority to determine whether an individual is mentally incapacitated and to appoint a guardian comes from the state's general authority to protect the welfare of its citizens. All states have given their courts authority to determine who lacks mental capacity, appoint a guardian, and oversee the acts of the guardian.

Traditionally, courts have viewed guardianship as a protective arrangement for the benefit of the incapacitated person. The view that guardianship is for the good of the incapacitated person often resulted in guardianship laws and standards that did not adequately safeguard the legal rights of vulnerable persons. In the last twenty years, advocates for vulnerable persons have recommended reform of guardianship laws to ensure that protection is provided in a manner that least restricts the rights and privileges of persons with diminished capacity.

Guardianship can indeed provide needed protection for a vulnerable person, but it is also a very intrusive, public intervention. Appointment of a guardian generally terminates the incapacitated person's right to make decisions about his or her own person and property. Furthermore, certain personal rights and privileges cannot be delegated to a substitute decisionmaker and are just lost when an individual is declared legally incapacitated. These include voting rights, driving privileges, the ability to make a will, and decisions about marriage and divorce. Thus, guardianship results in a significant loss of personal freedom and autonomy.

Due to the growing awareness of the intrusive aspects of guardianship, almost every state has now reformed its laws to make the process of obtaining guardianship more protective of the alleged incapacitated person's rights. These reforms include refining the definition of incapacity and creating procedural safeguards such as the right to notice of the hearing, the right to be present at the hearing, and the right to have legal representation. Today's guardianship statutes also require greater judicial supervision of the guardian. As a result of the guardianship reform movement, there are now new and more flexible forms of guardianship, more involvement of lawyers, and more awareness of the need to balance protection of individuals with diminished capacity with their right to autonomy. Although guardianship laws differ, several states have adopted, and many more have modeled their laws on, the Uniform Guardianship and Protective Proceedings Act (8A U.L.A. 429 [2003 and Supp. 2008]).

Guardianship reform has also resulted in more emphasis on individuals planning to avoid guardianship through the use of durable powers of attorney for property management and health care advance directives to guide future medical decisions. The increased use of these documents has significantly reduced the need for guardianship, which can be expensive, time consuming, embarrassing, and possibly contrary to the incapacitated person's wishes. Yet despite the availability of alternatives, most individuals fail to properly plan for incapacity. For them, guardianship is often unavoidable.

Guardianship Terminology

Guardianship is the legal process of providing a substitute decisionmaker for a mentally incapacitated individual. Every state and the District of Columbia has a statute that defines when a person is legally incapacitated and that authorizes courts to conduct guardianship hearings and appoint guardians. There is no federal law of guardianship.

Although "guardian" and "guardianship" are the most common terms for a court-appointed substitute decisionmaker and the arrangement under which that decisionmaker serves, a few states use the terms "conservator" and "conservatorship." In some states, "guardian" refers only to a decision-maker for personal matters, such as health care decisions, whereas the term "conservator" refers to a decisionmaker for property matters, such as investment decisions. In most states, however, the terms "guardian and guardianship" are used to describe the substitute decisionmaker for both person and property.

The incapacitated individual for whom a guardian or conservator has been appointed is often referred to as the "ward," although some states have adopted the term "incapacitated person," with a few states retaining the older term "incompetent." In this chapter, unless otherwise indicated, the terms "guardian" and "guardianship" are used to include the duties of a conservator and the concept of conservatorship. The incapacitated individual for whom a guardian has been appointed is referred to here as the "ward."

For Whom May a Guardian Be Appointed?

State law defines for whom and under what conditions a court can appoint a guardian. Although state laws differ in their definitions of what it means to be incapacitated, the most common description is someone who lacks the ability to make or communicate rational decisions. To determine whether a person is incapacitated, courts consider the individual's behavior and ability to care for essential needs. This functional approach to capacity is a sharp departure from past statutes that often labeled individuals as incompetent merely by virtue of their status, such as "old age."

The goal of functional-based definitions is to narrow the use of guardianship to only those persons who truly lack the mental capability to care for themselves. Just because a person is old, disabled, or mentally ill does not necessarily mean that the person should be considered legally incapacitated. It is how the individual functions, and whether that individual is capable of considering information, making decisions, and appreciating the possible consequences of those decisions, that is important. In short, under modern guardianship laws, courts should order the protection of guardianship only when it is clear that an individual is mentally incapable of caring for his or her own needs.

For Whom May a Conservator Be Appointed?

In some states, the terms "guardian" and "conservator" refer to individuals who serve quite different functions. In those states, guardians are appointed to make decisions about the person of the incapacitated individual, whereas conservators manage the incapacitated or disabled individual's property. Where this distinction is made, a conservator is appointed if for any reason, including severe physical disability, a person is unable to manage or direct the management of his or her property and as a result the property is at risk of being wasted or of being exploited by others. A conservator is often required to manage funds for the support, care, and welfare of the disabled person.

In states that make a distinction between guardianship and conservatorship, the standards for the two usually differ. A lower standard is used for conservatorship—something less than the mental incapacitation required for guardianship. For example, if it can be shown that an elderly person is easily influenced by a manipulative relative to turn over her Social Security funds or pension benefits each month, a conservator may be appointed to manage that individual's money even though she is not truly mentally "incapacitated." In contrast, states that use the term "guardianship" for protective arrangements that cover both person and property usually have a single definition of what it means to be an incapacitated person.

Demonstrating the Need for a Guardian

As a result of guardianship reforms, most state statutes no longer ask why the individual lacks capacity but whether he or she lacks capacity. Nevertheless, the need to identify the cause of incapacity may be important. Many states require a medical explanation for the incapacity as a way of distinguishing true incapacity from mere idiosyncratic behavior that might threaten the individual's health or well-being. For example, consider individuals who choose to participate in "extreme" sports where injury and even death are likely. Although such behavior carries a high probability of personal harm, an adult who chooses to engage in such behavior is not mentally incapacitated if he or she appreciates the possible consequences of the activity and knowingly accepts the risk. Laws that require a medical explanation for incapacity are an attempt to ensure that eccentric but mentally capable persons are not classified as incapacitated.

No matter how a state statute defines incapacity, anyone filing a guardianship petition should be prepared to present expert medical testimony that explains the loss of capacity. Although the burden of proof is on the petitioner, if the alleged incapacitated person believes that a guardianship is unnecessary, he or she should also be prepared to present evidence in rebuttal—that is, evidence that demonstrates his or her capacity to make rational decisions. The standard of proof can vary by state—some require only a "preponderance of the evidence"—in other words, enough evidence to show that it is more likely than not that the person is truly incapacitated. A growing number of states require "clear and convincing evidence" of mental incapacity. This standard requires the petitioner to produce evidence that demonstrates a high probability that the alleged incapacitated individual meets the state's definition of incapacity. The clear and convincing evidence standard is more difficult to meet than the preponderance of the evidence standard, but it is more protective of the alleged incapacitated person's rights and autonomy.

Establishing that an individual lacks mental capacity is only the first step toward obtaining a court-appointed guardian. Just because an individual is incapacitated does not automatically mean that a guardian is needed. If the incapacitated person's needs are being met by other arrangements, such as a durable power of attorney, the court may refuse to approve a guardianship. Again, although it is the petitioner's responsibility to prove the need for guardianship, a substitute decisionmaker who is already acting for the incapacitated person should be prepared to demonstrate that the present arrangement is adequate.

Not all courts, however, are willing to defer to a substitute decisionmaker already acting under a durable power of attorney. The reluctance of some state courts to give priority to a private arrangement for substitute decision-making reflects the concern that agents acting under a durable power of attorney, unlike guardians, are not under the supervision of the court. In theory, unsupervised agents, as compared with court-supervised guardians, can more easily exploit, neglect, or negligently handle the incapacitated person's affairs. However, in actuality, court resources for monitoring guardians are very limited, thus making the distinction between agents and guardians less significant in practice than in theory.[2]

Although state courts vary in their willingness to appoint a guardian, the underlying reality remains that a petitioner for guardianship must demonstrate to the court's satisfaction that a guardianship is truly needed; namely, that the appointment of a guardian would better serve the incapacitated person than existing arrangements. In most states, guardianship is based upon the twin pillars of mental incapacitation (or at least diminished capacity) and an unmet need for services and protection. Absent proof of either of these elements, a court may deny the petition for guardianship.

Types of Guardianship

The type of guardianship granted by a court depends on both the ward's needs and the court's jurisdiction. In order for a guardianship petition to fall under a court's jurisdiction, either the prospective ward or the ward's property, or both, must be located in the state where the court presides. A court can neither grant guardianship over the person of an individual who is not physically present in that state nor grant the guardian authority over property that is physically located in another jurisdiction.

If the alleged incapacitated person resides in the court's state of jurisdiction and has property there, the type of guardianship granted by the court will depend on the incapacitated person's needs and the suitability of the person who wants to be the guardian. Traditionally, there were three types of guardians: guardian of the estate with authority over the ward's property (sometimes referred to as a "conservator"), guardian of the person with authority over personal decisions for the ward, and plenary guardian with authority over both the property and person of the ward.

As a result of guardianship reform, there is now a fourth type of guardianship that operates as a modification of the three traditional types. This newer form of guardianship is known as "limited guardianship." As the name suggests, limited guardianship only grants the guardian power over the ward's person or property to the extent that the individual needs assistance. For example, a limited guardian might control the ward's investments, but the ward may be allowed to retain control over funds to pay for day-to-day expenses. The ward's abilities must be carefully evaluated by the court to determine where to draw the lines of authority between the limited guardian and the ward.

Guardian of the Estate

If the ward needs help with the protection and management of his or her property, the court can create a guardianship of the estate, also known in some states as a conservatorship. A guardian of the estate will usually have the same authority over the property as the owner would have, although there are some limits on a guardian's authority.

Limits on the Guardian of the Estate's Authority. Although the guardian of the estate generally has the right to act as he or she believes best, state law may limit or prohibit certain acts. For example, if the guardian wishes to transfer assets of the ward, state law may (1) permit the guardian to act without prior court approval, (2) require the court to grant authority to transfer such property at the time the guardian is appointed, (3) require the guardian to seek court approval before any transfer, or (4) prohibit the guardian from making a particular transfer. Acts that need prior court approval differ from state to state. Common activities that require prior court approval include selling the ward's real estate and liquidating the ward's investments.

Although a guardian of the estate has no official authority over decisions about the personal care of the ward (such as medical treatment), in reality the guardian's control of the purse strings can have a significant impact on personal decisions. Consider, for example, a situation where two adult children have been appointed as guardians for their mother—one, the guardian of the estate and the other, guardian of the person. The guardian of the person believes her mother should remain at home and be cared for by hired in-home caregivers. The guardian of the estate believes that such care is too expensive and refuses to authorize the payments. A guardian of the estate can also initiate actions that will result in significant lifestyle changes for the ward, such as insisting that the ward's house be sold. It may be necessary to petition the court for removal of a guardian of the estate or a guardian of the person if the two cannot cooperate for the ward's best interests.

Voluntary Conservatorship. In many states, a frail or vulnerable adult may choose to turn over control of assets and financial affairs to a conservator. Because of the voluntary nature of the arrangement, there is no need for incapacity to be proved. Thus, the individual in need of help can receive assistance without the stigma of being found incapacitated and without losing other important legal rights and privileges.

Guardian of the Person

A guardian of the person makes decisions that affect the person of the ward, including decisions about living arrangements and health care matters. State law determines the scope of authority that can be given to a guardian of the person and may prohibit certain acts or require prior court approval for them. For example, although a guardian of the person has the right to determine where the ward will live, the guardian may need prior court approval before moving the ward into a nursing home. Other aspects of the ward's life are considered so personal that no guardian may interfere with them, such as decisions to marry or divorce. No guardian can consent to a marriage, and in most states a guardian cannot initiate divorce proceedings. If the ward's spouse has initiated divorce proceedings, usually the guardian can consent only with prior court approval.

Whether a guardian can consent to mental health care treatment for a ward, even a ward who resides in a mental health treatment facility, varies from state to state. Given that individuals generally cannot be forced to take medication to alleviate the symptoms of mental illness, the guardian, as a substitute decisionmaker, usually cannot commit the ward to such treatment. A guardian of the person normally has the right, however, to make non–mental health care decisions for the ward, such as consenting to medical tests and treatment.

Much more controversial is whether a guardian, without prior court approval, can agree to withhold or terminate life-sustaining treatment. For example, state law varies on whether a guardian of a terminally ill patient may decide to discontinue a feeding tube or a respirator without prior court approval. Increasingly, guardians are permitted to make such decisions without going to court.

Plenary Guardianship

Plenary guardianship, which grants the guardian power to make decisions over both the ward's property and person, is the broadest type of guardianship and allows the guardian to make whatever decisions are necessary for the ward's well-being. Family members who serve as guardians are typically appointed as plenary guardians because they are viewed as well situated to know what the ward needs and how the ward would have made decisions if able. Plenary guardianship, however, can be a double-edged sword.

The plenary guardian has extraordinary power over the life of the ward but is subject to little supervision. Even though this extensive power can result in efficient decisionmaking, it also means that the guardian has a greater opportunity to exploit, neglect, or mistreat the ward. In contrast, where a separate guardian for the property and guardian for the person are appointed, there is a natural check-and-balance on the power of each.

Another challenge of plenary guardianship is finding someone with the ability, time, and desire to undertake the responsibility of acting in all matters for the ward. Although spouses are usually willing to take on such duties, they may be prevented by physical limitations or mental capacity issues. If the spouse cannot act as guardian or there is no spouse, adult children are commonly appointed as guardians. Unfortunately, many adult children do not live near their parents and have difficulties carrying out the duties of a guardian, especially those relating to the ward's property.

Appointing a nonfamily member as guardian is possible if someone is willing to accept that responsibility. If no one is willing to volunteer, professional guardians exist who, for a fee, will assume the role of guardian. Some attorneys are willing to serve as a guardian, as are some geriatric social workers. If the ward has enough income or assets, a bank or other financial institution may be willing to accept appointment as guardian because the ward can afford to pay the costs of the guardianship. Whenever a professional guardian is selected, care must be taken to ensure that the individual or entity is competent, experienced, and honest.

Limited Guardianship

In addition to the three traditional types of guardianship, most courts now have the authority to appoint limited guardians. In the past, individuals were thought of as being either competent or incompetent. Today it is understood that capacity runs along a continuum. In between complete capacity and complete incapacity, individuals may have varying degrees of ability to handle management of their property and persons. For those who are partially incapacitated, the courts can appoint a limited guardian whose powers are tailored to deal with the individual's particular needs. The authority of the guardian is limited in scope so that the ward can be as independent as is possible. For example, a court may appoint a limited guardian who has authority only over the individual's investments, with the individual making all other decisions about his or her life.

The goal of limited guardianship is to permit the ward to retain the maximum degree of independence while giving the ward the assistance he or she needs. Despite the apparent advantages, limited guardianships are not commonly used by courts. They are thought by many to be too time consuming and expensive to be of much practical value. If the ward's condition is one that is likely to deteriorate, opponents of limited guardianship argue that the court will be required to frequently reassess the ward's abilities and adjust the scope of the limited guardian's authority. Without question, evaluating the degree of diminished capacity and crafting a guardianship that least restricts the ward's life take time and money. It is far easier to appoint a traditional plenary guardian.[3]

The costs of limited guardianship aside, they are seldom sought for individuals who still retain some level of capacity because those individuals can most likely still create a durable power of attorney and avoid the courtroom. If they are so incapacitated that they cannot execute a valid power of attorney, then a full guardianship, rather than a limited one, is usually required.

Temporary or Emergency Guardian

A temporary or emergency guardian may be appointed when a quick response is necessary to protect the person or property of the alleged incapacitated person. The terms "temporary guardian" and "emergency guardian" usually have the same meaning. Temporary or emergency guardianships differ from the other types of guardianships. The petitioner does not have to meet all of the normal procedural requirements, and the guardianship is limited in duration. For example, notice requirements are often waived or shorter than for a full guardianship hearing, and the temporary guardianship may be granted without an independent evaluation of the ward's capabilities.

Temporary guardians may be appointed to deal with an immediate crisis, such as the need for a health care decisionmaker for a very sick individual or for facilitation of the discharge of an individual with reduced mental capacity from a hospital. If the patient is too confused to understand the release papers, the hospital or family may need to petition the court for the appointment of a temporary guardian whose authority is limited to signing the necessary discharge papers and moving the patient back home or into a nursing home or an assisted living facility.

Financial emergencies can also require the appointment of a temporary guardian. If an incapacitated person is being financially exploited, a concerned individual can file for temporary guardianship to stop the exploitation by taking control of the ward's assets and initiating civil or criminal proceedings against the party committing the exploitation.

Although there are fewer procedural formalities required for a temporary guardianship proceeding, the court must still find that the alleged incapacitated person meets the statutory definition of incapacity. If not, the petition for temporary guardianship will be denied. Courts will not approve a temporary guardianship merely as a convenience to the petitioner or as a means of avoiding the procedural requirements of a regular guardianship. Even where a temporary or emergency guardian is appointed, the court may conclude after a full hearing for permanent guardianship that the alleged incapacitated person does not need a guardian or that the need for assistance has passed.

Guardianship Procedures

The Petition

Guardianship is initiated by the filing of a petition that requests the court to find that the alleged incapacitated person is indeed incapacitated and in need of a guardian. In almost every state, any competent adult can file a guardianship petition, but usually only those concerned about the alleged incapacitated person's property or welfare are likely to do so. Institutions, such as hospitals, may file petitions because they need an individual who can sign consent, admission, or discharge forms on behalf of an incapacitated patient. Occasionally, bank officers or trustees may file a guardianship petition if they believe that a customer can no longer handle his or her financial affairs. The person who files the petition is known as the petitioner. Typically, the petitioner is, but need not be, the person nominated in the petition to serve as the guardian.

General Content Requirements. The contents of a guardianship petition depend on applicable state law and local court rules. As a result of guardianship reform, many states now have detailed requirements for what the petition must include. Usually, the petition must name the alleged incapacitated person; the cause, nature, and extent of the incapacity; and the type of guardianship sought (of the person or property, limited or plenary). The alleged incapacitated person's address and a description of his or her living arrangements (e.g., whether the person lives alone, with relatives, or in an institution such as an assisted living facility) are usually also required. The petition must explain the reason a guardianship is needed and how appointment of a guardian would benefit the alleged incapacitated person. The state may also require an explanation as to why no less-restrictive arrangement is appropriate. A petition that fails to meet all of the state or local requirements may be dismissed. Normally, an attorney is hired to draft and file the petition.

Nomination of the Guardian. State law or local court rules require the petition to contain the name and address of the proposed guardian. The requirement of naming a guardian can pose difficulties. If no family member or close friend is willing to serve as guardian, the petitioner may have to consider a professional guardian. Professional guardians, however, may be too costly and may not be available in all communities. Some states finance public guardians, but they are usually overworked and may be limited to acting as guardian only for the poor. The shortage of persons to serve as substitute decisionmakers is a growing problem in our aging society.

Where to File the Petition. Guardianship petitions are usually heard by the probate court (a court that hears matters of wills and estates). The proper place to file a petition is the county in which the incapacitated person lives or in which he or she happens to be physically present. A petition for guardianship of the estate can be filed in a county where the incapacitated person owns property.

Changing the Residence of the Ward. If the ward moves to a different state after a guardianship is established, a petition must be filed in the new state to have the guardian's authority recognized there or to have a new guardianship established in that state. State law varies as to whether the new state will accept the guardian's authority over the ward. Some states allow reappointment of a guardian merely upon proof of the original appointment in the prior state. Other states have laws permitting the transfer of a guardianship.[4]

Petitions Involving Property Located in a Different State. Often wards own vacation or rental property in a state other than the one in which they live and hold most of their property. If it is necessary to sell or rent that property for the benefit of the ward, a petition for guardianship over that property will have to be filed in the state where the property is located. The law of the state where the property is located may permit its court to rely upon a finding of incapacity in another state, or it may require a hearing to determine whether a guardian should be appointed. In any event, the authority of the guardian of the estate will be limited to dealing with the ward's property located in that state.

Notice

By statute, almost all states require that the alleged incapacitated person be given notice of the filing of the petition and the hearing date. Most states also require notice to be given to a variety of other persons, including the incapacitated person's spouse, family members, creditors, and heirs at law. Some states require notice to the person or entity that has physical custody of the alleged incapacitated person, such as a nursing home. States differ as to the amount of notice, but at least seven to fourteen days before the hearing date is common.

The Hearing

Before a guardian can be appointed, a judicial hearing must occur for the purpose of deciding whether the individual is mentally incapacitated and, if so, to what extent. To inform the court's decision, many states require a medical or psychological examination of the alleged incapacitated person. Incapacitation usually must be proved by clear and convincing evidence, which means that the judge or jury must be persuaded by the evidence that the claim of incapacitation is highly probable.

If the individual is found to meet the state's definition of incapacity, the court will have to decide whether a guardianship is in the best interests of the incapacitated individual. The petitioner must provide evidence that the needs of the mentally incapacitated person are not currently being met and that a guardian is needed. Based on this evidence, the court must determine what kind of guardianship will best serve the incapacitated person's needs — a guardianship for property, for the person, or both (plenary) — and whether that guardianship should be limited. Finally, the court must determine who should be named as the guardian or guardians. All of these decisions, of course, require evidentiary support. The purpose of the hearing is to consider that evidence.

Presence of the Alleged Incapacitated Person. The hearing requirements vary from state to state and even from court to court. Nevertheless, some standards are common. All states permit the alleged incapacitated person to attend the hearing; a few require his or her presence. Even if state law permits the court to hold the hearing without the alleged incapacitated person, most courts are reluctant to do so. To ensure the incapacitated person's presence, courts now commonly hold the hearing at the individual's residence, even in a hospital if necessary.

Right to a Jury. Though many states permit the alleged incapacitated person to request a trial by jury, most prefer an experienced judge to rule on the issue of incapacity. In some hotly contested guardianship hearings, however, counsel for the alleged incapacitated person may prefer that a jury, rather than a judge, determine the client's mental capacity in the belief that the jury may be more sympathetic to an older individual who is attempting to avoid the stigma and loss of autonomy that accompany guardianship. If the jury decides that the individual is incapacitated, the judge will then determine whether a guardian is appropriate and who will be named guardian.

Court Visitors. In some states, courts have the authority to seek information about the alleged incapacitated person before the formal hearing. Where permitted, the court can appoint a visitor who interviews the alleged incapacitated person, determines whether he or she should be present at the hearing, investigates his or her living conditions and financial well-being, and reports back to the court, perhaps with a recommendation as to what the court should do. The visitor may also interview the petitioner for information about why the petition was filed and talk to the proposed guardian to see if he or she is capable of carrying out the responsibilities of the position. Even though the final decision as to the alleged incapacitated person's mental capacity and need for a guardian is made by the court, the court visitor's findings can be critical in that determination.

Right to Legal Counsel. Because of the potential loss of autonomy for the ward, most, but not all, states require that the alleged incapacitated person be represented by legal counsel. The lawyer will be paid out of the assets of the ward whenever possible. If the alleged incapacitated person cannot afford a lawyer, the state provides one and will bear the cost. Counsel representing an alleged incapacitated person must pursue the client's wishes, even if the apparently incapacitated client wishes to resist guardianship.

Guardian ad litem. A guardian *ad litem*, though typically an attorney, is not the alleged incapacitated person's legal counsel. A guardian *ad litem* is an officer of the court who is expected to inform the alleged incapacitated person about the meaning of the guardianship hearing and to listen to that individual's concerns. The guardian *ad litem*, however, is not required to advocate for what the alleged incapacitated person wants, but rather is expected to make an independent decision about what would be in that individual's best interest and so inform the court. Therefore, because of their different obligations, the counsel to the alleged incapacitated person and the guardian *ad litem* should not be the same person.

Selection of the Guardian

If the individual is found to be incapacitated and in need of assistance, a guardian must be appointed. If more than one person or entity wishes to serve as guardian, the court is supposed to select the candidate who will best serve the needs of the ward. Several considerations influence how the court decides among competing candidates for guardian.

Guardian Nominated by the Petitioner. Given that the court does not have the power to force anyone to be a guardian, the court's choice is limited to those who are willing to serve. More often than not the court will appoint the individual or entity nominated in the petition unless there is a good reason not to do so. If no one is available to serve as guardian, the court may have the power to appoint a guardian who will be paid by the state.

Petitioners should identify the potential guardian before filing the petition. There are probably potential petitioners who do not file petitions because they are unable to locate a guardian. Many people do not want to serve as guardian because of the time it takes or because they are reluctant to assume the role of making critical life choices for another individual. Guardians of the estate are somewhat easier to find because the duties, although time consuming, are more manageable as they do not usually have the emotional burdens associated with being a guardian of the person.

Nomination of Guardian by the Ward. Some wards will have previously nominated a guardian, possibly in a durable power of attorney or a health care advance directive. In most states, if the ward has previously nominated someone for guardian, that individual, if qualified and willing, must be named as guardian, although an alternative individual can be named if the court finds good cause for doing so. If the ward has only modestly diminished capacity, the court may inquire as to whom the ward might wish to be named guardian. If the ward's choice is appropriate, the court will name that person as guardian.

Statutory Priorities. Some state statutes list possible guardians in order of their priority, usually beginning with the person nominated by the ward, followed by a spouse, children, and other relatives. A qualified individual with the highest priority is supposed to be named as guardian. If there are persons with equal priority, the court is directed to select the one best qualified to be the guardian. The court can pass over a person with higher priority to select someone with lower or no priority only for a good reason. The statutes also often exclude as candidates for guardian individuals with conflicts of interest, such as employees of the nursing home where the ward resides.

Even though circumstances may at times require the use of a professional guardian, courts prefer family members because they assume that family members, who are bound by ties of love and devotion, will perform better than a professional motivated only by professional standards and compensation. In contrast, even if a family member is willing to serve as guardian, the court may instead appoint a professional guardian if the court finds that to do so is in the best interest of the ward. Usually, the reason for a professional appointment is family discord—either discord between competing would-be guardians or discord between the ward and the proposed guardian. Conflicts of interest can also cause a court to reject a family member.

In recent years, state laws have been liberalized to permit nonprofit entities to serve as guardians. These social service entities are usually paid from the funds of the incapacitated person or by the county or state. They often serve as guardians for "friendless" individuals who do not have a willing or able family member, relative, or friend, and who do not have enough assets to afford the cost of a professional or institutional guardian such as a bank.

Several states have created public guardians to act as the guardian of last resort when no private individual or entity is available. Public guardians are agencies, offices, or public officials whose job it is to act as guardian of the estate or of the person. The cost of the public guardian is paid from the funds of the ward if there are sufficient assets, and if not, the state bears the cost. In a few states, public guardians are actively involved in the day-to-day details of the incapacitated person's life. In other states, because of a large caseload, the public guardian acts only to make major decisions in health care and living arrangements. Even when a public guardian exists, however, that office usually lacks the resources to assist all eligible elderly wards.

Costs of Guardianship

Guardianship is costly. Filing a petition requires hiring an attorney, paying for medical or other professional examinations, paying the fee of a court visitor or guardian *ad litem*, compensating witnesses such as physicians for their time, and perhaps hiring a social worker to prepare a care plan. If the case is appealed, additional legal costs will be incurred.

The costs of guardianship are borne by the ward subject to court approval. The attorney who represents the alleged incapacitated person is entitled to payment so long as the attorney rendered valuable services that were consistent with the alleged incapacitated person's wishes. Even the attorney for the petitioner is paid from the ward's funds provided that the petition for guardianship is successful. However, if the petition is denied, the petitioner is usually responsible for all fees and costs of litigation associated with pursuing the petition.

If the ward's funds are inadequate to pay the fee of his or her attorney, state law may provide for payment by the state or county. Unfortunately, the statutes often set a very low rate of fees, which tends to discourage attorneys from accepting appointment as counsel for alleged incapacitated individuals. Recently, some courts have requested that the legislature take steps to increase attorney fees to a more reasonable level.

Once appointed, the guardian is entitled to a fee for his or her services as well as reimbursement for out-of-pocket expenses. Often family members will decline any fee, though they are still entitled to any out-of-pocket expenses that they incur. Naturally, professional guardians expect to be paid, usually receiving an hourly fee, although if they act as guardian of the estate, they may be paid an annual fee equal to a percentage of the value of the ward's assets. Nonprofit entities that serve as guardian are usually paid a flat amount for each guardianship. Note that no fee can be paid to any guardian without prior court approval. If the court believes the requested fee is too high in comparison to the services performed by the guardian, the court will reduce the fee to a more appropriate amount.

Supervision of the Guardian

The actions of guardians are subject to the control and supervision of the court. Most states require annual reports to be made by the guardian. Reports by the guardian to the court are intended to promote guardian accountability for meeting the ward's needs. The guardian is expected to confer with the ward prior to making major decisions and then to make decisions consistent with the ward's expressed desires. If the ward cannot communicate, the guardian is expected to act in a manner consistent with the ward's preferences as they existed before the onset of the incapacity. If the incapacitated person never expressed a preference, the guardian is expected to act as a reasonable person would under the same or similar circumstances.

Initially, the guardian of the estate will be required to inventory the incapacitated person's assets and file an accounting with the court. Thereafter, the guardian will typically be required to provide an annual accounting with the court, although sometimes the court will insist upon more frequent reports. Usually, the guardian will have to account for all income received and expenses paid, and upon the termination of the guardian's term, the guardian will have to turn over all the assets of the ward. Mistakes, misuse, or intentional misconduct by the guardian can result in the guardian's personal liability for the ward's losses as well as penalties assessed by the supervising court.

Guardians of the person must also report to the court in most states. In many states, the guardian of the person must make an initial status report about the ward. The guardian may also be required to provide the court with a care plan and indicate how that plan will meet the ward's needs. The court can also require the guardian to report after a period of time about the ward's progress under the plan. In a report by the guardian of the person, the primary requirement is to describe any changes in the ward's mental and physical condition, note any unmet needs of the ward, and advise the court whether the guardianship should be continued or whether the powers of the guardian should be modified.

Guardians who fail to carry out their obligations may be removed by the supervising court or ordered to act in a more appropriate manner. Generally, state law permits any interested person, including the incapacitated person, to petition the court for the purpose of making it aware of guardian misconduct.

Termination of the Guardianship

A guardianship ends at the death of the incapacitated person. In the event of the death, mental incapacity, or resignation of the guardian, however, the guardianship does not terminate. Instead, the court appoints a successor guardian. Normally, no guardian will be permitted to resign unless there is an available successor guardian, because the incapacitated person cannot be left without a substitute decisionmaker.

If the incapacitated person regains capacity, the guardianship should be terminated. Generally, the incapacitated person must petition the court and request that it terminate the guardianship. Whereas in the past the burden was on the ward to prove that he or she had regained capacity, many states have reformed their guardianship statutes so that the burden of proof is now on those who want to continue the guardianship. If the ward petitions the court to end the guardianship, those who want it to continue must persuade the court that the ward is still incapacitated and that the continuation of the guardianship would be in his or her best interest.

Notes

1. For an in-depth analysis of the use of a durable power of attorney as an alternative to guardianship, see Linda S. Whitton, "Durable Powers as an Alternative to Guardianship: Lessons We Have Learned," *Stetson Law Review* 37 (2007): 7.

2. For an up-to-date overview of court guardianship monitoring practices in the various states, see Naomi Karp and Erica F. Wood, "Guardianship Monitoring: A National Survey of Court Practices," *Stetson Law Review* 37 (2007): 143.

3. For a discussion of the difficulties in getting greater use of limited guardianship, see Lawrence A. Frolik, "Promoting Judicial Acceptance and Use of Limited Guardianship," *Stetson Law Review* 31 (2002): 735.

4. The Uniform Law Commission approved in 2007 the Uniform Adult Guardianship and Protective Proceedings Jurisdiction Act (8A U.L.A. 1 [Supp. 2008]), the purpose of which is to resolve multistate guardianship jurisdiction disputes and to facilitate transfers of guardianship between jurisdictions where appropriate. For a list of states that have adopted the act, see the Uniform Law Commission website at http://www.nccusl.org.

For More Information

National Guardianship Association (877-326-5992)
(http://www.guardianship.org)

Find links to publications and other resources for family guardians.

9

Substitute Decisionmaking for Health Care and Property

Did You Know?

- If you lose capacity and have no substitute decisionmaker, you will likely need a court-appointed guardian.
- To avoid guardianship, you need a substitute decisionmaker for both health care decisions and decisions about your property and finances.
- You can name different substitute decisionmakers to handle health care and property decisions.
- You should carefully choose your health care agent because he or she may make life and death decisions for you when you can no longer decide for yourself.
- You should carefully choose your agent for property decisions because he or she will likely have access to all of your property, including your money.

All adults need to plan for management of their health care and property in the event they later lose the ability to make and carry out their own decisions. No one wants a guardianship, which involves public exposure, expense, and loss of control. Fortunately, for those who plan ahead, alternatives exist that can eliminate the need for guardianship.

Alternatives to guardianship allow you to appoint an individual or institution to act as your substitute decisionmaker or "agent." Because courts are generally not involved in these alternatives, they are less costly than guardianship. However, because these alternatives are not court supervised, the risk exists that your agent may take advantage of you. You should therefore choose an agent whom you wholeheartedly trust—someone who will act according to your expectations even if you cannot monitor what the agent is doing.

In order to prevent the need for guardianship, you must make sure that a substitute decisionmaking plan is in place for both health care decisions and property management. The name of the document for appointing a health care agent varies from state to state. The person appointed may be called your health care "proxy," "representative," or "agent," depending on the language used in your particular state's statute. Every state also has a power of attorney statute that allows you to give someone else authority to make your property and financial decisions. The person appointed to act for you under a power of attorney is called your "agent" or "attorney-in-fact."

You do not have to choose the same person to serve as the agent for both health care and property decisions. For example, Betty, a widow, feels that her daughter would be the best suited among her children to make decisions about her finances and property because the daughter is a certified public accountant. Although her daughter lives in another state, Betty is confident that her financial affairs can be handled long distance through online account management and telephone communication. With respect to substitute decisionmaking for health care, Betty chooses to make her son her health care agent because he lives in the same town and would likely be available in the event of an emergency.

Depending on the complexity of your property matters, you may decide to name an institution, such as a bank or trust company, rather than an individual, to serve as your agent. Whereas it is customary for family-member agents to serve without compensation, institutions charge a fee that is typically a percentage of the value of the property they are managing. Thus, an institutional agent may not be a good choice for seniors with only modest property and financial reserves.

The following discussion explains in greater detail how you can create a substitute decisionmaking plan for your health care and property management. Although a health care proxy and a durable power of attorney for property management are the primary tools for avoiding guardianship, there are other legal arrangements, such as a trust, joint account, or Social Security Representative Payeeship, that can serve a substitute decisionmaking function. These are also discussed.

Substitute Decisionmaking for Health Care

Creating a substitute decisionmaking plan for health care involves (1) stating in advance *what* kind of treatment you would want if you could no longer make those decisions for yourself and (2) selecting *whom* you would want to make decisions on your behalf. The first type of planning is sometimes called *directed* decisionmaking because you direct now—while you have capacity—what you would want later if you no longer have the ability to make decisions. The second type of planning is referred to as *delegated* decisionmaking because you delegate to someone else the authority to make decisions for you if later you cannot make the decisions for yourself.

In most states, the document used to direct what you would want if you later lose capacity is called a living will. The document that is used to delegate health care decisionmaking authority to someone else is usually called a health care proxy or power of attorney. The term "health care advance directive" is frequently used to include both living wills and health care proxies.

So long as you still have the mental capacity to make your own decisions, your wishes trump the opinions of anyone you have appointed as your health care agent. Likewise, if you change your mind about the choices stated in your living will or whom you want to serve as your health care agent, you can revoke your health care advance directives and create new ones.

Directed Health Care Decisionmaking

There are two basic types of health care documents that can be used to direct your medical treatment if you later lose the ability to make your own decisions. One is a directive that you can prepare without a physician's assistance, commonly called a living will. The other is a physician's order based on your wishes. Depending on state law, physician orders may include Do Not Resuscitate (DNR) orders, Out-of-Hospital Do Not Resuscitate orders, and Physician Orders for Life Sustaining Treatment (POLST).

Living Wills. Under all state laws today, you can sign a health care directive— commonly called a living will—that specifies whether you would want life sustaining treatment if you have a terminal illness or injury. Life sustaining treatment may include ventilators or respirators to help you breathe, cardiopulmonary resuscitation if your heart stops, and tube feedings to supply water and nutrition if you cannot eat or drink. The U.S. Supreme Court has recognized the right of all competent citizens to accept or decline medical treatment as well as the right of each state to set its own standard of evidentiary proof for whether an individual has made a choice about life sustaining treatment (*Cruzan v. Mo. Dep't. of Health*, 497 U.S. 261 [1990]). The much publicized cases of Nancy Cruzan (*id.*) and Terri Schiavo (*In re Guardianship of Schiavo*, 916 So.2d 814 [Fla. Dist. Ct. App. 2005]) illustrate the difficulties that can arise if a person has not clearly indicated in writing what his or her wishes are with respect to life sustaining treatment.

There is no right or wrong decision when it comes to a health care directive about life sustaining treatment. Each person should decide, based upon individual values and beliefs, what course of treatment would be preferable in a terminal situation. Whether you choose to accept or decline life sustaining treatment, you should discuss this decision with your health care providers and your family so that they will understand what you want if you can no longer participate in the decisionmaking process.

Under federal law, hospitals must ask patients whether they have health care advance directives, and if a patient does not, hospitals must offer the patient an opportunity to create them (Patient Self-Determination Act of 1990, Pub. L. No. 101-508, §§4206, 4751, 104 Stat. 1388). However, some physicians and religiously affiliated hospitals may not be willing to follow a health care advance directive that requests the discontinuation or the withholding of certain life sustaining procedures such as tube feedings. It is important to ask whether your physician or hospital has any policies that conflict with your wishes. If there is a conflict, you may need to seek care from providers whose policies are consistent with your preferences and values.

DNRs, Out-of-Hospital DNRs, and POLST. For patients who have terminal or serious, progressive chronic conditions, there are additional directed decisionmaking tools that may be important. These include DNRs, Out-of-Hospital DNRs, and POLST. Unlike a living will, which is created and signed by the patient, DNRs, Out-of-Hospital DNRs, and POLST protocols are directives about life sustaining treatments that are prepared by a physician after talking with the patient or the patient's health care agent.

The most common of these physician orders, the DNR, specifies that a patient should not be resuscitated in the event that the patient's heart stops. Because such orders are effective only for patients residing in a hospital or skilled nursing facility, an increasing number of states have enacted Out-of-Hospital DNR statutes that permit patients with terminal or serious, chronic conditions to have portable DNR orders. Such patients wear an Out-of-Hospital DNR identification tag to avoid resuscitation by emergency medical services if they happen to suffer cardiac arrest while outside of a hospital or skilled nursing facility.

Some states recognize a POLST protocol. POLST laws are aimed at ensuring that the wishes of those who have advanced, chronic progressive illnesses can be put in portable medical orders. These orders are more comprehensive than DNRs and cover, in addition to cardiopulmonary resuscitation, other medical treatment decisions such as hospitalization, tube feedings, antibiotics, and ventilation to assist breathing.

Delegated Health Care Decisionmaking

Whereas a living will and advance physician orders are important tools for stating today what you would want if you were terminally ill or in the end stages of a progressive illness, these directed decisionmaking tools do not cover all of the circumstances in which medical decisions might be needed on your behalf. For example, what if you were unconscious as the result of an automobile accident and could not participate in decisions about your care? Or what if you were conscious but unable to communicate due to the effects of a stroke? Because there are many nonterminal medical scenarios in which you might need care but lack the ability to participate in treatment decisions, it is important that you consider whom you would want to make those decisions for you.

If you do not select someone to act as your health care decisionmaker, most states have laws that allow certain family members (usually your spouse, adult children, and adult siblings) to give medical consent for you. However, these laws are at best a fallback method for substitute decision-making. You may not have relatives that qualify under the statute, or you may prefer that someone other than a relative act for you. Difficulties can also arise if the family members qualified by statute do not agree about your care. Most statutes do not give an order of priority among possible family decisionmakers. If qualified family members cannot agree about your treatment options, a guardianship may be necessary to resolve the dispute.

To avoid the problems that can result from reliance on family consent laws, it is usually better to appoint a substitute health care decisionmaker. The name for this person varies by state, as does the name of the document for appointing the person. Common names include health care representative, health care proxy, and health care agent. No matter what the name, this individual should be someone you trust and someone who is willing to carry out your wishes if you are unable to participate in your own treatment decisions.

The best way to ensure that your wishes will be followed is to discuss your values and preferences with your health care agent. Although incapacity and the possibility of serious or terminal illness are not pleasant topics of conversation, a candid discussion about these topics is the only way your health care agent can know your wishes. Knowing what you want will also reduce some of the stress for your agent if such decisions later need to be made.

How to Make Your Plan for Substitute
Health Care Decisions Work

Make Your Plan Known. Your health care decisionmaking plan will be effective only if your doctors and agents are aware of it. Discuss your wishes and values with your doctors, agents, and family members to ensure that they understand what you want and are willing to make decisions that are consistent with your wishes. If you have different agents for health care and financial decisions, make certain that both agents fully understand what you want. Even though your health care agent may have the authority to make your medical care decisions, the cooperation of your financial agent is necessary to pay for such care. Likewise, family members who do not have actual decisionmaking authority for you should be informed of your plan so that you can reduce the likelihood that they will later challenge the actions of your agents. Keep a card in your wallet that identifies the contact information for your health care agent and any successor agents.

Sign Multiple "Originals" of Your Documents. Although in most states your health care providers are allowed to rely on a copy of your living will and health care proxy or power of attorney, it is a good idea to sign several "originals" when your documents are prepared. Your agent and any successor agents should be given documents that contain an original signature, and you should keep a reserve set somewhere that is easily accessible in the event of an emergency.

Be Aware of Different State Law Requirements. The legal requirements for preparing a valid living will and health care proxy vary from state to state. Usually, state law requires that health care advance directives be signed and witnessed. Some state laws require two witnesses. Whether advance directives prepared in one state will be honored in another state varies state to state. Consequently, if you regularly live in more than one state, or plan to receive health care in another state, it is a good idea to prepare health care advance directives that meet both states' requirements. Another option is to prepare a separate set of documents for each state.

Substitute Decisionmaking for Property and Financial Management

The most common and cost-effective way to create a substitute decision-making plan for property and financial management is the durable power of attorney. All states have power of attorney laws that permit adults with decisionmaking capacity to give another person the authority to deal with their property and finances. The person who grants such authority is called the "principal." The person who receives authority from the principal is called the "agent" or "attorney-in-fact." All states allow these powers of attorney to be durable—that is, they continue to be effective even if the principal later loses decisionmaking capacity. Thus, a durable power of attorney is the most common technique for avoiding guardianship.

In addition to the durable power of attorney, there are other legal devices that can be used for limited substitute decisionmaking. In most instances, they are used in addition to a power of attorney rather than in its place. These include a trust, jointly held financial accounts, and a representative payeeship for management of a person's Social Security benefits.

Durable Power of Attorney

A durable power of attorney is a document that gives another person—known as your agent—authority to act on your behalf with respect to your property and money. In this arrangement you are known as the principal. If the power of attorney is *durable*, your agent will continue to have authority to act on your behalf even if you lose the ability to make and carry out your own decisions. Most people want their power of attorney to be durable so that they can avoid the need for guardianship if they later become incapacitated.[1]

In some states, all powers of attorney are durable unless stated otherwise in the document. In others, the power of attorney has to contain language that indicates the principal's desire that it remain valid even if the principal later loses capacity. A power of attorney can also be written so that it becomes effective only if the principal loses capacity. This is known as a springing power of attorney.

Whether you should choose an immediately effective power of attorney or a springing one depends on your objectives. If you are interested in giving an agent authority *only* as a precaution to avoid guardianship, then a springing power might be preferable. However, if you want your agent to be able to take care of your property and financial matters when you are out of town, or perhaps too ill to run errands, then the convenience of an immediately effective power of attorney may best suit your circumstances.

Regardless of when you want your power of attorney to become effective, the most important choice you must make is deciding who should serve as your agent. A power of attorney is no better than the trustworthiness of the agent acting under it. In order for your power of attorney to provide effective protection against the need for guardianship, you should also name a successor agent who can act for you if your first agent is no longer willing or able to act.

Almost as important as your choice of agent is the decision about how much authority to give to your agent. Although broad authority is usually a good idea if your goal is avoiding guardianship, you should exercise caution when giving your agent authority that could put your property at risk or impact your estate plan. For example, an agent with authority to make gifts, to create or revoke trusts, or to create or change beneficiary designations and survivorship interests could completely undermine your estate plan.

You may also want to consider whether your initial agent and successor agent should each have the same degree of authority. For example, you might feel comfortable giving your spouse unlimited authority to make gifts or to change beneficiary designations but would not want to see such authority in the hands of one of your adult children. The understanding that you and your spouse have with respect to gift making priorities among your children and grandchildren may not be shared by an adult child who sees sibling fairness issues differently.

In general, an agent is viewed as a fiduciary and is expected to act in the best interest of the principal. This means that an agent cannot use the principal's property for his or her own benefit unless authorized by the power of attorney. Some states have detailed provisions that describe an agent's duties. In states without such provisions, the courts rely on the common law of agency, which is based on case law decisions about the conduct of principals and agents.

In most states, an agent has either a common law or statutory duty to keep track of any dealings with the principal's property and to account for those transactions if requested by the principal, a court, or a representative of the deceased principal's estate. A principal can also include a provision in a power of attorney that requires the agent to make periodic accountings to a third person. Such a provision may operate as a safeguard on the agent's activities or as a way to prevent suspicions from arising where one child is selected over others to serve as the agent.

Although the law does not require a power of attorney to be prepared by a lawyer, it is advisable to seek out a lawyer's advice so that your power of attorney can be adjusted to fit your needs and objectives. Nearly one-half the states have an optional statutory form that can be used to create a power of attorney. Care should be taken to make sure that you satisfy the requirements for your state.

Some states require that the power of attorney be notarized. Others require one or two witnesses. Still others may require only the principal's signature. If your power of attorney may be used in a real estate transaction, notarization is advisable because it is required by county recorders' offices before documents such as deeds can be placed in the public record. Because powers of attorney are governed by state law, it may be necessary to do more than one power of attorney if you own property in more than one state. However, an increasing number of states are honoring out-of-state powers of attorney if they are valid under the law where they were created.

Advantages of a Power of Attorney. Compared with guardianship or a trust, a power of attorney is the most cost-effective and flexible form of substitute decisionmaking for property. There is no need for the principal to be officially declared incapacitated, and the transactions with respect to the principal's property can remain private. If the principal still has capacity and changes his or her mind about the choice of agent or scope of authority, the principal can simply revoke the power of attorney and create a new one.

Unlike a trust arrangement, which is effective only to deal with property titled in the trust, a power of attorney can authorize the agent to pursue personal entitlements and claims on the principal's behalf, such as those arising under Social Security, Medicare, and Medicaid laws, or under contracts and dealings with other persons. Another advantage of the power of attorney is that title to the principal's property remains in the principal, as opposed to trust assets, which have to be retitled in the name of the trust.

Disadvantages of a Power of Attorney. The greatest disadvantage of a power of attorney is that it is an unsupervised arrangement and susceptible to abuse. The very attributes that make it desirable—the privacy and flexibility with which the principal's affairs can be handled—make it potentially dangerous if placed in untrustworthy hands. Theoretically, it is a trustee's accountability to the terms of the trust document and a guardian's accountability to the court that protect vulnerable persons in those arrangements. In reality, however, these arrangements likely offer little more protection than the power of attorney. Court systems often lack the resources to monitor the activities of guardians, and a family trustee may have no one to whom the trustee must account other than the now incapacitated beneficiary. On balance, if care is taken in the selection of the agent and the scope of authority delegated to the agent, a power of attorney remains the best all-purpose tool for substitute decisionmaking.

Revocable (Living) Trust

Revocable trusts—also referred to as "living" trusts—are a common way to avoid probate (i.e., property passing under a will at your death) and provide incapacity planning for substitute management of property and finances. Property in a trust does not pass under your will at death because the property is titled in the name of the trust rather than in your name. A person called a trustee is responsible for managing the trust assets according to the instructions in the trust document. You can name yourself as the initial trustee, but a successor trustee should also be named to take over trust management responsibilities if you later lose capacity or no longer wish to manage the assets.

Consider the example of Sarah, an 85-year-old widow, who transferred her certificates of deposit, savings account, and a brokerage account into a revocable trust. Sarah named herself as the sole trustee and her 60-year-old daughter, Doris, as successor trustee. Two years after the trust was established, Sarah was diagnosed with early stage dementia and no longer felt comfortable managing the trust. She simply resigned as trustee, thus permitting Doris to take over as successor trustee. Doris now manages the funds in the trust and uses them to pay Sarah's living expenses.

Even though most people name spouses and children as successor or co-trustees, any adult with decisionmaking capacity can serve in that role. Individuals with considerable wealth often name professional trust companies to act as trustee. Institutional trustees charge a management fee based on the value of the trust and thus are not a good choice for persons with only modest assets.

No matter what the value of the property to be placed in trust, most people seek the assistance of a lawyer in creating the trust. The trust instrument sets out all of the terms of the trust, which can be as varied and creative as you like. You may also need assistance changing the titles on property that will be transferred to the trust, such as real estate, bank and brokerage accounts, and automobiles.

A trust creates a fiduciary relationship between the trustee, who has title to the property, and the beneficiary, who is the person who receives benefits from the trust. As a fiduciary, the trustee must follow the instructions in the trust document and act in good faith and the best interest of the beneficiary. Usually, the person who creates a revocable trust—called the settlor—is also a beneficiary of the trust during the settlor's lifetime. Thus, it is possible for the original owner of the property to wear three hats—settlor, trustee, and beneficiary during his or her lifetime.

The settlor of a revocable trust may amend or revoke it at any time so long as the settlor has mental capacity. The settlor can replace a trustee or change who will serve as successor trustee. The settlor can also change the beneficiaries. If the settlor becomes incapacitated, the trust becomes irrevocable for as long as the incapacity continues unless the settlor has given revocation authority to someone else. At the settlor's death, the trust continues until the time specified in the trust instrument for it to terminate. When that date is reached, which is often after all of the settlor's debts and estate taxes have been paid, the trust assets are distributed according to the instructions in the trust instrument. Because the assets do not pass through probate, the revocable trust serves as a will substitute as well as an alternative to guardianship.

Advantages of a Revocable Trust. One advantage of a revocable trust is that the property subject to the terms of the trust is clearly identified, as are the duties of the trustee. For those who can afford a professional trustee, the quality of the substitute property and financial management may be higher than under a less formal power of attorney arrangement. Furthermore, financial institutions are often more comfortable dealing with trustees than agents under powers of attorney.

A trust may also provide greater protection for your wishes should you later become incapacitated. You may make your expectations for property and financial management very explicit in the trustee's instructions. For example, if you have the resources to pay for in-home care and you are concerned that family members may move you to institutional care once you become incapacitated, your trust can be created to authorize only payment for in-home care. This directive must be respected, even if the arrangement is more expensive than nursing home care. Expenditures that might otherwise be considered imprudent—such as requiring the trustee to pay for a private room in a nursing home—will be permitted if the trust instrument authorizes them.

Disadvantages of a Revocable Trust. A revocable trust is the most expensive and complicated method of avoiding guardianship. Legal fees are incurred when the trust is created and increase with the trust's complexity. The cost of a revocable trust includes the expense of changing the title to all of the assets that must be transferred to the trust. Professional trustees charge an annual fee for their services, and accounting fees may also be incurred depending on the scope of the trust's activities.

A trust will not avoid the necessity of probate proceedings if the settlor fails to transfer all of her or his property to the trust. This risk is particularly high with respect to items that are obtained after the creation of the trust. Likewise, a revocable trust does not provide any income or estate tax savings for the settlor. The income of the trust is taxed to the settlor regardless of whether it is actually distributed to the settlor. And although the trust assets do not pass through probate, the assets are included in the deceased settlor's estate for purposes of state inheritance tax and federal estate tax.

Jointly Held Financial Account

Jointly held financial accounts can serve a variety of purposes. You may want to add the name of another person to your bank account for the sake of convenience only—that is, to permit the other person to conduct financial transactions on your behalf, but without transferring any ownership interest to that person. Or you may wish to give that person part ownership of the account and survivorship rights in the money held in the account. If you give a "true joint tenancy" interest in your bank or brokerage account to another person, that person is treated as receiving a present share of the account as well as survivorship rights in the total account.

Unfortunately, many financial institutions do not distinguish between a "convenience account" and a "true joint tenancy account" on the forms and signature cards used to open the account. The primary reason for this is that financial institutions want to avoid liability with respect to withdrawals made from accounts held in more than one name. Typically, any named owner on a jointly held account may access all of the funds in the account. Thus, a jointly held account is one way of providing for substitute management of account assets if one of the account holders later loses decisionmaking capacity. However, as the following examples illustrate, a power of attorney may be a better method of establishing a substitute decisionmaker if the sole purpose of a joint account is convenience.

Consider the example of Bob and Mary, both in their 80s and suffering from chronic health conditions that make it difficult for them to run errands. Bob and Mary have a joint-tenancy bank account that includes rights of survivorship. In part, they chose this type of account so that when one of them dies the survivor will have all of the account assets without the necessity of going through probate. Because it is physically difficult for them to go to the bank, Bob and Mary decide to add Tom, Bob's son from a former marriage, to the account so that he can help them with banking errands. This arrangement works well until Tom withdraws half of the money after Bob's death, claiming that it is his through rights of survivorship. Another problem can occur if Tom, who was added for convenience purposes only, has creditors who want to attach assets in the account to satisfy Tom's debts.

A few states have enacted laws that require banks to provide customers with the option of different account titles that distinguish true joint tenancy accounts from convenience accounts. Where such laws do not exist, courts generally permit the persons who contributed the money to the account (or their heirs) to offer proof that the other named person on the account was authorized for convenience purposes only.

Although it is possible to obtain a court ruling on the true intent of an account held in more than one name, lawsuits are time consuming and expensive. If a true joint tenancy is not intended, care should be taken to assure that the account title accurately reflects the convenience nature of the arrangement. If it is not possible to open an appropriately titled account, then use of a power of attorney to give the substitute decisionmaker authority over the account (but no appearance of ownership) better achieves the intended objective.

Social Security Representative Payeeship

If a senior who receives Social Security or Supplemental Security Income benefits needs assistance managing these payments, a representative payee can be appointed by the Social Security Administration (42 U.S.C. §§405[j], 1007, 1383[a]). A payee may be appointed either because the beneficiary wants assistance or because Social Security believes that the beneficiary needs assistance. If a family member or friend is not available to serve as payee, Social Security may appoint a qualified organization.

All children and legally incapacitated adults who receive benefits are required to have representative payees. Even if an incapacitated person has an agent who has been appointed to serve under a power of attorney, Social Security requires that the incapacitated person also have a representative payee. The agent under the power of attorney may apply to become the representative payee.

To become a representative payee, a person must submit an application at the local Social Security office and supply proof of identity. With limited exceptions, Social Security requires a face-to-face interview with the representative payee applicant. Individual representative payees may not charge a fee for their services, but they may be reimbursed for out-of-pocket expenses. Qualified organization payees must be authorized in writing by Social Security to charge a fee for representative payee services.

Representative payees must use payments solely for the benefit of the beneficiary, such as paying for food, shelter, clothes, and medical care. Any benefits not spent on past bills or current needs must be saved for the beneficiary's future needs. The representative payee must keep a record of all payments received and how they were spent or saved. The payee must also complete a Representative Payee Report, which Social Security sends out once a year.

A beneficiary who suspects that the payee has misused benefits should contact Social Security so that an investigation can be conducted. If Social Security was negligent in permitting misuse of the benefits, Social Security must repay the funds to the beneficiary. If Social Security was not at fault, the beneficiary is responsible for reclaiming the misused benefits from the representative payee.

If a beneficiary believes that he or she no longer needs a representative payee, the beneficiary may request that the representative payeeship be terminated, but the beneficiary must convince Social Security that the need for the arrangement no longer exists. Social Security may request a physician's statement that the beneficiary's condition has improved and that he or she is now capable of managing benefit payments.

How to Make Your Plan for Substitute Property and Financial Management Work

Choose Your Substitute Decisionmaker Carefully. Whether you are considering a power of attorney, trust, joint bank account, or representative payeeship, any substitute decisionmaking arrangement is only as good as the substitute decisionmaker. You should choose someone who is not only trustworthy but who will respect your wishes and carry them out even if you no longer have the ability to monitor what is happening. If you are using a power of attorney or trust, you should also choose a trustworthy successor agent or trustee so that your substitute decisionmaking plan does not fall apart if something happens to your original substitute decisionmaker.

Discuss Your Expectations. You should have a candid discussion with anyone who will have authority as your substitute decisionmaker and explain how you want your property and money handled. For example, under what circumstances would you want your property sold or given away? If you are using a power of attorney, do you want your agent to continue a pattern of gift giving or family maintenance if you lose the capacity to do so? Do you expect your agent to serve without compensation?

Carefully Consider How Much Authority to Give Your Agent. Although it is important to give your agent broad enough authority to avoid a guardianship, there are certain powers that may be particularly risky in the hands of an agent. These include the power to make or revoke a trust, to give a gift of your property, and to create or change beneficiary designations and survivorship interests. Such powers may be appropriate in the hands of your initial agent, but not a successor. For example, Bob may want his wife, Carol, to have such powers, but not his daughter, Anne, who is named as his successor agent.

Communicate Your Expectations to Family Members Who Might Challenge Your Plan. Although there is no sure defense against family members who might try to upend your substitute decisionmaking plan, candidly discussing your plan and choice of agent may make it more difficult for them to launch an attack. Creating a written record of your expectations and instructions for your substitute decisionmaker may also make it more difficult for others to argue that you wanted something (or someone) else.

Note

1. For a general discussion of the use and benefits of durable powers as an alternative to guardianship, see Linda S. Whitton, "Durable Powers as an Alternative to Guardianship: Lessons We Have Learned," *Stetson Law Review* 37 (2007): 7.

For More Information

ABA Commission on Law and Aging Consumer's Tool Kit for Health Care Advance Planning
(http://www.abanet.org/aging/toolkit/)

Find worksheets and resources that will help you consider your values and choices when preparing health care advance directives as well as suggestions about how to choose and communicate with your substitute decisionmaker.

Social Security Administration Internet Support for Representative Payees
(http://www.ssa.gov/payee/index.htm)

Find information for representative payees as well as information for beneficiaries who have a representative payee. A link is also provided for filing a representative payee accounting online.

10

Elder Abuse, Neglect, and Exploitation

Did You Know?

- Most abusers are people close to the victim—usually family members or caregivers.
- Most communities have agencies and programs to help abuse victims.
- Keeping vulnerable seniors connected to their communities with home visits and phone calls can reduce or prevent elder abuse.
- Your identity will be protected if you report suspected elder abuse.

"Elder abuse," as that term is used in the law, applies to more than just physical and psychological harm; it also includes neglect and financial exploitation. Many factors make it difficult to track how often elder abuse, neglect, and exploitation occur. Even though there is no central reporting system, the National Committee for the Prevention of Elder Abuse estimates that 4–6 percent of all elderly are abused. In the past, elder abuse was frequently hidden or dismissed as uncommon, but today government and social service agencies acknowledge that elder abuse, neglect, and exploitation occur frequently. This chapter looks at the nature and causes of elder abuse, the circumstances in which it often occurs, and what you can do if you, or someone you know, are victimized or in danger of becoming a victim.

What Are Abuse, Neglect, and Exploitation?

Abuse, neglect, and exploitation form the trio of what is usually just called elder abuse. Abuse can be conduct or statements that injure or threaten the physical or psychological well-being of an older person. Even onetime physical assaults, if harmful enough, are considered elder abuse. Inappropriate restraint of a person is a form of physical abuse. For example, a caregiver who ties an older person in bed for hours so that he or she will not get up unassisted and fall is committing an act of elder abuse. Nonconsensual sexual contact of any kind is also a form of physical abuse.

Psychological abuse, even though it may leave no physical injury, is no less serious than physical abuse. It can range from threatening to abandon the older person, or to put him in a nursing home, to threatening physical force if the person does not cooperate in daily tasks such as eating, bathing, and taking medication. Even repeated insults and shouting are a form of psychological abuse because they undermine the victim's sense of self-worth and security.

"Exploitation" is the term frequently used to describe financial abuse—that is, the misuse or theft of another person's property and money. Blatant forms of financial abuse include using the victim's ATM card without permission to withdraw money, or using the victim's power of attorney to steal the victim's property or money from bank accounts. More subtle forms of financial exploitation can occur when the abuser has close and frequent contact with the victim—such as where a relative caregiver shares the same home with the victim. The caregiver may be able to slowly siphon off the older person's assets. This can be accomplished by taking more than a fair share of that person's monthly retirement or Social Security benefits for the common household expenses or by spending the older person's money for the benefit of other family members. Abusive family members who pay for expensive vacations, houses, or automobiles with the elderly relative's money may justify the expenditures on the grounds that the money will be theirs someday anyway, or that the elderly victim is also benefiting from the expenditures.

Abusive acts often contain elements that are physical, psychological, and financial. For example, a family member may bring an elderly relative to his home for a "visit" and then seek permanent guardianship over that relative, arguing that he or she is no longer able to handle personal care and financial decisions. Using guardianship as a means to control the older person and his or her assets can be a form of legal "kidnapping" when that individual is not in a psychological position to freely object to the arrangement. Threats of nursing home placement or emotional abandonment may pressure the older person into going along with the arrangement. Domineering family members have also been known to cut off communication between elderly relatives and other family members or friends. The increasing frequency of adult children fighting over their parents and their parents' assets has prompted some elder advocates to call these guardianships "will contests while the person is still alive."

Unlike acts of physical, psychological, and financial abuse, which involve intentional threats or conduct, neglect is a failure to act that puts the older victim at risk. For example, it is elder neglect when a caregiver fails to provide essential medicine, food, or shelter to an older person. Liability for neglect is based on a legal "duty" to act. That duty is usually based on a contract when the neglect occurs in a nursing home or at the hands of someone hired to provide home care.

Neglect by family members who have volunteered to care for an elderly person at home may be more difficult to prove. No family member, with the exception of a spouse, has a duty to provide care to another adult. However, once that responsibility has been accepted and the vulnerable person has become dependent on that care, most states recognize that the volunteer caregiver has a duty to continue that care or to seek out an alternative caregiver. For example, Adam begins to provide daily help to his 88-year-old grandfather, Grant, who lives next door and must use a wheelchair. Having let Grant become dependent on his care, Adam cannot simply go on an extended vacation without making some provision for Grant's care while he is gone.

Most state statutes that deal with protection of vulnerable older persons also include "self-neglect" as a basis for protective legal intervention. This intervention may take the form of voluntary acceptance of protective services such as home-delivered meals or housekeeping assistance or involuntary measures such as guardianship. Appropriate protective intervention depends on the degree of self-neglect and the ability of the vulnerable adult to make rational decisions. Although self-neglect is often listed as a type of elder abuse that will trigger protective intervention, it is really not abuse in the technical sense. Rather, self-neglect is a descriptive term for a person's inability to care for herself or to make appropriate arrangements for such care.

Where Does Elder Abuse Occur?

Elder abuse occurs both in institutional settings, such as nursing homes, assisted living facilities, and board and care homes, and in noninstitutional settings, such as the victim's home or the home of a caregiver. Although the impact on the victim is essentially the same in either setting, where the abuse occurs is relevant to answering questions about how to effectively help victims and how to prevent the abuse from happening again. Whether in an institutional or noninstitutional setting, abuse occurs more frequently to seniors who are dependent and isolated.

Institutional Settings

Abuse in an institutional setting is usually perpetrated by individual employees. Physically abusive acts may include hitting uncooperative residents and using excessive physical restraints or drugs to keep residents contained and less demanding of staff time. Sexual assault is another form of physical abuse that can occur in institutional settings.

Neglect in an institutional setting usually takes the form of inadequate attention to resident needs, such as not responding to call buttons, providing substandard care, or failing to provide a decent emotional atmosphere of safety and concern for the older person's well-being. Signs of neglect in nursing homes range from residents who have infected bedsores due to lack of proper repositioning in their beds to residents who suffer severe weight loss and kidney failure from dehydration and inadequate assistance with eating.

Although residents are discouraged from keeping cash in their rooms, financial exploitation still occurs in an institutional setting. Financial abuse includes not only theft of whatever petty cash the resident might keep in the room, but also theft of residents' personal belongings, such as jewelry, radios, and televisions. As a result, the freedom to enjoy one's jewelry and other valuables can be compromised by the need to protect property from theft while residents are sleeping or out of their rooms for meals and activities.

Abuse and neglect are more common in institutions that serve the poor because such institutions often cannot afford to hire quality employees or to provide decent care. Undertrained, overworked, and poorly supervised employees too often lash out at the residents. Financially stressed institutions may cut corners on the amount of staff and other services in order to meet budget. The isolation and dependency of the residents and their lack of housing alternatives leave them no choice but to endure these unsatisfactory living conditions.

Even institutions that serve the middle class frequently have too few staff, pay low wages, and provide inadequate training. One of the primary reasons for this is inadequate public funding for those residents who have run out of money to pay for their own care. Medicaid, a hybrid program financed by both the federal and state governments, is the sole source of payment for a majority of nursing home residents. Unfortunately, the Medicaid reimbursement rates pay only about 70 percent of the actual cost of such residents' care, leaving nursing homes to find creative ways to balance their budgets.

Noninstitutional Settings

Abuse in a noninstitutional setting usually happens at the hands of a caregiver, often a family member. Because incidents of slapping or yelling at the victim often occur in the privacy of the victim's home or home of the caregiver, the victim's friends or other family members may be unaware that it is happening. Some victims put up with the abuse for fear they will lose the caregiver or that the caregiver—often an adult child—will get into trouble with the law. Other victims are too isolated or too physically or mentally incapacitated to seek help.

Some abuse occurs when caregivers fail to understand the older person's medical needs. For example, Judy is caring for her elderly aunt May, who suffers from diabetes. Judy does not understand the importance of diet in controlling Aunt May's diabetes and so fails to provide a proper diet or to monitor what Aunt May eats. Other abuse is just very negligent caregiving. It may range from failing to seek medical attention soon enough for the older person to more intentional abuse, such as leaving bedridden persons to lie in their own waste or refusing to feed them by hand because it is "too much work."

Financial exploitation by caregivers is fairly common and difficult to uncover. Some caregivers enter into the relationship specifically to financially exploit the victim. Often the victim is not even aware of the exploitation. For example, when the caregiver lives with the victim, it is easy to commingle funds and use the older person's money for the caregiver's support. The elderly victim may be lonely or depressed and believe that flattering attention by a caregiver or a "new best friend" is genuine. In such circumstances, the victim can be manipulated into making gifts or giving the abuser access to the victim's bank accounts and other property.

Causes of Abuse, Neglect, and Exploitation

Some who abuse the elderly are persons who have the specific, bad intent to exploit or injure their victims. They select the elderly as victims because they are available, vulnerable, and less likely to report the abuse. Others—usually family members—believe that they are entitled to use the victim's property and money as "payment" for caregiving or as part of the inheritance that will eventually be theirs. In other cases, caregivers simply become so frustrated with their duties and so angry with the older person that they lash out from the fatigue of caring for someone who may be uncooperative or even physically and verbally abusive to the caregiver. To be sure, the stress of caregiving can lead to despair, anger, and resentment, but abuse is never a proper response. Caregivers should seek available social services and other forms of support that will lessen their burden.

Studies have found that some abuse is revenge motivated—adult children retaliating against their older parents for abuse committed against them as children. Other abusers consider violence a normal and acceptable way of responding to someone who is uncooperative or burdensome. Many abusers suffer from alcohol or drug dependency and financially exploit the elder person to obtain money for their addiction. Caregivers who are financially dependent upon the older person may subconsciously resent their dependency and respond by abusing, neglecting, or exploiting the older person. For others, abuse is a way of gaining control and satisfying an emotional need to dominate the victim.

Solutions

Area Agencies on Aging and Adult Protective Services
Every state has enacted laws designed to protect the elderly from abuse, neglect, and exploitation. The federal government contributes limited funds to

states to help combat the problem. Federal grants are made to each state's agency on aging, which in turn provides money to local Area Agencies on Aging (AAAs). The state agency on aging serves as a general coordinator of all services and programs related to the assistance of elderly people within the state. The local AAAs supervise the actual delivery of services, usually at the county level.

The Older Americans Act Amendments of 1987 require state agencies on aging to assess the need for elder abuse prevention services and to create a state plan to prevent elder abuse within the state (Pub. L. No. 100-175, §144, 101 Stat. 926, 948-50 [1987]). Unfortunately, the federal funding to prevent elder abuse has never been sufficient, which explains in part why the problem is still so prevalent. Despite the lack of adequate funding, states have enacted adult protective services statutes as a means of establishing a comprehensive response to the problem of elder abuse. The statutes define elder abuse, provide ways to uncover it, establish the guidelines for protective interventions, and create punishments for the abusers.

All the statutes define elder abuse as physical harm. Some include the infliction of mental anguish or psychological injury, although that is sometimes limited to psychological abuse that is severe enough to require medical attention. A few states recognize unreasonable confinement as elder abuse, as well as neglect that rises to the level of a failure to provide for basic needs, including food, shelter, and care for physical and mental health. Self-neglect can be the basis for an investigation if the individual's personal safety is an issue. Financial exploitation is also included as abuse and is generally defined as the illegal or improper use of an elderly individual's resources or property for the benefit of the exploiter or another.

Many of the adult protective services laws require reporting of suspected abuse by professionals, such as health care personnel, social service providers, law enforcement officers, social workers, physicians, and nurses. To encourage nonmandatory reporting, all states guarantee to protect the identity of abuse reporters, although a few states permit limited disclosure of the reporter's identity under special circumstances. All states' statutes provide for some sort of initial investigation when a report of alleged abuse is received. The investigation will be carried out by a state or county agency. A few states require that the local law enforcement agency investigate elder abuse complaints.

After an investigation is completed, or if the older person requests assistance, the protective services agency is supposed to take the steps necessary to terminate the abuse and to meet the older individual's care needs. Usually, protective services include several types of assistance, such as a visiting nurse or home health aid, Meals-on-Wheels, light housekeeping, and legal assistance if necessary. The older person who is believed to be at risk for abuse, neglect, or exploitation must voluntarily accept assistance. If the person does not agree and adult protective services believes that the person is no longer capable of engaging in self-care or making rational decisions about needed care, adult protective services has authority to seek a temporary court order for emergency protective intervention and, when necessary, involuntary guardianship over the person.

Self-neglect often triggers services that the individual may not want. For example, Elaine, age 85, is found in poor condition living in her home, with a dozen or more cats, rotted food and trash all over the house, and no heat. Under many state adult protective services statutes, a state could force its way into the home, remove the animals, and either force Elaine to take care of herself or move her into a facility with supportive services, such as a nursing home.

The involvement of adult protective services can also lead to help for overstressed caregivers who may be well intentioned but who have snapped under the pressure of their caregiving responsibilities. If investigation reveals that the alleged abuser is generally a good caregiver but in need of support and a break, adult protective services may be able to arrange counseling and education for the caregiver as well as regular respite care for the vulnerable elder. Such services provide the caregiver with emotional support as well as periodic relief from caregiving so that the caregiver can attend to his or her own needs.

Criminal and Civil Law Remedies

Most elder abuse is also a crime under various state laws, including laws that criminalize assault and battery, theft, and extortion. In addition, a number of states have enacted statutes that specifically criminalize abuse of the elderly. Unfortunately, in many cases the abused older person will not report the crime out of a sense of loyalty if the abuser is a family member or caregiver or out of fear of retaliation by the abuser. Even if the abuse is reported, the criminal justice system may not respond quickly enough to protect the older person.

Another avenue for relief is a civil suit asking for a restraining or protective order against the abuser. Every state has special restraining orders and protective orders that can be invoked in the case of intrafamily abuse. These statutes, generally referred to as Domestic Violence Acts, permit the victim to obtain a court order forbidding contact between the abuser and the victim and requiring the abuser to leave the victim's household. Unfortunately, some of these statutes can be used only against a spouse. Even a protective order is not a guarantee that the violence or abuse will stop. If the abuser is also the older person's live-in caregiver, the older person may have no alternative other than moving to a nursing home for needed care. A surprising number of elderly would rather endure abusive or neglectful care than move into a nursing home.

Special Solutions for Abuse in an Institutional Setting

If abuse occurs in an institutional setting, there are several state offices whose responsibility it is to investigate complaints and find solutions. The local long-term care ombudsman is responsible for investigating reports of abuse in nursing homes and other residential care facilities (see Chapter 7 for more information about the Long-Term Care Ombudsman program). Although the long-term care ombudsman does not have direct authority to bring civil or criminal penalties against the nursing home or the abusive employee, the ombudsman often works with the nursing home to address and correct abuse problems. In very serious situations, including those involving a pattern of abuse, the ombudsman may assist the state agency that supervises nursing homes (often the state Department of Health or the state Department of Family and Social Services) and the state attorney general's office to pursue civil fines and criminal charges against abusers and the facilities in which abuse has occurred.

The victim, or someone who suspects that a resident has been victimized, may also make a complaint directly to the state regulatory agency for nursing homes or the state attorney general's office. State attorney general's offices have Medicaid fraud and control units that are required to investigate and prosecute patient fraud, abuse, and neglect in facilities that participate in Medicaid.

Community Programs

In addition to government offices that have a responsibility for investigating and addressing elder abuse, many communities have developed cooperative partnerships among seniors, law enforcement, and social service agencies for the purpose of preventing and redressing elder abuse. One such partnership is called Triad. The Triad concept was developed through the collaboration of AARP, the International Association of Chiefs of Police, and the National Sheriffs' Association. Each Triad is formed at the community level and comprises senior citizens, law enforcement agencies, and community groups that provide elder support and protection services.

Triads sponsor both educational programs and assistance in the community to help seniors avoid becoming the victims of elder abuse. Examples of such programs include the following:

- programs on how to avoid criminal victimization
- information on the latest fraud schemes and scams
- guidelines for dealing with telephone solicitations and door-to-door salespeople
- home security information and inspections
- Adopt-a-Senior visits for shut-ins
- safe shopping day programs that provide senior transportation to local grocers

- safe walks programs that arrange transportation to safe locations where seniors can enjoy weekly walking and exercise
- telephone reassurance programs

The success of these and other community-based programs has demonstrated that greater public awareness about the elder abuse problem, education of seniors, and services that keep seniors connected to their communities are essential components in preventing and reducing the incidence of elder abuse.

For More Information

AARP (202-434-AARP)
(http://www.aarp.org)

Find information about how communities can develop programs to fight fraud and abuse.

Eldercare Locator (800-677-1116)
(http://www.eldercare.gov)

Find information about local programs and services, including home-delivered meals, adult day care, caregiver support services, and legal assistance.

National Association of Triads (NATI) (800-424-7827)
(http://www.nationaltriad.org)

Find advice and technical assistance for local Triads.

National Domestic Violence Hotline (800-799-SAFE)
(http://www.ndvh.org)

Find local domestic violence shelters, other emergency shelters, legal aid programs, and social service programs.

National Committee for the Prevention of Elder Abuse
(http://www.preventelderabuse.org)

Find information and links to resources for elder abuse victims as well as for community groups and professionals who would like to improve programs and services for the prevention of crime and abuse against elders.

Index

About the Authors

Lawrence A. Frolik is Professor of Law at the University of Pittsburgh School of Law and an adjunct professor of law for the University of Miami School of Law LL.M. program in estate planning. He was one of the original academic creators of elder law as a scholarly discipline. A prolific author, in addition to his book, *Advising the Elderly or Disabled Client*, he has authored a dozen other books, including *Residence Options for Older or Disabled Clients, Elder Law in a Nutshell,* and the casebooks, *Elder Law: Cases and Materials,* and *Law of Employee Pensions and Employee Benefits.*

He is an elected fellow of the National Academy of Elder Law Attorneys, an academic member of NAELA's Certified Advanced Practitioners, and an academic member of the Special Needs Alliance. He is the past chair of the Pennsylvania Bar Association Elder Law Section, and he served as a policy advisor to the Executive Council of the Pennsylvania AARP. He now serves as a fellow of the TIAA-CREF Academic Advisory Board and as a trustee of the Achieva Family Pooled Trust. In 1995, he was a congressional appointed delegate to the White House Conference on Aging.

Linda S. Whitton, Professor of Law at Valparaiso University School of Law, is the Reporter for the Uniform Power of Attorney Act. She is a commissioner of the American Bar Association Commission on Law and Aging, an ABA representative to the National Conference of Lawyers and Corporate Fiduciaries, and a fellow of the American College of Trust and Estate Counsel. She is a past council member of the American Bar Association Section of Real Property, Trust and Estate Law and a past chair of the Association of American Law Schools Section on Aging and the Law. Professor Whitton teaches courses in elder law and property and frequently speaks and publishes on a variety of elder law topics.

Localism and Centralism in Europe

The Political and Legal Bases of
Local Self-Government

EDWARD C. PAGE

OXFORD UNIVERSITY PRESS
1991

Oxford University Press, Walton Street, Oxford OX2 6DP
Oxford New York Toronto
Delhi Bombay Calcutta Madras Karachi
Petaling Jaya Singapore Hong Kong Tokyo
Nairobi Dar es Salaam Cape Town
and associated companies in
Berlin Ibadan

Oxford is a trade mark of Oxford University Press

Published in the United States
by Oxford University Press, New York

British Library Cataloguing in Publication Data
Edward C. Page
Localism and Centralism in Europe: The Political and
Legal Bases of Local Self-Government
Comparative European Politics
ISBN 0–19–827727–X

Library of Congress Cataloging in Publication Data
Page, Edward.
Localism and centralism in Europe: the political and
legal bases of local self-government/Edward C. Page.
p. cm.—(Comparative European politics)
Includes bibliographical references and index.
1. Central-local government relations—Europe.
2. Local government—Law and legislation—Europe.
3. Comparative government.
I. Title.   II. Series.
JS3000.3.A3P34   1991   320.8'094—dc20   91–13235
ISBN 0–19–827727–X

Typeset by Taj Services Ltd., Noida. U.P. INDIA
Printed and bound in
Great Britain by Bookcraft (Bath) Ltd.,
Midsomer Norton, Avon

Acknowledgements

This book is part of a collaborative project, the first part of which appeared as a book jointly edited with Prof. Michael Goldsmith, *Central and Local Government Relations*, published by Sage in 1987. Prof. Goldsmith has offered immense encouragement to me in writing up this second part of the project. The project has also benefited from the help given by the European Consortium for Political Research, which organized a first meeting of the collaborative group. At this meeting we received invaluable guidance and advice from Kenneth Newton (Essex) and Jeanette Becquart-Leclercq (Lille). The Economic and Social Research Council funded further meetings of the group. The collaborators themselves—Peter Bogason (Copenhagen), Tom Clegg (London School of Economics), Trond Fevolden and Rune Sorensen (Oslo), Jan-Erik Lane and Tage Magnusson (Umeå), Enzo Santantonio (Rome), and Yves Mény (Paris)—provided material, some of which has already been published in the first edited volume, and critical advice on how to develop the themes that emerged from our discussions. Prof. Jack Hayward and Prof. George Jones have commented on drafts of various parts of the book. I am grateful to these people for their help.

Contents

Tables

Abbreviations

ACIR	United States Advisory Commission on Intergovernmental Relations
AMA	Association of Metropolitan Authorities
AMF	Association des Maires de France
ANCI	Associazione Nazionale dei Comuni Italiani
AP	Allianza Popular
CDU	Christlich-Demokratische Union
CISPEL	Confederazione Italiana dei Servizi Pubblici degli Enti Locali
DC	Democrazia Cristiana
ENA	École Nationale d'Administration
FEMP	Federación Española Municipios y Provincias
INU	Istituto Nazionale di Urbanistica
MRP	Mouvement Républicain Populaire
PCE	Partido Comunista de España
PDP	Partido Demócrata Popular
PSOE	Partido Socialista Obrero Español
SFIO	Section Française de l'Internationale Ouvrière
UCD	Unión de Centro Democrático
UGT	Unión General de Trabajadores
UPI	Unione delle Province d'Italia
USL	Unità Sanitaria Locale

Constitutional Subordination and Local Influence

By any measure local government everywhere in Europe is responsible for a large proportion of public services.[1] In addition to providing traditional services such as public health and cultural amenities, in most countries it is involved in major welfare state services like education, social services, and housing and in many it is also responsible for police, health, and even income maintenance. It thus affects, to a greater or lesser extent, the everyday lives of all citizens. The amount of 'government' that local government supplies can be readily measured through the amount of money it spends, the number of public employees it employs, or, somewhat less easily, the range of regulatory activity for which it is responsible. The degree to which this government is really 'local' cannot be so easily assessed.

To be local implies some control over decisions by the community. The principle of representative democracy suggests that this influence is exercised at least in part through democratically elected officials who may be expected to represent local citizens and groups. Local elected representatives can also provide the focus for forms of participatory democracy through direct citizen involvement or interest group activity.[2] However, these notions of local government as control by the community contrast with the fact that local government is essentially a subordinate institution. Local government is an 'integrating component of a greater state whole'.[3] In principle its structures and powers are subject to higher laws and can be changed by them. It is precisely this which distinguishes it from the states or provinces of a federal system which at least in some areas of their activity enjoy constitutional protection from the direct exercise of national authority. Local governments in federal systems, however, conform to the pattern of subordination; they are creatures of the province or state and can be reorganized and subjected to mandates and limitations imposed by state government.[4]

These two major characteristics of local government, its subordination and its susceptibility to control within the local community, create an inherent conflict. This conflict corresponds with what L. J. Sharpe calls the 'ineradicable ambiguity' of local government.[5] Local government is supposed to give expression to political preferences established in the locality. In this sense it is, in John D. Stewart's words 'the government of differences'.[6] Yet it is also ultimately subject to central government, which might constrain the pursuit of differences derived from locally established preferences. How can, then, the decisions of local political élites chosen through democratic elections shape the services for which they are at a minimum nominally responsible?

The answer to this question of the degree to which local government decisions are in fact local is likely to vary from one local authority to the next, and from one type of decision to the next. We know, for instance, that smaller local authorities in France are more likely to be vulnerable to central state intervention by virtue of the fact that they are unable to maintain a professional bureaucratic staff and in general rely more heavily upon central state specialists for advice.[7] We also know that some policy areas, such as income maintenance, are more likely to be centrally regulated than others, such as the provision of cultural activities.[8] A large variety of other factors might be argued or hypothesized to affect the extent to which local actors shape local decisions, including the degree of dependence on central grant, the party control of the locality, or the degree of controversy generated by the issue at stake.[9] The potential for variation across time, space, and issue is enormous.

It is quite clearly impossible, in view of the huge number of variables concerned, to generate any hard a priori rules concerning the precise circumstances under which decisions taken by any one local government at a particular time are likely to be truly local. However, it is also impossible to ignore the fact that the way in which local political élites shape public services appears to vary from one nation to another. For example, although all mayors are unique individuals, the repertoire of strategies and resources available to mayors, say, from Soviet, French, and American cities negotiating with national government varies in a manner in which generalizations are indeed possible.[10] To take another example, while there are great differences in the incidence and reactions to fiscal stress within nations, certain basic national institutional differences, such as the distinction between federal and unitary states, have a major and pervasive impact upon responses to stress.[11] The precise range of national and local influences on any one set of local government decisions is likely to be highly variable, complex, and amenable only to highly configurative explanations. Yet we can expect the opportunities for local political influence on public services to reflect broad features of a governmental system as a whole. In some systems local government is given greater opportunities to influence public policy either because it is given greater powers and responsibilities or because of the greater status that local political élites enjoy within the political system.

This book is concerned with understanding the differences between countries in terms of the opportunities available to local élites to shape public policy. But why should it matter that different countries demonstrate different broad approaches to the essential dualism of local government and offer their political leaders greater opportunities to influence decision-making? The issue is important because of the likely consequences such differences have for the nature of local politics and because an examination of the causes of cross-national diversity in this respect reveals basic and important aspects of national political development.

The opportunities available to local political élites to shape policy help define the nature of local political activity. To define what is at issue in political conflict is to have a decisive impact upon its subsequent course.[12] This is not only to be understood in the context of different functional issues creating different constellations of interests and different patterns of interaction between politicians, bureaucrats, and groups, as suggested by T. J. Lowi.[13] It also refers to the fact that in defining the nature of local political activity through the opportunities offered local élites to shape policy, local élites are constrained in the type of strategies they may pursue and the allies and supporters they seek in pursuing them. While this will be discussed more fully below, Jean-Pierre Worms's study of the prefect and the notable highlights how the 'brokerage' role of political leadership in France generates a distinctive relationship between local political élites on the one hand and state bureaucrats, provincial and national politicians, and the local electorate on the other.[14] We may thus expect the differences in opportunities offered local élites to have wide implications not only for the 'style' of local politics, but for relations between local political élites and other local political forces, and most importantly citizens, bureaucrats, and interest groups.

The question of the opportunities for influencing policy available to local political élites is also important since it leads us to ask about the causes of diversity and in doing so raises fundamental issues about the character of political development within European nations. Almost unnoticed in the literature on state- and nation-building, local government has played a crucial role in the development of political systems, from its function as the major if not only provider of public services for many centuries, through to its pioneering role in urban development and the welfare state of more recent years.[15] Transformations within local government systems of different nations reflect an array of experiences central to the wider process of nation-building, such as the experience of absolutism, the industrial revolution, the extension of mass suffrage, and the expansion of the welfare state. In accounting for differences in approach to the basic ambiguity within local government, it is possible to identify wider features of the development of political systems.

Such broad and fundamental questions do not generally feature in comparative studies of local government, which tend towards description. In contrast to truly comparative analysis, which seeks to develop and test theoretical propositions on the basis of cross-national evidence, there is far more descriptive material offering valuable information about local government and issues of central–local relations in different nations. However, by its nature this falls short of coherent comparative analysis. There are some extremely useful compilations of empirical characteristics of local government in different nations which devote little space to exploring the causes and implications of these differences.[16] Brian Smith offers an excellent exploration of the meaning of decentralization, drawing on examples from a wide variety of different nations, but the aim of the empirical discussion is, as the author states in his preface, primarily descriptive: to illustrate a variety of forms in which decentralization can be found.[17] Some particular aspects of local government which involve central—local relations have been the focus for genuinely comparative research across many nations.[18] However, the systematic study of wider aspects of central—local relations has been generally confined to paired comparisons.[19] Perhaps the most recent comparative work involving a significant focus on the general features of central—local relations in more than two countries is Montagu Harris's 1949 *Comparative Local Government*, which offers comparative reflections on his earlier account *Local Government in Many Lands*.[20] In this book I seek to apply a broad theoretical framework to a larger number of nations than is usual among comparative studies of local government.

LEGAL AND POLITICAL LOCALISM

A comparative approach which examines the causes and consequences of diversity must start from a framework which identifies the most important dimensions of diversity from the plethora of observable differences between countries. One can, in fact, identify two broad ways in which local government politicians can influence local decisions, and these offer a basis for distinguishing between different countries.

Local political élites can influence public policy through using their constitutional or legal position at the head of a government organization and directing it according to their own priorities. They might, for example, raise revenues, allocate spending, decide how and where the money should be spent, set out conditions of service and behaviour for employees, and make a variety of decisions affecting the quality of the services they deliver. In contrast to this, local élites can also influence public policy in a very different way by using their political authority as democratically legitimate representatives of the locality, or a significant section of its population, to influence national decisions in so far as they affect the locality. This might involve, for example, getting special legislation to allow a public works project, acquiring permission to borrow money, or altering proposed national legislation affecting local government powers, duties, structure, or resources.

A similar distinction between two broad ways in which local government can influence governmental policy can be found in the work of the Austrian legal philosopher Hans Kelsen, who distinguishes, to use his terms, 'static' decentralization from 'dynamic' decentralization. Static decentralization refers to the degree to which 'norms' are uniform throughout the territory of the state, while dynamic decentralization refers to the degree to which the ability to make such norms is dispersed.[21]

The notion that the opportunities available to local political élites to shape public service provision on these two dimensions vary systematically from one country to the next was made explicit in W. J. M. Mackenzie's work. Mackenzie argued that 'in different countries there are varying degrees of integration between local government and central government on two scales, a legal scale and a political scale'.[22] The legal scale has to do with the scope for action by the local authority in its freedom to run and shape public services. Of course, such freedom and scope for action are not defined by law alone, as will be discussed later on. However, the adjective 'legal' is a convenient shorthand since it refers to the range of powers and the level of discretion in fulfilling these powers which are significantly shaped by formal legal provisions.

The political scale has to do with ensuring that local interests are represented at the national level. Mackenzie illustrates this by citing the 'locality rule' in US politics as a 'means of bringing the parish pump to the Capitol'. The British position in this respect contrasts with the experience of a country such as France. 'It is a commonplace that in Britain the "carpet bagger" has been a great figure in politics from the time of Elizabeth I: and that in many other countries there is (by contrast with this) a political "career" which leads from a local assembly to a regional assembly and from there to a national assembly.' The 'close' integration that exists between central and local politics may actually be more important, Mackenzie argues, for understanding the nature of central—local relations than an understanding of the legal powers of central and local government. This close political integration 'may mean that the localities move the centre or that the centre moves the localities: a looser relationship may mean that local authorities are free—or simply that they are disregarded'.[23]

Thus localism, referring to the opportunities for local political élites to shape public services, may be political or legal. Likewise political and legal centralism refer to the absence of such opportunities on Mackenzie's two separate scales. To understand the character of the constraints upon local government in terms of the opportunities for influencing public service provision in any one country requires a comparative analysis; we can only consider the distinctiveness of such opportunities by comparing different political systems. A comparative analysis not only allows us to understand better the distinctive characteristics of different nations, it also provides a basis for going on to analyse why nations should have developed different patterns of local influence.

THE STUDY

This study explores the opportunities available to local political élites to shape public services on the basis of these two scales, the political and the legal, in seven unitary nations in Europe. It continues along the path first embarked on by a group convened under the auspices of the European Consortium for Political Research which produced *Central and Local Government Relations: A Comparative Analysis of West European Unitary States.*[24] The reasons for selecting France, Britain, Italy, Spain, Norway, Denmark, and Sweden were largely tactical rather than theoretical. In the first place, unitary systems of government were selected since I wanted to explore theoretical explanations for the development of different patterns of central—local relations without the complicating factor of federalism and the large and diverse literature that it has generated. Second, these seven nations were chosen since they represent forms of local government which from casual knowledge appear to be rather different: Britain with its long tradition of local self-government, the Southern European nations of Italy and Spain apparently sharing with France a 'Napoleonic' heritage of local government, and the three Scandinavian countries generally assumed to have many common institutional structures and political processes. Third, since this started as a joint venture which relied upon collaborators from different nations drawing on existing research in the field, these seven countries were ones about which considerable research had been done and appeared likely to provide sufficient material for cross-national comparison. Although the study concentrates upon these unitary states, the applicability of its conclusions to a wider range of countries will be explored in the final chapter.

This study focuses upon local government understood as county, provincial, or municipal government. In Italy, France, and Spain there has been a rapid development of a regional level of government. While the importance of the development of regional government cannot be denied and while its impact will be discussed in later chapters, it is not a focus for this study for two main reasons. First, the functions of elected regional governments have been so far rather limited in two of the three countries. In France and Italy, the regions account for well below one-half of the level of spending of the communes (already low in international comparison—see Chapter 2). Moreover, much of this spending is passed on to other government bodies; the regional work-force in Italy is under one-fifth the size of the communal work-force, and in France the regional work-force is under one-tenth the size of the communal work-force. Certainly, a number of centrally operated controls over local governments were 'regionalized' in each of these three countries. This did not involve significant allocation of supervisory roles to regional governments controlled by elected representatives, but rather to regional control bodies and divisions of national ministries, above all finance ministries. Of course, all of this could change, and it is by no means certain that this limited executive role will persist, but at present regions in these countries place many fewer demands on public resources than traditional units of local government.

A second reason for concentrating upon counties and municipalities is that the process of regionalization is an uncertain one and it is too early to predict how it will progress. While its momentum appeared strong in the earlier stages of regionalization in the 1970s and 1980s, the reversals that it has suffered in France, Italy, and Spain show that it is not ineluctable. In France the regional reforms of the 1960s produced few basic changes in the relationship between central and local government;[25] the socialist regional reforms of the 1980s experienced some reversals with the 'amelioration' of decentralization offered by the centre-right majority after 1986. Moreover, the impact of the reforms of the 1980s in France remain a matter of debate: according to one perspective, tutelage has re-emerged, albeit in a slightly different guise, and the functional transfers of authority have involved little more than a transfer of fiscal responsibility.[26] In Italy Nanetti shows how regions have gone through a variety of phases with the more recent phases characterized by a strengthening of state intervention which has

served to counterbalance much of the earlier regional decentralization laws.[27] In Spain there is still some uncertainty as to the future
of the regions. Sancho, for example, links the development of
regions with the thrust towards economic growth. He asks, 'will
Spain centralize when prosperity returns?', and answers in the
affirmative.[28] None of this is to attempt to play down the
importance of regions. Rather, it is to point to their recent origin,
their somewhat erratic development, and the likely prematurity of
any contemporary verdict on their significance. The most that one
can say on the basis of contemporary evidence is that regions may
bring about radical transformations of the patterns of relations
between central and local governments in these countries.[29]
Alternatively, they may become a source of yet further players in a
game in which the rules change very little to accommodate them.
They may even become more or less peripheral institutions in the
pattern of territorial politics, in much the same way as did the
regions of Italy under the 1947 constitution or the regions of France
in the 1960 reforms until the more recent wave of reforms in both
countries. As Michael Keating suggests in his comparative study of
Italy, France, and Spain, 'despite the radical ambitions of some of its
supporters, the capacity of regional government to transform the
unitary European state has yet to be demonstrated';[30] they may just
end up with the status of a 'planning and administrative arm of the
central government'.[31] The early 1990s do not offer a vantage point
which allows us to predict the outcome with any clarity. The
purpose of this work is, however, to understand and explain broad
patterns of central–local relations rather than evaluate recent
change.

There are three main questions addressed in this book. First, do
political systems in fact differ from each other according to the
opportunities that they offer local élites to shape public services on
the basis of the two scales, the legal and the political? Right at the
outset it must be stressed that the two different scales cannot be
collapsed to form some overall conception of 'decentralization'. The
'decentralization' that exists within the Italian context is no less real
than that which exists in the British context: it is simply different.
The features of 'decentralization' that any one commentator is
likely to highlight or value might differ: in the nineteenth century a
number of continental commentators regarded England as providing a model to be envied or emulated. English local self-government

was largely based upon the freedom of local government to undertake a wide variety of public services without the obstrusive intervention of the centre; that is to say, it was the tradition of legal localism that was much admired.[32] Ashford's comparison of Britain and France expresses admiration for the French system: the political localism of France resulting from the fact that 'the subnational system is more important to the political system' gives it its 'suppleness and ingenuity'.[33] However, no such general evaluation combining some overall notion of decentralization will be offered in this book. The two scales are simply different. Moreover, the development of local government's relations with national government on the two different scales can be understood as results of rather distinctive political processes (see Chapter 5).

As one compares nations one inevitably, to use Sartori's words, climbs the ladder of abstraction.[34] A whole wealth of detail, of itself intrinsically interesting and important, must remain neglected in order to make cross-national comparisons. It might thus be objected that in reducing the pattern of central–local relations to two dimensions or scales one is reducing their richness and complexity. Rhodes[35] for example uses over thirty different variables and dimensions to describe and explain the development of central–local relationships in Britain, which, he suggests, have changed significantly every seven or eight years. It is not claimed that the framework based on legal and political scales of local influence says everything of interest about central–local relations in any one country. There are aspects of the relationship that are barely touched on, such as the precise programmatic objectives of national and local political actors or the variety of strategies that they may use in their relationship, the conflict that exists between authorities and the implications this has for central–local relations, or the relationship between national government, local government, and the 'para-state' sector.

What is claimed for this framework is far more modest: that these two dimensions of legal and political scales as defined here are two very significant ones which encapsulate many of the important distinctions between the nations of this study in respect of the relationship between central and local government. Moreover, they serve as a basis for exploring a comparative explanation of these major differences. Mackenzie's scales, as this book shows, make valid distinctions which can then be used to highlight issues and processes which would not be possible, or at least would be far more difficult, using concepts at a lower level of abstraction. The two scales will not help us understand why precisely the Greater London Council was abolished in the 1980s nor will it explain why the French local fiscal system was restructured in the way it was in the late 1970s. The scales do, however, allow us to point to and document the most important and striking contrasts in central—local relations and help us begin to explain these contrasts.

This analysis is based on the experience of the seven unitary states which were explored in an earlier edited work: Norway, Sweden, Denmark, Britain, France, Italy, and Spain. The following two chapters draw together the empirical material and present it in a comparative perspective. In the Northern European nations, Norway, Sweden, Denmark, and Britain, the scope for local influence on the legal scale is greater than in the Southern European nations due to the wider range of functions and the lower level of detailed central intervention in these countries (Chapter 2). In the Southern European nations of Italy, Spain, and France, the possibilities for influence on the political scale, through local influence at the centre, are greater than in the North (Chapter 3).

The second question addressed in this book concerns the impact of different opportunities for local influence on public policy. What difference does it make whether a governmental system has greater or lesser degrees of political or legal localism? This is a very difficult question, since the record of political science and organizational sociology in producing hard and convincing evidence relating differences in institutional patterns to policy outcomes is poor. However, as one reviewer of the earlier comparative work has suggested, it is something that needs to be explored.[36] A variety of possible impacts of differences along the political and legal scales of local self-government are investigated, ranging from the impact on the structure of power within the local authority to the ways in which such differences might affect the distribution of public resources. Of particular importance here is the impact of the two different scales on the relative position of local political élites, as opposed to professional and bureaucratic élites at the local level, within the local decision-making process (Chapter 4).

The third question is that concerning the causes of different patterns of centralism and localism. Chapter 5 explores a variety of possible explanations for the different patterns of legal and political centralism. None of these offers satisfactory accounts for the differences between the Northern and Southern European nations. Chapter 5 then goes on to set out a historical explanation for the differences between our seven nations, linking the development of local government and central—local relations with longer-term patterns of the evolution of governmental institutions, as well as with the development of mass political parties. Chapter 6 reviews the principal conclusions of the study and explores their implications for the future of local government and for countries other than those included in the analysis.

The Legal Scale

MEASURING FUNCTIONS AND DISCRETION

The opportunities for local political élites to shape the nature of public services are in part a reflection of their capacity to use their legal or constitutional position as democratically elected heads of organizations responsible for delivering these services. This legal scale along which opportunities for local influence can be assessed thus reflects, broadly speaking, the degree to which local government authorities have 'hands-on' control over the nature of state services within their locality. Of course, this raises the question of whether local political élites as opposed to, say, professional or administrative élites actually exercise this hands-on control. While this question will be discussed below (Chapter 4), the ability of local elected élites to shape the public services they deliver is in large part a function of the degree to which services are delegated to the local level and the nature of this delegation.

This legal scale is closely related to two of the major dimensions of central–local relations used in an earlier comparative work.[1] In this work were explored the variations in the *functions* performed by local governments in different systems—local governments provided many services in some systems and very few in others—and the *discretion* or freedom that local political actors had in making decisions about delivering these services. A local government system in which a wide range of functions is carried out at the local level, and in which local political and administrative élites have wide discretion in making decisions about those services, is one of legal localism. How do our seven countries vary along this legal scale? To answer this question one must first derive the criteria according to which legal centralism and localism might be evaluated.

The first part of this chapter discusses variations in legal localism and centralism from the perspective of the allocation of functions:

does local government have hands-on control over a wider range of functions in one country than in another? The second section explores a number of institutional indicators of legal localism from the perspective of the discretion that local government has in exercising these functions. The third section discusses the concept of discretion and sets out the criteria used to assess the degree to which each of the seven countries varies according to this dimension of legal localism.

LOCAL GOVERNMENT'S CONTRIBUTION TO NATIONAL PUBLIC POLICY

One way of answering the question of what local government does is to list all the activities that are undertaken by local government in the seven countries. Such an exercise is likely to be long, tedious, and, given the great variability of descriptions of services cross-nationally, fruitless.[2] The purpose of this discussion of the variability of functions is to establish whether local government does more in one country than in another. This can be done in two ways: first, by examining the level of public resources, expenditure, and manpower channelled through local government authorities and, second, through describing which of the major functions of local government are found in different countries. Each of these can be elaborated in turn.

The level of public spending which is accounted for by local government is notoriously difficult to gauge cross-nationally due to differences in accounting conventions; for example, how nationalized industries are included in accounts varies across nations. Moreover, definitions of public spending are influenced by the design of service delivery systems. For example, where health insurance is paid for on the basis of an insurance system reimbursing patients for medical charges, only the net cost of the insurance system may be counted as public expenditure, in contrast to a system where direct payment of medical practitioners will ensure that the gross costs of health care are counted.[3]

Nevertheless, it is possible to give an approximate account of the contribution of local government to the total levels of government expenditure in each of the seven countries (Table 2.1). Local government authorities characteristically have a relatively stronger

TABLE 2.1. *Local government expenditure and national expenditure, 1980s*

	Local spending as %			
	Total expenditure (capital and current)	Total current expenditure	Total capital expenditure	Total current minus transfers
Norway (1984)	33.0	35.8	60.1	32.5
Sweden (1985)	39.5	42.1	68.4	37.8
Denmark (1985)	50.9	54.2	47.5	34.1
Britain (1984)	24.6	26.8	55.4	25.5
France (1985)	11.9	12.8	65.4	13.7
Italy (1980)	9.2	10.6	66.5	9.6
Spain (1983)	8.5	9.7	15.2	9.9

Sources: Organization for Economic Co-operation and Development, *National Accounts of OECD Countries* (Paris: OECD, 1987). Local government finance figures for Italy are from the *Annuario Statistico Italiano*.

role in capital spending, that is, spending on building and equipment, than they have in current spending: with the exception of Spain, local governments account for between one-half and two-thirds of total public capital expenditure. Yet since capital spending also characteristically involves smaller amounts of money than current spending (i.e. spending on wages and running costs), the overall contribution of local government to public spending is closer to the level indicated by current rather than capital spending. On the basis of capital plus current spending, there is a clear distinction between the three Scandinavian countries on the one hand and France, Spain, and Italy on the other. In the former, local government spends between one-third and one-half of total public spending, in the latter local government spends around one-tenth (Table 2.1). The Danish figure is particularly high since it includes a large sum for transfer payments delivered, but not determined, by the local authority. If we exclude these, the British figures appear closer to the Scandinavian—seven percentage points behind the Danish but twelve percentage points above France and nearly three times as large as Spain and Italy. On the basis of spending data, local governments in Southern European nations do less than those in Scandinavia and Britain.

This distinction between the Northern and Southern European nations of this study is reinforced by the analysis of public employment figures for central and local government (Table 2.2). The comparison of public employment figures is, of course, hazardous since great efforts have to be made to make figures from different national sources comparable—a major research project in itself.[4] However, the available figures, while approximate, show great differences in the levels of public employment by local government as between the North European nations and France, Italy, and Spain.

The proportion of public employees in the local government service is largest in the Scandinavian countries, and lowest in France, Italy, and Spain, with Britain occupying an intermediate position in our sevenfold ranking.

There is a whole host of services, relatively minor in spending and manpower terms, which are delivered by local government authorities by most, if not all, nations in the study. These include refuse collection and disposal, building control, and abattoirs. In order to present which of the major local functions are carried out by local government authorities it is useful to concentrate upon twelve broad groupings of major services for which generally comparable data exist across different countries: education, culture, health, police, social welfare, public health, transport, housing, utilities and

TABLE 2.2. *Local public employment and the public sector*

(Local employment as percentage of public employment)

Norway	64
Denmark	57
Sweden	54
United Kingdom	39
Italy	12
Spain	10
France	10

Source: Rose *et al.*, *Public Employment in Western Nations;* Page and Goldsmith (eds.), *Central and Local Government,* 157.

trading, general administration, with a residual other category (Table 2.3). Of course, these groupings are to some extent defined by the conventions used by statisticians and accountants in compiling statistics, and the major discrepancies between categories, such as the inclusion in the Italian figures of street cleaning (*nettezza urbana*) with social welfare (*azioni ed interventi nel campo sociale*), have been flagged.

Table 2.3 shows the relative spending of local government in the seven countries. The table shows the substantial weight of education in all local budgets—the only item taking consistently over 10 per cent of local budgets. However, a comparison on this basis is somewhat misleading since the levels of spending on education in Spain, Italy, and France reflect a lower involvement in education by local authorities, with their most important responsibility being that of building and maintaining schools (a financial rather than a planning responsibility). In order to compensate for the different levels of local involvement in major services one can multiply the percentages in Table 2.3 by the proportion of total public spending taken up by local government in each of the four countries (Table 2.4), to give a rough approximation of the percentage of total public expenditure accounted for by local spending on different functional services. While this is a crude means of presenting local government's contribution to public policy delivery, it does allow us to distinguish between those countries in which local government has a smaller contribution to make under a particular functional heading than under another.

From Table 2.4 it can be seen that local spending on education accounts for between 7 and 10 per cent of total public spending in Scandinavia and Britain, but under 3 per cent in France, 2 per cent in Italy, and under 1 per cent in Spain. The Scandinavian countries have major responsibility for health services, but in England, Italy, France, and Spain public spending on health is not channelled in any substantial way through local authorities. England is alone in having major local police functions, although in the three Southern European nations rural police are a function of local government. England and Sweden have local governments with major (but not exclusive) housing responsibilities while the other countries (if we exclude France, since the *Habitations à loyer modéré* (HLM), the housing authorities, are not directly run by the municipalities) do not. In Denmark, the responsibility for a wide range of social

TABLE 2.3. *The percentage share of local services in the 1980s*

Service	Norway	Sweden	Denmark	Great Britain	Italy	France	Spain
Education	20.6	16.0	14.9	36.1	20.2	22.5	9.3
Culture	6.6	5.7	3.2	3.6	2.4	7.5	
Personal Health	30.3	20.6	17.3	—	0.0	7.0	6.7
Police	—	—	0.4	9.4	3.9	4.5	
Social welfare	13.7	16.0	46.9[a]	7.2	—[b]	7.8	
Public health	0.9	4.0	—[c]	3.1	30.2	—[d]	40.9
Transport/highways	3.5	3.9	0.0	7.0	12.7	4.4	25.7
Housing	0.2	5.4	1.1	17.2	0.9	20.0[e]	1.3
Utilities/trading	14.6	10.4	6.6	2.6	6.7	4.8	3.0
General Admin.	3.9	5.6	4.0	—	17.6	23.0	
Other	5.6	12.4	5.6	13.8	5.4	3.5	12.2
TOTAL	99.9	100.0	100.0	100.0	100.0	100.0	99.1

[a] Includes income transfers.
[b] Included with public health.
[c] Included with personal health.
[d] Included with health.
[e] Includes HLM.

Sources: As Table 2.1.

TABLE 2.4. *Percentage share of total public spending taken up by local government by service*

Service	Norway	Sweden	Denmark	Great Britain	Italy	France	Spain
Education	7.4	6.7	8.1	9.7	1.9	2.9	0.9
Culture	2.4	2.4	1.7	1.0	0.2	1.0	0.0
Personal Health	10.8	8.7	9.4	0.0	0.0	0.3	0.7
Police	0.0	0.0	0.2	2.5	0.4	0.6	0.0
Social welfare	4.9	6.7	25.4[a]	1.9	—[b]	1.0	0.0
Public health	0.3	1.7	—[c]	0.8	2.9	—[d]	4.0
Transport/highways	1.3	1.6	0.0	1.9	1.2	0.6	2.5
Housing	0.1	2.3	0.6	4.6	0.1	2.6[e]	0.1
Utilities/trading	5.2	4.3	3.6	0.7	0.6	0.6	0.3
General Admin.	1.4	2.3	2.2	0.0	1.7	2.9	0.0
Other	2.0	5.2	3.0	3.7	0.5	0.4	1.2
TOTAL	35.8	41.9	54.2	26.8	9.5	12.9	9.7

[a] Includes income transfers.
[b] Included with personal health.
[c] Included with public health.
[d] Included with health.
[e] Includes HLM.

Sources: As Table 2.1.

benefits accounts for the high levels of social spending by local authorities.

Tables 2.1–2.4 show that local government in France, Italy, and Spain does less than its counterpart in Scandinavia and Britain. Moreover, the precise allocation of functions varies. Local authorities in France and Italy have some responsibilities in most major areas of government activity. However, they have few areas of competence in which they can provide the service without the collaboration of other public authorities; they play a part in the delivery of education, in economic regeneration, even in the running of public hospitals. However, the involvement is not that of actually running the service. In health in Italy and France the involvement is through affiliation to the governing boards of public hospitals; in Italy it is through representation on the *Unità Sanitari Locali*, the local health authorities. In short, though local government in Italy and France is involved with lots of services, it has direct responsibility for providing only a few.

In terms of allocation of functions then, there appears, not surprisingly, a reasonably clear divide between the Northern European nations and the Southern European. With the notable exception of housing, Scandinavian local governments are involved in many of the most important public services in terms of cost. In France and Spain these services are predominantly delivered through national or territorial organizations distinct from local government despite some connections between them such as the formal position of French mayors on local housing organizations (HLM) and publicly run hospitals. Local government in Britain makes a more modest contribution to public service delivery than in Scandinavian countries, largely because of the removal of health from local authority control following the creation of the National Health Service after the Second World War. Nevertheless, we can still include this as a country in which the possibilities for local influence through the legal dimension, as far as the range of functions given to local governments is concerned, are strong.

LOCAL GOVERNMENT DISCRETION

The concept of discretion appears simple: in using it to look at legal localism we are simply asking how much freedom local governments have to deliver those services for which they have formal executive responsibility. Yet it is a concept which is fraught with problems when one tries to apply it to local government. Discretion is a term that can be applied to individuals working within a municipality—a health inspector has discretion concerning how public health laws are to be interpreted, for example—or to groups—for example, a party committee in a municipality may have discretion to change standing orders—or to the municipality as a whole—it is for the municipality to decide how to allocate resources between a range of services. It can be applied to matters great and small: it can refer to the discretion of a garbage collector to refuse to pick up large items of waste or to the discretion of a municipality to fix tax levels without centrally imposed limits.

In this book discretion is understood to refer to the ability of the municipality as a collectivity to make decisions without the intervention of central government. To what extent are authorities free to make decisions about the services they provide?

While it is possible to use readily available indicators of spending and manpower to indicate differences in the range of functional responsibilities and distinguish between countries which are legally localist and centralist on this dimension, it is not possible to find such indicators of discretion. Although scholars such as Ashford have sought to impute levels of 'decentralization' from spending and central government grant data, the equation of greater decentralization with larger range of functions or smaller percentages of central government grants is clearly misleading.[5] The fact that services were taken away from British local authorities in 1948 and again in 1972 does not necessarily mean that the discretion of local government in providing its remaining services was affected. Moreover, the frequently cited case of the Netherlands, where local authorities are almost entirely dependent upon central grants yet appear to enjoy a substantial degree of discretion, remains a valid counter to the suggestion that local discretion is inversely related to the dependence of local governments on central grants.[6] There is no simple quantitative measure of local discretion. However, the frameworks for national government intervention in local government affairs do seem to vary. Do any of the distinctions between types of frameworks offer greater opportunities for local influence on public policies through this component of the legal dimension of localism?

One commonly used means of distinguishing between the frameworks of central intervention in local decisions is based on the different types of institutional mechanism involved in central–local relations. There is, of course, a variety of possible institutional indicators of discretion. Here the discussion will be confined to the three that feature most prominently in the literature on central–local relations in order to show the limitations of such an approach. The three indicators are: the general legal framework of local government, the arrangements for local authority supervision by the centre, and the intergovernmental grant structure.

THE GENERAL LEGAL FRAMEWORK

By definition, as we have observed, the constitutional status of local government is subordinate. However, in some constitutional systems local government appears to be given higher status than in others. Brian Smith suggests, for example, 'it seems reasonable to assume that it is more rather than less decentralized to give area governments the statutory right to do whatever they judge is in the best interests of their areas . . . rather than be required to find statutory confirmation for the right to take a decision'.[7] Here he is referring to the distinction between constitutional systems in which local government is assumed to have a general set of competences to deliver services unless otherwise specified by legislation and those in which a local government must have formal statutory power to undertake each and every one of its services. This latter type of system is usually referred to as one dominated by the principle of *ultra vires*. Therefore one might infer that presumed omnicompetence offers greater scope for influence by local political and administrative élites than are available in a system where the *ultra vires* rule applies.

As will be discussed below, all local government authorities are required to provide some services by law. However, Britain is the only one of the seven in this study to which the doctrine of *ultra vires* applies. The doctrine is somewhat weakened by the 'local interest' spending provisions of local government legislation since the nineteenth century. In article 137 of the 1972 Local Government Act, local governments in England and Wales are allowed to spend a defined small sum (the equivalent of 2 per cent of the notional local taxable property value) on matters 'in the interests of their area, or any part of it, or all or some of its inhabitants'; since that time the law has been modified to exclude economic development from the 'local interest' provision, and to adapt it to the new per capita local tax or community charge.[8]

In the other six nations local government is assumed to have a general competence, although this is more narrowly circumscribed in France, Spain, and Italy. In France, chapter three of the *Code municipal* sets out the principle of general competence for communes providing generally for the 'affaires de la commune' and competence for 'Tous les objets d'interêt locale' ('all matters of local interest').[9] It proceeds, however, to limit these through specifying those types of action that are not permitted without explicit state authorization: the incurring of loans or anything that interferes with the principle of 'libéralité' (or market competition). In Italy state supervision is likewise the major qualification to the principle of omnicompetence. Local authorities are given power to carry out all functions of 'local interest' as long as they are not in the sphere of competence of other public authorities.[10] In Spain, local government has long held general powers to intervene in 'all matters relating to local interests', a position confirmed by the 1985 *Ley de bases de régimen local* (Local Government Act), and the same act provides for the possible reduction of spheres of competence by provincial and regional bodies in the future.[11]

The omnicompetence of local government seems to have fewer conditions attached to it in the Scandinavian nations. All three are given competence to undertake any activity unless prescribed by law or falling within the province of other public authorities.[12] In Sweden there had been a tradition of limiting omnicompetence through specifying that the 'local interest' activities should be consistent with 'good order and economy'. This was replaced in 1948 by a more general provision that the local government could make provision for 'its affairs'. Nevertheless, the system of administrative justice in Sweden means that citizens can seek to challenge the right of local government authorities to undertake activities which violate the principle of the local interest, equal treatment of citizens, the notion that local should be non-profitable and non-speculative, according to the *kommunalbesvär*—challenges by citizens through the courts of the legality of local government actions. Such limitations are largely absent in the other two

Scandinavian nations. As Herlitz points out, in Denmark and Norway 'the powers that the municipality may exercise without the support of specific statutes have—though they are certainly limited—never been defined by statute as in Sweden'.[13]

In Britain, the doctrine of *ultra vires* means that local authorities may be challenged in the courts unless their actions can be justified by a specific statute. As Finer put it: 'The English system is to impose upon the municipalities the burden of proof that powers should be granted to them.'[14] There have been attempts, mainly by Labour MPs in the first half of the twentieth century, to introduce local government enabling bills extending the principle of omnicompetence (or near-omnicompetence) to Britain, but broad grants of powers were largely confined to enabling a wide range of actions in pursuit of specific services, above all public health (see the Public Health Acts 1890, 1907, and 1925, for example).

In sum, whatever the fine distinctions that may be drawn between different forms of grant of omnicompetence, Britain stands as the odd-man-out among our seven nations. However, the significance of this distinction between omnicompetence and *ultra vires* can be called into question. Since these general principles coexist with other firmer and more specific statutory controls, it is doubtful that they have any major effect on the opportunities for local political and administrative élites to shape public policies. In short, there is little reason to believe that constitutional guarantees of omnicompetence have any real meaning in practice.[15]

Omnicompetence implies high levels of discretion only in the absence of other forms of regulation which compel local governments to provide a service. If most major services are covered by statutes mandating services on local governments, local governments are then not effectively free to decide which services they should provide. If they are not free to decide which services they provide then the distinction between systems of *ultra vires* and omnicompetence assumes far less importance than a priori reasoning would suggest.

In all seven countries there is a more or less explicit distinction between obligatory and permitted functions. In the mainstream Civil Law countries of France, Spain, and Italy this distinction is formally enshrined in administrative law. The Italian system distinguishes between *funzione obbligatore* and *funzione facoltative* and the French between *services obligatoires* and *services facultatifs*.

In Spain, the 1985 Local Government Law distinguishes between the statutory functions of local government and those services which they are permitted to carry out to complement the provision offered by other levels of government. In Britain and Scandinavia, which are outside the mainstream Civil Law tradition, the services are not generally identified within a codified law, but rather there exists functional legislation which obliges local governments to undertake major tasks. In Britain and Scandinavia the distinction between different types of service (mandated or permitted) is one that can only really be found in individual laws. Using the categories of major public services we can see the degree to which services are mandated in the seven countries. Of course, such an examination cannot fully incorporate the diversity of the sets of discrete activities that go to make up some of the broad aggregates used here to describe major services. For example, social services may involve a mix of social work counselling, the assumption of parental rights in child care as well as cash assistance. However, on the basis of an examination of constitutional and legal texts as well as the contributions to our earlier volume, the functions of local government can be classified according to whether local authorities are mandated to provide them or whether they are merely permitted to do so (Table 2.5).

Two things must be borne in mind when interpreting Table 2.5. First, the precise obligations of local government in any particular policy area are defined by a vast array of legislation and court decisions; most services include both mandatory and permitted aspects to them, and the table offers a broad outline based on administrative codes and major legislation. Second, in some countries, notably the three Southern European ones, formal requirements as to the type of services that must be provided are poor guides to the range of services that are actually provided: many smaller communes in Italy, Spain, and France might, in fact, provide few services, even of the mandated kind.[16]

Nevertheless Table 2.5 shows a remarkable degree of continuity cross-nationally. The costlier services such as highways, education, social assistance, and personal health are mandated where there is a strong local government contribution to these services. The major exception to this general rule of the costlier services being mandated is in Britain, where housing and social services are both major functions provided on the basis of largely permissive legislation.

TABLE 2.5. *Mandated and permitted services*

	Norway	Sweden	Denmark	Great Britain	Italy	France	Spain
Housing	P	M	P	P[a]	M	n/a[b]	m
Education	M	M	M	M	p	m	p
Personal Health	M	M	M	n/a	M	m	p
Public health	M	M	M	P[c]	M	M	M
Social welfare	M	M	M	M	m	P	m
Police	n/a	M	n/a	M	P	m	m
Transport	P	P	P	P	P	p	M
Highways	M	M	M	M	M	M	m
Culture	P	P	P	P[d]	P	P	p
Utilities/trading	P	P	P	P	P	P	P

Note: P = permitted; M = mandated. Lower case used where local government has a relatively minor role in the service.

[a] Some homelessness mandates.
[b] HLM not included.
[c] Child care mandated.
[d] Libraries mandated.

Utilities and other marketed goods and services, including here passenger transport, are typically permitted rather than mandated. Apart from these, culture is the only other significant type of permitted function, and even in France where the relative import-ance of this function is greatest, it only accounts for one-fifteenth of local government spending. The bulk of local government expendi-ture in all countries appears to be directed towards the provision of mandated services, with permitted services taking up smaller portions of local spending.

Precisely why some services seem to be more likely to be the subject of mandatory legislation in most countries and others do not is open to a variety of possible explanations. The fact that costly services tend to be mandated may indicate central government's concern to exert greater control where the effects of local decisions on public finances are stronger and more immediate. Alternatively, mandates might be related to the degree of potential 'spillover' effects, that is to say the extent to which non-provision of a service in one locality is likely to affect citizens outside that locality. Another possibility is that mandates are linked to the political sensitivity of the service, or even to some other intrinsic feature of the service. For example, where the relevant clientele for a service can be specified, as in the case of school education, mandates may be more appropriate than in cases such as personal social services where the clientele cannot be identified in general or abstract regulations.

Whatever the reasons for the fact that there are cross-national similarities between what is mandated and what is permitted, the main conclusion to be drawn from such similarities is that the *ultra vires* principle has little real effect in terms of increasing the discretion of local political and administrative élites and on the legal dimension of localism. The major local services are mandated. If the omnicompetence principle means that local authorities have greater discretion because they can choose to provide services or not, then this choice does not exist for major services. Indeed, as far as the more expensive services are concerned Britain, with its *ultra vires* rule, has greater formal discretion to decide not to provide housing and social services, although no British local authority avails itself of such untested rights. Thus the distinction between omnicompetence and *ultra vires* provisions cannot be used to distinguish Britain from other countries in establishing the opportunities for local influence on public policy. For the purposes of any comparative evaluation of broad outlines of local government practice such a distinction is meaningless.

The prefectoral system has often been assumed to serve as the basis for centralization in countries such as France and Italy. A prefect is a central state official whose duties include the supervision of local government actions. The central state has a representative locally whose responsibilities include scrutinizing local government actions and resolutions for legality, and vetoing or approving them. The institution is likely to lead to greater central control, and therefore less local discretion. In so far as this limits the opportunities for local influence, it can be taken as an indicator of legal centralism. Despite the addition of a few reservations, such as the fact that prefects may to some degree serve as the representatives of the locality in the centre, the use of a prefectoral system as a factor to distinguish between degrees of decentralization is suggested by Smith: 'A prefectoral system will be assumed to reduce decentralisation since it adds to the degree of central control over both the field agents of functional departments and over any devolved institutions'.[17]

To what extent does the organization of central government in a prefectoral system necessarily limit the scope for local influence? There are, of course, different types of prefectoral systems which can be subdivided to such a degree that each country is unique.[18] However, broadly conceived, there are two major features of a prefectoral system: first, that there is a central official with responsibility for the local authorities of a defined area; second, that these responsibilities are relatively extensive, that is to say, they are not confined to one particular service, as is the case with central government inspectors, or one aspect of local administration, as is the case with centrally appointed auditors.

In formal terms, only Britain has avoided the institution of the prefect in recent history; there is no equivalent to the prefects of Italy and France or the civil governors in Spain. Scandinavian local government also knows the institution of the prefect through the county governors—*fylkesmann* in Norway, the *amtmand* in Denmark, and the *landshövding* in Sweden. The fact that the

Scandinavian countries also share a prefectoral system questions the assumption that French centralization, at least, is underpinned by the mere existence of prefects.

There are three possible interpretations that might be placed on this. The first is that the discretion allowed Scandinavian local governments is as much or little as allowed to French, Italian, and Spanish. The second is that such a conclusion is mistaken because Scandinavian prefects are fundamentally different from those of France, Spain, and Italy. They have far less power and instead of seeing themselves as representatives of the centre imposing discipline on the locality, see themselves as representatives of the localities in national arenas of decision-making.[19] There is unlikely to be much mileage in this argument. Certainly there are differences in the institution of the prefect or governor. For example, the prefect of a French *département* before the 1980s was likely to occupy that post for a relatively short period as part of the prefectoral corps, and thus have stronger national allegiances than the Scandinavian county governors appointed more or less for life after a career elsewhere. However, this should not be overstressed since a variety of classical studies of the institution in France and Italy has shown the importance of prefects promoting local interests to the advancement of their national careers.[20] If one starts to distinguish levels of discretion, or rather opportunities for local influence on locally delivered policies, by the powers that prefects or governors have, then one is moving away from the principle that it is the institution of the prefect that shapes local government discretion to the more general question of the range of powers of central government and its officials.

A third possibility seems more plausible: that the institution of the governor itself makes little overall difference to the discretion of local government in the political system. Fried's brief examination of the Italian prefect in comparative perspective argues that a prefectoral system does not necessarily produce greater centralization than other forms of central state organization, although historically it may have been designed to do so: 'The drive for greater local self-government has brought in its train a demand for the abolition of the prefectoral system—despite the fact that a prefectoral system is not necessarily tied to any particular level of centralization.'[21]

Chapman developed a similar argument somewhat earlier on the basis of a wider comparison. The alternative to prefectoral systems of supervision in unitary states is some form of supervision through central ministries themselves, whether through their local or regional offices or national headquarters. This suggests that the major difference between prefectoral and non-prefectoral systems is that the supervision in the one is supposed to be concentrated in the hands of a single authority based in close physical proximity to the local government authority, while in the other supervision is dispersed among different functional organizations of ministries without those necessarily being located in close physical proximity to the local government for which they are responsible. Since the defining characteristic of discretion is that local authorities can engage in activities with relatively less interference by central government than in systems where there is less discretion for local governments, there is no real reason to assume that spatial proximity of national supervisory officials to local government authorities should dispose central government to become more involved than it would be under a system in which supervision is spread throughout a variety of national bodies. Neither can it be assumed that the general supervisory competences of the prefect or governor involve greater overall intervention than the specific supervisory competences of diverse sections within the national or regional headquarters of ministries. As Chapman put it:

[One] justification for the prefect-governor is that decisions and activities of local authorities can be controlled locally, and not by remote control by central officials unaware of local circumstances and sentiments. It may be that Britain has developed into such a highly centralised state through lack of such an office. In the absence of a local organ of tested competence in which the central government has full confidence, control is inevitably concentrated in the ministries. . . . [There is] no way of measuring the compensatory elements of democracy and self-government. But anyone who has examined the work of the Swedish governors or Dutch commissioners is unlikely to be impressed by the view that these offices are harmful to local self-government.[22]

This also suggests that any refinement of different types of prefectoral system is unlikely to be fruitful.[23] If central control and limitation of discretion is exerted outside the prefectoral systems then there is no reason to assume that concentration on the prefectoral system alone will produce any satisfactory distinction between political systems. Moreover, as some commentators have observed, even where the institution of the prefect has been abolished or substantially modified, old patterns limiting local discretion can persist relatively unchanged.[24] There is, then, little real sense in pursuing the mere existence of a prefectoral system as a means of distinguishing between patterns of discretion in local government. As will be discussed below, the importance attached to the institution of the prefect among scholars of France, and to a lesser extent Italy and Spain, compared with the institution of governors in Scandinavia is more likely to reflect the pivotal role of prefects in the wider context of national–local relations than the simple existence of the prefect on its own. Of course, the powers of the prefects differ between countries, most obviously between the Southern European nations and Scandinavia but also among the Southern European nations themselves. However, to consider this institution in isolation as a means of assessing the opportunities it offers local political élites to shape the policies they deliver would be misleading since there is no reason to assume that what is done by one prefect could not be done, possibly even more effectively, by officials from national ministries.

FISCAL SYSTEMS

Systems of local finance are the most intensively studied aspects of local government cross-nationally. One method of assessing the discretion of local government, the degree to which its local élites can shape local services, is to look at the degree to which it can raise revenue locally—how far is local government free to set taxation levels?

In six of the seven countries the discretion to fix taxation rates locally has been subject to formal constraint at least at some point since the onset of fiscal stringency in the 1970s. The extent of the limitations, that is to say whether they are across the board limits, as found in Norway, or limits tailored to restrain the fiscal decisions of a few individual councils, as in Britain, varies. The circumstances under which the limitations have been brought in also vary, from occasional negotiated agreements, as in Sweden, to trade-offs in return for writing off debts, as in Italy. Given that sources of tax income are multiple, central restrictions affect some sources but not others, as in Spain, or affect the ratio of revenue from one tax to another, as in France. Only Denmark has not had firm limits imposed on local revenue raising at some point in the past fifteen years, and even here voluntary agreements between the associations and national government have served to place non-statutory limits on local fiscal decisions to reduce real growth in spending.

Tax structures and tax limitations are undoubtedly important constraints on local government decisions. Yet it is not possible to derive any a priori measure or criterion that determines whether one taxation system offers greater discretion than others. Revenue raising is bounded by a whole host of constraints; while a British local authority might fear the central imposition of an upper limit on its revenue following an 'excessive' rate (or now, community charge) increase, a Spanish local authority, in principle free to raise whatever level of taxation it likes, is constrained by the fact that its surcharge on the national income tax is massively unpopular and consequently has been very difficult to levy. Such constraints, in large part created by the legal framework of local taxation, are simply different. While comparative analyses have successfully shown the impact of taxation structures on the degree of fiscal stress, it is harder to relate taxation systems and limitations on local revenue raising to overall levels of local discretion.[25]

Grant structures are another intensively studied aspect of central–local relations. It has often been assumed that different grant types are associated with different degrees of local autonomy or discretion. The first possible measure of centralization introduced through dependence on grants is based on the assumption 'he who pays the piper calls the tune'. As Smith points out, this is 'such a widespread view that there is no need to elaborate on it here'.[26] The levels of local government dependence on central grants are presented in Table 2.6. From Table 2.6 it can be seen that in Britain and Italy around one-half of local income comes from central government grants; in France, Norway, and Spain this figure is around one-third, and in Sweden and Denmark around one-quarter.

Yet none of the available research conducted either within nations or cross-nationally supports the assumption that the level of grant dependence actually shapes the potential or actual control that central agencies may exert over the local government authorities. While this is not to suggest that grants are unimportant as tools in shaping the relationship between central and local government, the

TABLE 2.6. *Government grants: total and specific, mid 1980s*

	% expenditure financed by grants	Specific grants as % of total
France	36	15
Britain	44	20
Sweden	25	21
Norway	32	27
Denmark	27	23
Spain	36	90
Italy	53	n/a

Sources: Mouritzen and Nielsen, *Handbook of Comparative Urban Fiscal Data*; for Spain: R. J. Bennett, 'Tax Assignment in Multi-Level Systems of Government', *Environment and Planning C: Government and Policy*, 5 (1987), 267–85.

scope that they offer for central influence is unrelated to the level of grant dependence. The evidence from the United States and Britain suggests that in the United States one of the major roles played by grants is that they provide a forum for federal, state, and local administrators to talk about common service provision issues rather than providing a powerful means of federal supervision of state and local policy delivery.[27] This major role of grants does not vary directly in proportion to grant dependence. There is similarly no reason in unitary states to assume that, say, an extra 10 per cent dependence on grants in one country compared with another means a corresponding increase in the level of central control.

Another means of assessing local discretion in the grant system is through the structure of grant. We might expect that a general grant, unhypothecated to any particular service, is likely to offer greater discretion to local authorities than specific or categorical grants made to support specific local services—frequently with strings attached relating to the way the service should be provided. According to this logic, there would be greater discretion to be found among Swedish, French, and British local authorities than Danish, Norwegian, and, above all, Spanish (Table 2.6). However, comparative analysis has shown this to be a flawed assumption on two grounds. First, it is more accurate to argue that broader conditions of central–local government relationships shape the grant structure than vice versa.[28] The specific grants in Britain persisted long after they had ceased to have any measurable impact on the nature and level of services which they aided, and the move towards block grant reflected less a desire to offer greater freedom to local authorities than a wish by the Treasury to limit the amount of grant received by local authorities. Second, although specific grants serve to skew local spending priorities by making subsidized services relatively cheaper than others, this can scarcely be termed a limitation of local discretion on its own. In fact, the major limitations to local decision-making that result from specific grants in the United States, where they are a means of making up for the 'constitutional deficit' of the federal government through its incapacity to make direct federal regulations for state and local services, come from the strings or conditions that may be attached to such grants. Since such strings are not the only major source of national government influence on local government in unitary states, they are not particularly important. After all, if central government wishes to require uniform or common standards or procedures for service provision it can make regulations or laws irrespective of the structure or level of central government grants.

ASSESSING LEGAL LOCALISM

None of these three broad institutional measures of local discretion suggests great differences between nations in terms of the opportunities they present to local political élites to shape public services. The association of these indicators with levels of local discretion and decentralization does not stand up to cross-national comparison. Ultimately, discretion is likely to vary from time to time, place to place, and issue to issue within a nation. If there are salient institutional factors that produce systemic differences in levels of discretion they must be sought elsewhere. In order to explore variations in the degree to which different systems offer local élites greater opportunities to shape the services for which they are responsible we need to explore the concept of discretion and the valid role for a comparative analysis in assessing it.

The concept of discretion refers, as Dworkin suggests, to the scope for free action bounded by constraint.[29] He graphically suggests the analogy of discretion as the centre of a doughnut. The constraints that emerge from the legal system derive, of course, from constitutional norms, statutes, and administrative regulations of many kinds. Individually these legal documents are quite tangible: they can be touched, seen, read, and commented upon. They can form the basis of court action. Yet collectively they cannot be used to compare levels of discretion. First, the nature of legal constraints and therefore of discretion (i.e. the space not covered by legal constraints) cannot be defined simply by a textual analysis of statutes. The impact of statutes can only be evaluated on the basis of how they are interpreted by, for example, courts and auditors as well as local government politicians and officials, and this cannot be predicted or deduced on the basis of mere inspection of the text. Second, the mass of legal arrangements for even the major local services is so complex that to list them would be an impossible task: a huge variety of different aspects of particular services could be isolated (e.g. teacher recruitment, teacher training, school curriculum, curriculum for teacher training, timetabling, to mention a few out of possibly hundreds of areas in education alone). Third, even if such a task were attempted it would most likely be out of date before it was completed since the statutory arrangements for local services change with each new law passed which touches however tangentially on local services.[30] Fourth, even if one drew up such a list of statutory constraints, to try to aggregate these upwards to some sort of generalization about which countries have the most limiting constraints across a range of services would be at best impressionistic and at worst misleading. There is no common measure according to which, for example, the constraint on local authorities in Britain mandating them to sell council housing can be compared with the legal requirement that French communes divert the roads they build around buildings of major historical interest.

To engage in comparative analysis cannot be taken as licence to indulge in unsubstantiated generalization. Its purpose in this context is to identify important dimensions which underly the differences in the nature of discretion. Clearly any attempt to base such an examination upon detailed descriptions of individual forms of regulation is likely to be fruitless. However, it is possible to point to important differences in the way in which the boundaries of local government discretion, and hence legal regulation, are established, and it is these that allow us to distinguish between localism and centralism in terms of the degree of discretion that exists in each country.

There appear to be two broad methods of central government legal regulation of local government authorities: one in which central government involvement in detailed issues of local decisions is built into the form of regulation (administrative regulation) and one in which such detailed involvement is minimized (statutory regulation).[31] From the perspective of the centre, statutory regulation can be described as a method of 'remote control'; once the laws have been passed, local authorities can do as they please as long as their actions are within the law, with the only real form of central control consisting of quasi-judicial interpretation of legality through, above all, courts and auditors. This contrasts with administrative regulation under which the legality of local government actions is defined through the individual decisions of governmental officials themselves, with administrative approval of a legally binding nature being required in advance of actions of the local government (a priori control or approval) in addition to the quasi-judicial a posteriori validation found under statutory regulation. Administrative regulation is far from remote control since it involves the granting of state approval to local actions on a routine basis and therefore involves central government in details of local government decision-making. Administrative supervision is associated with prefectoral systems by virtue of the fact that prefects were, traditionally, at the heart of this system of central influence in countries such as France and Italy. However, it would be mistaken to associate this form of supervision simply with the prefect or even a strong prefect since it has become increasingly exercised by other ministries, above all the ministry of finance. In his comment on the decentralization measures in France, Mény writes that

On the suppression of the preliminary supervision, the Deferre law completes a development that began in 1959 and continued during the 1970s; that is, the reform consigns to oblivion an anarchic supervisory system that had become pointless. It is, for instance, hardly any use to check administrative financial measures for their legality when it is well known that in most municipalities they have been prepared by the field services of the government itself. The crucial question in recent years has not been supervision by the prefectures, but supervision by the Ministry of Public Works or the Treasury.[32]

What is important here is the general nature of the system of administrative control, which appears specific to the southern nations in this study, as opposed to the existence of a prefect-like figure, which is not.

These two types of supervision underly the distinctions between the countries' traditional patterns of central–local relations that existed until the 1970s at least. Moreover, these patterns do not appear to have altered radically despite the development of regional governmental structures in France, Italy, and Spain. There are two main features of the central–local relationship in Southern European nations which serve to organize central intervention into the details of local government policy-making.

The first feature of central–local relations distinguishing between those nations in which detailed intervention is built into the framework of local government concerns the allocation of functions. Local government authorities in Southern Europe do not have sole competence for the delivery of many of their major services. A prime example of this can be found in education. Unlike the Scandinavian and British cases, where most aspects of the detailed running of schools are a formal responsibility of local government, central and local government both have an important role to play in the day-to-day running of schools. The local role is distinctly a junior one, but its significance for local government finances is quite large (Table 2.3). Central government in the Southern European nations is responsible for planning schools, curriculums, training teachers, and paying teachers. This gives the centre the ability to direct, or at least have the dominant say in, the types of capital projects for schools. Such a directive capacity on the part of the central government extends to most of the obligatory functions of local government.

Moreover, the directive ability of central government in mandated services in Southern Europe highlights a salient distinction between the notions of 'mandated' and 'permitted' services as they apply to Northern and Southern Europe. In Britain and the three Scandinavian countries a mandated service is one which national law requires local authorities to carry out—a mandated service is one for which local government must make some sort of provision. In Southern European nations a mandated function is one in which the locality may act as an agent for central government bodies; in France obligatory services are described as obligatory expenditures.

Central involvement in these expenditures is usually very strong. Of course, such services are found in Britain and Scandinavia in the case of some transfer payments (e.g. income maintenance in Scandinavia and mandatory student grants in Britain). However, with the exception of social security payments in Denmark, most of the major services in these northern nations are not subject to such routine directive involvement by central state authorities as is found in the case of the obligatory services of the Southern European nations.

The second feature of central–local relations distinguishing between those nations in which detailed intervention is built into the framework of local government concerns the approval of details of local government decisions. Scrutiny of the budget for legality by either state officials or semi-independent auditors exists in all four Northern European countries, yet the controls exercised by the county governors in Scandinavia have become largely *post hoc* and concerned with broader questions of legality rather than with details of budgets. The Swedish County Administrative Board, headed by a county governor, a central government appointee (usually an ex-civil servant or Cabinet minister with a local connection in the county) is the representative of the central state. Its primary responsibilities are as a judicial and planning body. It supervises and inspects, among other things, the public health services of municipalities, and is the tribunal of first instance for formal citizen complaints against municipal decisions (*kommunalbesvär*). Its financial responsibilities are primarily those of tax assessment and collection, and not the supervision of the budget.

In Norway and Denmark the county governor, the *fylkesman* or *amtmand*, has traditionally been more powerful than the Swedish counterpart and, especially in Norway, remains so. Yet the emphasis of the work of the county governors in both countries is on securing conformity with general legal provisions, above all the requirement that the budgets are likely to balance. The reforms of local government in the 1960s and 1970s in Norway and Denmark, as well as Sweden, emphasized the planning function of state supervision of municipalities and counties.[33] The dominant concern in the transition from dozens of specific grants to a simplified (four-)block grant system in Norway was that of retaining general financial control while giving up detailed involvement in negotiating and allocating the 180 specific grants to local authorities.

In Denmark, Norway, and Sweden the centre does have some administrative control, above all approval of budgets in Norway and Denmark, yet the emphasis of control appears to have shifted under the post-war reorganizations to broader statutory forms aimed at influencing wider issues of legality and planning strategy rather than individual decisions. As Bogason argues

Central government changed its role from one that was primarily supervisory to one that is largely advisory . . . but continues to keep an eye on variations among localities and attempts to influence those local governments that are thought to deviate more from the norm than national politicians or influential professionals find acceptable. Central government supervision, then, has to a large extent changed from control over the legality of decisions and/or their approval, to a review of the adequacy of local initiatives and/or bargaining over the content of plans. Of course, heated controversies can still occur over the legality of specific decisions.[34]

In France, Spain, and Italy a priori supervision has traditionally been a function of the prefect. After the regional reforms of the 1970 in Italy and the 1980s in France and Spain these supervisory functions have passed on to a variety of regional bodies: the regional courts of accounts in France, to the regional offices of the ministry of finance in Spain and Italy. It must be stressed that though the controls over municipalities are regional in location, they are distinct from, and not subject to, the elected regional level of government.

Even in areas in which a priori central approval is required in the Northern European nations, as in the case of capital spending approval in Britain, central state officials have generally exerted less detailed scrutiny of local authority proposals. While central state approval is required in Britain and Scandinavia, such approval generally comes after the details of capital programmes have been worked out at the local level. In France and Italy, major investment programmes are likely to have involved cntral state officials at a much earlier stage in drawing up the municipal capital project. Such was the central involvement in details that standardized designs for things such as swimming pools, modelled on those known to have received central approval in the past, were fairly commonplace in the smaller French localities unable to devote resources to more innovatory projects.

This has not been changed substantively by the reforms of the

1970s and 1980s in the Southern European nations. Although frequently hailed as a major move towards decentralization, the changes have probably affected the communes least. The direct involvement of the prefect in local government decisions, according to which the prefect passes judgement on the legality of budgets and resolutions, has been replaced by central government approval at the regional level through the regional committees of control in Italy and the regional courts, above all the regional courts of accounts, in France. Moreover, in Italy and France the prefect still retains an important role as an intermediary between the communes and the regional supervisory bodies, using the sanction of referring decisions to these regional bodies as a means of shaping local decisions. In Spain, the return to democracy brought about the demise of the powerful civil governors. However, many of their supervisory functions were given to other national or regional bodies: the Ministry of Finance supervises budgets, and the regional prefect, the *delegado del gobierno*, can suspend council decisions if they entail 'grievous harm for non-local interests'. While the modes of administrative supervision may have changed, in France, Italy, and Spain the ability of central officials, whether prefects or civil servants from local branches of ministries, to become involved in detailed matters of local decision-making has presisted.

CONCLUSIONS

France, Italy, and Spain could be regarded as exemplary cases of legal centralism before the reforms of the 1970s and 1980s. Here the opportunities for local élites to shape public policies through their 'hands-on' power over the local governmental apparatus appears more limited than in Britain and Scandinavia. Even after the reforms of the 1970s and 1980s the signs of legal centralism are still clearly visible. In this context legal centralism does not mean that there is a single source of all major policy initiatives, or that governments merely passively carry out central directives. Rather it means that local government finds it difficult to undertake any major actions without involving central state officials at an early stage in the process. It means also that local government undertakes relatively few major functions, and many of these are of a mandatory nature giving central government power to direct local government. Even in permissive functions many aspects of local government activity, above all finance, have to be negotiated with central government. Conversely, even though recent statutes have served to limit the scope for local influence, above all in taxation levels, Britain can be regarded as an exemplary case of legal localism: broad grants of power over wide areas of public policy leading to a remote control approach to local government in which the extension of control requires statutory change rather than administrative intervention. The powers of the Scandinavian governors, especially in Norway and Denmark, and the fact that the possibilities for detailed central involvement in local decision-making appear far greater than in Britain, make these countries less easy to place on the legal scale of centralism and localism. However, when one considers the range of local government functions, as well as the fact that central intervention appears more concerned with broad strategic and legal issues, then we might place the three Scandinavian countries closer to the British end of the scale than to the Southern European end.

3

The Political Scale

The localness of local government is in part a function of the range and extent of its functional responsibilities. It is also related to the influence that local political élites have in national decision-making arenas in so far as these affect the locality. This form of influence through participation in national policy arenas was discussed as 'access' in the earlier stages of this study.[1] In the terms borrowed from Mackenzie in Chapter 1, the greater the influence of local political élites in national decisions affecting local government, the greater the degree of political localism.

There are two broad forms or routes of local government access to the centre. One type of route is direct: there may exist bilateral relationships between national politicians and officials and the officials or politicians from an *individual* local government authority. Thus, for example, a mayor establishing direct contact with a national politician in order to secure extra resources for a capital project would be an example of such a direct form of access. The second type of route is indirect through some form of *collective*, usually national, organization. An association of mayors or councillors seeking to secure, say, a change in legislation affecting local services, would be an example of this indirect route.

Of course the precise routes of access and the importance attached to each of them varies from one country to the next. For example, direct access may be afforded via regional offices or provincial prefects, and such routes of access may be dominated by political élites alone, or, on the contrary, may resemble a dialogue between national and local administrators and technocrats or some mix of technocrats and politicians. Similarly, indirect patterns of access may be dominated by groups composed of bureaucratic actors, political actors, or a mix of both. The first purpose of this chapter is to describe patterns of central—local access in our seven countries. The second purpose is to go beyond description and evaluate whether some patterns of central—local access offer greater opportunities for local political influence than others. While one can point to differences in the precise routes of access, it is not possible to deduce from these alone whether one route is likely to afford local government authorities greater participation in national policy—making. Unfortunately, conventional means of measuring the local involvement in national politics, such as the local government background and involvement of national politicians, offer poor guides in evaluating the impact of different patterns of access. Consequently, this chapter develops a more satisfactory set of criteria for understanding the importance of different patterns of access in so far as they affect the opportunities for local influence in the centre.

INDIRECT PATTERNS OF ACCESS

Local government interest groups constitute an indirect means of access between central and local government. Since this chapter is concerned with exploring variations in political centralism and localism, examining the degree to which local élites have more privileged access to central processes of decision-making in some countries than others, on what criteria might one distinguish between different systems of indirect access?

The literature on pressure group theory is well developed and offers a variety of different criteria which might be used to explain why some interest groups are more successful than others. The potential determinants of interest group influence produce a very long list indeed.[2] Some of the more conventional ones, the amount of money available to the group and the degree to which its members have skills relevant to effective contact with government officials, are more appropriate in accounting for differences between smaller organizations, possibly run by volunteer or part-time staff, and large national professionally staffed organizations such as the local authority associations in each of our countries, rather than explaining cross-national differences between them. Consequently, this chapter focuses upon five possible dimensions along which our seven nations appeared to differ. Moreover, these dimensions are also held responsible for explaining strengths and weaknesses of specifically local government interest groups in individual nations.[3]

The first dimension to be explored in looking at the nature of access offered to local governments by pressure groups is whether such pressure groups exist. The second dimension refers to the inclusiveness of the interest group. Interest groups claim to speak for a particular constituency, usually a certain type of local authority. How far does their membership cover the potential membership? Those groups with a higher coverage of the population they claim to represent are likely to have greater legitimacy than those with only a fraction of the potential members belonging to their organization. The third dimension is related to this, and to some extent the effect of extensive membership may even countervail it: the internal cohesion of the group. In many countries interest groups of local politicians represent diverse types of local government unit; this diversity may spring from the fact that different sorts of local government, say, counties and municipalities, find themselves in the same local authority association, or from the fact that there is diversity among the same sort of local government units such as reflected in the differences between urban and rural communes. These different types of local government units may have very different interests: a small commune in Italy with a Christian Democratic mayor might have little in common with a large Communist-run urban commune. Differences in geographical location, socio-economic composition, and political control may serve to fragment any attempt to aggregate interests and weaken the possible influence of the group. The question however remains: how far does this appear to be a ubiquitous phenomenon or does it suggest that national interest groups of local government are especially weak because of this in some states only? A fourth dimension derives from the degree to which the pressure group has authority to direct or coerce its members. It is this dimension that distinguishes between interest group consultations and negotiations. Without the ability to direct its members to act in the agreed way, it cannot directly bargain, and therefore will be expected to be weaker.

There are other factors that contribute towards explaining the variable impact of pressure groups, such as the nature of the demands that the groups make of government. We might expect that the greater the congruence between the views expressed by the group and the values of the government the greater the group's influence. However, our systematic knowledge of local authority associations in a comparative context is very limited, and the analysis must confine itself to those areas about which some information is available. Hence this chapter cannot claim to provide a discussion of all the general institutional factors contributing to the strength or weakness of local authority associations as pressure groups, only some of the most important.

NATIONAL LOCAL INTEREST GROUPS

Included in this discussion of groups are the major interest groups which are formally independent of political parties. Of course there are groupings of councillors, some with formal status, some informal, operating to deal with local government matters in many of the major parties in our seven countries. Ashford discusses the different local government organizations of the main parties in France, and Rhodes does the same for Britain.[4] Looking at the major associations, however, there is no difference between our seven countries in terms of the existence of national groups representing local government authorities. Table 3.1 presents the major local authority associations which will form the basis of the analysis in the remainder of this chapter. It excludes some of the smaller local authority associations (e.g. the London Boroughs' Association and the Association of London Authorities) as well as those which are not primarily the representatives of elected local government authorities (e.g. the Confederazione Italiana dei Servizi Pubblici degli Enti Locali). No major theoretical justification is called for in making such a decision: we would expect any similarities or differences to be found within the major associations if anywhere. Each country has at least one local authority association. Certainly, the precise functions of the associations vary; some have more extensive information services than others. Some are responsible for wage negotiation for local government employees, more a general reflection of union and wage negotiating structures nationally than a significant feature of central–local relations alone. In addition, the internal structure of groups varies; for example Italian associations have a more developed regional organization than the British. Moreover, in the case of France, the

TABLE 3.1. *Major local authority associations: target and actual membership*

	Target	Actual	% Density
Italy			
Associazione Nazionale dei Comuni Italiani	8,085	5,168	64
Unione Nazionale			
Comuni ed Enti Montani	4,125	3,571	87
Unione delle Province d'Italia	92	92	100
Britain			
Association of District Councils	333	333	100
Association of Metropolitan Authorities	77	77	100
Association of County Councils	47	47	100
Convention of Scottish Local Authorities	65	65	100
Spain			
Federación Española			
Municipios y Provincias	8,022	c.4,000	50
Norway			
Norske Kommuners Sentralforbund	472	472	100
Denmark			
Kommunernes Landsforening	14	14	100
Amtsradsforeningen	281	281	100
Sweden			
Svenska Kommunförbundet	27	27	100
Svenska Landstingsförbundet	276	276	100
France			
Association des Maires de France	36,433	c.28,000	77

Sources: Page and Goldsmith (eds.), *Central and Local Government Relations*; ISAP, *Le relazioni centro-periferia* (Milan: Giuffre, 1984); R. A. W. Rhodes, *The National World of Local Government* (London: Allen & Unwin, 1986).

associations are not strictly speaking local government associations, but associations based on the individual membership of mayors rather than the corporate membership of the local government authority. Yet for our purposes, each country has a formal system of interest groups which exist to aggregate and articulate the views of local political élites in central policy-making processes. These groups are all at least consulted or informed as a matter of course by central government whenever legislation or other central instruments are about to be used, amended, or dropped. Hence the existence of pressure groups of local authorities does not distinguish between the patterns of relationship between national and local government in our seven countries.

COVERAGE OF THE GROUPS

The membership of groups (Table 3.1) does vary throughout our seven nations. In Scandinavia and Britain there is virtually full membership of the associations. In Italy, the associations represent 72 per cent of potential members, although just over a third of the potential members of the major organization of the communes, the Associazione Nationale dei Comuni Italiani, are not in fact members. In France a similar portion of mayors are members of their national association. In so far as we might suspect on the basis of interest group theory that, *ceteris paribus*, the larger the portion of the target membership represented by a group, the more powerful it is, then we might expect such groups to be more powerful in Britain and Scandinavia. We must bear in mind, however, that not all other things are equal, and that in practice the representativeness of the associations does not appear to make a great difference to the role they have played in national policy-making (see below).

INTERNAL UNITY WITHIN THE ORGANIZATIONS

The available evidence makes it very difficult to evaluate whether the associations of one country are more divided than those of another. The empirical information about the associations in our seven countries is sparse and patchy, and there is no common measure which can be used to measure or even describe intensity or levels of cohesion across nations. Faced with this, any examination of the divisions within and among local authorities in the context of national interest organizations must be very tentative. Let us look at the evidence that does exist on the matter.

Apart from an amicably settled division between the Copenhagen municipalities and the Kommunernes Landsforening in the early 1980s over the distribution of block grant, there is little evidence of internal divisions in the Scandinavian countries. Whether this is due to a 'consensual style' of policy-making in Scandinavia or something peculiar to central–local relations cannot be determined here.[5] The scope for conflict certainly exists in Scandinavia; the Norwegian Kommuners Sentralforbund consists of both municipalities and counties; municipalities vary in population from Oslo's 450,000 to several smaller rural municipalities with fewer than one thousand inhabitants, and Norwegian counties range from 77,000 (Finnmark) to 400,000 (Hordaland). Similar potential for diversity exists within the Swedish and Danish local government organizations even though in these two countries there are separate associations for counties and municipalities. In fact, prior to the 1970s there were separate organizations for different types of local government in Scandinavia: the Norske Kommuners Sentralforbund was created in 1972 out of the Norges Byforbund (Norwegian Association of Cities) and the Norges Herredsforbund (Norwegian Association of Rural Municipalities and Counties); the Danish Kommunernes Landsforening was created in 1970 out of the three associations—the Danish Town Association, the Federation of District Council Associations (rural parishes), and the Urban Districts Association; and the Swedish Standsförbundet (city) and Landskommunsförbundet (rural districts) were merged in 1968.[6]

In France, the most important of the associations, the Association des Maires de France (AMF) is dominated numerically by small communes, although the most influential positions within it are held by the larger towns, and this influence is increasing.[7] This has led to conflicts within the association in the past, most visibly when forty mayors of large cities set up their own Association des Maires des Grandes Villes in 1974, although remaining in the AMF. As Mény says, 'cleavages based on party lines, ideology and interests prevent the associations from presenting a common front'.[8] Such conflicts are, however, less frequent in some areas, such as extracting finance from the centre or resisting central encroachment, than in others.

In Italy and Spain the major associations have managed to present a united front despite being associated with distinct parties; the Federación Española de Municipios y Provincias works as if it were

part of the municipal lobby within the PSOE.[9] Yet despite this, and
despite the fact that the FEMP represents all types of local
authorities: urban and rural, provincial and municipal, the association managed to find an agreement among its members and present
a united front to the government in 1985 over the potentially highly
divisive question of the allocation of block grant resources to local
communes (the larger city authorities in fact sacrificed some of their
income to smaller ones in return for aid from other sources). In
Italy the Associazione Nazionale dei Comuni Italiani is headed by a
Christian Democrat, the Unione delle Province d'Italia by a
Socialist, leaving to the Communists the association of municipally
owned firms (CISPEL).

In Britain Rhodes describes the conflicts and cleavages within the
'national community of local government' as 'awesome to
behold'.[10] The differences may be geographic in origin or related to
party political differences. Both forms of cleavage are demonstrated
in the fact that the separate (Conservative) Association of London
Authorities and the Labour-dominated alternative it was set up to
rival, the London Boroughs' Association, comprise members who
also belong to the AMA. Certainly there is a potential for conflict,
although in Rhodes's case-studies of central−local bargaining in fire
and education these conflicts are not greatly apparent.[11]

The evidence from successful local authority group representation outside the routine processes of day-to-day consultation
suggests that local government wide issues, such as the structure or
powers of local government, appear to evoke the greatest cohesion
within the associations in the seven countries. Of course, this
assumption cannot be invariably made, as Rhodes shows in the case
of local government reform proposals in Britain in the 1970s.
Although it might appear that the longer-term interests of local
government as a whole were at stake here, the issue gave rise to
diverse views from the different local authority groups involved as
each tried to promote the interests of its members.[12] Whether local
government wide issues evoke the greatest potential for unanimity,
or whether such issues simply do not exist, to raise the question of
the circumstances under which unanimity is likely to be greater
underlines the limitation of the associations in each of the countries.
Local governments are diverse with diverse interests. A national
organization is singular; there are relatively few occasions when
there is likely to be unanimity or near unanimity among local

governments, and as a route for influencing national decisions, national associations must be rather limited.

If we base our expectations upon interest group theory and identify strength with cohesion, we would anticipate local government associations to be weakest in France and Britain, where there is substantially more evidence of dissension within the groups than elsewhere. However, such evidence is itself rather weak. On the basis of the potential for division we might presume British associations to be more powerful than the Italian, given the strength of partisan and regional cleavages in Italy.

GROUP AUTHORITY

Much has been made of the notion of 'corporatism' in relation to pressure group activity in recent years. One of the distinctive features of corporatism is that it suggests that a group has the capacity to coerce its members into actions; it has some form of binding authority over them. This may have the result of strengthening the hand of groups in their relationships with the state since the groups can *negotiate* arrangements to which they can keep their members instead of merely being *consulted* or asked for their views. In consequence the power of the group may be strengthened, although on the other hand this might involve further modification of the group's aims as it seeks to maintain good relations with the state.

Leaving aside the role of the associations in wage and conditions of service negotiations through which the associations participate in producing binding agreements (although these are not enforced by the associations as such), there is little evidence of this aspect of corporatism in the work of local authority associations. The associations in all seven countries represent views in consultations with central government in addition to providing consultancy, information, and advisory services. In some areas the associations of some countries do have quasi-executive functions: in Britain they have some role in the distribution of capital funds among members and in the allocation of grants to voluntary bodies, and in Denmark the Kommunernes Landsforening has *de facto* responsibility for the state commission on local government career structures. However, these functions where they do exist are narrowly circumscribed, and

cannot be construed as offering the national associations broad
authority or coercive power over their members. It is instructive in
this context that the most exhaustive attempt to find corporatism in
British central–local relations initially came up with the much
weaker 'corporate bias' and later suggested that even this was too
strong a term: the associations had no hierarchical control over their
members or anything remotely resembling it.[13]

THE IMPACT OF THE ASSOCIATIONS

In all seven countries there have been more or less radical attempts
to shape the powers of local authorities and their relations with
central government in the post-war period. By examining the role of
the local authority associations in these changes we may offer some
case-study evidence derived from the processing of issues in which
we may not only assume that the local authorities have a vital
interest, but also that the cohesion within the associations will be
strongest. As regards the general structure and powers of local
governments throughout the country as a whole we might expect to
find a greater degree of concern and unanimity within the
associations than over issues such as the distribution of financial
resources among local governments or over more specific functional
policy proposals.

Of course, given the range of actors and interests involved in local
government reorganization, it is impossible to assess directly the
impact of any one organization, especially when its members have
recourse to many other avenues to influence the policy—through
party contacts, MPs, ministers, and so on—in addition to interest
group activity. However, if we look at the way that these groups
have participated in the process of reorganization we can make
some broad distinctions.

The French Association des Maires de France has had a
particularly important role to play in debates surrounding the
restructuring of French local government. In both defending the
status quo to maintain the power of mayors and the boundaries of
communes and in advocating change to enhance the powers of the
communes not only has it been on the sides of the argument that
eventually won, its impact has been direct. The importance of the
Association des Maires de France has been in no small part due to

the importance of the French second chamber, the Senate, as a forum for the expression of the views of local notables (it is termed the 'Grand Conseil des Communes'). This link between communes, Senate, and the Association of Mayors is underlined by the fact that many leading figures within the Association have also served as senators. Most notably Alain Poher, now serving his eighth consecutive term as President of the Senate, a post he has occupied since 1968, was also Assistant Secretary-General of the Association (1945–60), then its President (1974–83), and now its Honorary President (since 1983). Such links with the Senate have been used to help modify or block changes that would reduce the status of local mayors. In 1969 a Republican Minister of the Interior, Marcellin, proposed that very small communes be compulsorily merged under the direction of the prefect. The Association opposed this proposal, and in the event it managed to have the proposal substantially diluted so that local elected representatives rather than the prefect alone would make the recommendations for mergers. Since mergers remained effectively non-compulsory, plans for merger could be ignored; as Ashford states 'communes could veto action by not responding'. In fact, according to Ashford, one of the major contributions of the Association des Maires de France was that it used its influence indirectly on the centre to ensure that direct forms of communication or access were used to establish where mergers should take place. Unlike Britain, where 'indirect consultation and administrative orders' could be used to ensure reform, 'the French had to employ individual consultations with each département and commune'.[14] While the impact of the Association on the decentralization reforms under the Mitterrand presidency is less apparent, the impact of the Senate is more so. The Senate appears to have been influential in the drafting of the precise decentralization proposals since one of the authors of the legislation 'confided in private that the measures had been derived in part from those put forward by the government of President Giscard d'Estaing in 1980–81, as amended by the Senate'.[15]

We know less about the role of the associations in Italy and Spain. In Italy, the enabling legislation for the creation of regions in 1970 reflected ANCI and UPI desires to restrict the powers of the regions by making the 1970s law 'of the creation of the regions . . . a point of arrival (rather than departure) for regional decentralisation and exclud[ing] any future development in the process'.[16]

Following the expansion of the regional government responsibilities in the mid-1970s as a partial consequence of Communist electoral strength, the ANCI and the UPI were actively campaigning to have the powers of the regional governments reduced: 'the national associations ... pushed for the central state to pass reforming legislation. These associations saw in such a law a form of guarantee against the "imperialist" tendencies of the region. . . . This reaction was encouraged in an underhand way by the central government, which maintained a direct link with local government in financial matters and looked like supplanting the regional level.'[17] Clegg reports that the Spanish FEMP has scored successes in the regionalization law of 1985, especially in the area of the internal organization and powers of local authorities.[18]

In the three Scandinavian nations, with the major exception of the reform of the municipalities (but not counties) in Norway, reorganization appears to have generated very few major political controversies. The actual reforms of local government which, for the most part, involved the merging of small local communes, ending the distinctions between rural and urban communes and increasing the powers of the counties, were certainly potentially conflictual. Yet it is difficult to find any evidence of local authority association opposition to the whole process of reform. In fact, in Denmark and Sweden the local authority associations were active members on some of the commissions that decided the shape of the new local authorities under the reorganized systems of government: the 1958 municipal law commission of Denmark; the 1952 Local Government Commission in Sweden; and the 1959 commission in Sweden advising the government on local government mergers. In Denmark, Harder showed how the only real problem of the amalgamations into larger local authorities came with the unwillingness of the smaller suburban authorities which were to become part of larger authorities: 'this pressure, however, had very little effect.'[19] Brand, in his comparison of local government reform in England and Sweden, puts this lack of major effective opposition to reform down in part to the 'consensual' political culture of Sweden as well as the fundamental avoidance of political conflict found among the Swedish local authority associations:

The Swedish local government associations were unlike the [English] County Councils Association and the Association of Municipal Corporations, being more oriented towards technical advice for members (for which they maintained staffs much larger than their English counterparts) and less oriented towards political maneuvering vis-à-vis the government. The small size of their membership made this technical emphasis necessary and also made their political force rather weak. In England the Rural District Councils Association and the Urban District Councils Association were also weak politically as compared with the associations of the larger local authorities: the counties and county boroughs or even the boroughs.[20]

In Norway, where local government associations were not represented on the Municipal Amalgamation Commission first set up in 1946, local government boundary reform 'seems to have aroused a stronger local reaction than in the other Scandinavian countries'.[21] In Norway the rural and urban municipalities' associations managed to stall the implementation of proposals to merge parts of rural with parts of urban municipalities in order to avoid producing what were regarded as over-large authorities, and in the late 1960s an Association of Compulsorily Amalgamated Municipalities was set up to re-establish some of the older abolished local authorities. This had a limited success in the mid-1970s when parliament recreated ten older municipalities.

In England and Wales the impact of the major local authority associations on reorganization has been rather limited. Frank Smallwood's extensive study of the reform of London government in the early 1960s showed that the local authority associations, after their initial reluctance to consider any radical change to the existing structure, played little part in the subsequent debate and conflict surrounding reform.[22] The Local Government Act of 1972, which reorganized local government outside London, also contained few signs of local authority association influence. The divergence between the recommendations of the Royal Commission on Local Government and the actual proposed legislation certainly reflected the views of the associations dominated by the rural districts and counties. Yet it owed less to negotiating success than to the change-over from a Labour to a Conservative government nationally. Rhodes concludes that the main contours of reorganization in England and Wales were formed 'by unilateral exercise of executive authority'. Although there were discussions with the associations 'the government controlled the agenda of, access to and the timing and content of consultation . . . the government took a firm decision in favour of a two-tier system and then allowed extensive discussions.'[23] In Scotland, reorganization involved even less participation by the local authority associations. In fact, the Convention of Scottish Local Authorities was created during the process of reorganization, and the Scottish Office, the government department responsible for local authorities, took a leading role in its creation.

EVALUATING INDIRECT ACCESS

It is difficult to distinguish between the seven countries on the basis of the power that the national associations of local authorities actually have to shape national policy-making. Certainly, they are routinely consulted on most issues affecting local government. They are even represented on a whole range of joint bodies with central government. They also provide information, expertise, and advice to members. As with interest groups more generally, it is difficult to generalize across a whole range of issues and argue whether one group in one country is politically more powerful than that of another. However, surveying the available evidence about relations between groups and central government suggests that where there are strong conflicts between central government and local government, or where there is strong local authority dissatisfaction with the status quo, then mobilization of political support within the national legislative or political executive arena rather than the use of routine contacts between local authority association representatives and national officials is likely to bring about success.

We can however, distinguish 'normal' interest group strengths and those that are in principle available to representatives of local government nationally. Normal interest group strengths are conventionally related to factors such as size, finances, expertise, cohesion, and such like. One of the distinctive features of groups of local authority associations is their status as 'legitimate' representatives of democratically elected public authorities, as Haider states in his study of US state and local interest group lobbying in Washington: 'The chief distinction between public and private lobbying groups is "officiality", which means essentially legitimacy in standing. The legitimacy of governors, mayors and county officials within the general-purpose governments over which they preside is unquestionable ... [T]his legitimacy remains the essential resource which members seek to capitalise upon.'[24] All seven countries, again, have associations with this legitimacy, and while it may be argued that the status or legitimacy of local government in one country might be less than in another, we have no real way of assessing this beyond reciting anecdotal evidence.[25] Yet this legitimacy, often cited as one of the special strengths of these associations, can easily be overrated.[26] As Haider points out, 'This legitimacy bestowed at one government level carries over to the superior level, but not without a certain political devaluation in transference.'[27] What distinguishes French from British groups is that local legitimacy appears, in Haider's term, to lose far more in the process of transference in Britain than it does in France. The legitimacy of the local system is directly translated into national power in the French Senate; the legitimacy of local political office is further strengthened by the near-convention that those who wish to pursue a national political career and who have aspirations to senior political office seek some form of local mandate, usually by being elected mayor (see below). The successes of the local authority associations in reform relied to a large extent upon the exploitation of such linkages. In Britain the process of transference of local legitimacy to national arenas appears to lose a lot; the local authority associations cannot call upon the active support of their nominal supporters in Parliament on anything other than non-controversial issues.[28] Nevertheless, we still have grounds for expecting that indirect forms of local influence, through interest group activity, are enhanced through direct patterns of access. The possibility of immediate and direct contacts between national and local politicians distinguishes interest groups of local authorities and most other interest groups and gives them their distinctive source of power.

DIRECT FORMS OF ACCESS

Consideration of interest group activity suggests that direct forms of access are particularly important in shaping the influence that might be exerted through local authority associations. Another weakness of indirect forms of access, from the perspective of the local politician, is that direct forms of central−local interaction offer local authorities greater scope for influence than indirect forms. From the perspective of an individual authority, its influence is reduced because it has to aggregate its views with those of the other members of the association, introducing the possibility of dilution or even of complete incongruity between its views and that of its national association. From the perspective of local government authorities collectively, interest group activity at the national level is frequently competitive, and above all generalist associations of local government appear to fit uneasily into a national world of group politics dominated by functional groups.

In the section on local authority associations I concluded that direct forms of access significantly shaped the relative power that such associations have on government in Britain and France. How does one assess such differences in the context of the seven-nation study? How does one go about distinguishing between those countries in which the access to national decision-making by local élites is more privileged and those where it is less so? We must explore the question more generally of how much support local administrators or politicians can count upon within the national executive and legislature. There are a variety of indicators which are used to illustrate the strength of such national support for local political élites, of which legislators' backgrounds and the *cumul des mandats* are the most important. While these two specific methods have weaknesses they help point the way to a more satisfactory set of criteria to distinguish between levels of local influence within the centre.

STATISTICAL ANALYSES OF ACCESS

On what basis can local government claim to have representation in the national arenas of decision-making? One conventional method of illustrating the amount of support for local government, frequently used in Britain, is to study the degree to which members of national legislatures have served as representatives in local government. The logic behind this argument, rarely explicitly set out, is that to have served as a local councillor makes one sympathetic to local government and likely to represent it on occasions when local government affairs are discussed in the national legislature. In one way or another the overlap between national and local political careers is frequently considered as an important indicator of the national importance of local politicians in many countries. Since such career details are quantifiable they are easily compared. However, as will be discussed below, statistical analyses of political backgrounds are misleading when taken as indicators of access. It is, however, worth exploring them further since both by elimination and by consideration of the shortcomings of such measures we can get closer to a satisfactory set of criteria by which patterns of access can be distinguished.

W. J. M. Mackenzie's attempt to measure this conception of local government representation in parliaments is perhaps the most important general comparative attempt to come to grips with the question of the different levels of importance attached to local politics in different nations. Its importance goes beyond the rather inconclusive results it yields.[29]

The context of the article helps to develop the point. In 1952 Mackenzie argued that on the basis of the figures he had to hand, local government in Britain was not very well represented in Parliament—referring to the fact that relatively few MPs had been councillors. David Butler replied to this using more satisfactory data: 'when at least 36 per cent of MPs have served in local government, local authorities cannot really claim that they lack representation.'[30] Mackenzie replies, with disarming honesty

My original hypothesis, not very clearly framed, was that forms of British law give local government a status of exceptional freedom, but that legal autonomy was overridden in practice by party discipline and the prevalence of the carpet bagger. I had hoped, after reading Mr Butler's note, that it might be possible to put this in more exact form by statistical comparison with other countries: but on the whole I have to report failure . . . The (available) figures seem to me to illustrate my point, but it is clear that they do not prove it.[31]

The figures for the 1980s in our seven countries do not prove this either (Table 3.2). From Table 3.2 it can be seen that in Italy there is relatively little local government experience among Italian deputies. The fact that strong national support for local government does exist in Italy can be adduced from a variety of other sources.[32] The fact that many Cabinet ministers in Britain were once elected councillors similarly cannot be taken as an accurate indicator of the importance of local government in national arenas of power. Such equations of previous experience with current behavioural and attitudinal predispositions is erroneous because, like the analogous

TABLE 3.2. *Percentage of members of lower chambers and cabinets having local government background*

| | Percentage[a] of national politicians who have held locally elected offices | |
	MPs (1980s)	Cabinet ministers (1987)
Britain	35	14
France	75	53
Italy	48	20
Sweden	80	n/a
Norway	85	50
Spain	19[b]	29
Denmark	44	26

[a] As percentage of relevant officials for whom detailed biographical data are available.

[b] Under Franco regime.

Sources: Page and Goldsmith, *Central and Local government Relations*, *Keesing's Contemporary Archives*, *Who's Who in Italy 1983* (Milan: Who's Who AG, 1983); *Hvem er Hvem?* 1984 (Aschenhoug-Gyldendal: Kunnskapsforlaget 1984); *Kraks Bl Bog 1985* (Copenhagen: KRAK, 1985); *Quien es Quien en España Edición 1989* (Madrid: Geranios, 1989); *Who's Who 1989* (London A. & C. Black, 1989); *Who's Who in France 1984-5* (Paris: Éditions Jacques Lafitte, 1984); unpublished information on Italian MPs supplied by Paul F. Furlong, University of Hull.

'representative bureaucracy' thesis which assumes that the views officials in government bureaucracies represent are shaped through social background, it confuses past environment with current motivation.[33] Just as top civil servants who come from privileged backgrounds cannot be assumed to be Conservative, neither can all politicians who have served as councillors be presumed active supporters of the views which dominate among local politicians and officials. This is clearly shown by the fact that despite the generally low level of local representation within the British Cabinet indicated in Table 3.2, the three ministers who presided over what are widely seen as the most severe attacks on local government in Britain in over 150 years were all former councillors: Patrick Jenkin (introduced rate capping, councillor for Hornsey 1960−3), Kenneth Baker (among other things removed many local authority educational powers, councillor in Twickenham 1960−2), and Nicholas Ridley (introduced poll tax, rural district councillor, Castle Ward 1952−5).

Another popular indicator of local influence in the centre, the degree of local support which can be mobilized within the centre, is offered by French analyses.[34] The basis of this argument is the identification of the *cumul des mandats*, the practice of accumulating national and local elective office simultaneously, as an important feature of the French territorial governmental system. As the often quoted arguments of Crozier and his colleagues showed, central state prefects depended upon the collaboration of mayors, and deputies and ministers in turn depended upon the collaboration of prefects, so that there existed a web of interdependencies which served to limit the scope for any one set of actors—mayors, prefects, departmental notables, national politicians, and officials— to act independently.[35] The network of interdependencies limits the powers of actors, and the major opportunity to evade such limits is to occupy more than one strategic position in the network: mayor, departmental councillor, and deputy. This strategy is especially adopted by the mayors of the larger cities and brings material rewards for the local commune and enhances the political careers of the cumulants.

Becquart-Leclercq takes on a task suggested by other studies and seeks to determine how far the *cumul* principle applies in other countries. The methodology she uses is simple. Using as an indicator the number of members of the European Parliament who also hold office in national legislatures she concludes that 'apart from Ireland (where 6 out of 15 hold dual mandates) and Luxembourg (4 out of 6), France is at the forefront of the accumulation stakes with 17.28 per cent of its 81 Euro-MPs having elective office at home, followed by Italy (16.05 per cent of 81) and the United Kingdom (11.52 per cent of 81) while Germany has only 2.47 per cent (out of 81).'[36]

The problem with this, of course, that there is no reason to suppose that accumulation as between national legislatures and the European Assembly is an indicator of, or is in any way related to, accumulation as between local and national office. Becquart-Leclercq's logic appears to be that a 'culture' of accumulation will be reflected at all levels. That this is fallacious is shown by the experience of Italy where, according to the European Assembly indicator, there is a high propensity to accumulate. Yet membership of the national assembly is incompatible with membership of a local council in Italy.[37] The *cumul des mandats* is, at least in the context of our seven-nation comparison, not a significant factor affecting direct patterns of access between national and local officials: only in France is the mechanism of the *cumul* so central to the system of territorial government.

EVALUATING DIRECT ACCESS

How, then, might one assess and understand differences in patterns of direct access? Mackenzie's original study, which sets out the distinction between a political and legal scale of local self-government, recognizes that

The legal situation may not correspond closely to the political situation, and the latter may be difficult to assess, because close and loose integration may both work in two ways. Close integration may mean that the localities move the centre or that the centre moves the localities: a looser relationship may mean that the local authorities are free—or simply that they are disregarded. The matter is one of political structure, and is too delicate to be measured by the very crude statistics available. . . . [Political influence] is obviously related to differences in cabinet systems and party systems as well as in the tradition of administrative law.[38]

This suggests an underlying principle in both Becquart-Leclercq's and Mackenzie's work that needs to be made explicit and might serve as a basis for comparison. Both local government background and the *cumul* offer, or are believed to offer, some mechanism which ensures that national politicians pay special attention to the demands and interests of local governments: the MP with a background in local government because he retains local government sympathies, the cumulant because using his position to gain benefits for his commune enhances his national and local career.

It follows, then, from this that what we are looking for is not any indirect link such as background, since we have little reason to assume that mere past experience of local elective office shapes subsequent parliamentary or ministerial behaviour—a point implied by Mackenzie. Rather we need to know whether there is any incentive to represent localities once politicians have arrived in the national policy-making arena. This does not entail looking for any common mechanism such as the *cumul*, since the *cumul* only appears to be important in France but not in the other six nations. What is needed are indicators of the degree to which national political careers are built up through the mobilization of local political support.

Such a mechanism is clearly present in Italy. Local élites do not have to rely upon the mere goodwill of national politicians or the fading memory of local political service that the national politicians may have when, as Tarrow's study shows, local élites negotiate with and extract benefits from the centre using party political channels of access, as opposed to the politico-administrative route of access to the centre in the French system.[39] Rather they can deal in a more fungible commodity: votes. While the conventional wisdom has it that proportional representation on the basis of large multi-member constituencies strengthens the powers of national party organizations, in Italy the system of proportional representation as it operates serves to enable local political leaders to exert great influence over national politicians.

The importance of local government to political parties has been well documented: control of local government along with other public or parastate organizations offers jobs which can be used to reward party supporters through intricate networks of patronage. Moreover, parties in Italy rely heavily upon government employment as a means of paying party workers from public funds. As Santantonio summarizes:

Decentralisation and regionalisation, which the parties themselves advocated because they offered new areas of control and fresh outlets for an expanding group of professional politicians, have further helped to integrate political forces within all the administrative structures and organisations, allowing them to extend their network of influence. The parties are now deeply rooted within the system and pervade public activity to such a point that complaints about a 'spoils system' and of parties taking over all aspects of public life are common.[40]

These local networks of clientelistic relationships which focus upon the party, and which are sustained by the patronage resources offered by local political office, affect national politics and offer well-placed local political élites national influence through the party mechanism. Percy Allum's study of post-war Naples analyses this phenomenon in some detail. [41] The electoral system of Italy for the chamber of deputies is one of proportional representation with preference voting in multi-member constituencies. Whether an individual gets elected depends upon the number of preference votes received. The choices of the electorate are, however, shaped by the recommendations of local notables: the *grandi-elettori* and the *capi-elettori*. The *grandi-elettori* are distinguished from the *capi-elettori* through having influence over a broader range of groups. Support by *grandi-elettori*, usually local priests, mayors, and councillors, is important to lesser-known candidates in order to ensure that they receive high enough preference rankings to be elected. Consequently, *grandi-elettori* are extremely important figures in the development of national political careers. Allum quotes one Christian Democrat Councillor who talks of certain deputies 'who always come here to ask for votes full of fawning obsequity'.[42] In all, the local network of clientelism is part of a much larger national one in which the aspiring national politician constantly has to prove to *grandi-elettori* that he can provide them with benefits and that he can earn their support. Consequently, as Allum concludes: 'This explains why even the most important national party leaders are often more interested in parochial issues and particular interests than broad national problems.'[43]

Since, as Guiseppe DiPalma suggests, clientelistic links of the form found in Italy should be found throughout Mediterranean politics, we might expect to find such important local clientelistic links in Spain too which also serve to make local power bases important for national politics.[44] Certainly, there has been a tradition of such links before the Franco dictatorship (see also Chapter 5). Carr details the 'bossism' or *caciquismo* which reached its heyday in the late nineteenth century and early years of the twentieth when it provided the necessary resources for electoral management to sustain the *turno pacifico*, the alternation in office of the liberals and liberal-conservatives to the exclusion of other political forces.[45] Municipal-based clientelism was the basis of the *turno pacifico*, and consequently local government reform was one of the key objectives of its opponents (consisting of those parties excluded from this convenient arrangement). *Caciquismo*, of course, itself existed before this period; local *caciques* were important in the appointment of provincial governors in the 1840s. Moreover, Pitt-Rivers offers anthropological evidence for the persistence of this phenomenon in Andalucia well into Franco's rule (see also Chapter 6), although without electoral competition such local power bases could not be directly translated into national power.[46]

A more difficult question is how far such patterns of the importance of local power bases for national political careers have survived in Spain. Existing work offers some general indications that the transition to mass democracy in Spain has been based upon older clientelistic patterns established under Franco and upon the development of new clientelistic patterns. Clegg writes, 'The main parties of the centre and right UCD (now defunct), AP and PDP appear to have absorbed many of the clientelistic networks that existed under Franco, and these now operate within the context of democratic politics.'[47]

There are also signs that local bases of power at least had a role in explaining the two remarkable features of the post-Franco era: the sudden demise of the UCD, a party that looked set to become a catch-all party for the centre-right much as the CDU in Germany or the DC in Italy, between 1979 and 1982 and the impressive rise of the Spanish Socialists, the PSOE, since the end of the Franco era. It was above all the ideological diversity of the UCD and the inept style of leadership of Suarez, who wanted to turn the UCD into an authoritarian party, offending key notables within the party in the process, that broke the party and made its share of the vote fall from 35 per cent in 1979 to under 7 per cent in 1982. Yet among the party's internal conflicts were conflicts surrounding candidate selection, with local political leaders, above all in Galicia, resenting the central party's attempts to foist candidates upon it. The PSOE on the other hand managed to expand its share of the vote from 29 per cent in 1977 to 48 per cent in 1982 remaining at 44 per cent in 1986. Heywood attributes this in part to the management of the PSOE organization by its leaders, above all Guerra and Gonzales. They managed to exclude potentially electorally damaging left-wing groups from significant influence within the PSOE. They have managed to 'dispel dissident elements with relative ease, while loyalty has been rewarded with posts as party officials, or appointments within local governments'.[48] These observations are, of course, indicative of something that might develop rather than suggestions that control of local government has the sorts of national political rewards that it appears to have in Italy and France. Above all, democratic elections in Spain's municipalities are so recent (the first elections were held in April 1979) that even if they had already eradicated or transformed pre-existing systems of municipal clientelism, we have no evidence of it yet. Certainly one of the most pressing demands of the Socialists in the early period after Franco was for municipal elections; because 'The party needed to secure two additional pillars of its power: it had to consolidate the UGT as a powerful socialist trade union and to gain local bases of power. Thus the PSOE pressed the government to return to the UGT the property that had been confiscated by the Franco regime . . . and it called for municipal elections to replace mayors and councillors appointed by the dictatorship.'[49] Precisely how important such local power bases become for the Socialists and the parties of the centre and right remains to be seen.

In Britain and the Scandinavian countries such direct national career consequences of local political support are largely absent. This is not necessarily due to the absence of opportunity for local parties to shape candidate selection rather than national party organization.[50] The activity of local politics is, however, seen as largely separate from national politics in these countries. While local experience and local ties might promote a general predisposition among MPs to assist the local community through, among other things, taking an interest in local government problems, such national career incentives as are found in Italy and France are simply not there in Denmark, Norway, Sweden, and Britain. In Britain, local government experience is advantageous within both parties primarily in so far as it attests to the prospective parliamentary candidate's willingness and skill to stand for public election. Within the Conservative party such local government background was, according to Rush's study of candidate selection 'viewed as a limiting factor, as an indication of the applicant's parochial outlook and lack of wider experience'.[51]

CONCLUSIONS

Opportunities for local political élites to shape policies within their locality through influencing decision-making by national politicians and officials are offered both by indirect interest group participation and through direct contacts with the national level. The evidence suggests that direct contacts are particularly effective, not only in themselves but also in strengthening the influence of national associations of local authorities. Such direct links result not from a specific phenomenon, such as the *cumul des mandats*, or the local government background of ministers and parliamentarians. Rather, political career structures in different countries place varying degrees of emphasis upon national politicians maintaining local support. Consequently, direct political contacts which are characteristic of political localism are far more marked in Italy, France, and possibly Spain than in the other countries.

The closeness of direct links between national and local politics in France and Italy, and the possibility of the development of such links in Spain may, as Mackenzie suggests, lead to greater national political influence over local politicians rather than greater local influence at the centre. Such links may enable national party leaders to monopolize appointments to local offices and to suppress local political dissent. While Kesselman's study of the 'ambiguous consensus' in France reminds us that the links between local and national politics tend to create incentives for local political actors to downplay political controversies in their communes, it is difficult to construe the close links between national and local politics as producing the dominance of a national party organization over local politics, as Mackenzie argues to be the case in the Soviet Union.[52] Above all, the Senate as well as the reservoir of local support enjoyed in the National Assembly and in major ministries has helped local government in France resist major incursions into its power and at least contributed to some expansion of its powers in the 1980s. In Italy, the direct linkages through the party structure and electoral system have also helped block major attempts at reorganization and have helped win back some of the ground lost to the regions after 1970. In the countries included in this study, close political linkages between national and local government do, in fact, appear to produce opportunities for local officials to influence policies that affect them in national decision-making arenas.

Since this is the case, one must raise the apparently awkward question of why political localism seems to coincide in our seven cases with legal centralism. While the relationship between the two scales will be discussed in more detail in Chapter 6, if political localism were an important component of the role of local government in France and Italy then one might expect local authorities to use this influence to gain more functional responsibilities and greater discretion (i.e. more legal localism). However, in France and Italy at least legal centralism has persisted despite the decentralization reforms of the 1970s and 1980s. Why local élites should not have used their influence in the centre to produce far greater legal localism in these two countries is a question that cannot be answered on the basis of the available evidence.

A number of hypotheses may be advanced. One would be that political localism is an inherently defensive and conservative influence in the political system due to the inability of diverse local government units to agree to positive reforms. Another might be related to the strength of the potential opposition for greater legal localism, above all the undoubted strong prestige of the civil service in France. A third hypothesis could be that local political élites have little to gain from greater legal localism, and might even suffer from the greater demands on their time and skills that legal localism might bring. French mayors derive their political power from the status attached to local government rather than to the range of public services they can shape, so the benefits to the mayors in particular of a wider range of functions and greater discretion to carry them out directly may not be immense. In Italy an important benefit of control of local government to the party and individuals that control it is in the patronage that it offers: yet a greater range of functions would be unlikely to extend the range of political patronage given that it is widespread throughout the public and semi-public sector. A fourth hypothesis may simply be that the lack of demand for greater legal localism is cultural; that there is a broad consensus on the nature of local government in France and Italy as an intermediary between centre and periphery rather than as a major provider of services in its own right.

We have no way of evaluating these and other hypotheses adequately at present. For this reason we cannot simply assume that because local élites in Italy and France have not pressed for far greater powers on the legal scale of local self-government this reflects a basic error on the part of observers of these countries who have identified the importance of political localism there over the past twenty-five years. The weight of available evidence is not consistently heavy, especially in the Scandinavian countries and

Spain. However, it does suggest that there are clear differences between France and Italy on the one hand and Britain and the three Scandinavian countries on the other in terms of the influence that local political élites may bring to bear on decision-making processes within central government.

4

The Consequences of Localism and Centralism

Apart from the direct implications for our understanding of the nature of democracy in any particular country, the degree and nature of localism might be expected to have some impact on the quality and nature of decision-making. A number of authors such as Dahl, Sharpe, and Stewart have argued that decentralization, usually understood to refer to the capacity to make decisions locally without the intrusion of the centre over a wide range of issues, brings a number of benefits such as policies which reflect more closely citizen preferences and policy innovations.[1] In this chapter I do not intend to restate or add to the list of benefits that result from greater decentralization, still less to offer any criticism of calls for greater decentralization.[2] Rather this chapter is concerned with exploring some impacts of the different forms of localism and centralism on patterns of political and administrative behaviour.

What types of administrative and political behaviour might we expect to be affected by different forms of centralism and localism? One suggestion comes from Douglas Ashford, who suggests that political localism is associated with pragmatic decision-making and legal localism with a more dogmatic approach. He makes little secret of his admiration for the interpenetration of central and local administration and politics. For Ashford political localism and legal centralism give France its 'flexibility'. French 'pragmatism' is contrasted with British 'dogmatism', characterized by the separate and unequal spheres of central and local politics and administration.[3] It is not, however, clear from whose perspective the British system is inflexible and dogmatic and the French pragmatic and flexible (see also Chapter 5). The requirement, for example, that ministerial approval be sought for swimming pool designs in France, a feature of the French model of centralization according to a body of theoretical and empirical literature from which Ashford draws heavily, seems intuitively far more inflexible than the less direct controls over capital expenditure in Britain.[4] Such broad evaluative terms are unlikely to get us any closer to assessing a wider impact of different patterns of localism and centralism.

The two different dimensions of centralism and localism entail, above all, two distinct types of political activity. To influence local policy through bringing benefits to the locality through bargaining and negotiating with other state politicians and officials is very different from heading a large bureaucratic organization. If the bargaining and negotiation that characterize the lives of successful mayors in Italy and France are 'brokerage', local elected leaders of countries such as Britain, to extend the metaphor, have to run a business.[5] Of course many political skills and activities will be common to élites under both political and legal localism. However, legal localism brings local elected élites into far greater dependence on a powerful professionalized bureaucracy than political localism.

There are three main areas in which the different forms of leadership implied by shaping policy as head of a large local welfare bureaucracy on the one hand and manipulating non-local political and administrative structures on the other might affect the nature of local government more widely. First, we might expect them to affect relationships within the local government authority, above all the relationship between elected politicians and non-elected officials. Since local governments under legal localism have developed more extensive bureaucracies, we might expect these to be both more professionalized and more powerful and serve to limit the role of the elected representative to a far greater degree than under legal centralism.[6] Second, we might expect types of localism to reflect relationships between citizens and elected representatives since, among other things, the criteria according to which citizens may evaluate the performance of their elected leaders varies. Success under political localism is a function of the ability to bring in benefits from the outside, while success under legal localism can only be evaluated primarily in terms of the use and allocation of local resources. Third, given that political localism is based upon local political élites securing at least the appearance of exceptional treatment for local citizens, we would expect this to affect the nature of the distribution of public services under political and legal localism, with universalistic criteria for subnational resource allocation being far more common under legal localism. Each of these three areas will be explored in turn.

RELATIONSHIPS WITHIN THE LOCAL GOVERNMENT AUTHORITY

On the basis of the well-developed Anglo-French comparative literature one can conclude that the French mayor is primarily a 'policy-broker'. As such he is a figure in negotiating, bargaining, or otherwise attracting scarce resources such as money or legal powers, and this gives him a key role in local political decisions which his counterpart in Britain is less likely to enjoy. In Britain not only is political leadership more fragmented, since its role is dominated by the administration of functional services, even within the functional policy-making arenas it is likely to be weaker due to the development of professionalism and bureaucratic influence in specialized fields of policy-making.[7] In short, political localism tends to define a specific key role for political élites in local government, brokerage, which is absent where there is political centralism. This brokerage role is remarkably resilient to the development of those factors which may be expected to erode the power of elected representatives: functional specialization, professionalism, and bureaucratization. Moreover, with greater legal localism come wider functional responsibilities and greater discretion in carrying them out. This may be expected to increase the degree of fragmentation in political leadership and increase the power of local bureaucrats and professionals as local government authorities are more reliant on their own expertise to carry out their functions.

While this might appear a justifiable conclusion on the basis of Anglo-French comparisons, does it apply more widely as a characteristic of the difference between political and legal localism? There are two main areas that need to be looked at here: the fragmentation of political leadership and the relationship between local politicians and bureaucrats. Any evaluation of these two issues must of necessity be tentative since there is little systematic evidence about the relationship between officials and politicians and between local political figures cross-nationally.

POLITICAL LEADERSHIP AND POLITICAL LOCALISM

Political localism involves the manipulation of desired local political resources to extract benefits from national political actors. In France and Italy these resources are predominantly individual: in France popular legitimacy at the local level and the claim to be able to forge consensus; in Italy the position within the party, the control over patronage, and the ability to deliver preference votes.[8] Since these resources are primarily concentrated in the hands of individuals, it is likely that political localism tends to concentrate power in the hands of individuals.

In France this concentration of power is quite clearly seen in the dominant role of the mayor in the commune. In his brief comparative survey of mayors, Mény points to the uniqueness of the French mayor. The 'caesaristic' authority and power of the political leadership 'so strongly contested during and after the Second Empire in France has never been seriously in danger. The legal position of the French mayor protects him from both collegiality and direct democracy. Whether conceived of as "monarque au petit pied" or magnanimous paterfamilias, dictator of little Clochemerles or efficient manager, the French mayor enjoys a breadth of scope for action which is the envy of his foreign counterparts.'[9] This power of the mayor is not found only in the smaller communes, more characteristic of Kesselman's study, but also in larger communes.[10] Claude Sorbets points to two 'ideal typical' models of mayor who have tended to replace the old rural notable mayor: the 'technician mayor' who plays 'with the dependencies within the state apparatus as a privileged intermediary between everyone' and ensures that mayoral office 'constitutes a key centre of decision making'; and the 'militant mayor'—in communes where parties have sought to avoid 'presidential' forms of local leadership through greater participatory mechanisms, the mayor emerges with his presidentialism enhanced as the only person in a position to claim to provide a 'synthesis', to integrate diverse policy proposals into municipal policy.[11] The position of the mayor in France is strong, among other reasons, because executive authority is concentrated in his hands, he is generally unencumbered by a deliberative council, and because the mayor of a large French town is likely to be an important figure in national politics, in contrast to mayors in other Western nations who are likely to, in Ted Lowi's terms, 'go nowhere'.[12]

The concentration of authority in the hands of an individual contrasts strongly with the collegial nature of political leadership in Britain. In Britain, the involvement of politicians in decision-making, whether of routine or what may be termed policy-making character, takes place within functional council committees. There are, of course, 'coordinating' institutions, such as policy and resources committees, as well as inner circles of the political parties which control the local authorities. As such it is impossible to deny the existence of actors who may make strategic decisions about local authority policy. However, the central point is that these actors are multiple and not singular; committees and caucuses rather than single individuals. The case of Liverpool in the mid-1980s offers a good, if extreme, example of this. Liverpool council was quite clearly steered by its political leadership into a confrontation with the Conservative national government through seeking to avoid the legal requirement that its expenditures should be covered by its income. Eventually this brought Liverpool into conflict with the Labour party nationally as well as sections of its own work-force too. Yet this decisive direction for Liverpool was achieved through mobilizing collective support within the governing Labour party by a collective leadership in which there were several, not one, leading figures.[13]

Eileen Martin-Harloff conducted a comparative analysis of local authority structures under the auspices of the International Union of Local Authorities.[14] Using the text and figures she provides it is possible to summarize the nature of political leadership in our seven countries. Three major types of political institutions may head the executive of local authorities: a mayor or chairman of the council, a collective executive board, and a series of committees. It is further possible for executive power to be shared between these groups. Table 4.1 outlines the executive political leadership of municipalities in our seven countries from the perspective of whether each of these three institutions has executive authority over departments of the local authority.

In France, executive power is concentrated in the hands of the

TABLE 4.1. *Executive structures in local government*

	Executive authority vested in		
	Committees	Board	Mayor/Chairman
Denmark	Yes	No	Yes
France	No	No	Yes
Italy	No	Yes	Yes
Norway	Yes	Yes	No
Spain	No	Yes	Yes
Sweden	Yes	Yes	No
United Kingdom	Yes	No	No

mayor. Furthermore, we might also include Spain as a country in which local executive power is concentrated in the hands of the mayor since the executive board of the municipality, the *comisión de gobierno*, is appointed by the mayor and serves at the mayor's pleasure. This concentration of executive power in a single position contrasts with the practice in Britain where the mayor has no executive powers, these being in practice vested in the committees of the council. Sweden and Norway also contrast with France and Spain, as chairmen have no executive authority and council affairs are run by executive committees which in principle direct the functional committees.

The two apparent exceptions to this tendency for fragmentation of authority under legal localism and concentration under political localism are Italy and Denmark. Denmark vests local government executive power in a mayor and committees, while in Italy it is divided between the mayor and the governing board or the *giunta*. The Italian *giunta* can be considered as equivalent to a committee structure since the *assessori* who make up the *giunta* have specific functional responsibilities in addition to acting as a form of local cabinet structure.[15] Mayors are thus in all countries bar France and Spain, in principle, forced to share executive power with colleagues from the council with defined functional responsibilities.

However, in practice the role of the mayor in the Italian system, while certainly far weaker than that of his French counterpart, is stronger than the role of the Danish *borgmester*. In Italy mayors can be and are not infrequently censured by their councils following clashes with their *giunta* and even forced to resign.[16] However, the potential for conflict reinforces the point that Italian mayors are active policy-makers enjoying a legitimacy that may bring them into conflict with political colleagues.[17] In Denmark the role of the mayor is far more limited. The mayor has a variety of non-executive functions, presiding over the council meetings and publicizing decisions, yet the executive capacity is narrowly confined to taking emergency decisions. Harder points out that

The Burgomaster's position as head of the local authority's administration gives him no powers, however, to take decisions in matters which are under consideration within the authority. More especially, the Burgomaster has no power to take decisions in matters which, under standing orders, are the responsibility of a committee . . . [or] matters which have been delegated by a committee to a department of the local authority.[18]

Since in Italy the power of the mayor offers an individual politician far greater power than is generally found in Britain and the Scandinavian countries, the nature of executive leadership in our seven countries tends to fit our expectations about the nature of leadership under political localism and centralism. This is not to suggest that cities with lower political localism never enjoy great leaders, still less that cities with higher political localism invariably or even frequently enjoy them. Rather, it is to suggest that the structure of executive power is concentrated in the hands of a single figure—a mayor—to a greater degree where political localism is stronger. Of course, coincidence does not establish a causal relationship, and it would be mistaken to interpret the evidence of the preceding paragraphs as proof that political centralism shapes leadership structures. However, some additional circumstantial evidence comes from the temporal coincidence in France between the origins of the *cumul des mandats* in the 1870s onwards and the emergence of the mayor as a political leader of the commune as evidenced by the progressive erosion in 1876, 1882, and 1884 of the state's power to nominate mayors in favour of election from the municipal council.[19] However, while causation can never be proven in this context, it is nevertheless possible to make a plausible link between the degree of political localism and the nature of executive leadership.

BUREAUCRATS AND POLITICIANS

The relationship between officials and politicians is crucial for understanding the nature of local government. Since the localness of local government is based upon its legitimacy, established in the modern era through elections, it is also a function of the degree to which what is done in the name of local government is shaped by a political as opposed to professional and bureaucratic élite. However, hard evidence is difficult to come by in any systematic way cross-nationally. The issue of relations between elected politicians and bureaucrats is still more difficult to deal with, not least because it has generated remarkably little empirical work.[20] There does appear to be, from the evidence that exists, some support for the expectation that the countries with greater legal localism and less political localism are likely to have more professional and powerful bureaucracies.

One indicator of the power of local bureaucracies can be seen in the status of their professional expertise. In Britain, the expertise of local bureaucrats enjoys a rather high status: in the period since the Second World War they have come to dominate the entry into local government professions. Bodies such as the Chartered Institute of Public Finance and Accountancy, the Institute of Housing, and the Royal Town Planning Institute grant qualifications to aspiring senior officials in these areas. Moreover, local government offers senior employment to legal practitioners, who tend to dominate in the most senior management positions of local government: the town clerk or chief executive. The national organizations of local officials are routinely contacted by national government on questions of a technical character and they are also involved in negotiations surrounding pay and conditions of service.[21] Of course, the actual wider social status of local officials does not correspond to the status of their expert advice. One popular and generally accurate describer of British civil service culture, the television and radio series *Yes Minister*, alluded to the popular image of worthy pomposity which attaches to almost anything to do with local government when the Minister, puzzled as to what environmental health officers did, was told bluntly by his civil servants that they were 'ratcatchers'.[22]

In France, despite their expertise and competence, local government bureaucrats enjoy a far lower status. This is not only because of their presence in the shadows of the immense technical reputation of the national bureaucratic élite but also because of the failure of local government employees to professionalize.[23] The Interior Ministry and the Ministry of Economy and Finances determine questions of qualification and pay for officials of the communes, and have kept communes from creating the sorts of senior posts that would attract high-fliers into local government employment.[24] Moreover, it is not uncommon to find national civil servants seconded to local government posts in cases where there are sensitive issues at stake, where expertise is unavailable locally. The decrease in national civil service recruitment has made communal public service more attractive for the better educated in the past few years—traditionally few with higher educational qualifications could be found among the top levels of the municipal civil service, which tended rather to be filled with those who had worked their way through the administration. In short, the whole picture of French local government bureaucracy is one of a low level of professionalization, not only in relation to the national civil service, but also in relation to their British counterparts.

The evidence on the other five countries is far more patchy. In Italy, without a national civil service of the status and prestige of the French, local government officials appear to have a relatively low degree of professionalization if this is measured by the status of their expertise and by the ability of officials to regulate entry to their profession.[25] Fried's study of Rome in the 1960s highlights the low status of municipal planners—professionals who enjoyed a particularly high status in Britain at around the same time.[26] While the planners of Italy did have a professional organization, the Istituto Nazionale di Urbanistica (INU), these were not in the main local government employees. As Fried explains:

fascist planners left the city offices . . . Since that time there has usually been a split between, on the one hand, the professional planners in INU, who work for government mostly as private consultants and are often deeply involved in the evolution of planning theory, and, on the other hand, the planners who work regularly for the City Planning Department who have been less caught up in the postwar climate of revisionism and more absorbed in their day-by-day administrative responsibilities. Since the early postwar period, INU planners have tended to be critical of the competence, integrity and outlook of the City Planning Department.[27]

Consistent with our expectation that politicians are less likely to decline in influence *vis-à-vis* professionals, it was only when sympathetic assessors were elected to the *giunta* that the INU managed to increase its influence in Rome; a feature also found in Bologna.[28] In both cities pro-planning assessors faced difficulties in putting through progressive plans for their cities in the face of council opposition which grew to such an extent that they fell from grace showing, as Fried says, that 'planners have experienced difficulties and failure even in Italian cities run by parties ostensibly favourable to planning. Italian planning journals tend to look outside Italy for examples of effective planning.'[29]

The contrast between the role of politicians and bureaucrats at the local level in Italy and Scandinavian countries is made by Kjellberg who argues that one general characteristic of Italian local government is the 'dominance of political elements in local government'. This he contrasts with Sweden, quoting from Tom Anton:

Apart from coalition government, the greatest structural source of support for unity among city politicians in Stockholm was and remains the dominance of professional administrators in city politics. The city's career public service—large in number, well trained and well rewarded—had traditionally enjoyed a very high degree of access to the political elite . . . The result has been an elite extraordinarily receptive to administrative definitions of issues and to professionally prescribed solutions to problems.[30]

Kjellberg adds that 'by and large this picture would also seem to fit Norwegian city politics, as evidenced by the attitudinal homogeneity of the municipal political elite across party lines, and the role played by the professional administrators in Norwegian local government.' Anton's conclusion for Sweden is that 'administrator influence means far more than control over information and expertise. Forced to seek nonembarrassing criteria of choice, but limited by their own multitude of responsibilities, city politicians move in the direction of least resistance by learning to think in administrative terms.'[31] Lane and Magnusson have also emphasized the importance of the local bureaucracy in local policy-making in Sweden and have offered quantitative evidence to show the increasing importance of bureaucratic actors in Sweden since the 1960s.[32]

The evidence, then, such as it is, suggests that where there is a higher degree of political localism, elected leaders are more likely to maintain their influence within the locality since they have a resource that can be constantly cashed—their legitimacy. This is consistent with the findings of scholars in the United States such as Greenstone and Peterson, who looked at the relationship between elected and non-elected city officials and contrasted machine cities, which have political authority based upon clientelism, with the more professionalized reform cities. In machine cities 'local politicians still have the capacity to control local bureaucracies', while in reform cities 'local administrators are guided more closely by federal legislation and administrative guidelines, even to the point of adopting the national mission as their own'.[33] Of course, decisions taken in the name of local politicians in any country reflect a strong influence of permanent officials whose experience offers them technical, political, and administrative expertise. In all countries the strength of politicians in this relationship is that democratic constitutions have placed them in positions of formal authority over permanent officials. Yet the way in which these democratic constitutions work in France and Italy gives local political élites something that is largely absent in Britain and Scandinavia: an additional source of authority. In France and Italy, elections do not only decide which party will govern the city, they provide individuals and networks with an affirmation of their worth to national officials. Since this affirmation can be used to extract resources from the centre, it offers something to political élites to maintain their position in the locality in spite of the universal pressures towards the increasing bureaucratization of political life.

LOCAL POLITICIANS AND CITIZENS

What differences might we expect different patterns of localism and centralism to make to the relationship between local citizens and their elected and non-elected officials? Two possible impacts might be explored. First, we might expect higher levels of participation where there is greater legal localism. This is based on the assumption that citizens are likely to perceive that they are influencing a more important institution where that institution has a wider range of powers. This observation follows on from the suggestion by Robert Dahl that effective participation is greater, other things being equal, where the institution in which citizens participate has itself greater power. Almond and Verba suggest 'in general, one would expect that the extent to which the local government is open to citizen participation in decisions would be closely related to the extent of local autonomy', a view that they feel was supported by their data and 'impressions of community life' in the nations they studied.[34] A second possible expectation would be that under political localism the means by which local citizens participate, other than through the electoral system, is mediated through political actors while under legal localism participatory mechanisms are channelled through bureaucratic actors. This is a corollary of our expectations about the power of local bureaucrats and politicians; since the literature on pressure groups suggests that groups target their attentions on the more powerful institutions and actors in government, we might expect participation to be geared towards political actors in the Southern European nations and towards bureaucratic actors in Northern Europe. If substantiated, this distinction between bureaucratic and political routes of access of local citizens to local officials is likely to shape differences in the relationship between citizens and their local government more widely. We can look at each of these issues in turn.

THE LEVEL OF PARTICIPATION

How far is the level of participation greater under greater legal localism? Unfortunately, there is no general cross-national indicator of levels of participation in local government. Participation is a complex phenomenon and can be manifested in activities as diverse as responding to a questionnaire conducted by a city council to taking part in a demonstration outside the city hall.

The only convenient means of comparing levels of participation is through electoral participation. The figures for local government electoral turnout for our seven nations are presented in Table 4.2. From Table 4.2 it can be seen that the major distinction is found between Britain and the remaining six countries. It is beyond the scope of this study to explain why electoral turnout should be so low in Britain. However, turnout appears unrelated to legal localism or to the range of powers given to local authorities and the freedom they

TABLE 4.2. *Municipal election turnout, averages (%)*[a]

Britain	40
Norway	81
Sweden	90
Denmark	80
Spain	69
Italy	85
France	70

[a] Spain; 1987; others late 1970s.
Source: M. Goldsmith and K. Newton, 'Local Government Abroad', in Committee of Inquiry into the Conduct of Local Authority Business Cmnd. 9797, *Research* iv, *Aspects of Local Democracy* (London: HMSO, 1986), 146; *Keesings Contemporary Archives*.

have in making arrangements to carry them out since both the highest and the lowest level of turnout are found among our nations where local functions and discretion are more extensive. Of course, electoral turnout is just one measure that fails to tap the whole range of possible modes of citizen participation. It would certainly be wrong to place too much emphasis upon it. However, the figures lend no support to the expectation that levels of participation are higher under greater legal localism.

STYLES OF PARTICIPATION

Where the power of professional local bureaucrats is stronger we can expect groups and individuals to channel their participation directly through local bureaucrats. Where politicians are in a more powerful position, we may expect citizens and groups to channel their participation through politicians. This much is suggested by pressure group theory. This might lead to different forms of participatory institutions. In one set of countries we would expect to find a predominance of forms of participation, such as direct contact with local politicians, emphasizing the role of the politician; in the other we would expect to find other more bureaucratic forms of participation, such as public inquiries, which emphasize the role of permanent professional officials. Moreover, we might expect citizen participation to be greater where channelled through the politician than through the bureaucrat since the bureaucrat has not the incentive to listen to the local citizenry, or sections of it, that the elected representative has through the pursuit of its vote.

It is not possible to make direct comparisons between degrees of citizen participation in our seven countries. The degree of participation itself is a function of at least three distinct features; the opportunities available for participation, the 'take-up' rate of the citizenry of these opportunities, and the impact of participation on public decisions. Systematic and comparable evidence on such issues is simply unavailable. We have some comparative studies which do, however, show differences in levels of participation. Hansen and Newton[35] show similar levels of interest group membership in Tromso, Norway, and Birmingham, England, yet interest group activity in Tromso politics was much higher. Interest groups were more than twice as likely to seek to influence political decisions in the Norwegian city than they were in the English. Miller suggests the insignificance of participatory mechanisms in Swedish urban government marks it off from many other Western nations including Britain and Denmark.[36]

Generally, however, there is no evidence to suggest that the relative positions of politicians and bureaucrats are likely to produce radically different institutions of public participation. Apart from the universal electoral mechanism, citizen participation is usually channelled through a variety of statutory as well as non-statutory processes of open meetings (as in the case of planning) or user/client representative bodies (such as in education). The basic principle here is that all interested citizens, or all affected citizens, have equal access to decision-makers. Usually such decision-makers are local government officials. This basic principle of equal access to all affected citizens is shown above all in the nature of the process of *kommunalbesvär* in Sweden, according to which complaints can be made against local government decisions to a higher authority. It is also found in planning inquiries, in council initiatives to promote public involvement in plans, and in user groups such as school boards of governors found in Britain as well as Scandinavia.[37]

The emphasis upon universalistic approaches to participation contrasts strongly with the general absence of such mechanisms in

France. It does not, however, contrast strongly with the principles of participation introduced in Italy. In Italy, neighbourhood government and *cogestióne* (co-management by users) of municipal institutions has developed significantly since the 1970s to such a point where 'in today's context of tighter communal budgets, the contribution to the management of services by users has become indispensable.'[38] By contrast, in France neighbourhood democracy and *cogestion*, management of municipal activities by clients and citizens, has been weak not only in terms of its take-up but also in terms of its promotion by local governments. In France, the traditional picture of the level of participation is outlined by Kesselman: group activity at the local level is 'unknown', and demands from citizens for services were 'infrequent and rarely organised'.[39] Such a judgement fits neatly into the view of French political relationships which has dominated the literature on France since its publication in 1964: *The Bureaucratic Phenomenon* of Crozier which suggests that a dominant cultural trait of the French system is that policy-makers are isolated from the influence of those over whom they govern.[40] In France the lack of group life within the commune has been a constant theme of sociological, anthropological, and political studies since at least Tocqueville.[41] It is also a view supported by more recent research. In his study of Villeneuve, Meyers shows how attempts to set up institutions of public participation first enjoyed substantial success in the 1970s, with large numbers of citizens attending public meetings, but very rapidly participatory goals faced lack of organized citizen involvement, apathy, and eventual exclusion of citizen groups from managing municipal services in the only true case of self-management that did emerge.[42] In short, if political localism through its impact on the position of political actors in the locality affects patterns of citizen participation, then the Italian and French contrast shows that the impact is not a simple one that equates greater politician influence with greater opportunity for citizen participation.

The factors which affect citizen participation in local government remain to be isolated empirically. Many authors suggest that levels of participation are products of 'culture'.[43] It is therefore a safe conclusion that political and legal centralism and localism, although they may certainly have a bearing on the subject, do not affect levels and styles of participation profoundly.

THE PURSUIT OF LEGITIMACY

However, it is possible that the ascendancy of the politician has a rather greater effect on the style of relationship between the local government authority and its citizens than on participation conceived largely as group activity. The literature on reformed government in the United States was less about the ability to participate than about the nature of the groups who are given access to decision-makers. Research on American cities has found that the distinction between reformed and unreformed municipal structures influences the relationship between the city authority and citizens. A reformed structure, with its emphasis upon institutionalizing technical expertise and eradicating the favour-trading that went on under political bosses, has generally been shown to be less responsive to citizen demands than the unreformed structures of local government.[44]

The thrust of Lineberry and Fowler's research was based on the distinction made several years earlier by Banfield and Wilson between 'public regarding' policies (i.e. policies that affect the population of a city at large) and 'private regarding' policies (i.e. policies that benefit a segment of the population of the city). Although this distinction, and in particular the assumptions about ethnic culture on which it was to some extent based, has been criticized widely, their general thesis 'pointing to the existence of two broad orientations about government, one emphasizing the search for a common good and the other emphasizing the role of government as a mechanism for deciding whose interests are to prevail when those interests conflict' is still widely accepted.[45] Using this distinction Lineberry and Fowler found statistical evidence to support the hypothesis that unreformed structures were more likely to be receptive to 'private regarding' policies than unreformed cities.[46] In an important refinement to the Lineberry and Fowler thesis, Karnig found that the level of community organization—broadly the degree to which there were active groups making private regarding demands on the city—was a crucial intermediating factor affecting the relationship between the city structure (reformed and unreformed) and the level of private regarding policy outputs.[47]

The reasoning behind this assumption is that 'a system of government based upon specific material inducements' as characterized the city machines of the United States 'is wholly at odds with that conception of democracy which says that decisions ought to be made on the basis of reasonable discussion about what the common good requires. Machine government is, essentially, a system of organized bribery.'[48] This stresses the role of the city as a manufacturer of 'gravy'—the goods that can be distributed unequally to different groups. The reform ideal, on the contrary, stresses impartiality, professionalism, 'particular regard for the public virtues of honesty, efficiency and impartiality; and a disposition to encourage the consumption of "public goods" like schools, parks, museums, libraries and, by extension, urban renewal'.[49]

When applied to our European cases, this suggests rather distinctive patterns of relationship between local governing élites and citizens in political systems where the governing élite is primarily bureaucratic and where local governing élites are primarily political. One cannot push the analogy too far, certainly not in the case of France, yet like the bosses of the US city machines, the day-to-day authority of the mayor in France and Italy depends upon the maintenance of public legitimacy within the commune. Legitimacy is not simply something that has to be acquired once every few years; it is something which has to be constantly nurtured. While local political leaders in all nations must fear the verdict of the electorate at the next election, the position of mayors in France and Italy is somewhat different from that of their counterparts in Scandinavia and Britain because the former are unable to act without it. In Britain and Scandinavia the power of political leaders, such as it is, derives from their formal control of an organization structured, in principle, on hierarchical lines. In France and Italy the power of political leaders depends heavily on their ability to act as mediators; their authority within the commune is contingent upon bringing external benefits, and their access to external benefits is contingent upon their authority within the commune. This distinction needs some elaboration.

Tarrow's study of mayoral leadership in Italy and France shows that the power of the mayor in each country rests upon his brokerage role with institutions outside that locality.[50] The role is a mediating one. His local power is based upon his access to institutions higher up. His access to institutions outside is based upon his ability to command resources at the local level. That is why there was a significant positive correlation between the extensiveness of a mayor's local contacts within the local community and the extensiveness of his contacts with provincial, regional, and national political actors. In Italy this command of resources is linked, as we have seen, to the mayor's position within the party as an intricate network able to influence votes in national elections. In France, the resource that the mayor can deliver is an 'ambiguous consensus'—a claim to speak for the commune either by helping to suppress political conflicts (a pattern of leadership associated with the rural mayors) or the ability to stand above political conflicts and offer a 'synthesis' of the general interest of the commune (a pattern of leadership associated with urban mayors).[51]

This form of legitimacy puts the French and Italian mayors in a rather different position from British and Scandinavian political leaders *vis-à-vis* their citizens. The legitimacy of politicians in British and Scandinavian local government is derived from the fact that public election has placed them in formal command of the local government apparatus. While, of course, under such a system it might be possible for the local administration to offer electoral bribes to particular groups, we would expect at least a far less direct style of local coalition-building and local support generation than in France and Italy.

If we look at the way in which mayors in France and Italy seek to build up their legitimacy we may see some rather divergent strategies. In France, studies largely of small towns have tended to emphasize an apolitical strategy of establishing legitimacy: the mayor establishes himself as a person who may 'speak for the commune' by suppressing political conflicts where they occur. This is the meaning of the 'ambiguous consensus' of Kesselman's study. To be re-elected a mayor must 'work to create the impression that he is working in the general interests of the population of the commune, that the benefits local citizens receive are the products of his personal action, and nobody else would have been able to achieve the same results'.[52] The mayor bases his apolitical character as the father of a united family—the metaphor frequently used by mayors to describe their relationship with the local community—on the apparent unity and consensus that obtain within the commune, yet mayors have to manufacture this unity and consensus. As Becquart-Leclercq's study shows, this is achieved in the smaller communes through establishing personal contacts with citizens, placating enemies by means such as getting their children into a desired school, pouring oil on troubled waters, and resolving differences over a cup of tea.[53] In the larger communes this is not a strategy that can stand alone. Instead, the repertoire of contacts between a mayor and his citizenry must be more diverse. This gave rise to the political machines of the earlier part of this century, similar in many respects to those of the US, being based upon jobs and public favours (such as licences) in return for electoral support.[54] With the drying up of the gravy provided by job patronage 'clientelism reappeared in a new guise' suggests Médard, a point best illustrated by the career of Chaban–Delmas in Bordeaux. His style was based upon maximizing personal contacts with citizens. He successfully courted the Bordeaux notables, the Catholic Church, and commercial interests to help sell his image to the electorate. He developed an active social policy targeted at the elderly and channelled it through a social worker adjoint mayor whose 'role as a go-between is inseparable from the close personal ties with the elderly and the notables'[55] and he pursued a strategy of co-opting political enemies—by patronizing enemies he managed to 'vassalize' them. The co-optation of political enemies appears to be particularly important. It would, of course, be wrong to suggest that populist strategies are the only strategies for establishing mayoral legitimacy. Another method, usually part of a wider repertoire in larger towns, is that of establishing a technical expertise. Nevertheless, there exists enough evidence to show that maintaining popular legitimacy is a constant concern of mayors in France, not merely something to be worried about as election time approaches, and that such strategies adopted in pursuit of legitimacy involve direct appeals to the local citizenry or the provision of what might be termed 'private regarding' policies in Banfield and Wilson's terminology.[56]

In Italy the relationship between political leaders and citizenry seems more straightforwardly clientelistic. Chubb's discussion of Palermo contrasts the importance of bureaucracy to the everyday life of Palermo citizens with the sluggishness of Italian administration as the major reason for the prevalence of what might be termed 'graft', both petty and large.[57] Policemen can turn a blind eye to minor offences, vending licences can be given or withheld, for example. This is in addition to the important but ultimately more limited patronage offered by offering employment. 'In such a situation ordinary citizens, and in particular the poor, disadvantaged by their illiteracy and lack of experiences in dealing with bureaucratic institutions are constrained to seek assistance from a higher status "patron" who can intervene directly on their behalf.' Membership of the DC in Palermo offers citizens access to this clientelistic network of favours. 'Once again,' Chubb continues, 'consensus is rooted in the critical intermediary role of the party or the individual politician in every transaction between the citizen and the state.'[58] The importance of patronage in jobs and other favours in the Italian South is shown by the fact that determined efforts by the Communists to eradicate them in another city, Naples, were unsuccessful; the Communists were ultimately led to introduce employment policies that could equally be regarded as based on patronage.[59]

This network of clientelistic ties, then, makes it easier to appreciate how what Fried terms 'private planning processes' were possible in Rome. The 'private planning process' was one in which

Individuals and agencies acted much as they wished and often in contrast to the policies emerging . . . from the public planning process. Public agencies and private corporations preferred central to peripheral sites and acted accordingly. Private individuals, for their part, found it desirable to build illegal extra stories on the old buildings in the center and to build five-storey apartment houses on suburban land not zoned for development; they found the lack of a building permit no hindrance to the implementation of *their* plans. These private planning activities, undertaken without regard to the dictates of public plans, were the major form of citizen participation in the planning process in postwar Rome.[60]

The Roman position does not appear to be one distinctive to the South—similar problems of enforcement of plans were reported in northern cities such as Milan, Turin, and Bologna.[61]

As Tarrow concludes, much of an Italian mayor's time is spent untangling red tape and doing other favours to build up political support.[62] This, he suggests, helps explain relatively high rates of turnover in the office. The evidence suggests that participation in Italian local government, whether in respect of trivial issues such as an individual licence or a broad planning issue, is likely to offer a powerful mediating role to political parties and through them to local politicians who preside over networks of influence within them.

The importance of the party channel in Italy forms the basis of

Kjellberg's examination of participatory institutions in Italy and Scandinavia.[63] While, as we have seen, the formal institution of neighbourhood government is certainly not uniquely Italian, Kjellberg distinguished the relatively greater influence of neighbourhood government in Italy from the experience of Sweden and Norway where there have been a 'few short-lived experiments'. This could not be explained by ideological differences between local élites in the two countries or by the fact that the Communists have greater strength in Italian cities, since neighbourhood groups have emerged in non-communist cities of Italy. Neither is it due to the fact that local governments appear to do less in Italy since, as Kjellberg suggests, this implies that they are little more than symbolic—something belied by their extension to a whole range of social and health services as well as cultural services. He suggests that 'the trend toward municipal decentralization in Italy is a function of the dominance of *political* elements in local government; it is the pervading political perspective which has fostered the neighbourhood group innovation and left its mark on its development.'[64]

Kjellberg points to the weakness of 'political elements' in Scandinavian local participation. This is, of course, not to say much about the degree of participation which, as we have seen, varies in a way unrelated to levels of political and legal localism. Rather, it suggests that while in Britain, Denmark, Norway, and Sweden the opportunity, take-up rate, and even impact of participation is variable, the relationship between citizen and local government is above all channelled through what might be termed bureaucratic or universalistic participatory mechanisms—user groups, neighbourhood groups, consultative procedures. In Italy and France such universalistic forms of participation can be found, but it appears they are in addition to a more direct relationship between local politicians and citizens. In Italy, the importance of party appears to have strengthened the influence of formal universalistic channels of participation, such as neighbourhood organizations, in addition to providing informal particularistic channels of influence, of the form suggested by Banfield and Wilson as producing 'private regarding' policies. In France, given the traditional weakness of voluntary organizations at the local level, particularistic channels of citizen influence appear to constitute the dominant link between the mayor and the local citizenry. In both Italy and France the structures of participation appear to be distinctly less bureaucratic, more particularistic and selective than the mechanisms that are stressed in discussions of participation in Britain and Scandinavia.

DISTRIBUTIVE CONSEQUENCES

One reviewer of the earlier book resulting from this project suggested that it would be useful to explore whether variations in central—local relations had some consequences for the distribution of public services.[65] By this he meant one should look at whether there exists, due to patterns of central-local relations, any systematic bias in the way in which goods and services are delivered such that certain groups, whether this be, say, the poor, the rural inhabitants, political enemies, tend to be advantaged or disadvantaged.

There are two reasons that one might expect patterns of central—local relations to have an impact on the distribution of public services. First, the legal dimension means that some services are administered by the central state and others by the municipalities. In so far as central and local governments have distinctive strategies, methods, or formulas for distributing services we might expect systematically different biases in the distribution of any set of benefits associated with a particular service, depending on whether the service was carried out by national or local government organizations. To illustrate this point: if it were found that national government were more likely to be redistributive to the poor than local government (a familiar enough argument in the context of federal—state relations in the USA), we might expect the provision of educational benefits to be more redistributive in systems such as France, where education is largely provided by national government organizations, than in systems such as Britain, where delivery of the service is largely in the hands of local authorities.

Of course, there is no such evidence of such a bias. Certainly, taking the nation as a whole, redistribution of resources from richer to poorer areas is almost by definition a function that can only be undertaken by a national government. Such redistribution is possible, however, through a grant system. National organization and redistribution of services cannot guarantee redistributive outcomes, nor is it the only way that they can be achieved.

Let us try to think about how bias may enter into the distribution of a service where the service is administered by local governments. It helps to have a clear type of bias in mind for this discussion, so let us take the case of education and think of some hypothetical ways in which distribution might be skewed against the poor where education is administered by local government. The bias can come from the spatial allocation of resources—a poorer locality gets less grant from the national government than a richer one or they both get the same amount of grant but the poorer one has fewer taxable resources. The bias might come from a set of *local* political decisions according to which councils in poorer areas for some reason devote smaller portions of their budgets to education. Or the bias might come from what in the American literature is termed the 'bureaucratic decision rules'—the norms and rules which govern who receives how much of a service.

The first two sources of bias are unlikely to be significantly related to the degree to which a service is delivered by national or local government, whether we conceive of national government as redistributive and local government as non-redistributive or vice versa. The possibility of bias through the territorial distribution of resources is just as great in many nationally administered services, such as the National Health Service in Britain or the education service in France.[66] The possibility of political bias through political decision is just as great through nationally administered services since political decisions taken nationally can target beneficiaries or losers; social security is a good example of this since national political decisions can change eligibility rules making the service more or less redistributive.

Bureaucratic decision rules have been subjected to much research in US urban political studies. Broadly this literature suggests that the types of decisions, norms, and assumptions that surround service distribution have implications for equity in service distribution. For example, one good indicator of police services is the response rate to calls for police help. Mladenka and Hill found in their study of Houston, Texas, that variations in response rate were related to the perceived seriousness of the crime and the perceived chances of arresting the offender.[67] Such decision rules have the potential of systematically skewing the distribution of police services. In fact Mladenka and Hill found no systematic bias against the poor or blacks in this set of decision rules. Some studies have managed to discover the decision rules governing the allocation of services and found no bias towards specific social, ethnic, or racial groups. Other studies, such as Levy and his colleagues' examination of service delivery in Oakland, found evidence of such a systematic class-related bias in which the poor were disadvantaged.[68] Jones cites the case of Detroit where the decision rule in the refuse collection department to assign extra resources to areas where there are alleys behind residences (because refuse placed in front of houses is generally kept tidier than refuse placed behind them) discriminates in favour of the poor.[69]

The point about discussing these cases of decision rules, the third possible source of bias in service provision, is that it is highly variable and dependent upon factors largely unrelated to the prevailing pattern of central–local relations. As Jones concludes: 'the distributional consequences of a bureaucratic decision rule depend on the nature of the rule.'[70] While political science research in Europe has not devoted much attention to such rules, the American research suggests that the bias that they introduce is related not to broad features of national political systems but to more specific issues of detail such as the precise nature of the decision rule (itself a function of a possible variety of past events) and the distribution of the population throughout the territory. Consequently, it is likely to be inappropriate to expect any broad characterization of central–local relations to affect such decision rules, still less their impact in terms of service equity.

There is, however, a second way in which we might expect the broad pattern of central–local relations to affect resource distribution. The literature on federalism, above all in the United States and Germany, has suggested that there is a link between political localism and the absence or presence of equalizing grants. According to such a view, the more powerful the voice of individual subnational governments at the national level, the less likely the development of a national policy that equalizes fiscal resources, since radical change produces losers as well as winners, and the potential losers have influence on government at the centre. Possibly the potential losers are also the most powerful; they are, after all, by definition the richer areas. Reissert points to the antagonistic interests of local government groups as one of the reasons for the failure to reform local finances in Germany.[71] While there are complex equalization formulas, they achieve only partial equalization.[72]

Unfortunately there is no available data enabling one to test the link between grants and the resources of the locality, as measured conventionally by variables such as per capita income or more general tax capacity.[73] Moreover, the degree to which grants equalize inequalities in local resources depends not only on the way the grant is distributed but also on the size of the grant. Two conditions then have to be filled for us to believe that grants compensate for inequalities in resources: they must have an equalizing design and they must be large enough to make an equalizing impact. In the absence of firm quantitative evidence, an examination of the equalizing properties of grant systems will offer some a priori support or criticism of the hypothesis linking political centralism to equalization.

In Britain, the central grant to local authorities is distributed on the basis of a formula that emphasizes two features: first, the assessed level of need for spending and second, the tax base of the locality. The method implies a high degree of equalization since it is based on the assumption that if all local authorities spent at the level of centrally assessed need, then the local tax rate charged would be uniform throughout England (outside London). Certainly the correspondence between local tax base (up until 1990 a function of the notional assessed rental value of property in the early 1970s) and more conventional indicators of wealth is an imperfect one. Moreover, the assessment of need as well as the penalties imposed for overspending assessed need also affect the equalizing impact of grants in Britain; however, from available evidence it appears that the impact of grants in Britain is significantly equalizing.[74]

In the Scandinavian countries, where specific grants generally make up a larger portion of total central grants receipts, there are equalization funds which ensure greater equity in grant distribution. Wolman and Page found that Denmark has a comparatively highly equalizing grant distribution effected through a centrally distributed equalization grant in addition to a horizontal fiscal equalization scheme.[75] In Sweden, the general state grant making up around one-fifth of total grant, is distributed on the basis of a formula based on the taxable resources of the municipality. In Norway, there exists an income support grant which is distributed to localities with low income tax yields. In all three Scandinavian countries, however, equalization grants are small by comparison with specific, service-related grants (see Table 2.6).

In France, the major general grant is the *Dotation Global de Fonctionnement*. It consists of three main elements: the *dotation forfaitaire*, which is paid in relation to tax effort (the tax paid by households); and two *dotations de perequation* (equalization) one distributed in inverse proportion to the tax potential of the commune (calculated as the tax yield of the national average local tax rates applied to the particular commune) and another distributed in inverse relation to business tax yields. In Spain and Italy, on the other hand, the absence of any true equalization grants has been indentified as a major problem of public finance in these countries.[76] In Spain, the dominant criterion for the distribution of the general national grant to the communes is population size. In Italy, despite some nominal and very crude equalization elements in the grant distribution formula, there has been 'no commitment to equalisation', and the bulk of grants are distributed on the basis of past expenditure.[77]

The available evidence does not suggest that equalization is impossible in systems where there is greater political localism. Above all, France since 1979 shows that equalizing grant formulas can be used as the basis for distributing significant amounts of money among municipalities even where local political élites have great power at the centre. To be fair, the actual results of this equalization in France seem singularly unimpressive—the correlation between taxable wealth, as approximated by per capita income was +0.72 in 1982, indicating that richer areas tend to get more grant despite equalization. This compares with negative correlations for Denmark and Britain (−0.83 and −0.34 respectively), indicating richer areas get less grant, especially in Denmark.[78] We do not have comparable figures for the other countries. Moreover, the French figure is based upon data aggregated up to the region, while in Denmark and Britain the unit of analysis is the county, so even these results must be treated with caution.

The most that we can say of the hypothesis that links political localism with lack of equalization is that it makes equalization a difficult objective to achieve. In France, the major exception to our hypothesized rule, Mény argues that

Too many interests unite in favour of a more or less amended status quo: the locally elected officials, who despite their ritual protests do not blame the state for their failures or the iniquity of the tax burden: the rich communes who refuse to share their windfall gains ... Thanks to the possibility to manipulate and nationalise the local system, France responded to the challenge of industrialisation and urbanisation in spite of communal fragmentation .... The need for an equalisation of resources in time of crisis has made the intervention of the state more acceptable.[79]

If we were to find that political localism was associated with the inability to produce redistributive grant formulas and coupled this with the clientelistic orientation towards citizens typical of local government within such systems, this would indeed constitute a powerful bias against promoting equality via service provision; such systems would appear to be incapable of targeting services on the basis of general indicators of need as opposed to relations of political power. This conclusion would be premature for three main reasons. First, local government in systems based upon political localism typically only account for a small portion of public spending and cannot contribute greatly to the maintenance of social inequality more widely. Second, and following on from this, we lack clear comparable evidence about redistribution through major public services, the most important of which in Italy, Spain, and France would be delivered outside local government. The evidence that does exist in Britain suggests that inequalities have persisted despite decades of spending and service growth.[80]

A third reason for doubting that political localism combined with clientelistic relations between élites and citizens can explain inequalities in service provision is that it is clearly not impossible to devise schemes containing significant degrees of equalization in systems with nationally powerful local political élites. It might be that the actual impact of these redistributive grants in France is more apparent than real, yet the considerable data requirements and methodological difficulties that must be encountered to test this adequately are beyond the means available for this study. It might also be that equalization is difficult under higher levels of political localism. Yet here again it might equally be that the low level of equalization in Italy and Spain and the late and apparently modest introduction of equalization in France reflect the fact that local governments spend less and therefore this means that the consequences of the persistence of fiscal inequalities are by no means as evident as in systems where local government does more. On the weight of existing evidence, then, we must conclude that fiscal equalization is not only found in governmental systems character-ized by relatively high levels of political centralism.

CONCLUSIONS

Our quest for the wider significance of patterns of centralism and localism can only be suggestive. This is not only because systematic comparative evidence is hard to come by, but also because causal links between a particular feature of central–local relations and other aspects of politics are difficult to substantiate given the fact that we have only a few countries in the comparative analysis.

Political localism, in its impact on the standing of the politician within the locality, appears to be the most important of our two dimensions in this respect. There is some evidence to suggest that political localism can enhance the power of the politicians *vis-à-vis* the professional administrators. This seems to have some implica-tions for the relationship between citizens and political leaders. The implications are hardly straightforward ones of greater participation under certain types of central–local regime. Such regularities in institutions or levels of participation simply cannot be detected. However, under greater political localism local politicians not only need to win elections, they need to be able to claim legitimacy in dealing with those outside the locality. This appears to create a greater incentive for direct appeals to the citizenry through 'private regarding' policy outputs. In turn the fact that such direct appeals take place in the context of a party organization in Italy means that they are part of a wider linkage structure which in turn strengthens citizen influence through the formal mechanisms of participation.

5

Explaining Patterns of Centralism and Localism

THEORETICAL APPROACHES TO CENTRALISM AND LOCALISM

Why should countries differ in their patterns of centralism and localism and consequently the opportunities that they offer local political élites to shape policy? There have been few systematic attempts to explain different patterns of national–local relations in different countries. Most of the recent theoretical work in the field of national–local relations, in fact, leads one to expect a high degree of similarity cross-nationally in the patterns of access that constitute our political scale of local influence as well as in terms of patterns of functional allocation that make up the legal scale.

The interorganizational approach which has been so influential in the study of national–local relations throughout the West since the 1970s, with its focus on complexity, interdependence, and bargaining, has tended to imply that patterns of policy-making vary so much within an individual nation across policy sectors and across time that broad generalizations about nations would be very difficult.[1] In probably the most systematic application of this genre to date, Rhodes finds it difficult to draw substantive cross-sectoral generalizations from his study of different policy networks and cases. To draw 'macro-level' conclusions from his analysis he has to go outside his framework and 'place networks in their context' by offering an interpretation of the nature of central–local relations and changes in this relationship over time. In doing so he postulates a number of interrelationships (for example, the relationship between 'policy mess' and 'partisan de-alignment') for which there is scant elaboration or evidence and which, more importantly, are quite remote from the concerns of his discussion of policy sectors and could have been derived independently of it.[2] In such an approach, which emphasizes detailed appreciation of the configuration of interests and power prevailing in any one set of national—local interactions, generalization must remain difficult. Consequently this body of literature is of little help in explaining differences in general patterns of national—local interaction.

Some other theories which have a bearing on national—local relations are also likely to be of little help in explaining differences cross-nationally since they are more or less based on the hypothesis that such differences do not exist, or if they do, they do not matter since the theories are only abstract constructs or ideal types. Into this category would fall the 'fiscal federalism' literature which suggests that the allocation of functional responsibilities to local government should be based upon criteria derived from economic theory such as efficiency in allocation, maximizing citizen choice over the quality and quantity of the good or service provided, and minimizing the externalities or spillovers, that is to say making sure that the advantages of the service provided or the disadvantages of poor services are primarily felt by the inhabitants of that area rather than a wider constituency.[3] While such an approach touches on the legal dimension of localism, it offers no explanation as to why functional allocation should not follow these principles.

Similarly, the 'dual state' thesis of Peter Saunders and the thesis put forward by Peterson in *City Limits* which flatly contradicts it do not address the question of cross-national variability.[4] According to these two arguments, the division of labour between national and local government and the resulting types of functions allocated to the local level shape the type of politics at the local level. For Saunders, writing of Britain, the local level is characterized by pluralism inherent in the nature of providing social welfare type services. For Peterson, writing of the United States, the local level is characterized by the dominance of business as a consequence of the prime role of local government as an attracter of industry and investment. Both of these theories, although framed in broad theoretical terms, are highly country specific and do not identify cross-national differences, let alone explain them.

There have been a number of writers who have sought to highlight and explain differences. Douglas Ashford's *British Dogmatism and French Pragmatism* offers an analysis of the differences between France, dominated by 'pragmatic' bargaining relations characteristic of political localism, and Britain with its 'dogmatic' refusal by national élites to become drawn into such relations.[5] Margaret Archer's *The Social Origins of Educational Systems* seeks to analyse and explain the different degrees of legal localism in so far as they are reflected in the educational system in Britain, France, Russia, and Denmark, with reference to experience elsewhere in addition.[6] Another important comparative analysis which seeks to explain different patterns of political localism, different patterns of linkage between national and local élites, is Sidney Tarrow's study of Italy and France, *Between Center and Periphery*.[7]

This chapter first examines these approaches to understanding cross-national variation in centralism and localism. While none of them offers a satisfactory explanation for divergent patterns of centralism and localism, the shortcomings of such theories have to be established before one can and should move on to develop an alternative. Moreover, in considering the shortcomings of existing theoretical works it is possible to learn a great deal about the more and less promising avenues of enquiry to be followed in developing an alternative. This chapter will then go on to develop such an alternative.

COMPARATIVE THEORIES OF NATIONAL—LOCAL RELATIONS

Margaret Archer has explored the development of centralization in the educational systems of four countries: Britain, Denmark, France, and Russia.[8] While not directly about local government itself, an examination of different administrative arrangements for education must be of interest to a comparative study of local government more generally since education is one of the largest local responsibilities in those countries where it is not nationally administered.

The central question of Archer's work as far as we are concerned in this chapter is the question of how centralized systems of education developed. A centralized system is 'centripetal in nature, for the negotiation of change depends upon the aggregation of grievances, the acquisition of political sponsorship and the percolation of these demands into the central decision making arena'.[9] A decentralized system is one in which there are multiple levels at which change can be negotiated and there is 'no necessity for demands to be cumulated or passed upwards, since changes can be introduced locally or internally'.[10] Centralization and decentralization, in Archer's work, are the major form of distinction between educational systems.

The degree of centralization and decentralization of an educational system is related to the nature of its development. Archer begins by asserting that education in all countries was at one time 'mono-integrated'. That is to say one group 'virtually monopolized formal instruction', which resulted in the fact that 'education was firmly linked to only a single part of the total social structure, namely that group with which the dominant group was associated'.[11] The differentiation between centralized and decentralized systems of education comes about in the process of development of a state system of education. In this process 'assertive groups' seek to wrest control of education from the dominant group. In doing so they could use two strategies: substitution and restriction. Substitution

consists in replacing the supply of educational facilities, which the dominant group had monopolized, by new ones. In practice, this means devaluing their monopoly by building and maintaining new schools and recruiting, training and paying new teachers to staff them. Here domination is challenged by competition on the educational market—the aim of the assertive group being to price the dominant party out of it or relegate it to a small corner of the market.

Restriction, on the other hand, means coercive appropriation of the means of educational production: buildings, funds, and personnel. 'Here domination is challenged, not by market competition but by coercive power—the aim being the forcible transfer of educational control.'[12]

In France and Russia the challenge to dominant groups in education came through restrictive strategies; the state forcibly removed control of schools from the church. In Britain and Denmark the dominance of the church was challenged through the setting up of competitive educational systems: non-denominational and vocational schools. From restrictive origins emerge highly 'unified' or 'centralized' systems of education:

Restriction itself involved manipulation of the state machinery in order to terminate educational practices which were harmful to the operations of the elite. . . . If the aims of the political elite are to be satisfied, unification must be intense and extensive. What is significant about such systems is that this group is in a position to *design* the unified administrative framework in accordance with its goals. The central administrative agencies formed . . . have a strong, hierarchical distribution of authority in which each lower administrative level is subject to a higher one and ultimate control is exercised at the apex by a political officer. In turn this means a very low degree of autonomy of decision making in the various regions or in individual schools.[13]

Correspondingly, substitutive origins are not liable to develop such strong centralized forms of administration: '*forceful* political initiatives in favour of a *strongly unified* system are lacking in such countries.'[14] A large portion of the remainder of Archer's book sets out how each of the systems in the four countries develops, yet from the perspective of centralization, as seen as a strong form of 'unification', the distinction between France and Russia on the one hand and Britain and Denmark on the other largely persists into the contemporary era.

This is a very attractive theory, impressively argued and backed up with almost encyclopaedic knowledge of the development not only of the four relevant educational systems, but also their social and political systems too. Such a theory quite clearly helps us to understand the development of the educational powers of local authorities on a legal scale, although the decentralization to which Archer refers is not solely about institutions of local government but rather refers to the potential access of a variety of groups (e.g. the teaching profession) to the educational policy process. Can it be used to understand the centralization or decentralization of a wider range of government services?

Education is a distinctive service since it has generated major political conflict; above all it was the arena in which was fought out, as Rokkan puts it, one of the fundamental issues of nation building—the relation between church and state.[15] Certainly, other ancestors of contemporary local services were also involved in this conflict—poor relief, solemnization of births, deaths, and marriages—but education was clearly the most important issue to both the church and the state. It is difficult to find struggles for control between political or social groups for any other service currently administered by local governments. For example, Gerald Rhodes looks at the development of weights and measures inspectors in Britain and finds that there was no evidence of any thought, let alone debate, about whether the service should be controlled or administered locally or centrally.[16] In roads administration too it would be hard to explain the relative decentralization of the early British road system and the centralization of the French in terms of specific struggles between assertive or dominant groups. In both France and Britain government was the only real provider of roads, so there is no dominant group from which the state apparatus may wrest monopoly control.[17] Moreover, the extension of the provision of roads (characteristically in France the motives for more extensive state road provision appeared to be military, in Britain they were rather commercial)[18] scarcely involved any major national controversies, let alone any of a scale to match the church—state controversy in education.

There is a second and more important reason for doubting that Archer's approach can be extended to embrace an explanation for the development of differences in the legal scale of local self-government. The patterns of 'centralization' and 'decentralization' found in education appear to be found in other areas without this reflecting such past conflicts between dominant and assertive groups. As has been shown in Chapter 2, legal centralism applies to a whole range of services in France, Italy, and Spain. Now, it may be that the factors which caused assertive groups to go for substitutive strategies or coercive ones also obtain for other services. As Archer states, 'it remains quite possible that a broader web of social relations, spun in other parts of the social structure, in fact, envelops educational interaction.'[19] I have already argued that one is unlikely to find conflicts of the same magnitude, importance, or nature in many other local services. This would, then, suggest that there are other causes for the fact that the form of centralization about which Archer writes, legal centralism in the terminology of this study, appears to apply more generally in each country and not to education in particular. Kogan made this point:

Although it would be old fashioned to think in terms of national characteristics determining educational systems, the question might be asked as to whether prevailing cultures which embody views of the educational process are not at least part of the reason why, for example, education in Britain works within a polity that is permeable, accessible in its structures and styles while Russia, come Tsar, come Soviet, hardly changes at all.[20]

In short, the patterns of centralism and localism about which Archer writes in the context of education appear to be reflected outside the educational sphere to such a degree that one might question whether differences in patterns for the government of education result primarily from the interaction between groups and interests involved in the educational sphere alone.

Ashford's comparative study of France and Britain concentrates upon what I have referred to in this book as the political scale of local self-government. In fact, Ashford is critical of what he understands as an overemphasis in British studies of local government upon 'local autonomy' (legal localism in the terms of this book) as the 'only acceptable evidence of local democracy'.[21] French pragmatism resides in the fact that 'the subnational system is more important to the political system and the formalities of administrative and political behaviour can easily cloak the more flexible and diverse ways that political actors have devised to influence each other.' This pragmatism results from the complicity between national and local administrative and political élites of the form well documented by Kesselman, Crozier, and Worms among others.[22] In Britain, dogmatism is characterized by the fact that 'policies concerning the subnational system tend to isolate interdependent choices, to fix on rather narrow goals, and to arrive at relatively singular strategies for change.'[23] This results from the nature of local politics in Britain: 'The national and local electoral systems, the relationship of national and local parties, and very different orientations of national party leaders serve to attenuate local issues and to isolate local politics from higher level decisions.'[24]

Ashford makes a claim that his 'structural' analysis offers some general means of 'dealing with the historical and institutional diversity of political systems'.[25] However, the approach, rich though it is in factual detail, does not offer a general theoretical approach. His broad comparative conclusions are that as the welfare state develops, different polities must cope with the problems of central–local relations that emerge, and that Britain and France cope with these problems in different ways. The resulting patterns of central–local policy-making are 'embedded in the institutional and political fabric of the two countries'.[26]

In one sense Ashford's approach is descriptive rather than explanatory; it describes the way in which local government has developed within the welfare state. However, this book has set itself the task of explaining differences in the opportunities for local influence on the legal and political scale. Moreover, Ashford's approach appears incapable of being extended to a wider comparative context. Above all this is because the criteria for defining systems as pragmatic or dogmatic are nowhere set out clearly. In fact, in discussing dogmatism and pragmatism Ashford tends to conflate two aspects of central—local relations: the process and the outcomes. Britain is dogmatic because of the absence of influential local actors participating in national policy-making arenas in contrast with the pragmatic French. The pragmatic French produce 'more durable, more acceptable and more effective policy changes'.[27] Now of course, there are problems with the view that the French pattern is necessarily 'good' or even 'democratic'. Kesselman underlines the tendency endemic in the French system for local élites to suppress political conflicts; for Crozier the central—local relationship is one of the dominant features characterizing the immobility of the 'Stalled Society'.[28]

These evaluative considerations aside, there is the implicit assumption within Ashford's approach that only where local government has close political ties to the national policy-making system can one secure 'durable, acceptable and more effective policy changes' as far as national policies for local government are concerned. Such a conclusion is not altogether self-evident. In fact, the propensity to produce consensual policies is an often praised feature of the Scandinavian system of government. Since, as we have seen, the national importance of local government is far less in the three Scandinavian countries, the notion of pragmatism as an outcome (type of policy) appears unrelated to pragmatism as a process (integrating national and local politics). This might, however, mean there are alternative pragmatic procedures for incorporating local government in national policy-making, such as interest group negotiation at the national level or even 'corporatist' consultative bodies. If this is the case, then it is something that has to be deduced from Ashford's work rather than found within it; the theory itself is not sufficiently elaborated to enable one to apply it elsewhere.

Tarrow introduces his comparative study of Italy and France with a general analytical framework which seeks to combine rather divergent approaches to the integration of peripheral areas in modern economic, social, and political systems. Tarrow highlights two major variables in the relationship between centre and periphery: the 'elite coalitional strategy' and the 'strength of institutional linkages'. Élite coalitional strategies shape the general ideology that central government élites have in respect to their roles in making policies for the peripheries. One of these élite ideologies, he argues, is one of 'normative equality', viewing the periphery as an area to be 'liberated from the artificial shackles of poor education, isolation and traditional local elites'.[29] An alternative ideology is that of 'technocratic reformism' which stresses 'the periphery's poor organisation' for productive economic enterprise; the 'welfare ideology' emphasizes the use of nationally designed social and economic programmes to relieve the problems of underdeveloped peripheries.

The ideology dominant in any country will be shaped by the coalitions existing between dominant national élites and local or peripheral élites. Just as the 'alliance between the iron and the rye' in Germany and the deal between the North and South of Italy around the time of unification gave national ruling élites political support from peripheral élites, under modern conditions such support must be broader and can take one of two forms: populist coalitions or productive coalitions. Under populist coalitions national élites seek support from a provincial petty bourgeoisie, peasants, and artisans. Under productive coalitions national élites seek alliances with 'the most productive groups on the periphery on the theory that they will be most likely to generate a multiplier effect out of the public resources that are expended'.[30] State benefits in the form of grants to local government should, he argues, be targeted towards these coalition partners.

Another dimension, however, that has to be brought into the model is the degree to which the centre is actually capable of targeting benefits, in most cases central grants, to the social groups that correspond to its coalition strategy. A territorial system might be integrated, meaning that there is sufficient capacity at the centre to direct benefits to coalition partners, or it might be diffuse allowing local political élites to change national policy priorities. Combining institutional strength (diffuse or integrated) and the two élite coalitional strategies (populist or productive) Tarrow arrives at four types of policies: redistributive policies where an integrated state apparatus directs benefits to its petty bourgeois, peasant, and artisan coalition partners; clientelistic policies where benefits targeted to the same group come under the influence of peripheral élites in their distribution; *dirigiste* policies where the central state can direct its benefits to productive peripheral forces through an integrated state apparatus; and (less well defined) extractive policies meaning, in Tarrow's words, that the 'state's links to the periphery are permeated by the market . . . [and] the periphery's regulation may actually take the form of economic extraction, as in the United States in the long period of peripheral decline between the New Deal and the 1960s'.[31]

Tarrow's theoretical approach is interesting and appealing for three main reasons. First, it distinguishes between different forms of relationship between centre and periphery according to a clear and logical framework. Second, it suggests, albeit tentatively, some factors that might account for differences between different patterns of centre–periphery relationships; for example, he suggests that 'productive' coalition strategies are more likely where there is a higher level of economic development. Third, it suggests some empirical policy consequences of different patterns of centre–periphery relations.

There are, however, several problems in the application of the approach in a cross-national study which includes more than the two nations Tarrow examines, France and Italy. First, the approach applies most readily where there is a rather limited range of local government functions. Take, for example, education. Education is one of the largest, in some cases the largest, single local government service in those countries where public education is not provided through central state organizations. In so far as central grants take account of spending needs, among other things, they are likely to be targeted toward local authorities with larger numbers of pupils of school age. Thus we find, for example, that grant per head of population in Britain correlates positively with the percentage of the population made up of pupils of school age.[32] This grant distribution has less to do with the political allegiance strategies of national élites than with the fact that education is in Britain, as in all developed nations, a major governmental responsibility. In Britain, unlike places like France and Italy, running schools is a large and major responsibility of local government, and national support for this service is reflected in grant distribution. Grants cannot simply be taken as indications of national–local élite relations. Consequently, Tarrow's analysis cannot be extended to a wider array of local government authorities since the benefits distributed to the periphery and the way in which they are distributed are likely to be crucially shaped by the distribution of functions between central and local government.

A second problem with Tarrow's approach is related to this: one can doubt the appropriateness of local government as a vehicle for exploring the hypotheses he raises. The analysis is designed to look at the channelling of resources between centre and periphery. Yet local government expenditure constitutes only a small proportion of total public expenditure in France and Italy (see Chapter 2), and central grants to local government only a small portion of the totality of central government resources expended in the periphery. If, to take Britain as an example, one were looking for evidence of a 'productive coalition', one would not look at central grants to local government, but rather at the wider question of industrial incentives, very few of which are channelled through local government. Tarrow's theory is not about local government *per se*, but about peripheral development and integration in its entirety. Consequently one can doubt that local government is an appropriate laboratory for testing such broad hypotheses, especially when one extends the comparison to include countries with great dissimilarities in the ways in which central funds find their way to the periphery or provinces.

A third problem with extending the Tarrow thesis is that its assumption that peripheral élites remain important coalition partners for central political élites is based very much on conditions that obtain in France and Italy. The notion of the 'productive coalition' in France is one that corresponds very closely to recent experience. De Gaulle, through regionalization, hoped to enlist the support of local economic élites, the *forces vives*, in economic modernization.[33] Clientelism is a term that has nearly become extremely closely identified with Italy, as has *dirigisme* with France. Yet Tarrow's model does not apply to countries where there is no great incentive for national politicians to engage in the sort of allegiances which produce distinctive patterns of policy distribution. In Britain, as Bulpitt has argued, the 'dual polity'—involving the separation of national from local politics—that has characterized the British 'territorial code' for the past century at least has been based upon taking for granted the fact that local political élites, regarded by national politicians as at best worthy provincial sorts, would run local government without generating any embarrassing controversies for national politicians.[34] British national élites have made no determined effort to coalesce with local political élites; neither have they sought consistently to garner support for economic modernization among identified peripheral élites in the same way that de Gaulle sought to recruit the *forces vives* to his vision of economic modernization.

For these three reasons, then, Tarrow's masterful comparison of France and Italy does not offer a general framework which can be used to explain variations along my two scales of localism. Tarrow's work, like that of Ashford and Archer, points to the importance of the historical dimension in understanding differences in local government. Archer, above all, devotes a large portion of her work to the early involvement of the state in educational provision. Ashford writes about the 'two paths from monarchy to democracy' in France and Britain and draws parallels between the nineteenth century and the contemporary scene. The importance of the historical dimension is less pronounced in Tarrow's empirical material, but it is certainly present in the theoretical discussion: his is after all a theory about the political *development* of national and local relationships. It is to an exploration of differences in historical development, as far as central–local relationships are concerned, that the remainder of this chapter is devoted.

HISTORICAL APPROACHES TO UNDERSTANDING CENTRAL–LOCAL RELATIONS

Archer, Ashford, and Tarrow are of course not unique in discussing the importance of historical dimension in the explanation of distinctive features of national–local relations. A number of authors have pointed out similarities between contemporary patterns and those prevailing many years, even centuries, ago. Thoenig, for example, discusses the development of a particular brand of centralization in France in the late nineteenth century.[35] One could even point to the fairly direct and conscious link between Tocqueville's description of centralization under the *ancien régime* in France and Crozier's analysis of the 'local politico-administrative system' published a century and a quarter later.[36] The whole basis of Ashford's study of 'British dogmatism' and 'French pragmatism' is that central–local relations in Britain and France have retained their own respective distinctive features over a century of development.[37] All of this lends further weight to the suggestion that it would be fruitful to look for historical explanation of differences in central–local government relations.

One fairly attractive historically based explanation for differences between central–local relations in different European nations is the argument that the Southern European nations display the legacy of the Napoleonic era and the Northern European ones the lack of such an influence. Such an explanation is attractive for a variety of reasons, not least because the origins of the modern forms of local government in France, Italy, and Spain are Napoleonic: the terms 'prefect' and 'department' are very clearly Napoleonic whatever their more distant provenance. Moreover, there appears to be a neat coincidence between features of local government, such as the existence of a powerful prefect, and the extent of Napoleon's Europe.

Sharpe's essay contrasting local government reorganization in the United Kingdom with the pattern elsewhere in Western Europe distinguishes between the 'Napoleonic States' of Belgium, France, Italy, Spain, Portugal, and Greece, and non-Napoleonic states.[38] Sharpe points out, in the context of a study of structural reform, that these Napoleonic states share much in common that has been discussed in this book as legal centralism and political localism. Use of Napoleon's name suggests some form of causal link between inclusion in the French First Empire and the form of local government.

There are a number of problems with such an approach which links such a historical experience with contemporary local government structures. First, the type of structure associated with Napoleonic rule was widespread in Europe until the earlier part of this century in countries other than those forming part of the First Empire. Sharpe offers a useful definition of what we usually regard as characteristic of a Napoleonic system:

the division of the state into fairly uniform jurisdictions that are larger than the basic units of local government and over which nominally presides an appointed civil servant—the prefect—as a kind of *primus inter pares* in relation to both the elected local government and a series of out-stationed central technical personnel who provide local services within the jurisdiction.[39]

If we look at Montagu Harris's survey we find that such a structure could be found earlier this century in the countries included by Sharpe as Napoleonic, some parts of the First Empire not included by Sharpe as Napoleonic, such as the Netherlands and parts of Germany West of the Rhine, as well as countries outside it such as Norway and Denmark.[40]

The experience of Napoleonic rule appears to be neither a necessary nor sufficient condition to develop a Napoleonic system of government. Some of the German portions of the empire developed in ways that differed markedly from the French 'Napoleonic' pattern after Napoleon's defeat.[41] In addition to this, as suggested above, the origins of many of the territorial governmental institutions associated with Napoleon date from at least the seventeenth century and sometimes even much earlier. In some cases these institutions have declined in importance or disappeared altogether, and in others they have persisted. This suggests another problem with a 'Napoleonic' explanation of the differences between nations: such an explanation begs the question of what it was about a period of two decades, during which much of Europe was ruled by Napoleonic governmental structures, that should determine the development of local government for such a long time to come.

What, then, in the absence of a simple explanation that perceives local government structures to be a function of Napoleon's military and diplomatic successes, might explain different patterns of development in the relations between local and central government, the development of different modes of local self-government? There is no general theory. Perhaps the closest to a general theory of the development of central–local relations in Europe can be found in Otto Hintze's works on state formation and local government, including studies of institutions of territorial government such as the Kreis or the commissary in comparative European perspective. While Hintze's work is fascinating and useful it makes no claim to offer an explanation for modern patterns of local self-government, since it focuses primarily on the period up to 1800.[42]

While Hintze's work will be used as an important component in this exploration of causes for differences, such an exploration must take us further ahead in time. The basic argument of this chapter is that there developed by the end of the eighteenth century a common pattern of central–local relations in five of the six continental

European nations in this study: a pattern of administrative control of local government by a central state official. Such a pattern did not apply in Britain and only to a limited extent in Sweden. The reforms of the nineteenth century which virtually created systems of local government in each of the countries did not alter this basic distinction between Britain and Sweden and the remaining countries. However, in the twentieth century such a pattern of administrative control only persisted in the three Southern European nations due to the importance of local government in networks of clientelism on which major political parties based their support in these countries after the introduction of mass suffrage. I will present this argument in four stages: first, looking at development to 1800, second, looking at the reform of local government in the nineteenth century, third, looking at patterns of clientelism in the twentieth century, and finally bringing all the parts of the explanation together. In outlining the argument I do not offer a discussion of the history of local government in these seven countries, rather I concentrate on those aspects of the development of local government that have a particular bearing on the relationship with national government.

THE PERIOD TO 1800

Otto Hintze distinguishes between two great epochs in the history of local government. In the first epoch, starting in the medieval period, local government institutions were shaped by 'actual relationships'. Their development was not planned or consciously designed but evolved 'organically'. In the second epoch, starting at the beginning of the nineteenth century, the development of local government was based upon 'theories', by which he means the conscious planning of administrative organizations. Stein and Turgot are early examples of the administrative organization theorists he has in mind. In the first epoch, explanations for patterns of local self-government reflect historical patterns of social stratification and relationships between political and social groups. If we look at this early period we can see some important differentiation among our seven countries. Let us first look at the patterns of territorial administration in this period before turning to Hintze's explanations of them.[43]

The French system of central supervision of territorial government through the institution of the intendant, the predecessor of the Napoleonic prefect, can be traced back to the fifteenth century. It only became significant in the 1630s onwards following the civil wars of the late sixteenth century, and was expanded under Colbert in the late seventeenth century so that by the early eighteenth century the whole of France became subject to the institution of the intendant.[44] The intendant was a royal agent empowered to collect taxes, administer justice, and supervise the actions of the municipalities.[45]

The institution of intendant was also found in Spain and Italy. In pre-unification Italy probably the most important of the states for our purposes is Piedmont since, as Fried suggests, 'The roots of Italian Administration are Piedmontese: for it was Piedmont that led the process of fusing the seven states of the peninsula into the united Kingdom of Italy and that bequeathed to the new nation-state its dynasty, its constitution, and its laws.'[46] The Duchy was divided into provinces during the period of absolutism under Emanuel Philibert in the latter half of the sixteenth century. While the specific arrangements for each province and each municipality might actually differ, in general each province was headed by a referendary, primarily a judicial position, and a military governor with law and order functions. The position of referendary was expanded, especially in the last decade of the seventeenth century, to include supervision of local budgets, decisions, and elections and was relabelled 'intendant'. Unlike the position in France, where the military governors (the old *prévôts de maréchaux*) lost their functions to the intendants above all after their support for the insurgents in the Fronde uprising in the middle of the seventeenth century, central state organization in Italy remained under two principal central state officials.[47]

Under Fernando VI, Spain was divided into provinces which were the responsibility of the royal governor, the intendant also given the judicial position of *corregidor*, who became increasingly powerful in the latter half of the eighteenth century. By the end of the century he was the most important figure in the locality, 'very powerful, seldom loved but generally respected', having responsibilities for policing, justice, economic regulation, revenue collection, and avoidance of food shortages.[48] Furthermore, these intendants could not, after Carlos III's ordinance of 1783, be natives of the provinces for which they were responsible. The position in Spain, however, differed significantly from that of France and Italy in the eighteenth century since the control over the municipality was much weaker. As Carr states, 'The fatal flaw was the last link in the chain of command—municipal government. It was here that the Caroline reformers achieved nothing because the crown could not recapture the powers it had made over to local municipal oligarchs. The impetus of reform and modernization was dissipated in the town hall where the government failed to insert effective instruments of its will. . . . The destruction of these "little republics" was left to the liberal statesmen of the nineteenth century.'[49]

Royal governors were not unique to Southern Europe. In Norway, Sweden, and Denmark they were county-based officials owing their origins to the period of absolutism in the seventeenth century. Moreover, the English justice of the peace was a central government appointee with a powerful role in territorial government. Yet in Britain central state supervision of local government, such as it was, emerged as far weaker by the beginning of the nineteenth century than in Norway and Denmark and certainly weaker than in Spain, Piedmont, and France.

In Denmark, the rapid development of absolutism under Frederick III between the Diet of Copenhagen in 1660 and the codification of the powers of the monarch in the Kongelov of 1665 had a major impact on the system of territorial government. Under Hannibal Sehested, the Grand Chancellor, the new territorial division, the *amt*, replaced the feudal *len*. These were governed not by provincial *lensmenn* but the new central officials, the *amtmenn*.[50]

In Norway, the old Germanic forms of territorial organization, counties and townships, remained formally in place by the end of the eighteenth century, as Hovde explains, for 'feudalism had never become so strong as to obliterate them entirely.'[51] As in Denmark, the *len*, or counties, were units which could be traced back to medieval times. Under Danish absolutism the *len* and the *lensheere*—the old designation for counties and their noble leaders—were replaced by the terms *amt* and *amtmand*, reflecting a change away from these as units of local self-government and towards their nature as units of central administration. This change was reinforced through the transformation of the *amtmand* into a royal appointee responsible for the administration of the *amt*. By all accounts this was the only form of territorial government, since local government, outside the towns at least, was extremely weak. The counties, as indirectly elected assemblies, were powerless. Residents of towns and villages normally held general meetings, either on the initiative of citizens or of the government, which had no official power other than advisory influence. Frequently these took the form of consultations with royal officials after church services on a Sunday. Where felt, the influence of parochial government on public policy appeared also to be highly conservative—Derry discusses the preoccupation of the peasantry with curbing perceived government excesses in spending.[52] In the cities there developed the practice of committees forming to take the place of the mass meeting; this development was formalized in 1687 by a law which provided for the selection by government officials of 'best citizens', later 'deputized citizens', to consult with royal authorities. The law also provided for 'best parishioners' to help oversee church administration and provide a pool of possible appointees for poor relief and schools. Yet, on the whole, local government was extremely weak: 'since there was no class of country gentry and (until 1837) no regular form of rural self-government, the resident officials were not much hampered by local opinion in the interpretation of laws and regulations.'[53]

In Sweden, a significantly different picture emerges. As in Denmark and Norway the *lan* or county units of government reflected territorial divisions of a medieval era (the *landskap*). In the 1630s these had grafted on to them the characteristics of a central royal agency through the creation of the *landshövding*. Also in the seventeenth century were created the subdivisions of counties for administrative purposes, the *fogderier* with the *haradshövding* as the state representative. The original impetus for creating this level of government was similar to the creation and expansion of the intendants in Southern Europe: for military and highway purposes. So far the Swedish experience differs little from the experience of Norway and Denmark. However, in the eighteenth century the role of the county and *härad* eroded—the *härad* became a district for strictly judicial purposes. The *landshövding* remained important for central administration in the provinces yet from the seventeenth century onwards parochial government appears to have occupied a greater role in territorial administration than the district or the *lan*. Swedish county government appeared to have little importance by the end of the eighteenth century.[54] In contrast, however, local self-government in the parish (the *socken*) appeared to thrive—so much so that in the course of the century it adopted many more functions. As Andren suggests, the parish not, as in England, the county is the 'backbone in Swedish local government'.[55]

In England the shire or county was the main territorial unit of government at the beginning of the nineteenth century. Despite the existence of parish and town government, it would have appeared preposterous, as Webb and Webb argue, to assert anything other than that 'the government of the various parts of England and Wales rested, under King and Parliament, with the official dignitaries of the County—the Lord Lieutenant, the High Sherriff and the Justices of the Peace.'[56] The county was the area of jurisdiction for the major institutions of subnational government in England from the medieval period prior to the early part of the nineteenth century. The *custos rotulorum*, the Lord-Lieutenant, the sheriff, the high constables, coroners, and justices of the peace were county officials. Operating both within and outside the institutions of the Quarter Sessions, these justices had wide powers which extended beyond their law and order functions. These included, for example, the passage of regulations concerning the administration of relief to the poor; the Speenhamland system is perhaps the most famous example of the exercise of power by county justices.[57] Moreover, despite their formal integration into the British legal system and despite their formal subservience to the Crown, the justices of the peace enjoyed a high degree of autonomy. Webb and Webb write:

In spite of all forms and appearances, the rulers of the English county felt themselves at liberty to administer the local affairs as they thought fit. If we were asked to name a period in English history during which the county possessed the largest measure of self-government, when its local administrators were most effectively free from central control ... we would suggest the years between 1689 and 1835, or, more precisely, the century that elapsed between the accession of the House of Hannover and the close of the Napoleonic wars.

The Quarter Sessions developed into a powerful legislative body within the county which was rarely under any obligation to subject its resolutions to central government agencies. It was, Webb and Webb continue, an 'inchoate provincial legislature'.[58]

Otto Hintze suggests an explanation for this apparent difference between Sweden and England on the one hand, where central government supervision appeared relatively light, and our remaining five nations of Spain, Italy, France, Norway, and Denmark on the other. The central thesis of Hintze's work on the development of local government is that Europe can be divided into two broad groups: the 'core' of the Franconian empire—France, Germany to the Elbe, Aragon, and North Italy, in which county government disappeared by the beginning of the nineteenth century, and the peripheral areas of England, Scandinavia, Poland, Hungary, and Bohemia where county government formed the basis for government after the nineteenth century. Three things, he argues, shaped this development.

First, the system of military conscription of the Carolingian Empire. 'All constitutions are originally constitutions for wars and armies.' It was the personal contracts between the monarchy and the nobility that characterized the heartland of the Carolingian Empire, according to which land was granted explicitly in exchange for making up the military, and the strict hierarchical character of constitutional arrangements that this produced destroyed the old county levels of government. Despite the development in England of a similar system after the Norman Conquest, 'the water that brought Franconian feudalism did not penetrate very deeply and soon receded. In the twelfth century a feudal military structure was abandoned, in the thirteenth century the feudal economic structure was modernised through the introduction of leaseholds, and the parliamentary constitution took over from the feudal in the fourteenth century.'[59]

It was the particular feudal system of the Carolingian Empire that destroyed the old county levels through its creation of a power base for a territorial nobility to challenge the authority of the monarchy. In the process of state building the counties had to be destroyed:

in France and Germany the new territorial units of government are based on the destruction and dissolution of the old Gau and County structures, of which only fragments, such as parishes (Kirchspiele) and Goes (Hundreds) became part of subsequent territorial organisations. But such small fragments were too small to form the basis for a larger gentry-based local government; at most they could lead to the involvement in public affairs of the commune or parish by its agrarian inhabitants, which in any case only happened very rarely.[60]

This was replaced in the heartland of Europe by new administrative districts created by the state and supervised by state officials. Local self-government in the county was thus destroyed.

However, local self-government could also be destroyed if there were not the type of people able to run it reasonably efficiently and without seeking to use local government as a means of obstructing or opposing the national government. In particular Hintze suggests that a petty nobility forms the most important type of social class that is, in Hintze's words, capable of carrying it. 'Local self-government in large areas has only developed in places where a broad and strong stratum of lower knightly nobility as a landed aristocracy is the most decisive social factor of the rural areas of the countries concerned.'[61] The powerful higher nobility—the lords in England, the noble families of Scandinavia, and the grandees of Spain—have too high ambitions of national power to remain as reliable leaders of institutions of local self-government. The conservatism of the peasantry equips them simply for communal or parochial forms of self-government. In short, the peasants were too narrow in mentality to do anything more than be concerned with affairs that affected an area within sight of their local church tower, the high nobility had little interest in the affairs of these areas, but the lower nobility 'had the time and the means to offer military and public services, they had broad enough horizons to see out beyond the shadow of their church tower and were in a position due to their flexibility and availability to participate in public affairs'.[62]

While it is not possible to offer a comprehensive picture of the nobility in all seven countries, it appears that the Swedish and English nobility were the most likely of all the seven to be 'carriers' of local self-government. In Sweden and Britain the *landshövding*, *häradshövding*, and the justices of the peace in the eighteenth century were landowning nobility, passing on to the gentry or *anstandspersoner*—'professional men, small gentry, rural industrialists, non-noble civil servants'.[63] In parts of Italy, Spain, France, and Denmark—Norway on the other hand, the nobility could be termed 'useless' by one leading authority. There was gambling and drinking. There was 'plenty of opportunity for love-making and gossip and petty political intrigue, which kept a great many nobles in expensive, sometimes highly cultured but always politically ineffective attendance in France, Spain, the two Sicilies, Denmark, and many small German courts'.[64]

On the other hand Lindsay contrasts these with the more powerful working nobility of eighteenth-century Hungary, England, and Sweden. Rosén makes a contrast between absolutism in Denmark and Sweden precisely in terms of the different impact absolutism had on the nobility:

> In both countries absolutism led to the creation of a new service nobility, but in Sweden this nobility did not remain as separate from the old nobility as it did in Denmark. Members of the old Swedish families continued to serve the state in various capacities, and the new families were quickly assimilated.[65]

While Hintze's first factor affecting the development of a centralized territorial apparatus and a weakening of institutions of local self-government, exposure to the military organization of the Carolingian Empire, was only found in Piedmont and France, the absence of a nobility suitable for 'carrying' local self-government accounts for the nature of central territorial control in Norway, Spain, and Denmark.

While Hintze's explanation appears convincing, the most important point for the development of the argument of this book is that, in short, France, Piedmont, Denmark, Norway, and Spain entered the nineteenth century with local government systems in which there was direct central administrative control through a centrally appointed official, owing little allegiance to the locality and with the power to scrutinize and veto such actions that the communities within his sphere of responsibility might take. Britain and Sweden did not.

REFORM IN THE NINETEENTH CENTURY

Any account of local government containing even a smattering of historical context in most countries will contain something along the lines that the system of local government that operated for most of the twentieth century had its foundations laid in the nineteenth. By this observation one has generally in mind factors such as the creation of local government units in Scandinavia, the creation of a 'system' of local government from the bewildering array of bodies collectively known as local government in England, and the restructuring of local government in the Spanish and Italian constitutions of the nineteenth century or the 1884 *Code municipal* in France.

This importance attached to the nineteenth century is undoubtedly justified in any general description of the development of local government. The importance of changes in local government is further highlighted by the close relationship between local government reform and parliamentary and electoral reform and thus its relationship in a wider process whereby access to political power was extended to the middle and later working class.

Yet from the perspective of central−local government relations, it is striking how little was changed by the great transformations of the local government system. The French revolutionary reform of local government in the 1790 municipal laws opened municipalities to·elections with a relatively wide suffrage despite the restrictions on voting based on a tax qualification. They also created eighty-nine *départements* headed by the prefects—as so many observers have commented this appeared less a substantial change and more a continuation of the system of the *généralité* and the *intendant.*[66] Under the Directory after 1795 the departmental councils were abolished, and the cantons were effectively to replace municipalities in some small communes and take over many municipal functions throughout France. Under Napoleon the prefect replaced the intendant in 1800 and acquired greater supervisory powers, and a centrally appointed subprefect was given responsibility for a new subdivision of the *département* (based on the old districts of the *généralité*; and the role of the subprefect was analogous to a role held by the *sub-délégué* of the *ancien régime*). The mayors and municipal councillors, according to the laws of 1800, also became appointed by central state, usually by prefects and subprefects from lists which local voters participated in preparing. This system lasted in essence until after the end of the restoration in the 1830s.

In 1831 the elective principle was introduced again for municipal councils, and central state officials chose the major executive positions of mayor and mayor-adjunct from the elected council. The constitution of 1848 brought an extension of popular election into local government through allowing smaller municipalities to select their own senior executives. The central government retained the right to appoint mayors for the larger towns. This voter selection of mayors in the smaller communes was reversed under

Napoleon III in the 1850s; the nominees for mayor did not even have to be members of the municipal council although these councils themselves remained directly elected bodies. After the Second Empire the elective principal for major municipal offices was reinstated to a limited degree under legislation of 1871 in towns of under 20,000 inhabitants which could choose their own mayors. Legislation at the start of the Third Republic also increased the powers of the *conseil général*—the elected body of the *département*. In fact, in the Third Republic there were strong pressures in the National Assembly for a widening of the electoral principle and greater relaxation of central controls. Yet these were resisted quite vigorously and largely successfully by President Thiers.

Perhaps the most important change of the nineteenth century in France came with the 1884 municipal code. Among the enduring contributions of this law was the codification or consolidation of diverse laws passed at different epochs into one code. Its main innovation was to provide for an increase in power of the municipal councils which could henceforth choose the mayor and the mayors-adjoint. It standardized the size of the municipal council and the number of executive posts according to the size of the municipality, and set out a whole range of standing orders and regulations about the range of services that can or must be provided by the communes.

Throughout all of this, the basic principle that local government requires central approval for its actions, through the principle of tutelage, was never actually challenged. While there were certainly pressures under the Second Empire for reformers to stress the need to dismantle the French system of centralization, under the Third Republic the experience of the Paris Commune and the real fear that municipalities might prove to be the seedbed for monarchist opposition helped both liberals and conservatives to accept the status quo of a powerful central government control over the affairs of the municipalities.

The Piedmontese system of local government at the turn of the nineteenth century corresponded closely to the French as it was divided under French rule into *départements* and *arrondissements* governed by prefects and subprefects who appointed mayors and council members.[67] After 1814, Victor Emanuel sought a faithful reconstruction of the constitutional system of the *ancien régime* including the restoration of the military governor. The Napoleonic influence could be detected in some aspects of the new structure of local government: in addition to communes grouped into provinces which were in turn grouped in divisions, there was a level of government equivalent to the Napoleonic cantons (*mandamenti*) between the provinces and communes. Under the constitutional monarchy which lasted for the decade after 1848 there were substantial changes in local government. The 1848 Local Government Act gave corporate powers, such as the right to own and dispose of property, to the divisions, provinces, and communes, set out powers and duties of local governments, and provided for local government elections. However, as Fried suggests, the increased powers of local government also brought increased power for the intendant, above all through giving him responsibility for supervising those expanded functions. In addition, in this period the intendant was given responsibility for public education.

The 1848 law was amended by royal decree in 1859 to prepare the ground for national unification. Some of the changes were cosmetic, making the territorial system of government less distinctively Piedmontese, such as renaming the provinces 'districts' and the divisions 'provinces'; others were more substantive. The intendant was made, in principle, subordinate to a governor who was to be more a party politician than a bureaucrat; the intendant became a vice-governor, and the sphere of authority was extended to include responsibility, again in principle, for all ministries in the locality. The military governor lost, during this period, most of his civil powers. The local government franchise was extended, the communal mayor still remained appointed, but was subject to greater formal accountability to a local executive committee, a *giunta municipale*. In the same decree, provinces were no longer allowed to formulate their own budgets.

In 1861, the first national parliament after unification drafted legislation acknowledging the diversity of the new nation by giving highly decentralized powers to regional levels of government. Such proposals were eventually defeated, above all because of the fears that regions with substantial autonomy would offer great scope for opponents of Italian unity. The resulting decree of 1861 merely changed the nomenclature of the governors to prefects and abolished the post of vice-governor. A Law on Administrative Unification of 1865 created nationally uniform laws on local government which were 'only slightly modified versions of the

Piedmontese legislation of 1859'.[68] The system of local government, and more importantly the uniform pattern of central–local relations, created by the 1865 law was the system that persisted for at least the remainder of the century. Under the liberal regime of 1870–1922 the powers of the prefect in fact increased with the growth of public services. As Fried concludes on the administrative provisions for unified Italy: 'The fundamental importance of the 1865 Act lay . . . in the fact that it established a highly centralised structure of government in the new kingdom.'[69] Taxation powers were circumscribed, spending was limited by provisions determining what revenues must be met by local government (including footing the bill for national government functions) and central powers over the local commune included powers of appointing the mayor and dissolving the council.

In Norway, the first of the Scandinavian countries to experience major local government reforms, a system of local government was created in 1837 in response to pressure from peasants concerned about the possible profligacy of county government authorities run by state bureaucrats. The 1837 law created an indirectly elected *fylkesting* for the county and elected municipalities. The 1837 legislation created around 700 *herreds* (rural districts based on the parish in many cases) and separate provision for the major towns of Oslo and Bergen, the forty provincial towns (*kjopstader*), and twenty ports (*ladesteder*) which were removed from the administrative jurisdiction of the twenty *fylke* or counties (since in two cases *fylke* were combined this meant in practice there were only eighteen). They were still subject to central supervision through the governor or *fylkesman* (in fact, the Danish terms *amt* and *amtmand* were used in Norway until they were changed to the old Norwegian *fylke* and *fylkesman* in 1919). For the following ninety years after 1837 in Norway there were no significant changes in the local government structure or its functions.

In Sweden the major local government reform took place after a royal decree of 1862. There had been some important legislation affecting parish government before this, above all the 1843 laws enabling parishes to raise revenues for non-church functions such as public health, education, and poor relief. The reform of 1862, however, provided a common local government structure. The cities and the rural areas were to be governed by general assemblies of the whole population or representative systems of government

could be substituted for these general meetings. The local authorities, rural communes, and cities were empowered to raise taxes. It
further separated the ecclesiastical and the civil functions of the
parish, although the school board remained in the ecclesiastical
organization until 1930. It also created an elected county council.
One of the important factors leading to the setting up of the county
as a unit of government was that it formed the basis for election to the
Upper House proposed in the 1860s in the wake of the constitutional settlement abolishing the old system of representation of estates.
Yet none of these changes fundamentally affected the relationship
between central and local government from the perspective of
weakening or strengthening the controls exercised by central
government. As Verney argues 'the 1862 decree which inaugurated
these Councils did not, however, affect the status of the Provincial
Governors who were appointed by the Crown and whose offices
carried on provincial administration.'[70]

Of the three Scandinavian countries local government in
Denmark in the nineteenth century was the most restricted. The
elective principle for local government, introduced primarily after
the 1840s, remained based on a narrow suffrage (involving less than
one-fifth of the population by 1900) right up until the end of the
century. The Country Communal Law of 1867 and a law on market
towns in 1868 set up the system of local government that persisted
until 1970: a system of around 1,300 parish communes (*sognekom-
mune*), 80 market towns (*kobstad*), and Copenhagen, in a class of its
own. The county councils (*amt*) were indirectly elected until 1933,
and the centrally appointed *amtmand* or governor had wide powers
of scrutiny of local government actions, including the power to
approve budgets and dissolve disobedient councils, in addition to
presiding over the duties of the county and public boards within the
county (e.g. school boards) which collectively provided more of the
important public services than the towns or districts.

English local government reform in 1834 and 1835 followed the
extension of the suffrage in 1832. The 1834 Poor Law Act provided
for the election of local Poor Law Commissioners and the 1835
Municipal Corporations Act gave municipal boroughs corporate
powers to buy property. The powers of the corporations were
extended throughout the nineteenth century, expanding local
government functions (especially in the area of public health).
Legislation in 1888 extended the principle of elected local

government to the counties, reshaped city government through the creation of a London County Council, and created the county boroughs—city councils carrying out most local functions in their area. In 1894 the urban and rural sanitary authorities outside the county boroughs were transformed into elected rural and urban district councils.

Throughout this process the nature of central control did not change dramatically; local and general acts defined the sphere of local government action, rather than the administrative control exercised by central government agents in much of Continental Europe. Despite some experiments in 1848 with the creation of a General Board of Health with extended powers over local poor boards (in fact, these powers, as Smellie argues were more by way of 'opportunity to irritate local interests' than 'power to overcome obstruction'), and a short-lived attempt by auditors to extend their influence into supervising the policy decisions of local government authorities, there developed no really detailed control of local decisions over and above the requirement of ministry approval for loans.[71] Such approval, moreover, was apparently easily obtained.[72] In fact, the classic portrayal of the development of local services in the nineteenth and twentieth centuries is that such services were initiated locally in one or a few pioneering local authorities, and then made the subject of general legislation mandating or permitting these services to be provided elsewhere.[73]

In Spain, the restoration of absolutism under Ferdinand VII voided the 1813 liberal constitution of the Cortes of Cadiz, which never actually came into effect but which provided for election of municipal officials but interestingly no dimunution of the powers of central officials over the communes.[74] 'Insofar as Ferdinand had a system,' writes Carr,[75] 'it was the restoration of the machinery of government he had known in 1808.' The constitutions of 1837 and 1869, both quite short-lived, introduced changes in local government, widening its franchise and diminishing the power of the provincial governor, the *jefe político*, yet throughout the nineteenth century the centralized pattern of local administration faced few challenges. Carr writes:

Through later liberals were to divide on issues of the election or selection of local government officials . . . all liberals . . . accepted two propositions: that the Cortes as 'sole representative of the sovereign nation' must enforce a uniform and centralised system and that, within this sytem, the municipalities were 'subaltern corporations'. This conception of the relationship between local and central government, derived from the French model, stamped the whole subsequent history of Spain.[76]

The 1837 constitution was reversed in 1845, but the 1869 constitution was not substantially altered by the 1876 constitution and the following 1877 Local Government Law in so far as local government was concerned. This lasted at least up until the period of dictatorship between 1923 and 1930. According to this system there were 9,500 communes and 49 provinces. The provinces were headed by the *jefe político*, later to become the civil governor with supervisory powers very similar to those of the French prefect.

To sum up, five of our seven countries had comparable patterns of central–local relations in the nineteenth century—legal centralism from the perspective of the range of functions of local government as well as the nature of central supervision of local government, which was administrative rather than statutory in nature. These patterns were to all intents and purposes already established by the beginning of the nineteenth century. The divergent pattern of legal localism in England and to a lesser extent Sweden was already established in the early nineteenth century, with regard to county government in England and parish government in Sweden.

CLIENTELISM, THE DEVELOPMENT OF MASS PARTIES, AND LOCAL GOVERNMENT

The observation that five of the seven countries displayed patterns of legal centralism throughout the nineteenth century raises three interrelated questions: why did three of the nations retain these patterns of legal centralism right up to the present? Why did two of them lose these patterns? Why did England and Sweden not develop these patterns? In order to explain this we need to switch our attention away from the institutional development of local government and towards more general features of political development, especially the development of mass parties. Political localism, that is to say the importance of local government for national politics and national political careers, helps explain developments in legal localism and centralism. Moreover, since it is an aspect of the local government system this book has set itself the task of explaining, it is useful to introduce the issue now.

The links between local and national politicians in France, Spain, and Italy broadly reflect clientelistic patterns of political interaction. According to Waterbury, patron–client relations 'provide discriminatory access to desired goods. The desired good may simply be to be left alone or protected from a worse fate than is one's own already, or it may be of a more positive nature consisting in material rewards or strategic resources. Access is governed by a patron who may have varying degrees of control over the resource.'[77] The observation that clientelistic strategies are extremely important for mobilizing political support in Spain and Italy, and that municipal government plays an important part in these strategies, is widely accepted. Less well-accepted is the applicability of the social scientific concept of clientelism to France and the territorial system of administration.

Clientelism in Italy is especially associated with governing parties: the liberals from 1870 to 1922, the DC and its allies after the Second World War, above all in the South of the country. The ability to dispense political favours, above all jobs in the public sector, is a powerful resource on which power within the Christian Democrats is frequently based, not only in the South but throughout Italy. Each major faction leader within the DC is 'supported by solid and large groups of local leaders each linked to him by ties of mutual advantage and personal loyalty'.[78] Tarrow's analysis of Italy shows the importance of local–national party linkages as channels through which local élites gain resources from the central government (see also Chapter 3).[79] As Santantonio points out in his discussion of Italian local government, local government not only provides a source of patronage but also a source of 'hidden finance' for parties nationally as well as locally.[80] Although many of the case-studies refer to the Italian South, Zuckerman shows that 'Field studies in central and northern Italy directly corroborate the view that clientelism is found and is of major importance throughout Italian society.'[81]

Clientelism is also a term which can be applied to Spain, at least before the death of Franco, without generating any controversy. Kenny writes that 'each official, major or minor, weaves himself a web of influence and support with the object of absorbing the maximum possible power into his own hands . . . The mayor, the priest, the Civil Guard sergeant, the doctor, the rich landlord are well-known leaders who play, as the mood moves them, an innovating or controlling role in local affairs. Their friendship, their interest, their benevolence, indeed their services must be courted in case of need or difficulty. They in turn are linked to the towns through more powerful urban patrons as clients themselves.'[82]

In France, Tarrow's influential comparison of centre–periphery relations in Italy and France suggests that the use of partisan channels for directing peripheral demands to the centre constitutes 'clientelistic' integration in Italy, while French centre–periphery relations, conducted not through party contacts represented '*dirigiste*' integration.[83] However, following Médard, it is possible to show that the centre–periphery bargaining can be accurately described as clientelism. Moreover, this clientelism can be linked to party structures. As Médard argues, 'although political clientelism may operate even in the absence of strong party structures, such structures are of crucial importance for an understanding of center–periphery relations in contemporary France.'[84]

In each of these three political systems, parties built up support in the nineteenth century through clientelism—offering specific rewards to their supporters. Shefter shows how early in the history of the unified Italian political system patronage was used to maintain support for the *blocco storico*, the coalition of northern bourgeoisie and southern landowners. This coalition, he argues, has persisted into the present. The *blocco storico*, the 'logrolling' arrangement by which the northern bourgeoisie was 'able to work through the Southern landlords to keep the peasants at bay ... received the support of Southern Deputies for the economic policies it favoured' in return for patronage provided by the southern gentry. The process of *trasformismo* according to which deputies opposed to the government became supporters once granted access to patronage is generally associated with the liberal government of Depretis of 1876. Shefter adds, 'the techniques perfected by Depretis were used by the governments which ruled Italy for the next forty years.'[85]

In post-war Italy, the DC built up its base of political support through the use of patronage. The type of patronage employed in the post-war period changed, however, from one based upon economic and social notables to one more firmly based upon the official of the political party discussed by Tarrow in his *Peasant*

Communism.[86] Patronage started to come under challenge following economic modernization in the 1960s as one of the major factors in Italy's 'backwardness'. The left in Italy, which gathered strength in the 1970s, has not relied upon patronage to maintain political support in the same way as the DC. On the one hand, the Communists managed to gain control of the local governments of large cities such as Turin, Rome, and Naples, and thus in principle contributed to the decline of clientelism and patronage. However, as Chubb shows in the Naples context, the limitations on the Communists in achieving their aims within the city show its strengths outside the local government system: 'The combination of continued DC domination of the state apparatus and the DC monopoly of local economic power has made it virtually impossible for the PCI to transform the fundamental structure and constraints of the Neapolitan situation . . . The most it can do is to attempt to use local institutions as levers of pressure to extract resources from the state and the regional government.'[87] The success of the left within local government does not necessarily entail a commensurate decline in the importance of clientelism.

In Spain, the term *caciquismo* is used to describe the networks of patronage which were used to mobilize electoral votes from the extension of suffrage in the late nineteenth century and lasted for at least the first two decades of the twentieth century. As in the French Second Empire, the prefect became a mobilizer of support for national political parties. The selective enforcement of regularly flouted laws, the ability to appoint and dismiss municipal employees, as well as to vary and withhold wages, were important incentives in patron–client relations which gave power to local bosses or *caciques*.[88] 'Spanish municipal politics,' Carr adds, 'are incomprehensible unless we realise that the understrappers of the politicians, like the American Ward Secretaries, were distributors of doles, knowing the needs of each family and each voter, protecting the most favoured against the law and the tax collector . . . The highest price Spain paid for her electoral system was inefficient local government and a legal system working through influence.'[89]

Médard outlines the development of clientelism in France since the Third Republic. The Republicans developed new networks of patronage, above all the schoolteachers of the expanding school system, to bolster their support against the conservatives who could call upon traditional patron–client networks, above all those connected with the church. The prefects, who had been throughout the nineteenth century a vehicle for securing political support and suppressing political opposition, had as their first task 'to insure the electoral victory of the incumbents'.[90] A particularly important new network of patronage was set up in 1881 with the creation of the Ministry of Agriculture, which became crucial in the territorial distribution of state resources.[91] As Médard puts it, state resources were mobilized to win over peasants to the cause of the Republic. This strategy did not entirely eliminate conservative traditional clientelistic ties, and the effect of the coexistence of traditional and new clientelistic ties was to divide the peasantry.

Under the Fourth Republic this division of the peasantry started to change. Under the Fourth Republic the traditional notables were to a large extent replaced by the 'resistants'—those who had participated in the resistance to Nazi occupation during the Second World War. Until the Communists left the coalition in 1947 patronage became instituted along functional lines, with different parties controlling particular ministries and newly nationalized industries—with education being the preserve of the radicals and socialists and the interior coming under the MRP. However, later in the Fourth Republic the apparent centralization of parties and patronage began to reverse. One indicator of this was the transformation of the socialist SFIO from a mass party to one based on local notables and another was the increasing sway that major personalities within the parties held at the local level, not least because personal factors appeared to shape voting behaviour.[92] The influence of the personality in elections became more important after the introduction of fixed lists in 1951 and parties nationally had to pay attention to politicians with local strength. Médard concludes that 'at the end of the Fourth Republic a new political class had come into existence. Recruited from the parties which made up various coalitions, it had strong local roots at the municipal and departmental levels and maintained strong connections with the Administration . . . During its short life, the Fourth Republic brought to light a combination of party clientelism and a clientelism of notables rather similar to that of the Third Republic.'[93] In the Fifth Republic clientelism was also a strategy for building up support for the Gaullists: many of the Gaullist deputies who were elected on the strength of their association with de Gaulle had to have more enduring local bases of support. One way of doing this was to create notables whose main strength lay less in their local economic or social power but in their access to national political resources. Above all this was shown in the phenomenon of the *Jeunes Loups*: bureaucrats, usually ENA trained, who were launched into political careers which involved the acquisition of local mayoral office and election to the National Assembly. Access to state resources became the basis of political power of the new notables of the post-war period. Multiple office-holding, the *cumul des mandats* whereby a mayor may also be a departmental and regional councillor and a deputy (see Chapter 3), increased access points to national power. This in turn increased the local electoral strength of the cumulant as his dominance of the local political scene was translated into political power in national arenas of decision-making.

Patterns of clientelism and their importance for political parties in Spain are rather more difficult to discern because of the recency of the return to democratic elections. Despite the erosion of local government and the absence of competitive elections, the life blood of *caciquismo*, clientelistic relationships still appeared to persist under Franco. The system of *caciquismo* had declined in the early decades of the twentieth century, yet clientelism persisted. In 1973 Kenneth Medhurst wrote that

Caciquismo as a system no longer exists. Growing urbanisation and political awareness were in the process of undermining the basis of the system before Primo de Rivera's regime and the Republic . . . Nevertheless, caciquismo . . . embodied or fostered attitudes and administrative practices that have outlived the system itself. They are deeply embedded in the fabric of Spain's local political life and signify the existence of an underlying continuity in the Spanish state's approach to the management of local affairs.[94]

The Franco regime, although generally stripping local government of many powers, helped maintain the institution of the provincial governor and of the mayor as major sources of political patronage through their fusion with the provincial and local leadership of the Falange Movement.

Clegg shows the importance of regional and local party groupings in the development of national party policy after Franco, and suggests that clientelism persisted in the parties of the right:

The main parties of the centre and the right, UCD (now defunct), AP and the PDP, appear to have absorbed many of the clientelistic networks and agents that existed under Franco, and these now operate within the context of democratic politics. The formation of autonomous regional governments has vastly expanded the possibilities for distributing political patronage. In some cases this means that regional funding available to local councils has been directed almost exclusively to councils controlled by certain parties, excluding the opposition. The president of the regional government or a leading national deputy from a province usually plays a key role in these networks, uniting groups of local elected officials around them.[95]

Moreover, use of local patronage does not appear confined to the centre and right: Heywood shows how the Socialist PSOE managed to use locally based patronage to overcome attacks by the Gonzalez and Guerra leadership and to construct a more effective form of 'democratic centralism' in the Socialist party than was possible in the more hierarchically structured communist PCE.[96]

In Spain, Italy, and France, then, clientelism with local government as a significant focus has played an important part in the development of major political parties. The same cannot be said of the parties in Scandinavia and Britain. Of course, patronage exists in each of these countries, as in any country where a politician has discretion or influence over appointments to desired positions. Yet this does not constitute the form of clientelism, based upon the existence of locally based centres of power which form part of a wider national network of political power relations as found in Italy and France. Of course, such locally-based (or more accurately family-based) national clientelistic relations assumed great importance in a country such as Britain in the eighteenth century, as discussed by Namier, and remained so within the Conservative party at least until the elaboration of a mass organization at the end of the nineteenth century.[97] Yet in the development of mass parties, whether Conservative, Socialist, Liberal, or Peasant, there is no evidence that the mass parties in Denmark, Sweden, Norway, or Britain relied upon local office-holders to furnish political support in the way they did in Italy and France. Barnes's study of the social and political structure of a Norwegian parish in the early 1950s offers a striking contrast to the images of municipal politics in Italy and France. Unlike the position in Italy and France Barnes observed 'no one person in a key position who articulates the parish with a wider social system' as the mayoral 'policy-brokers' of Italy and France. There is no one individual in a parish 'with overall leadership valid in a wide range of contexts'.[98] Moreover, individual parish councillors displayed scrupulous honesty through their genuinely great reluctance to discuss any issue in which through kinship or otherwise they may be said to have some interest.

Why should the importance of clientelism vary? There are many different types of approach that seek to explain the incidence of clientelism. Some explore it from an anthropological perspective, seeing it as related to kinship structures; some see it from the point of view of economic development, associating clientelism with particular paths to modernization or particular transitional stages; some regard it as a more general feature of a national or subnational culture. Explaining the variable importance of clientelism in party development cross-nationally is not something that can be pursued here.[99] Here we must be satisfied with the relatively less contentious conclusions of the research into clientelism as they concern this study: that it was and remains especially important in Spain, France, and Italy.

In conclusion, then, with the development of mass parties in France and Italy came the elaboration of patterns of clientelism which tied local politics in very closely with national politics. Local office-holding and influence throughout the whole machinery of government at the local level became important to national politicians, although the patterns of clientelism varied significantly, as suggested by Tarrow as between France and Italy. They also varied over time. By contrast, in the Northern European countries of Denmark, Norway, Sweden, and Britain such clientelistic patterns that created close links between national and local politics cannot be found: instead parties sought to extend their appeals by promising universalistic rather than particularistic benefits to their supporters.

AN EXPLANATION OF DIFFERENCES

Across most of Europe, local government in the early nineteenth century was structured hierarchically in terms of its relations with the centre: central government through governors or prefects had direct administrative control over the actions of local government bodies. In Britain and Sweden, central government in principle controlled local government, as it does in any unitary state at any time by definition, yet the control was far less direct and far less obtrusive than in the other five countries in our study. Britain and Sweden were not alone in their absence of extensive and direct hierarchical control over local government: the central–local regimes in Poland and especially Hungary (which had a system of local government very similar to Britain in terms of its central–local relationships throughout the nineteenth and the first part of the twentieth century) also lacked institutions for exercising direct detailed administrative control. The nineteenth century saw the creation of modern local government, by which I mean formalization of the powers and duties of local government, establishment of regular procedures for raising and spending money, the election of council members, and so on. Yet in terms of central–local relations the basic difference between Britain and to a lesser extent Sweden on the one hand and the remaining five countries on the other persisted. In Britain local government was reformed and expanded on the basis of a statutory relationship of control according to which parliamentary approval was required to ensure the legality of local government actions, either through individual or general legislation (the latter becoming more important around the end of the nineteenth century). In Denmark, Norway, Spain, France, and Italy local government was reformed and expanded on the basis of an administrative relationship of control according to which the approval of a state official was required to ensure the legality of local government.

Such a hierarchically structured system persisted in France and Italy but not in Denmark and Norway. The reason for the persistence in France and Italy can be related to the patterns of clientelism that became so important in these countries in the nineteenth and twentieth centuries as means of building support for political parties. The importance of local patronage created a block to local government reform.[100]

Taking our three Scandinavian countries, primary local government units, that is to say, districts, parishes, and towns, were numerous and contained relatively small populations. The extension of local government functions in Scandinavia, and the relaxation of central controls over local government units by governors in Denmark and Norway followed a process of local government consolidation, increasing the size of local government units and ending the distinctions between rural and urban municipalities, in the post-war period. In Sweden the number of municipalities and towns decreased from 2,498 in 1951 to 278 in 1974, in Denmark the decrease was from 1,388 urban and rural districts in 1957 to 277 communes by the early 1970s. In Norway the decline was not so great, from 744 in 1960 to 451 by 1970. Nevertheless, the aims behind these reorganizations was to 'establish units capable of implementing new public services'.[101] The period of consolidation of local government also coincided with a period of the expansion of local government functions. Also in the process of local government reform the position of the governors in these nations has become weakened. In Denmark the 1970 Local Government Act redefined the *amtmand*'s control over the municipalities: the *amtmand* was to chair a supervisory committee with four county councillors with the major responsibility of scrutinizing budgets for 'illegality'.[102] Moreover, since the 1970s there has been a consistent effort by the central administration to reduce the detail of national regulations. Bogason concludes, 'it seems fair to say that the role of local government in many fields was changed from one of policy implementation to one of policy planning and implementation, giving new possibilities for variations in service among localities due to differing priorities and use of capabilities.'[103] In Norway the *fylkesmann*'s main responsibility has developed to one of scrutinizing the municipal budget to ensure that it is balanced: it is not uncommon for a budget to be referred back because of unrealistically high revenue projections.[104] In Sweden the *landshövding* or governor is the chairman of a county administrative board which appears to have planning and some limited *post hoc* supervision as its most important roles in relation to local government, and it also hears appeals in first instance by individuals against planning decisions of municipalities. While the institution of the governor was retained in each of the three Scandinavian countries, his powers have diminished, above all in Denmark and Norway (they appear to have been traditionally much weaker in Sweden), and have become far less extensive than those held by his counterparts in France, Italy, and Spain.

In contrast, in Italy and France attempts to increase the size of local government units to make them financially and professionally capable of delivering modern services had failed due to the importance of local power bases for national politics. Attempts to encourage mergers of local authorities, even for limited purposes, through *communautés urbaines* in the 1960s, produced few results.

One alternative to the problems of service delivery created by the existence of a plethora of small communes was to rely upon units outside the local government structure, trying to bypass the local notables through the regions.[105] Yet by the 1970s governments had given up any serious attempts at reforming the territorial structure. Characteristically, the reforms of territorial government of the 1980s did not represent a head-on clash with the entrenched interests of the notables within the communes. In fact, local government within the commune was least affected by the changes of Mitterrand's administration. Instead the legislation increased the powers of the larger units of non-central government: the *départements* and the regions. Unlike the position in Scandinavia and Britain, the importance of local government for the power of national politicians meant that the communes could not be amalgamated and reformed to fit central government conceptions of efficiency. Instead, any attempt to use non-central agencies for the delivery of significant public services outside the direct supervision of state officials required the use of the departmental and regional level of government.

Similarly in Italy, the expansion of non-central administration has not produced any great expansion of communal activity. In the early post-war years there were attempts to deal with the large numbers of small communes through introducing *consorzi*, local authorities uniting to provide specific services. Yet the political difficulties of reforming local government in Italy have meant that expansion outside the central sphere has also taken place outside the communes. The regions, institutions envisioned in the post-war constitution, were given more substantive powers in the 1970s, as were the provinces. The reorganization of the national health service in 1978 placed health service administration in the hands of local health boards (USLs), which are larger than communes and which are only indirectly under the influence of municipal politicians, and created *comprensori*, planning districts at a level above the commune. The commune's share of public spending, already low in 1970 at 23 per cent, declined to 14 per cent in 1981.[106] In short, as in France, the small primary local government units of Italy have not become significant service providers.

Along with larger size, as we noted in the case of Scandinavia, especially Denmark and Norway (since Sweden had less of a tradition of obtrusive central interference in the affairs of the parish), came a relaxation of the direct administrative controls over local government. Again, in France and Italy it appears that the relaxation of central control by prefects has primarily been to the benefit of central ministries, above all finance ministries, as well as of the regions in which the new supervisory bodies (the Regional Courts in France and the regional control bodies of Italy) are located. For the smaller units of local government in both countries detailed administrative control by a superior authority has remained.

The absence of close ties based upon networks of what may be termed clientelism leaves central government freer to shape local government according to its perceived needs. This is shown by the relative ease of wide-scale reorganization in Britain in the 1960s and 1970s as well as the highly consensual process by which local government units were cut to a fraction of their pre-war number in Scandinavia. In Britain this process did not involve the acquisition of extra functions; in fact in the 1970s' reorganization, health services were taken away from local government, but in Britain local government functions were already quite extensive. Neither did reorganization in Britain coincide with a change in central supervision as it did in Norway and Denmark, although 'policy planning' experiments of the 1970s sought to reduce central intervention still further in the field of capital spending approval, which still required the submission of plans to the central ministry.

To be malleable as an institution of public service delivery is, paradoxically, to be highly vulnerable to central perceptions of the role of local government. In the post-war period in Scandinavia, and for a century in Britain, the conception of the role of local government has been that of an institution with sufficient financial and economic capacity to deliver major public services. Most of the post-war reforms in these countries contained this conception of the role of local government, even if one can detect other motives, such as the maximization of party political advantage.[107] Yet in Britain the perception has changed importantly under the Conservative government, which views local government increasingly as an institution which stifles the expression of individual preferences—it is a layer of government which raises and allocates resources bureaucratically or politically rather than in response to the preferences of individuals. It is this malleability of local government, resulting from the insignificance of clientelistic ties within national politics, which makes it especially vulnerable to the type of centralization imposed by the Thatcher government. Characteristically this has been imposed not through detailed administrative supervision but through general laws taking powers and responsibilities away from local government.

6

Conclusions

Whereas the distinction between Northern and Southern European forms of local government is certainly not uncommon, older studies of comparative local government usually made a distinction between English and 'Continental'—especially French—forms of local government. Montagu-Harris summarizes his review of local government in many lands with the observation that apart from Britain and Switzerland,

The countries of Europe are generally attached to the more centralised and bureaucratic system of which France was the model and the most complete exemplification until the introduction of the Fascist regime in Italy. Spanish legislation, however, has noticeably broken away from this tradition, while the local authorities in Sweden, Finland and, to a lesser extent, some of the other northern countries, enjoy a decidedly fuller freedom than do those in the centre and south of Europe.[1]

Another even earlier comparer of local government, Albert Shaw, whose previous work on Britain focused upon Glasgow City Corporation, prefaced his survey of municipal government in Europe with the observation that

if Glasgow is the convenient threshold to a comparative knowledge of British municipal affairs, Paris in a far more essential way holds the key to an intelligent survey of municipal progress on the Continent. Whether one goes to the Low Countries and Scandinavia, to Switzerland and Italy or to Germany and Austria-Hungary, he finds evidences on all hands of the abounding influence that the modern Paris has exerted upon the outward forms of European cities. And some study of the history and characteristics of administration will soon make plain to him the remarkable influence that the symmetrical statutory schemes of France has exerted upon the law-making bodies of other countries.[2]

In the late twentieth century, there has grown a greater distinction between Continental forms of local government than was apparent in Montagu-Harris's day. As local government has been modernized in Scandinavia, it has come to resemble British local government to a greater extent.

Following the framework suggested by Mackenzie, the preceding chapters have pinpointed the major differences in terms of the opportunities for local politicians to shape public policies between our seven countries on the basis of two dimensions: the legal and the political.[3] Certainly, local government in its many aspects is such that no two, twenty, or even two hundred distinctions will capture its reality. The intention has not been to force this diversity into the confines of a grand overarching theory. The basis of the distinction between legal and political dimensions made by Mackenzie and used in this book is an inductive one—something that was derived from the observation of different systems of government—rather than grand theory. Moreover, to point to areas of commonality and diversity and to compare them cannot be taken to imply general similarity and dissimilarity in the local government system across the board, or even in central–local relations, but merely similarity on these two dimensions. There are many other dimensions and issues involved in central–local relations, ranging from the intricacies of local finance to professional organization, that have only been touched on in previous chapters. However, the importance of the two dimensions and the nature of the process by which they appeared to develop makes them especially significant.

The central argument is that there are two major fault lines distinguishing systems of national–local relations—political and legal dimensions—and that three processes have affected this development: the development of state structures prior to the nineteenth century; the development of mass parties; and the post-war expansion of governmental activities. The progress of these developmental processes separates out three groups of countries.

First, there are those systems with a long tradition of local self-government (Britain and Sweden) in which national administrative supervision has generally been weak, as has the interrelationship between national and local political activity. Second, there are those where political relations between national and local élites have been intensive and central supervision has traditionally been strong (France, Spain, and Italy). Third, there are those without strong political localism which have nevertheless moved from a system of control based upon administrative supervision in the post-war period towards greater degrees of legal localism, above all in terms of the degree of administrative control and the range of functions provided (Denmark and Norway). In these two countries the basis of local government discretion is in the relaxation of administrative supervision of the 'Continental' form identified by earlier writers in favour of more generalized statutory controls and planning instruments. Legal localism in these two countries is arguably more a matter of national administrative expediency than the result of a tradition of local self-government.

Understanding the process of this development, above all the origins of political localism in clientelistic patterns of electoral competition, helps us to understand why the close interpenetration between national and local politics should necessarily offer advantages to local political élites. After all, as Mackenzie suggests, the close relationship may mean that 'the centre moves the localities or the localities move the centre'. There are certainly some signs of the centre, through the party structure, moving the locality. One obvious sign of this is France is the possibility of parties 'parachuting' in a national politician to local office to provide him with the electoral legitimacy required for a national politico-administrative career. However, evidence of such central influence over local politics is rare in our three Southern European nations. Moreover, even in the French case the 'parachuted' politician has to secure and maintain his legitimacy in the local sphere. The local élites, above all the outgoing mayor, must be offered a *quid pro quo* for supporting the nationally sponsored candidate.[4]

Of course, where national and local politics are intertwined, such as in the Soviet Union, and the basis of the power of the local élites is primarily their access to goods and benefits located at regional and national level, this produces a centripetal network of relationships quite unlike that of our Southern European nations.[5] Since, as has been shown, the quest for mass electoral support plays an important part in maintaining a national role for local élites, they have a resource which national political élites cannot control and cannot take for granted. It is the basis for the intertwining of national and local politics, rather than the fact that they are intertwined, that produces political localism.

WIDER APPLICATIONS OF THE APPROACH

Does this argument apply to a wider group of nations? Perhaps the most significant omissions from this analysis of Europe are two unitary states, Belgium and Holland, and the federal states of West Germany, Switzerland, and Austria. Comparison is difficult in the case of the federal systems because they represent a distinctive form of constitution that has not explicitly been brought into this analysis. Moreover, with the exception of West Germany, the territorial and local government structures of these countries have been significantly affected by strong linguistic or religious conflicts for which the framework developed in this book has not catered.

Taking the unitary states of Belgium and the Netherlands first, Belgium appears on a priori grounds to come into the category of legal centralism and the Netherlands into the pattern of legal localism. In part this is because of the narrower range of functional responsibilities of Belgian local government. Belgian local authorities account for around 11 per cent of total current spending and 18 per cent of total capital spending, which places Belgium in a similar position to France, Italy, and Spain (see Table 2.1). By contrast, in the Netherlands 25 per cent of total public current spending and 37 per cent of capital spending is channelled through local government, making it close to Britain, at least in the larger item of current spending.[6] In Belgium one also finds the French form of hierarchical division of labour between national and local government, giving the locality few major services for which it alone is responsible, which contrasts with the Netherlands where the division of functions follows the pattern of separation found in Scandinavia and Britain.

In terms of our political dimension, available evidence again suggests including Belgium with our Southern European group, since as Mughan suggests, 'communes have long enjoyed high popular esteem in Belgium, and election to local office is almost a prerequisite for a political career in Brussels.' The holding of dual mandates, by which around four-fifths of deputies hold local elective office, 'has always provided an informal but intimate link between local and national politics in Belgian political life'.[7]

One feature of the system in the Netherlands which does not so neatly conform to our expectations of localism is the rather extensive administrative control over local government authorities.

The prefectoral institution in Holland, the *Commisaris van de Koningin*, as well as the powers to scrutinize budgets and administrative actions, are characteristic of administrative forms of control. In fact, the Netherlands appears to resemble Norway and Denmark before the major reforms of the 1970s. In a sense this confirms the link between size and relaxation of administrative controls found in these two countries. The most recent (failed) attempt at decentralization also incorporated the proposal that the number of communes be halved to 400.[8] The other point where these two countries do not fit neatly is that unlike the Southern European nations, Belgium experienced a massive reduction (from 2,359 to 596) in the number of communes in 1975.

The linguistic and religious peculiarities of the Netherlands and Belgium mean that the central–local relationships in these countries are highly distinctive. The a priori evidence suggests that Belgium might have features in common with France, Italy, and Spain and that the Netherlands share many features in common with Britain and Scandinavia—above all with those countries which had a tradition of administrative control which has tended to disappear in the post-war era (Denmark and Norway).

What about federal systems? It is inappropriate to apply this approach as it stands to federal systems. For one reason, it is not entirely clear how the two fault lines would be applied. They could in principle be applied, as in this book, to distinguish the territorial patterns of government in one country from those in another. This would be inappropriate for two reasons. First, in so far as we have in mind distinguishing between federal and non-federal countries, these two fault lines fail to incorporate what must be the central feature of any discussion of federal–unitary differences—the existence of a state/provincial level of government with some forms of constitutionally guaranteed autonomy. As indicated in Chapter 1, the discussion in this book is derived from a conception of local government as subordinate, which state government in federal systems clearly is not. Second, in so far as we wish to distinguish federal systems from each other, the focus must be primarily on federal–state relations due to the diversity of state–local relations. Our major dimensions, legal and political localism and centralism, simply do not distinguish between major federal systems of the West. In Canada, the United States, and Germany the administrative forms of control found in Italy and France are simply not present in federal—state relations, while state and local politics (if not necessarily state and local legislators) occupy a vital position in national policy-making.

It is possible that the two dimensions of political and legal centralism and localism might be used to point to variations in state—local relations. However, even here we must expect the approach to be of limited use. If we take the US case, about which most has been written, there are few significant cases of what I have termed 'administrative' control over local government by the state—perhaps the relationship between some states and their counties comes closest to this. Moreover, perhaps the most exhaustive comparative study of state—local relations in the fifty states concluded that in the cities the differences in 'local discretionary authority' were generally small.[9] The political localism of the United States is represented by the importance of local affiliations and issues in Congressional elections.

However, some of the general principles of the analysis of unitary systems do appear to apply to federal systems even if the whole approach cannot be directly applied there. Chapter 5 argued that the development of the welfare state produced changes in the nature of local government in those countries where it became a large-scale employer of welfare state service deliverers. One of the major distinctions between the Northern and Southern European nations is the development of local government as a *welfare state bureaucracy*. The absence of the high cost and high manpower services such as health and education from direct local government responsibility marks off Scandinavia and Britain on the one hand from France, Italy, and Spain on the other. Moreover, the development of the welfare state had implications for the nature of central control. While legal localism in terms of the nature of statutory supervision pre-dated the development of the welfare state in Britain and Sweden, in Norway and Denmark the trend towards such patterns of supervision coincided with the growth in welfare state services. In these northern countries the weakness of political localism made unproblematic the reorganization of local government to provide, from the centre's perspective, more efficient units of service delivery. The local units of government in Italy and France, by contrast, could not so easily be recast to fill the functions of an expanding public sector.

Parallels to such developments can be found in federal systems.

The tendency for reorganization in the form of the enlargement of the size of local government units to coincide with welfare state expansion has parallels in federal states in the timing of reorganization in West Germany, where the most important reductions came during the period of rapid expansion in the late 1960s and early 1970s. In addition this linkage of welfare state to reorganization can be found in the United States where the expansion of welfare bureaucracies tended to produce consolidation and enlargement of some local authority areas. The only major type of local government that has experienced the scale of territorial consolidation witnessed in many parts of Europe is the school districts (declining from 109,000 in 1942 to 15,000 in 1988), which with nearly one-half of local government employment makes them the most important single type of local welfare bureaucracy. Other local government units have remained at around the same level over nearly half a century (counties at around 3,000, municipalities increasing gently from 16,000 to 19,000, townships declining gently from 19,000 to 17,000) or grown (special districts increased from 8,000 to 29,000 over the period). The attraction of large units of local government for national government in unitary states is also reflected in the nature of US county government (average population 71,500) compared with other compendious forms of local government (municipalities 7,800, townships 3,100). Counties have, throughout this century but especially over the past three decades, expanded their functions away from the traditional functions of state administration (law and order, registration of population) into public welfare activities, 'services that previously had been considered appropriate only for municipalities'.[10]

Moreover, the tendency for growth in welfare state functions to coincide with changes in modes of higher level supervision, as was noted above all in Denmark and Norway, also has parallels in the case of US counties. While these were never generally under a strictly administrative form of supervision, in many areas states made counties dependent upon specific grants of powers from them. According to the US Advisory Commission on Intergovernmental Relations this

has sometimes involved requesting the legislature not only for power to carry on the added functions, but also to improve internal structure and procedures—whether to cope with the increasingly complicated and technical requirements of their traditional activities or those of newly assumed urban-type services. . . . Some states have given their counties varying degrees of discretionary authority or home rule. Over half of the states have granted to them the power to adopt local charters, whether by constitutional provisions, by general state law, or by both.[11]

Certainly, the ACIR adds, it is important not to overstate the developing county role, but nevertheless many counties 'have moved far beyond their historic roles as the local arm of state government'.

While legal localism appears to be associated (although not exclusively) with the provision of costly services which require large bureaucracies and political localism with inhibiting such a development, the federal structure prevents the two principles from producing a system based more on one form of localism than another. The boundaries of local governments are hard to change because of political localism; the number of counties has remained virtually the same since the 1930s because of the 'political and legal obstacles to subdividing, merging or otherwise altering the boundaries of those that exist'.[12] The cities too have legal and political powers which have prevented any major consolidations and this to some extent accounts for the development of counties; restrictive annexation laws prevented cities from expanding their boundaries to include their newly urbanizing fringes, and the smaller cities preferred to transfer functions to counties rather than face domination by the centre city.[13]

THE THREATS TO LOCAL POLITICS

The precise localness of local government decisions within one nation or many cannot be summarized since it must remain a function of the specific configuration of contraints, power, and interests surrounding particular issues. This book has been concerned with the different opportunities for local influence offered by different political systems rather than the magnitude of such opportunities since we have no common metric to compare levels of freedom and power among such a wealth of different actors.

If we look at the sets of opportunities for local influence, not only do they vary, but the nature of this variation suggests two very different and in some ways conflicting types of local politics. The differences between systems of local government in unitary states, as well as the tensions within the local government systems of other states, seem to be between a form of local government where the role of political leadership is predominantly one of giving direction to a welfare bureaucracy, and a form where the role of leadership is predominantly that of mobilizing political support. One style is based upon making decisions about priorities from a wide range of functions and contrasts with one based primarily on maintaining a traditional range of local services such as culture and public health, and developing public works and attracting industry and investment; one is based upon collegial leadership and the other emphasizes the role of powerful individuals; one stresses good and sound management, the other stresses entrepreneurship and skill in negotiation; one stresses universalistic distribution of benefits, while the other is based on particularistic benefits; in one few appeals can be made to traditional citizen identification with the area covered by the political community while in the other basic local loyalties can be invoked.

Of course, an incompatibility or tension between the two types of local political leadership does not mean that political and legal localism cannot coexist as they do in the United States. In fact the two styles of local politics reflect the well-established American distinction between machine systems, based upon clientelism, and more bureaucratic reform systems. The tension between machine politics and the development of welfare state services is found in the machine's unreliability as a means of channelling universalistic benefits to citizens. The study by Greenstone and Peterson suggests that reformed local governments as opposed to the more clientelistic machine cities 'permit bureaucrats to implement policies efficiently and fairly in the manner determined by the national authorities'.[14]

Each of these distinctive types of local politics appears to be under rather different types of threat. For political leadership under political localism one possible threat is the increase in functional responsibilities and the consequent generation of a large communal bureaucracy, possibly professionalized, which in turn creates a demand for a different type of leadership, a more managerial than political leadership, within the large cities. As Chapter 3 discussed, this appears to have occurred to a certain extent in Marseilles. Another is that the development of the welfare state will undermine the clientelism on which such political leadership is based. The development of benefits and their distribution according to general and universal formulas, and to an increasing extent outside the traditional local government structures, could serve to erode the 'brokerage' role of the local politician. The literature on clientelism, or rather bossism, in American cities suggests that over time we should expect a decline in the degree to which local politicians can rely upon the favours that they can do for their constituents as a means of building political support. The growth of the welfare state, with its emphasis on universality in the provision of major benefits, means that there is less 'gravy' on which local political entrepreneurs can base their public support. Banfield and Wilson quote Mayor Clark of Philadelphia, 'when word gets round that you can't get things done by favor any more there tends to be a sort of channeling of complaints and desires to get things done away from the legislative branch and into the executive branch.'[15] Exposure to political and cultural influences through the mass media can further weaken the bond between local citizens and local élites, as shown by Banfield and Wilson when they relate the episode of a precinct captain in Chicago calling on a voter on a Sunday afternoon 'and finding him with three newspapers spread out on the floor and the TV set on. "What can you tell me that I don't already know?" the voter asked.'[16]

Where leadership roles emphasize giving direction to a welfare state bureaucracy the threat to legal localism, or in particular local political leadership within it, might come from the development of professional power. The tendency for legal localism to be associated with greater professional influence has already been noted (see Chapter 4). Greater professionalization can be expected further to diminish the role of the elected politician. Perhaps more important, the more local government becomes identified as a welfare state institution, the more likely it is to be evaluated according to functional criteria both by national political élites and local citizens. As a welfare bureaucracy, with an emphasis upon the norms if not necessarily the practice of universal benefits administered equitably, the degree to which patterns of allocation are consistent with the preferences of local élites is likely to be a peripheral issue. In this sense the functional importance of local government, and the professionalism and efficiency which it brings to bear on delivering public services, make it a prime target for limitations on its discretion, partly because its role as an efficient service provider displaces or even undermines its role as a representative of local political forces. Moreover, according to the classical Weberian definition of the term, the creation of an efficient bureaucracy itself allows it to serve any master, thus imposing tighter national restraints on a service or even removing it from local government becomes easier. In addition local government is more likely to become subject to the inertia pattern of public policy development: if, as current British experience suggests, national government policies for local government services are more likely to increase restrictions on local decision-making rather than decrease them, then government legislation restricting local government discretion is likely to accumulate since governments relatively rarely repeal or reverse legislation of previous governments.[17]

It is, of course, very easy to overestimate the inevitability and unilinearity of change in both types of local government system. It is also easy to underestimate the adaptability of local political élites to such changes. On the threat to political localism through the demise of clientelism, the Italian political system has shown itself to be able to resist attempts to remove systems of patronage through universal welfare state benefits, and, as discussed in Chapter 4, one should not underestimate the capacity of French mayors to define new sets of clients. Moreover, as Sacks's study of the *Donegal Mafia* shows, clientelism can outlast immediate reasons for its existence.[18] On the threat to legal localism, the removal of functions and the drastic reduction in local government discretion through tightening the statutory framework for raising local revenue appear to be characteristic of Britain but not the other Northern European nations. Moreover, even if professionalization of public services has not yet reached saturation point, it is quite possible that it has already had all or most of the impact on local government it is ever likely to.

There is, however, a danger in extrapolating long-term trends from changes introduced within a short time span. How, for example, local government in Britain will develop after Mrs Thatcher's administration is by no means certain. While the Thatcher administration made major inroads into the discretion of local government, above all through tightening the limits on local financial decisions, we simply cannot assume this represents an inexorable trend. Similarly, there is still a long way to go before major services such as education, housing, health, and police are in the hands of locally elected officials acting within a broad statutory framework and without the intervention of central state officials in France, Spain, and Italy. Given the persistence of administrative patterns of supervision in these countries it is not even certain that this is the direction in which they are moving.

Notes

Chapter 1. Constitutional Subordination

1. See S. Humes and E. Martin, *The Structure of Local Governments throughout the World* (The Hague: International Union of Local Authorities, 1961); E. Martin Harloff, *The Structure of Local Government in Europe* (The Hague: International Union of Local Authorities, 1987).
2. For a discussion of democratic theory and local government see W. Hampton, *Democracy and Community: A Study of Politics in Sheffield* (London: Oxford University Press, 1970); D. M. Hill, *Democratic Theory and Local Government* (London: Allen & Unwin), 1974.
3. O. Hintze, 'Staatenbildung und Kommunalverwaltung' (first published in 1927) in id., *Staat und Verfassung: Gesammelte Abhandlungen zur allgemeinen Verfassungsgeschichte*, ed. G. Oestreich (Göttingen: Vandenhoeck & Ruprecht, 1962), 218.
4. In the United States, for example, Dillon's Rule implies that local government is subordinate to the state as local government in unitary systems is subordinate to national government. See United States Advisory Commission on Intergovernmental Relations, *State and Local Roles in the Federal System* (A-88) (Washington, DC: Government Printing Office, 1982). For Germany see A. B. Gunlicks, *Local Government in the German Federal System* (Durham, NC: Duke University Press, 1986).
5. L. J. Sharpe, 'Is There a Fiscal Crisis in European Local Government?', in id. (ed.) *The Local Fiscal Crisis in Western Europe* (London and Beverly Hills, Calif.: Sage, 1981).
6. J. D. Stewart, *Local Government: The Conditions of Local Choice* (London: Allen & Unwin, 1983).
7. See Y. Mény, *Centralisation et décentralisation dans le débat politique français* (Paris: Librairie Générale de Droit et de Jurisprudence, 1974).
8. See e.g. M. Kochen and K. Deutsch, *Decentralization* (Cambridge, Mass.: Oelgeschlager, Gunn, & Hain, 1980).
9. See e.g. Royal Commission on Local Government in England, *Report*, Cmnd. 4040 (London: HMSO, 1969), 132; L. Strömberg and

J. Westerstahl, *The New Swedish Communes: A Survey of Local Government Research* (Lerum: Lerums Boktrykeri AB, 1984), 16.

10. See Y. Mény, 'Le Maire ici et ailleurs', '*Pouvoirs*, 14 (1983), 19–28

11. H. Wolman and M. J. Goldsmith, 'Local Government Fiscal Behaviour in a Period of Slow National Growth: A Comparative Analysis', *Environment and Planning C: Government and Policy* 5/2 (1987), 171–82. See also P. E. Mouritzen and B. J. Narver, 'Fiscal Stress in Local Government: The Danish and American Cases', in T. N. Clark (ed.), *Research in Urban Policy*, ii: *1986.* (Greenwich, Conn.: JAI Press, 1986).

12. E. E. Schattschneider, *The Semi-Sovereign People* (New York: Holt, Rinehart, & Winston, 1960).

13. T. J. Lowi, 'American Business and Public Policies: Case Studies and Political Theory', *World Politics* 16/4 (1966), 677–715.

14. J.-P. Worms, 'Le Préfet et ses notables', *Sociologie du travail*, 3 (1966), 249–75.

15. The major exception here is the work of Otto Hintze. See his 'Staatenbildung und Kommunalverwaltung' and also 'Der Commissarius und seine Bedeutung in der allgemeinen Verwaltungsgeschichte' (first published 1910), *Staat und Verfassung*, p. 218, repr. in id., *The Historical Essays of Otto Hintze*, ed. and trans. F. Gilbert (New York: Oxford University Press, 1975).

16. See e.g. D. E. Ashford (ed.), *Financing Urban Government in the Welfare State* (London: Croom Helm, 1980); Y. Mény and V. Wright (eds.), *Centre Periphery Relations in Western Europe* (London: Allen & Unwin, 1985).

17. B. C. Smith, *Decentralisation: The Territorial Dimension of the State* (London: Allen & Unwin, 1985).

18. On finance see L. J. Sharpe (ed.), *The Local Fiscal Crisis in Western Europe* (London and Beverly Hills, Calif.: Sage, 1981); K. Newton, *Balancing the Books: The Financial Problems of Local Government in Western Europe* (London and Beverly Hills, Calif.: Sage, 1980); on education see M. S. Archer, *The Social Origins of Educational Systems* (London and Beverly Hills, Calif.: Sage, 1979).

19. D. E. Ashford, *British Dogmatism and French Pragmatism: Central–Local Policy Making in the Welfare State* (London: Allen & Unwin, 1982); S. Tarrow, *Between Center and Periphery: Grassroots Politicians in Italy and France* (New Haven, Conn.: Yale University Press, 1977).

20. G. Montagu-Harris, *Local Government in Many Lands* (London: D. S. King, 1933); id., *Comparative Local Government* (London and New York: Hutchinson, 1949).

21. H. Kelsen, *General Theory of Law and State* (Cambridge, Mass.: Harvard University Press, 1949), 303 ff.

22. W. J. M. Mackenzie, 'Local Government in Parliament', *Public Administration*, 32 (1954), 423.

23. Ibid., p. 418.

24. E. C. Page and M. J. Goldsmith (eds.), *Central and Local Government Relations: A Comparative Analysis of West European Unitary States* (London and Beverly Hills, Calif.: Sage, 1987).

25. P. Grémion, *Le Pouvoir périphérique* (Paris: Éditions du Seuil, 1976).

26. See *Le Monde*, 17 Dec. 1987; A. Terrazzoni, *La Décentralisation à l'épreuve des faits* (Paris: Librairie Générale de Droit et de Jurisprudence, 1987). For an alternative view, however, see V. A. Schmidt, 'Unblocking Society by Decree: The Impact of Governmental Decentralization in France', *Comparative Politics* 22/4 (1990), 459−81.

27. See R. Y. Nanetti, *Growth and Territorial Policies: The Italian Model of Social Capitalism* (London: Frances Pinter, 1988); see also R. L. King, 'Regional Government: The Italian Experience', *Environment and Planning C: Government and Policy*, 5 (1987), 327−46.

28. J. R. L. Sancho, 'The Autonomous Communities: Politics and Economics', *Environment and Planning C: Government and Policy*, 5 (1987), 251−7.

29. See especially M. Hebbert, 'Regionalism: A Reform Concept and its Application to Spain', *Environment and Planning C: Government and Policy*, 5 (1987), 239−50.

30. M. Keating, 'Does Regional Government Matter? The Experience of Italy, France and Spain', *Governance*, 1/2 (1988), 200.

31. Ibid., p. 202.

32. R. von Gneist, *History of the English Constitution* (London: Clowes, 1891).

33. Ashford, *British Dogmatism*, p. 367.

34. G. Sartori, 'Concept Misformation in Comparative Politics', *American Political Science Review*, 64 (1970), 1033−53.

35. R. A. W. Rhodes, *Beyond Westminster and Whitehall: The Sub-Central Governments of Britain* (London: Hyman Unwin, 1988), ch. 5.

36. R. A. W. Rhodes's review of Page and Goldsmith, *Central and Local Government* in *Political Studies*, 36 (1988), 387.

Chapter 2. The Legal Scale

1. E. C. Page and M. J. Goldsmith (eds.), *Central and Local Government Relations: A Comparative Analysis of West European Unitary States* (London and Beverly Hills, Calif.: Sage, 1987).

2. See the Council of Europe's list in 'Council of Europe Study Session on Local and Regional Authorities in Europe No. 13 Vol. II. The Financial Structures of Local and Regional Authorities in Europe' (Strasbourg:

Council of Europe, 1976). As will be discussed later in this chapter, one of the main problems with such a list is that it assumes that 'responsibility' for a service means the same thing in different countries—it does not. Responsibility for education in Italy and France, for example, includes maintaining and building schools but not employing teachers as it does in Britain.

3. For an excellent discussion of the problems of measuring public expenditure see D. Heald, *Public Expenditure* (Oxford: Martin Robertson, 1983).

4. See R. Rose *et al.*, *Public Employment in Western Nations* (Cambridge: Cambridge University Press, 1985).

5. D. E. Ashford, 'Territorial Politics and Equality: Decentralisation in the Modern State', *Political Studies*, 27/1 (1979), 71–83.

6. See K. J. Davey, 'Local Autonomy and Independent Revenues', *Public Administration*, 49 (1971), 45–50.

7. B. C. Smith, 'Approaches to the Measurement of Decentralisation', *International Review of Administrative Sciences*, 3 (1979), 218.

8. See *Local Government and Housing Act 1989* C 42 (London: HMSO, 1989); see also Committee of Inquiry into the Conduct of Local Authority Business, *Report*, Cmnd. 9797 (London: HMSO, 1986), 175 ff.

9. *Droit administratif* (13th edn.; Paris: Dalloz, 1975).

10. G. Llandi and G. Potenze, *Manuale di diritto amministrativo* (Milan: Giuffre, 1974), 235.

11. See T. Clegg, 'Spain' in Page and Goldsmith, *Central and Local Government Relations*, p. 137.

12. See the chapters on Denmark by P. Bogason, on Sweden by J. E. Lane and T. Magnusson, and on Norway by T. Fevolden and R. Sorensen in Page and Goldsmith, *Central and Local Government Relations*.

13. N. Herlitz, *Elements of Nordic Public Law* (Stockholm: Norstedt, 1969), 160.

14. H. Finer, *English Local Government* (4th edn.; London: Methuen, 1950), 210.

15. See also ibid., pp. 206 ff.

16. See e.g. J. Kobielski, 'L'Influence de la structure des communes urbaines sur leurs dépenses de fonctionnement' (Rennes: Université de Rennes Laboratoire d'Economie des Villes et des Collectivités, 1975).

17. Smith, 'Approaches to the Measurement of Decentralisation', p. 217.

18. F. F. Ridley, 'Integrated Decentralization: Models of the Prefectoral System', *Political Studies*, 21 (1973), 13–25; B. C. Smith, *Decentralisation: The Territorial Dimension of the State* (London: Allen & Unwin, 1985).

19. Similar to Otto Hintze's distinction between the *Hofkommissar* and

the *Landkommissar* in his 'Der Commissarius und seine Bedeutung in der allgemeinen Verwaltungsgeschichte' (first published 1910) in id., *Staat und Verwaltung*, ed. G. Oestreich (Göttingen: Vandenhoeck und Ruprecht, 1962).

20. R. C. Fried, *The Italian Prefects: A Study in Administrative Politics* (New Haven, Conn., and London: Yale University Press, 1963); P. Grémion, *Le Pouvoir périphérique* (Paris: Éditions du Seuil, 1976).

21. Fried, *Italian Prefects*, p. 311.

22. B. Chapman, *The Prefects and French Provincial Administration* (London: Allen & Unwin, 1953), 72–3.

23. For a discussion of different prefectoral systems see Ridley 'Integrated Decentralization'.

24. See Y. Mény, 'France' and V. Santantonio 'Italy', in Page and Goldsmith, *Central and Local Government Relations*.

25. One of the earliest comparative works in this field was J. W. Grice, *National and Local Finance* (London: D. S. King, 1910). Finance has been the focus of the 'Fiscal Austerity and Urban Innovation' project initiated by Terry Clark, the data for which is available in P. E. Mouritzen and K. H. Nielsen, *Handbook of Comparative Urban Fiscal Data* (Odense: Dansk Data Arkiv, 1988). See also K. Newton, *Balancing the Books: The Fiscal Problems of Local Government in Western Europe* (London and Beverly Hills, Calif.: Sage, 1980).

26. Smith, 'Approaches to the Measurement of Decentralization', p. 220.

27. See E. C. Page, 'The New Gift Relationship: Are Central Government Grants Only Good for the Soul?', *Public Administration Bulletin*, 36, (1981), 37–52.

28. See E. C. Page, 'Grant Consolidation and the Development of Intergovernmental Relations in the United States and the United Kingdom', *Politics* 1/1 (1981), 19–24; J. Rattsø, 'Local Government Allocation of Labour and the Grant System: An Applied Model Analysis of Local Government Behaviour in Norway', *Environment and Planning C: Government and Policy*, 7/3 (1989), 273–84. This analysis also discusses the change-over to a grant system almost entirely dependent upon a block grant in 1986 in Norway.

29. R. Dworkin, *Taking Rights Seriously* (London: Duckworth, 1977).

30. See E. C. Page, 'Laws and Orders in Central–Local Government Relations' (Glasgow: University of Strathclyde Studies in Public Policy, No. 106, 1983).

31. See H. Kelsen, *General Theory of Law and State* (Cambridge, Mass.: Harvard University Press, 1949).

32. Y. Mény, 'Radical Reforms and Marginal Change: The French Socialist Experience', in B. Dente and F. Kjellberg (eds.), *The Dynamics of Institutional Change: Local Government Reorganization in Western Democracies* (London and Beverly Hills, Calif.: Sage, 1988), 147–8.

33. F. Kjellberg, 'Local Government Reorganisation and the Welfare State', *Journal of Public Policy*, 5 (1985), 215–40.
34. Bogason, 'Denmark', in Page and Goldsmith, *Central and Local Government Relations*, pp. 54–5.

Chapter 3. *The Political Scale*

1. E. C. Page and M. J. Goldsmith (eds.), *Central and Local Government Relations: A Comparative Analysis of West European Unitary States* (London and Beverly Hills, Calif.: Sage, 1987).
2. H. Eckstein, *Pressure Group Politics: The Case of the BMA* (London: Allen & Unwin, 1960).
3. R. A. W. Rhodes, *The National World of Local Government* (London: Allen & Unwin, 1986); K. Isaac-Henry, 'Local Authority Associations and Local Government Reform', *Public Administration Bulletin*, 33 (Aug. 1980), 21–41; C. Craig, 'COSLA: A Silent Voice for Local Government', in H. M. Drucker and N. L. Drucker (eds.), *The Scottish Government Yearbook 1981* (Edinburgh: Paul Harris, 1980).
4. D. E. Ashford, *British Dogmatism and French Pragmatism: Central-Local Policy Making in the Welfare State* (London: Allen & Unwin, 1982), 384; Rhodes, *The National World of Local Government*, pp. 50 ff.
5. See T. J. Anton, *Administered Politics. Elite Political Culture in Sweden* (The Hague: Martinus Nijhoff, 1980); N. Elder, A. J. Thomas, and D. Arter, *The Consensual Democracies? The Government and Politics of the Scandinavian States* (Oxford: Martin Robertson, 1982).
6. See B. Molin, L. Mansson, and L. Strömberg, *Offentlig förvaltning* (Stockholm: Bonnies, 1975), 178–81.
7. A. Laurens, *Le Métier politique ou la conquête du pouvoir* (Paris: Éditions Alain Moureau, 1980), 53–4; P. Garraud, *Profession: homme politique. La carrière politique des maires urbains* (Paris: L' Harmattan, 1989), 186.
8. Y. Mény, 'France' in Page and Goldsmith, *Central and Local Government Relations*, p. 103; see also Ashford, *British Dogmatism and French Pragmatism*, p. 291. Garraud in his *Profession: homme politique,* pp. 187 ff. points to the factors leading to cohesion in the AMF.
9. T. Clegg, 'Spain' in Page and Goldsmith, *Central and Local Government Relations*, p. 149.
10. Rhodes, *National World of Local Government*, p. 299.
11. Ibid., p. 347.
12. Ibid., p. 246.
13. Compare R. A. W. Rhodes, *Control and Power in Central–Local Government Relations* (Aldershot: Gower, 1981) with R. A. W.

Rhodes *et al.*, 'Corporate Bias in Central–Local Relations' (Colchester: University of Essex Department of Government, SSRC Central–Local Relations Discussion Paper, 1982) and Rhodes, *National World of Local Government*, pp. 244–6.

14. Ashford, *British Dogmatism and French Pragmatism*, p. 112.
15. Mény, 'France', p. 103.
16. R. Y. Nanetti, *Growth and Territorial Policies: The Italian Model of Social Capitalism* (London: Frances Pinter, 1988), 81.
17. E. Buglione, F. Merloni, V. Santantonio, and L. Torchia, 'L'Italie', in Y. Mény (ed.), *La Réforme des collectivités locales en Europe* (Paris: La Documentation Française, 1984), 70.
18. Clegg, 'Spain', p. 149.
19. E. Harder, *Local Government in Denmark* (Copenhagen: Det Danske Selskab, 1973), 129.
20. J. A. Brand, *Local Government Reform in England 1888–1974* (London: Croom Helm, 1974), 50–1.
21. F. Kjellberg, 'Local Government and the Scandinavian Welfare State: Structural and Functional Reforms in Denmark, Norway and Sweden since 1945', Colloquium on the Reforms of Local and Regional Authorities in Europe, Council of Europe, Linz, 5–6 Nov. 1981.
22. F. Smallwood, *Greater London: The Politics of Metropolitan Reform* (Indianapolis, New York, and Kansas City: Bobbs Merrill, 1965).
23. Rhodes, *National World of Local Government*, pp. 244–5; for a discussion of reform see B. Wood, *The Process of Local Government Reform 1966–74* (London: Allen & Unwin, 1976).
24. D. H. Haider, *When Governments Come to Washington: Mayors, Governors and Intergovernmental Lobbying* (New York: Free Press, 1974), 255.
25. For an attempt to discuss the 'cultural disdain' of local government in British élite political culture see R. Greenwood, 'Pressures from Whitehall' in R. Rose and E. C. Page (eds.), *Fiscal Stress in Cities* (London: Cambridge University Press, 1982).
26. See Rhodes, *National World of Local Government*, p. 94.
27. Haider, *When Governments Come to Washington*, p. 255.
28. Isaac-Henry, 'Local Authority Associations', p. 31.
29. W. J. M. Mackenzie, 'The Conventions of Local Government', *Public Administration* 29 (1951), 345–56.
30. D. E. Butler, 'Local Government in Parliament', *Public Administration*, 31 (1953), 46–7.
31. W. J. M. Mackenzie, 'Local Government in Parliament', *Public Administration* 32 (1954), 409–23.
32. See S. Tarrow, *Between Center and Periphery: Grassroots Politicians in Italy and France*, (New Haven, Conn.: Yale University Press, 1977); S. Tarrow, 'Introduction' in S. Tarrow, P. J. Katzenstein, and L.

Graziano (eds.), *Territorial Politics in Industrial Nations* (New York: Praeger, 1978); B. Dente, 'Centre-Local Relations in Italy', in Y. Mény and V. Wright (eds.), *Centre-Periphery Relations in Western Europe* (London: Allen & Unwin, 1985).

33. See E. C. Page, *Political Authority and Bureaucratic Power: A Comparative Analysis* (Brighton: Wheatsheaf Books, 1985).

34. J. Beqcuart-Leclerc, *Paradoxes du pouvoir local* (Paris: Presses de la Fondation Nationale des Sciences Politiques, 1976).

35. M. Crozier *et al. Où va l'administration française?* (Paris: Èditions d'Organisation, 1974). For a recent statement see F. Dupuy and J.-C. Thoenig, *Sociologie de l'administration française* (Paris: Armand Colin, 1983).

36. J. Becquart-Leclercq, 'Le Cumul', in A. Mabileau (ed.) *Les Pouvoirs locaux à l'épreuve de la décentralisation* (Paris: Pédone, 1984), 222.

37. Santantonio, 'Italy', p. 126.

38. Mackenzie, 'Local Government in Parliament', p. 423.

39. Tarrow, *Between Center and Periphery*.

40. Santantonio, 'Italy', p. 125.

41. P. Allum, *Politics and Society in Postwar Naples* (London: Cambridge University Press, 1973).

42. Ibid., p. 171.

43. Ibid., p. 334. For a discussion of clientelism and elections in the Italian South see also C. White, *Patrons and Partisans: A Study of Politics in Two Southern Italian Comuni* (Cambridge: Cambridge University Press, 1980), 50 ff.

44. J. Linz, 'The New Spanish Party System', in R. Rose (ed.), *Electoral Participation: A Comparative Analysis* (London and Beverly Hills, Calif.: Sage, 1980), 125.

45. R. Carr, *Spain 1808–1975* (2nd edn., Oxford: Clarendon Press, 1982), 366 ff.

46. J. A. Pitt-Rivers, *People of the Sierra* (London: Weidenfeld & Nicolson, 1954).

47. Clegg, 'Spain', p. 148.

48. P. Heywood, 'Mirror Images: The PCE and the PSOE in the Transition to Democracy in Spain', *West European Politics* 10 (1987), 207.

49. J. M. Maravall, 'The Socialist Alternative: The Policies and Electorate of the PSOE', in H. Penniman (ed.) *Spain at the Polls 1977, 1979 and 1982* (Washington, DC: American Enterprise Institute, 1985), 137–8.

50. See Lane and Magnusson, 'Sweden'; Sorensen and Fevolden, 'Norway'; Bogason, 'Denmark'; and Goldsmith and Page, 'Britain' in Page and Goldsmith, *Central and Local Government Relations*.

51. M. Rush, *The Selection of Parliamentary Candidates* (London: Nelson, 1969), 79.

52. M. Kesselman, *The Ambiguous Consensus* (New York: Knopf, 1967); Mackenzie, 'Local Government in Parliament'.

Chapter 4. *The Consequences of Localism and Centralism*

1. R. A. Dahl, 'The City in the Future of Democracy', *American Political Science Review*, 67 (1961), 953–70; J. D. Stewart, *Local Government: The Conditions of Local Choice* (London: Allen & Unwin, 1983); L. J. Sharpe, 'Theories and Values of Local Government', *Political Studies*, 18/2 (1970), 153–74.
2. See E. C. Page, 'The Value of Local Autonomy', *Local Government Studies*, 8/4 (1982), 21–42.
3. D. E. Ashford, *British Dogmatism and French Pragmatism: Central–Local Policy Making in the Welfare State* (London: Allen & Unwin, 1982).
4. J.-C. Thoenig, 'State Bureaucracies and Local Government in France', in K. Hanf and F. W. Scharpf (eds.), *Interorganizational Policy Making* (London: Sage, 1978); N. P. Hepworth, *The Finance of Local Government* (4th edn.; London: Allen & Unwin, 1984).
5. C. C. Hood, 'The Machinery of Government Problem', *Studies in Public Policy*, 28 (Glasgow: University of Strathclyde, 1979).
6. E. C. Page, 'The Marginalisation of Local Political Elites in Britain', *Environment and Planning C: Government and Policy*, 2 (1984), 167–76.
7. See S. Tarrow, *Between Centre and Periphery: Grassroots Politicians in Britain and France* (New Haven, Conn.: Yale University Press, 1977), 111 ff.
8. See J.-P. Worms, 'Le Préfet et ses notables', *Sociologie du travail*, 3 (1966), 249–75; M. Kesselmann, *The Ambiguous Consensus* (New York: Knopf, 1967); P. Allum, *Politics and Society in Postwar Naples* (London: Cambridge University Press, 1973).
9. Y. Mény, 'Le Maire ici et ailleurs', *Pouvoirs*, 24 (1983), 20–1.
10. Kesselman, *Ambiguous Consensus*.
11. C. Sorbets, 'Est-il légitime de parler d'une présidentialisme municipale?', *Pouvoirs*, 24 (1983) 105–16.
12. Cited in Mény, 'Le Maire', p. 27.
13. P. Taafe and T. Mulhearn, *Liverpool: The City that Dared to Fight* (London: Fortress Books, 1988).
14. E. Martin Harloff, *The Structure of Local Government in Europe* (The Hague: International Union of Local Authorities, 1987).
15. See also S. Humes and E. Martin, *The Structure of Local Government throughout the World* (The Hague: International Union of Local Authorities, 1969).
16. See Mény, 'Le Maire ici et ailleurs', p. 23. On political leadership in

Italy see F. Kjellberg, *Political Institutionalisation: A Political Study of Two Sardinian Communities* (London and New York: Wiley, 1975); C. White, *Patrons and Partisans: A Study of Politics in Two Southern Italian Comuni* (Cambridge: Cambridge University Press, 1980).

17. See also Tarrow, *Between Center and Periphery*.
18. E. Harder, *Local Government in Denmark* (Copenhagen: Det Danske Selskab, 1973), 42.
19. A. J. Tudesq, 'De la monarchie à la Republique: le maire petit ou grand notable', *Pouvoirs*, 24 (1983), 5–18.
20. For exceptions see J. Dearlove, *The Politics of Policy in Local Government* (London: Cambridge University Press, 1973); K. Newton, *Second City Politics* (Oxford: Oxford University Press, 1976); S. Leach et al., *The Political Organization of Local Authorities: Committee of Inquiry into the Conduct of Local Authority Business Research*, i, Cmnd. 9797 (London: HMSO, 1986).
21. R. A. W. Rhodes, *The National World of Local Government* (London: Allen & Unwin, 1986).
22. J. Lynn and A. Jay, *Yes Minister: The Diaries of a Cabinet Minister*, iii (London: British Broadcasting Corporation, 1983), 159.
23. E. N. Suleiman, *Politics Power and Bureaucracy in France: The Administrative Elite* (Princeton, NJ: Princeton University Press, 1974).
24. F. Dreyfus and F. d' Arcy, *Les Institutions politiques et administratives de la France* (Paris: Economica, 1985), 346.
25. P. F. Furlong, 'Policy Elites and Public Administration in Italy', Paper prepared for the European Consortium for Political Research Joint Sessions, Rimini, 1988.
26. R. C. Fried, *Planning the Eternal City: Roman Politics and Planning since World War II* (New Haven, Conn.: Yale University Press, 1973); M. Goldsmith, *Politics, Planning and the City* (London: Hutchinson, 1980).
27. Fried, *Planning the Eternal City*, p. 250.
28. Ibid., p. 252.
29. Ibid., p. 254.
30. Kjellberg, *Political Institutionalisation*, p. 109.
31. Anton, *Governing Greater Stockholm: A Study of Policy Development and System Theory* (Berkeley, Calif.: University of California Press, 1975), 155;
32. J.-E. Lane, T. Magnusson, and A. Westlund, 'Kommunernas byråkratisering', *Tväsnitt* 2 (1982).
33. J. D. Greenstone and P. E. Peterson, *Race and Authority in Urban Politics: Community Participation and the War on Poverty* (New York: Russell Sage Foundation, 1973), 224–5.
34. G. Almond and S. Verba, *The Civic Culture* (Boston: Little Brown, 1963), 125.

35. T. Hansen and K. Newton, 'Voluntary Organizations and Community Politics: Norwegian and British Comparisons', *Scandinavian Political Studies*, 8 (1985), 1–21.

36. T. Miller, 'The Emergence of Participatory Ideas on Swedish Planning and Local Government', *Scandinavian Political Studies*, 2 (1979), 313–32.

37. N. T. Boaden *et al.*, *Public Participation in Local Services* (London: Longman, 1982); J. C. Birch and H. Christoffersen (eds.), *Citizen Participation in America and Scandinavia* (Gentofte: Kommunernes Landsforening, 1981).

38. R. Y. Nanetti, *Growth and Territorial Policies: The Italian Model of Social Capitalism* (London: Frances Pinter, 1988), 150.

39. Kesselman, *Ambiguous Consensus*, pp. 156 ff.

40. M. Crozier, *The Bureaucratic Phenomenon* (London: Tavistock, 1964).

41. J. Fauvet and H. Mendras (eds.), *Les Paysans et la politique dans la France contemporaine* (Paris: Armand Colin, 1958); Kesselmann, *Ambiguous Consensus*; L. Wylie, *Village in the Vaucluse: An Account of Life in a French Village* (New York: Harper & Row, 1957).

42. G. G. Meyers, 'Villeneuve: A Community Study in French Political Subculture and Public Policy', Ph.D. thesis, Stanford University, Calif., 1982.

43. See Miller, 'The Emergence of Participatory Ideas'; Hansen and Newton, 'Voluntary Organizations'; Boaden *et al.*, *Public Participation*.

44. For a discussion of the literature see B. D. Jones, *Governing Urban America: A Policy Focus* (Boston: Little Brown, 1983), 347–80.

45. Jones, *Governing Urban America*, p. 243.

46. R. Lineberry and E. P. Fowler, 'Reformism and Public Policies in American Cities', *American Political Science Review*, 61 (1967), 701–16; E. C. Banfield and J. Q. Wilson, *City Politics* (New Haven, Conn.: Yale University Press, 1963), 38–43.

47. A. Karnig, 'Private Regarding Policy, Civil Rights Groups and the Mediating Impacts of Municipal Reforms', *American Journal of Political Science*, 19 (1975), 91–106.

48. Banfield and Wilson, *City Politics*, p. 125.

49. Ibid., p. 330.

50. Tarrow, *Between Center and Periphery*.

51. See J. F. Médard, 'Political Clientelism in France: The Centre–Periphery Nexus Reexamined', in S. N. Eisenstadt and R. Lemarchand (eds.), *Political Clientelism, Patronage and Development* (London and Beverly Hills, Calif.: Sage, 1981).

52. Kesselman, *Ambiguous Consensus*; P. Garraud, *Profession: homme politique. La carrière politique des maires urbains* (Paris: L'Harmattan, 1989), p. 175.

53. J. Becquart-Leclercq, *Les Paradoxes du pouvoir local* (Paris: Presses de la Fondation Nationale des Sciences Politiques, 1976), 188–9.

54. J. Y. Nevers, 'Du clientèlisme à la technocratie: cent ans de démocratie dans une grande ville, Toulouse', *Revue française de science politique*, 33 (1983), 428–54.

55. Médard, 'Political Clientelism in France', p. 142.

56. Banfield and Wilson, *City Politics*, pp. 38–43.

57. J. Chubb, 'The Social Bases of an Urban Political Machine: The Christian Democratic Party in Palermo' in Eisenstadt and Lemarchand, *Political Clientelism, Patronage and Development*.

58. Ibid., p. 80.

59. J. Chubb, 'Naples under the Left: The Limits of Local Change', in Eisenstadt and Lemarchand, *Political Clientelism, Patronage and Development*.

60. Fried, *Planning the Eternal City*, p. 258.

61. Ibid., p. 263.

62. Tarrow, *Between Center and Periphery*, p. 200.

63. F. Kjellberg, 'A Comparative View of Municipal Decentralisation: Neighbourhood Democracy in Oslo and Bologna', in L. J. Sharpe (ed.), *Decentralist Trends in Western Democracies* (London and Beverly Hills, Calif.: Sage, 1979).

64. Kjellberg, 'Comparative View of Municipal Decentralisation', p. 109.

65. R. A. W. Rhodes's review of Page and Goldsmith, *Central and Local Government* in *Political Studies*, 36 (1988), 367.

66. C. Ham, *Health Policy in Britain* (London: Macmillan, 1985), p. 166.

67. K. Mladenka and K. Hill, 'The Distribution of Urban Police Services', *Journal of Politics*, 40 (1978), 112–33.

68. F. Levy, A. Meltsner, and A. Wildavsky, *Urban Outcomes* (Berkeley, Calif.: University of California Press, 1974).

69. Jones, *Governing Urban America*, p. 364.

70. Ibid., p. 364.

71. B. Reissert, 'Federal and State Transfers to Local Government in the Federal Republic of Germany: A Case of Political Immobility', in D. E. Ashford (ed.), *Financing Local Government in the Welfare State* (London: Croom Helm, 1980).

72. D. King, *Fiscal Tiers: The Economics of Multi-Level Government* (London: Allen & Unwin, 1984), 186.

73. H. Wolman and E. C. Page, 'The Impact of Intergovernmental Grants on Subnational Resource Disparities', *Public Budgeting and Finance*, 7 (1987), 82–98.

74. Ibid.

75. Ibid., p. 89.

76. R. J. Bennett, 'Tax Assignment in Multilevel Systems of Government—

A Political-Economic Approach and the Case of Spain', *Environment and Planning C: Government and Policy*, 5 (1987), 267–85; G. Pola, 'Recent Developments of Central–Local Financial Relations in Italy', *Environment and Planning C: Government and Policy*, 4 (1986), 187–98.

77. B. Dente, 'Intergovernmental Relations and Central Control Policies: The Case of Italian Local Finance', *Environment and Planning C: Government and Policy*, 3 (1985), 383–402.
78. Wolman and Page, 'The Impact of Intergovernmental Grants', p. 87.
79. Y. Mény, 'Financial Transfers and Local Government in France: National Policy Despite 36,000 Communes', in D. E. Ashford (ed.), *Financing Local Government in the Welfare State* (London: Croom Helm, 1980), 156.
80. J. LeGrand, *A Strategy of Equality* (London: Allen & Unwin, 1982).

Chapter 5. Explaining Patterns of Centralism and Localism

1. See K. Hanf and F. W. Scharpf (eds.), *Interorganizational Policy Making* (London and Beverly Hills, Calif.: Sage, 1978); R. A. W. Rhodes, *Control and Power in Central–Local Government Relations* (Aldershot: Gower, 1981); D. S. Wright, *Understanding Intergovernmental Relations* (2nd edn.; Monterey, Calif.: Brooks Cole, 1982).
2. Rhodes, *Beyond Westminster and Whitehall: The Sub-Central Government of Britain* (London: Hyman Unwin, 1988), 371 ff.
3. For an excellent discussion of this literature see D. King, *Fiscal Tiers: The Economics of Multi-Level Government* (London: Allen & Unwin, 1985).
4. P. Saunders, 'Rethinking Local Politics', in M. Boddy and C. Fudge (eds.), *Local Socialism* (London: Macmillan, 1984); P. E. Peterson, *City Limits* (Chicago: University of Chicago Press, 1981).
5. D. E. Ashford, *British Dogmatism and French Pragmatism: Central–Local Policy Making in the Welfare State* (London: Allen & Unwin, 1982).
6. M. S. Archer, *The Social Origins of Educational Systems* (London and Beverly Hills, Calif.: Sage, 1979).
7. S. Tarrow, *Between Center and Periphery: Grassroots Politicians in Italy and France* (New Haven, Conn.: Yale University Press, 1977).
8. Archer, *Social Origins of Educational Systems*.
9. Ibid., p. 271.
10. Ibid., p. 266.
11. Ibid., p. 22.
12. Ibid., pp. 106–7.

13. Ibid., p. 200.
14. Ibid., p. 185.
15. S. Rokkan, *Citizens, Electors, Parties* (Oslo: Universitetsforlaget, 1970), 131.
16. G. Rhodes, *Central–Local Relations: The Experience of the Environmental Health and Trading Standards Services* (London: Royal Institute of Public Administration, 1986).
17. S. and B. Webb, *The Story of the King's Highway* (London: Frank Cass, 1963); J.-C. Thoenig, *L'Ère des technocrates* (Paris: Éditions d'Organisation, 1973).
18. See Webb and Webb, *Story of the King's Highway*, pp. 166–7.
19. Archer, *Social Origins of Educational Systems*, p. 36.
20. M. Kogan, review of Archer's *Social Origins of Educational Systems* in *Journal of Social Policy*, 9/2 (1980), 243–5.
21. Ashford, *British Dogmatism*, p. 362.
22. M. Kesselman, *The Ambiguous Consensus* (New York: Knopf, 1967); M. Crozier *et al; Où va l'administration française?* (Paris: Éditions d'Organisation, 1974); J.-P. Worms, 'Le Préfet et ses notables', *Sociologie du Travail* 3 (1966), 249–75.
23. Ashford, *British Dogmatism*, p. 359.
24. Ibid., p. 360.
25. Ibid., p. 352.
26. Ibid., p. 361.
27. Ibid., p. 362.
28. Kesselman, *The Ambiguous Consensus*; Worms, 'Le Préfet et ses notables'; M. Crozier, *La Société bloquée* (Paris: Le Seuil, 1970).
29. Tarrow, *Between Center and Periphery*, p. 34.
30. Ibid., p. 36.
31. Ibid., p. 38.
32. In N. Boaden's *Urban Policy Making* (London: Cambridge University Press, 1971), the correlation in +0.38.
33. See P. A. Gourevitch, *Paris and the Provinces: The Politics of Local and Regional Reform in France* (London: Allen & Unwin, 1980), 99 ff.
34. J. Bulpitt, *Territory and Power in the United Kingdon* (Manchester: Manchester University Press, 1983).
35. J.-C. Thoenig, 'Local Subsidies in the Third Republic', in D. E. Ashford (ed.), *Financing Local Government in the Welfare State* (London: Croom Helm, 1980).
36. A. de Tocqueville, *The Ancien Regime and the Revolution* (Oxford: Blackwell, 1949); M. Crozier, *The Bureaucratic Phenomenon* (London: Tavistock, 1964).
37. Ashford, *British Dogmatism and French Pragmatism*, p. xiii.
38. For a good discussion of 'Napoleonic' systems see L. J. Sharpe, 'Local

Government Reorganisation: General Theory and United Kingdom Practice', in B. Dente and F. Kjellberg (eds.), *The Dynamics of Institutional Change* (London and Beverly Hills, Calif.: Sage, 1988).

39. Sharpe, 'Local Government Reorganisation', pp. 95–6.

40. G. Montagu-Harris, *Local Government in Many Lands* (London: D. S. King, 1933); see also O. Hintze, 'Staatenbildung und Kommunalverwaltung', in id. (ed.), *Staat und Verfassung: Gesammelte Abhandlungen zur allgemeinen Verfassungsgechichte*, ed. G. Oestreich (Göttingen: Vandenhoeck and Ruprecht, 1962); E. Harder, *Local Government in Denmark* (Copenhagen: Det Danske Selskab, 1973).

41. See E. Becker, 'Entwicklung der deutschen Gemeinden und Gemeindeverbände in Hinblick auf die Gegenwart', in H. Peters (ed.), *Handbuch der kommunalen Wissenschaft und Praxis*, i: *Kommunalverfassung* (Heidelberg: Springer Verlag, 1956), 87. As Becker points out, one of the distinctive and most important features of the Napoleonic system of local government was the equal treatment of town and country.

42. See Hintze, *Staat und Verfassung*; see also E. C. Page, 'The Political Origins of Bureaucracy and Self-Government: Otto Hintze's Conceptual Map of Europe', *Political Studies*, 38/1 (1990), 39–55.

43. This section draws heavily on Hintze, 'Staatenbildung und Kommunalverwaltung'.

44. R. Mousnier, *État et société en France au XVIIe et XVIIIe siècles: Le gouvernment et le corps* (Paris: Centre de Documentation Universitaire, 1968).

45. V. R. Gruder, *The Royal Provincial Intendants* (Ithaca, NY: Cornell University Press, 1968).

46. R. C. Fried, *The Italian Prefects: A Study in Administrative Politics* (New Haven, Conn., and London: Yale University Press, 1963), 1.

47. See P. Viollet, *Histoire des institutions politiques et administratives de la France*, iv: *Le Roi et ses ministres pendant les trois derniers siècles de la monarchie* (Darmstadt: Scientia Verlag, 1966, repr. of 1912 edn.).

48. W. N. Hargreaves-Mawdsley, *Eighteenth Century Spain 1700–1788: A Political, Diplomatic and Institutional History* (London: Macmillan, 1979), 11.

49. R. Carr, *Spain 1808–1975* (2nd edn., Oxford: Clarendon Press, 1982), 65.

50. See. J. Rosén, 'Scandinavia and the Baltic', in *The New Cambridge Modern History: The Ascendancy of France 1648–1688* (London: Cambridge University Press, 1981); see also E. Ekman 'The Danish Royal Law of 1665', *Journal of Modern History*, 29 (1957), 102–11.

51. B. J. Hovde, *The Scandinavian Countries 1720–1865* 2 vols. (Port Washington, NY: Kennikat Press, 1943), ii. 567.

52. T. K. Derry, *A History of Modern Norway 1814–1972* (Oxford: Clarendon Press, 1973), 138.

53. Derry, *History of Modern Norway*, p. 29.

54. F. Kaiser, '1862 ars kommunalforordningar', in Svenska Landstingsforbundet, *Hundra ar under Kommunalforfattningarna 1862–1962* (Stockholm: Svenska Stadsforbundet, 1962), 29.

55. N. Andren, 'Local Government in Sweden', University of Stockholm Texts in Political Science, (1953), 1.

56. S. and B. Webb, *English Local Government from the Revolution to the Municipal Corporations Act: The Parish and the County* (London: Frank Cass, 1924), 279.

57. J. J. Clarke, *The Local Government of the United Kingdom* (London: Pitman, 1939), 30–1.

58. Webb and Webb, *English Local Government*, p. 535.

59. Hintze, *Staat und Verfassung*, p. 103.

60. Ibid., p. 214.

61. Ibid., p. 230.

62. Ibid., p. 231.

63. M. Roberts, 'Sweden', in A. Goodwin (ed.), *The European Nobility in the Eighteenth Century* (London: Adam and Charles Black, 1953), 153.

64. J. O. Lindsay, 'The Social Classes and the Foundations of States', in J. O. Lindsay (ed.) *New Cambridge Modern History of Europe* vii: *The Old Regime* (Cambridge: Cambridge University Press, 1957), 55.

65. Rosén, 'Scandinavia and the Baltic', p. 536.

66. Tocqueville, *Ancien Regime*.

67. See Fried, *Italian Prefects*, from which this account draws heavily.

68. Ibid., p. 86.

69. Ibid., p. 89.

70. D. V. Verney, *Parliamentary Reform in Sweden* (Oxford: Clarendon Press, 1957), p. 49.

71. K. B. Smellie, *A History of Local Government* (4th edn., London: Allen & Unwin, 1969), 46.

72. See E. S. Griffith, *The Development of Modern City Government*, 2 vols. (Oxford: Oxford University Press, 1927), i. 225.

73. R. M. Gutchen, 'Local Improvements and Centralisation in Nineteenth Century England', *Historical Journal*, 4 (1961), 85–96. Indeed, this pattern appears to have persisted well into the twentieth century. B. Swann, 'Local Initiative and Central Control: The Insulin Decision', *Policy and Politics*, 1 (1972), 55–63 shows how local practice in the provision of insulin became national policy.

74. Carr, *Spain*, p. 98.

75. Ibid., p. 121.

76. Ibid., pp. 98–9.

77. J. Waterbury, 'An Attempt to put Patrons and Clients in their Place', in E. Gellner and J. Waterbury (eds.), *Patrons and Clients in Mediterranean Societies* (London: Duckworth, 1977), 332.

78. A. S. Zuckerman, 'Clientelistic Politics in Italy', in Gellner and Waterbury, *Patrons and Clients*, p. 73.

79. Tarrow, *Between Center and Periphery*.

80. E. Santantonio 'Italy' in E. C. Page and M. Goldsmith (eds.) *Central and Local Government: A Comparative Analysis of West European Unitary States* (London and Beverly Hills, Calif.: Sage, 1987).

81. A. S. Zuckerman, *The Politics of Faction: Christian Democratic Rule in Italy* (New Haven, Conn., and London: Yale University Press, 1979), 56; see also A. Weingrod in Gellner and Waterbury, *Patrons and Clients*; Tarrow, *Between Center and Periphery*.

82. M. Kenny, *A Spanish Tapestry: Town and Country in Castile* (London: Cohen & West, 1961), 37.

83. Tarrow, *Between Center and Periphery*.

84. See J. F. Médard, 'Political Clientelism in France: The Center-Periphery Nexus Reexamined', in S. N. Eisenstadt and R. Lemarchand (eds.) *Political Clientelism, Patronage and Development* (London and Beverly Hills, Calif.: Sage, 1981), 125.

85. M. Shefter, *Patronage and its Opponents: A Theory and some European Cases* (Cornell University Western Societies Program Occasional Papers No. 8, 1977), 72.

86. S. Tarrow, *Peasant Communism in Southern Italy* (New Haven, Conn.: Yale University Press, 1967).

87. J. Chubb, 'Naples under the Left: The Limits of Local Change', in S. N. Eisentadt and R. Lemarchand (eds.), *Political Clientelism, Patronage and Development* (London and Beverly Hills, Calif.: Sage, 1981), 117.

88. Carr, *Spain*, pp. 368–70.

89. Ibid., p. 371.

90. Médard, 'Political Clientelism in France', p. 153; see also B. le Clère and V. Wright, *Les Préfets du Second Empire* (Paris: Armand Colin, 1973).

91. M. Faure, *Les Paysans et la politique dans la société française* (Paris: Armand Colin, 1966).

92. P. M. Williams, *Crisis and Compromise: Politics in the Fourth Republic* (3rd edn., London: Longmans Green and Co., 1964), 99.

93. Médard, 'Political Clientelism in France', p. 158.

94. K. N. Medhurst, *Government in Spain: The Executive at Work* (Oxford: Pergamon, 1973), 186.

95. T. Clegg, 'Spain', in E. C. Page and M. J. Goldsmith (eds.), *Central*

and Local Government Relations: A Comparative Analysis of West European Unitary States (London and Beverly Hills, Calif.: Sage, 1987), 148.

96. P. Heywood, 'Mirror Images: The PCE and the PSOE in the Transition to Democracy in Spain', *West European Politics*, 10 (1987), 193–210.

97. L. B. Namier, *The Structure of Politics at the Accession of George III* (London: Macmillan, 1929); R. T. Mackenzie, *Political Parties* (2nd edn., London: Heinemann, 1963), 252.

98. J. A. Barnes, 'Class and Communities in a Norwegian Island Parish', *Human Relations*, 7/1 (1954), 53.

99. See Shefter, *Patronage and its Opponents*.

100. A point also developed by B. Dente, 'Local Government Reform and Legitimacy', in B. Dente and F. Kjellberg (eds.), *The Dynamics of Institutional Change* (London and Beverly Hills, Calif.: Sage, 1988).

101. T. Fevolden and R. Sorensen, 'Norway', in Page and Goldsmith, *Central and Local Government Relations*, p. 30; P. Bogason, 'Denmark', ibid., p. 47; and J. E. Lane and T. Magnusson 'Sweden', ibid., pp. 12–13.

102. National Association of Local Authorities in Denmark, *Economic and Political Trends in Danish Local Government* (Copenhagen: National Association of Local Authorities in Denmark, 1981), 115.

103. Bogason, 'Denmark', p. 54.

104. Fevolden and Sorensen, 'Norway', p. 38.

105. Y. Mény 'France' in Page and Goldsmith, *Central and Local Government Relations*.

106. Santantonio, 'Italy', p. 114.

107. L. J. Sharpe, 'Reforming the Grass Roots: An Alternative Analysis', in D. E. Butler and A. H. Halsey (eds.), *Policy and Politics* (London: Macmillan, 1978).

Chapter 6. Conclusions

1. G. Montagu-Harris, *Local Government in Many Lands* (London: D. S. King, 1933), 391.

2. A. Shaw, *Municipal Government in Continental Europe* (New York: The Century Co., 1895), p. vii.

3. W. J. M. Mackenzie, 'Local Government in Parliament', *Public Administration*, 29 (1954), 423.

4. See P. Garraud, *Profession: homme politique. La carrière politique des maires urbains* (Paris: L'Harmattan, 1989).

5. C. Ross, *Local Government in the Soviet Union* (London: Croom Helm, 1987).

6. Source: Organization for Economic Co-operation and Development, *National Accounts for OECD Countries* (Paris: OECD, 1987).

7. A. Mughan, 'Belgium: All Periphery and No Centre?', in Y. Mény and V. Wright (eds.), *Centre Periphery Relations in Western Europe*, (London: Allen & Unwin, 1985), 280.

8. A. Hoogewerf, 'Les Pays-Bas', in Y. Mény (ed.), *La Réforme des collectivités locales en Europe: Stratégies et résultats* (Paris: La Documentation Française, 1984), 141.

9. See US Advisory Commission on Intergovernmental Relations, *The Question of State Government Capability* (Washington, DC: US Government Printing Office, 1985), ch. 12, 'The States and their Local Governments'.

10. US Advisory Commission on Intergovernmental Relations, *State and Federal Roles in the Federal System* (Washington, DC: Government Printing Office, 1982), 237.

11. Ibid., p. 239.

12. Ibid., p. 238.

13. Ibid. See also T. J. Anton, 'The Political Economy of Local Government Reform in the United States', in B. Dente and F. Kjellberg (eds.), *The Dynamics of Institutional Change: Local Government Reorganization in Western Democracy* (London and Beverly Hills, Calif.: Sage, 1988).

14. J. D. Greenstone and P. E. Peterson, *Race and Authority in Urban Politics: Community Participation and the War on Poverty* (New York: Russell Sage Foundation, 1973), 225.

15. E. C. Banfield and J. Q. Wilson, *City Politics* (New Haven, Conn.: Yale University Press, 1963), 122.

16. Ibid., p. 122.

17. R. Rose, *Do Parties Make a Difference?* (2nd edn., London: Macmillan, 1984).

18. P. M. Sacks, *The Donegal Mafia: An Irish Political Machine* (New Haven, Conn.: Yale University Press, 1976); see also A. S. Zuckerman, *The Politics of Faction: Christian Democratic Rule in Italy* (New Haven, Conn., and London: Yale University Press, 1979).

Bibliography

ALLUM, P., *Politics and Society in Postwar Naples* (London: Cambridge University Press, 1973).

ALMOND, G., and VERBA, S., *The Civic Culture* (Boston: Little Brown, 1963).

ANDREN, N., 'Local Government in Sweden', University of Stockholm Texts in Political Science (1953).

ANTON, T. J., *Governing Greater Stockholm: A Study of Policy Development and System Theory* (Berkeley, Calif.: University of California Press. 1975).

—— *Administered Politics: Elite Political Culture in Sweden* (The Hague: Martinus Nijhoff, 1980).

—— 'The Political Economy of Local Government Reform in the United States', in B. Dente and F. Kjellberg (eds.), *The Dynamics of Institutional Change: Local Government Reorganization in Western Democracy* (London and Beverly Hills, Calif.: Sage, 1988).

ARCHER, M. S., *The Social Origins of Educational Systems* (London and Beverly Hills, Calif.: Sage, 1979).

ASHFORD, D. E., 'Territorial Politics and Equality: Decentralization in the Modern State', *Political Studies*, 27/1 (1979), 71–83.

—— (ed.), *Financing Urban Government in the Welfare State* (London: Croom Helm, 1980).

—— *British Dogmatism and French Pragmatism: Central–Local Policy Making in the Welfare State* (London: Allen & Unwin, 1982).

BANFIELD, E. C., and WILSON, J. Q., *City Politics* (New Haven, Conn.: Yale University Press, 1963).

BARNES J. A., 'Class and Communities in a Norwegian Island Parish', *Human Relations*, 7/1 (1954), 39–58.

BENNETT, R. J., 'Tax Assignment in Multilevel Systems of Government: A Political-Economic Approach and the Case of Spain', *Environment and Planning C: Government and Policy*, 5 (1987), 267–85.

BECKER, E., 'Entwicklung der deutschen Gemeinden und Gemeindeverbände in Hinblick auf die Gegenwart', in H. Peters (ed.), *Handbuch der kommunalen Wissenschaft und Praxis*, i: *Kommunalverfassung* (Heidelberg: Springer Verlag, 1956).

BECQUART-LECLERCQ, J., *Paradoxes du pouvoir local* (Paris: Presses de la Fondation Nationale des Sciences Politiques, 1976).

BECQUART–LECLERCQ, J., 'Le Cumul', in A. Mabileau (ed.), *Les Pouvoirs locaux à l'épreuve de la décentralisation* (Paris: Pédone, 1984).

BIRCH, J. C., and CHRISTOFFERSEN, H. (eds.), *Citizen Participation in America and Scandinavia* (Gentofte: Kommunernes Landsforening, 1981).

BOADEN, N. T., *Urban Policy Making* (London: Cambridge University Press, 1971).

—— GOLDSMITH, M., HAMPTON, W., and STRINGER, P., *Public Participation in Local Services* (London: Longman, 1982).

BOGASON, P., 'Denmark', in E. C. Page and M. Goldsmith (eds.), *Central and Local Government Relations: A Comparative Analysis of West European Unitary States* (London and Beverly Hills, Calif.: Sage, 1987).

BRAND, J. A., *Local Government Reform in England 1888–1974* (London: Croom Helm, 1974).

BUGLIONE, E., MERLONI, F., SANTANTONIO, V., and TORCHIA, L. 'L'Italie' in Y. Mény (ed.), *La Réforme des collectivités locales en Europe* (Paris: La Documentation Française, 1984).

BULPITT, J., *Territory and Power in the United Kingdom* (Manchester: Manchester University Press, 1983).

BUTLER, D. E., 'Local Government in Parliament', *Public Administration*, 31 (1953), 46–7.

CARR, R., *Spain 1808–1975* (2nd edn., Oxford: Clarendon Press, 1982).

CHAPMAN, B., *The Prefects and French Provincial Administration* (London: Allen & Unwin, 1953).

CHUBB, J., 'The Social Bases of an Urban Political Machine: The Christian Democratic Party in Palermo', in S. N. Eisenstadt and R. Lemarchand (eds.), *Political Clientelism, Patronage and Development* (London and Beverly Hills, Calif.: Sage, 1981).

—— 'Naples under the Left: The Limits of Local Change', in S. N. Eisenstadt and R. Lemarchand (eds.), *Political Clientelism, Patronage and Development* (London and Beverly Hills, Calif.: Sage, 1981).

CLARKE, J. J., *The Local Government of the United Kingdom* (London: Pitman, 1939).

CLEGG, T., 'Spain', in E. C. Page and M. Goldsmith (eds.), *Central and Local Government Relations: A Comparative Analysis of West European Unitary States* (London and Beverly Hills, Calif.: Sage, 1987).

Committee of Inquiry into the Conduct of Local Authority Business, *Report*, Cmnd. 9797 (London: HMSO, 1986).

Council of Europe, 'Council of Europe Study Session on Local and Regional Authorities in Europe No. 13 Vol. II. The Financial Structures of Local and Regional Authorities in Europe', (Strasbourg: Council of Europe, 1976).

CRAIG, C., 'COSLA: A Silent Voice for Local Government', in H. M. Drucker and N. L. Drucker (eds.), *The Scottish Government Yearbook 1981* (Edinburgh: Paul Harris, 1980).

CROZIER, M., *The Bureaucratic Phenomenon* (London: Tavistock, 1964).

—— *La Société bloquée* (Paris: Le Seuil, 1970).

—— *et al.*, *Où va l'administration française?* (Paris: Éditions d'Organisation, 1974).

DAHL, R. A., 'The City in the Future of Democracy', *American Political Science Review*, 67 (1961), 953–70.

DALLOZ, *Droit administratif* (13th edn; Paris: Dalloz, 1975).

DAVEY, K. J., 'Local Autonomy and Independent Revenues', *Public Administration*, 49 (1971), 45–50.

DEARLOVE, J., *The Politics of Policy in Local Government* (London: Cambridge University Press, 1973).

DENTE, B., 'Centre–Local Relations in Italy', in Y. Mény and V. Wright (eds.), *Centre-Periphery Relations in Western Europe* (London: Allen & Unwin, 1985).

—— 'Intergovernmental Relations and Central Control Policies: The Case of Italian Local Finance', *Environment and Planning C: Government and Policy*, 3 (1985), 383–402.

—— 'Local Government Reform and Legitimacy', in B. Dente and F. Kjellberg (eds.), *The Dynamics of Institutional Change* (London and Beverly Hills, Calif.: Sage, 1988).

DERRY, T. K., *A History of Modern Norway 1814–1972* (Oxford: Clarendon Press, 1973).

DREYFUS, F., and D'ARCY, F., *Les Institutions politiques et administratives de la France* (Paris: Economica, 1985), 346.

DUPUY, F., and THOENIG, J.-C., *Sociologie de l'administration française* (Paris: Armand Colin, 1983).

DWORKIN, R. M., *Taking Rights Seriously* (London: Duckworth, 1977).

ECKSTEIN, H., *Pressure Group Politics: The Case of the BMA* (London: Allen & Unwin, 1960).

EKMAN, E., 'The Danish Royal Law of 1665', *Journal of Modern History*, 29 (1957), 102–11.

ELDER, N., THOMAS, A. J., and ARTER, D., *The Consensual Democracies? The Government and Politics of the Scandinavian States* (Oxford: Martin Robertson, 1982).

FAURE, M., *Les Paysans et la politique dans la société française* (Paris: Armand Colin, 1966).

FAUVET, J., and MENDRAS, H. (eds.), *Les Paysans et la politique dans la France contemporaine* (Paris: Armand Colin, 1958).

FEVOLDEN, T., and SORENSEN, R., 'Norway', in E. C. Page and M. Goldsmith (eds.), *Central and Local Government Relations: A Comparative Analysis of West European Unitary States* (London and Beverly Hills, Calif.: Sage, 1987).

FINER, H., *English Local Government* (4th edn.; London: Methuen, 1950).

FRIED, R. C., *The Italian Prefects: A Study in Administrative Politics* (New Haven, Conn., and London: Yale University Press, 1963).

—— *Planning the Eternal City: Roman Politics and Planning since World War II* (New Haven, Conn.: Yale University Press, 1973).

FURLONG, P. F. 'Policy Elites and Public Administration in Italy', Paper prepared for the European Consortium for Political Research Joint Sessions, Rimini, 1988.

GARRAUD, P., *Profession: homme politique. La carrière politique des maires urbains* (Paris: L'Harmattan, 1989).

GNEIST, R. VON, *History of the English Constitution* (London: Clowes, 1891).

GOLDSMITH, M. J., *Politics, Planning and the City* (London: Hutchinson, 1980).

—— and PAGE, E. C., 'Britain' in E. C. Page and M. Goldsmith (eds.), *Central and Local Government Relations: A Comparative Analysis of West European Unitary States* (London and Beverly Hills, Calif.: Sage, 1987).

GOUREVITCH, P. A., *Paris and the Provinces: The Politics of Local and Regional Reform in France* (London: Allen & Unwin, 1980).

GREENSTONE, J. D., and PETERSON, P. E., *Race and Authority in Urban Politics: Community Participation and the War on Poverty* (New York: Russell Sage Foundation, 1973).

GREENWOOD, R., 'Pressures from Whitehall', in R. Rose and E. C. Page (eds.), *Fiscal Stress in Cities* (London: Cambridge University Press, 1982).

GRÉMION, P., *Le Pouvoir périphérique* (Paris: Éditions du Seuil, 1976).

GRICE, J. W. *National and Local Finance* (London: D. S. King, 1910).

GRIFFITH, E. S., *The Development of Modern City Government*, 2 vols. (Oxford: Oxford University Press, 1927).

GRUDER, V. R., *The Royal Provincial Intendants* (Ithaca, NY: Cornell University Press, 1968).

GUNLICKS, A. B., *Local Government in the German Federal System* (Durham, NC: Duke University Press, 1986).

GUTCHEN, R. M., 'Local Improvements and Centralisation in Nineteenth Century England', *Historical Journal*, 4 (1961), 85–96.

HAIDER, D. H., *When Governments Come to Washington: Mayors, Governors and Intergovernmetal Lobbying* (New York: Free Press, 1974).

HAM, C., *Health Policy in Britain* (London: Macmillan, 1985).

HAMPTON, W., *Democracy and Community: A Study of Politics in Sheffield* (London: Oxford University Press, 1970).

HANF, K., and SCHARPF, F. W. (eds.) *Interorganizational Policy Making* (London and Beverly Hills, Calif.: Sage, 1978).

HANSEN, T., and NEWTON, K., 'Voluntary Organizations and Community Politics: Norwegian and British Comparisons', *Scandinavian Political Studies*, 8 (1985), 1–21.

HARDER, E., *Local Government in Denmark* (Copenhagen: Det Danske Selskab, 1973).

HARGREAVES–MAWDSLEY, W. N. *Eighteenth Century Spain 1700–1788: A Political, Diplomatic and Institutional History* (London: Macmillan, 1979).

HEALD, D., *Public Expenditure* (Oxford: Martin Robertson, 1983).

HEBBERT, M., 'Regionalism: A Reform Concept and its Application to Spain', *Environment and Planning C: Government and Policy*, 5 (1987), 239–50.

HEPWORTH, N. P., *The Finance of Local Government* (4th edn.; London: Allen & Unwin, 1984).

HERLITZ, N., *Elements of Nordic Public Law* (Stockholm: Norstedt, 1969).

HEYWOOD, P., 'Mirror Images: The PCE and the PSOE in the Transition to Democracy in Spain', *West European Politics*, 10 (1987), 193–210.

HILL, D. M., *Democratic Theory and Local Government* (London: Allen & Unwin, 1974).

HINTZE, O., *Staat und Verfassung: Gessammelte Abhandlungen zur allgemeinen Verfassungsgeschichte*, ed. G. Oestreich (Göttingen: Vandenhoeck and Ruprecht, 1962).

—— *The Historical Essays of Otto Hintze*, ed. and trans. F. Gilbert (New York: Oxford University Press, 1975).

HOOD, C. C. 'The Machinery of Government Problem', *Studies in Public Policy*, 28 (Glasgow: University of Strathclyde, 1979).

HOOGEWERF, A., 'Les Pays–Bas', in Y. Mény (ed.), *La Réforme des collectivités locales en Europe: Stratégies et résultats* (Paris: La Documentation Française, 1984).

HOVDE, B. J., *The Scandinavian Countries 1720–1865*, 2 vols. (Port Washington, NY: Kennikat Press, 1943).

HUMES, S., and MARTIN, E., *The Structure of Local Governments throughout the World* (The Hague: International Union of Local Authorities, 1961).

—— —— *The Structure of Local Government throughout the World* (The Hague: International Union of Local Authorities, 1969).

ISAAC–HENRY, K., 'Local Authority Associations and Local Government Reform', *Public Administration Bulletin*, 33 (Aug. 1980), 21–41.

JONES, B. D. *Governing Urban America: A Policy Focus* (Boston: Little Brown, 1983).

KAISER, F., '1862 ars kommunalforordningar', in Svenska Landstingsforbundet, *Hundra ar under Kommunalforfattningarna 1862–1962* (Stockholm: Svenska Stadsförbundet, 1962).

KARNIG, A., 'Private Regarding Policy, Civil Rights Groups and the Mediating Impacts of Municipal Reforms', *American Journal of Political Science*, 19 (1975), 91–106.

KEATING, M., 'Does Regional Government Matter? The Experience of Italy, France and Spain', *Governance*, 1/2 (1988), 200.

KELSEN, H., *General Theory of Law and State* (Cambridge, Mass.: Harvard University Press, 1949).

KENNY, M., *A Spanish Tapestry: Town and Country in Castile* (London: Cohen & West, 1961).

KESSELMAN, M., *The Ambiguous Consensus* (New York: Knopf, 1967).

KING, D., *Fiscal Tiers: The Economics of Multi–Level Government* (London: Allen & Unwin, 1984).

KING, R. L., 'Regional Government: The Italian Experience', *Environment and Planning C: Government and Policy*, 5 (1987), 327–46.

KJELLBERG, F., *Political Institutionalisation: A Political Study of Two Sardinian Communities* (London and New York: Wiley, 1975).

—— 'A Comparative View of Municipal Decentralisation: Neighbourhood Democracy in Oslo and Bologna', in L. J. Sharpe (ed.), *Decentralist Trends in Western Democracies* (London and Beverly Hills, Calif.: Sage, 1979).

—— 'Local Government and the Scandinavian Welfare State: Structural and Functional Reforms in Denmark, Norway and Sweden since 1945', Colloquium on the Reforms of Local and Regional Authorities in Europe, Council of Europe, Linz, 5–6 Nov. 1981.

—— 'Local Government Reorganisation and the Welfare State', *Journal of Public Policy*, 5 (1985), 215–40.

KOBIELSKI, J., 'L'Influence de la structure des communes urbaines sur leurs dépenses de fonctionnement' (Rennes: Université de Rennes Laboratoire d'Économie des Villes et des Collectivités, 1975).

KOCHEN, M., and DEUTSCH, K., *Decentralization* (Cambridge, Mass.: Oelgeschlager, Gunn, and Hain, 1980).

LANE, J.-E., and MAGNUSSON, T., 'Sweden', in E. C. Page and M. Goldsmith (eds.), *Central and Local Government Relations: A Comparative Analysis of West European Unitary States* (London and Beverly Hills, Calif.: Sage, 1987).

——, ——, and WESTLUND, A., 'Kommunernas byråkratisering', *Tväsnitt* 2 (1982), pp. 20–30.

LAURENS, A., *Le Métire politique ou la conquête du pouvoir* (Paris: Éditions Alain Moureau, 1980).

LEACH, S., *et al.*, *The Political Organization of Local Authorities: Committee of Inquiry into the Conduct of Local Authority Business Research*, i, Cmnd. 9797 (London: HMSO, 1986).

LE CLÈRE, B., and WRIGHT, V., *Les Préfets du Second Empire* (Paris: Armand Colin, 1973).

LE GRAND, J., *A Strategy of Equality* (London: Allen & Unwin, 1982).

LEVY, F., MELTSNER, A., and WILDAVSKY, A., *Urban Outcomes* (Berkeley, Calif.: University of California Press, 1974).

LINDSAY, J. O., 'The Social Classes and the Foundations of States', in J. O. Lindsay (ed.), *New Cambridge Modern History of Europe*, vii: *The Old Regime* (Cambridge: Cambridge University Press, 1957).

LINEBERRY, R. L., and FOWLER, E. P., 'Reformism and Public Policies in American Cities', *American Political Science Review*, 61 (1967), 701–16.

LINZ, J., 'The New Spanish Party System', in R. Rose (ed.), *Electoral Participation: A Comparative Analysis* (London and Beverly Hills, Calif.: Sage, 1980), 125.

LLANDI, G., and POTENZE, G., *Manuale di diritto amministrativo* (Milan: Giuffre, 1974).

Local Government and Housing Act 1989 C 42 (London: HMSO, 1989).

LOWI, T. J., 'American Business and Public Policies: Case Studies and Political Theory', *World Politics*, 16/4 (1966), 677–715.

LYNN, J., and JAY, A., *Yes Minister: The Diaries of a Cabinet Minister*, iii (London: British Broadcasting Corporation, 1983).

MACKENZIE, R. T., *Political Parties* (2nd edn.; London: Heinemann, 1963).

MACKENZIE, W. J. M., 'The Conventions of Local Government', *Public Administration*, 29 (1951), 345–56.

—— 'Local Government in Parliament', *Public Administration*, 32 (1954), 409–23.

MARAVALL, J. M., 'The Socialist Alternative: The Policies and Electorate of the PSOE', in H. Penniman (ed.), *Spain at the Polls 1977, 1979 and 1982* (Washington, DC: American Enterprise Institute, 1985).

MARTIN HARLOFF, E., *The Structure of Local Government in Europe* (The Hague: International Union of Local Authorities, 1987).

MÉDARD, J.-F., 'Political Clientelism in France: The Centre–Periphery Nexus Reexamined', in S. N. Eisenstadt and R. Lemarchand (eds.), *Political Clientelism, Patronage and Development* (London and Beverly Hills, Calif.: Sage, 1981).

MEDHURST, K. N., *Government in Spain: The Executive at Work* (Oxford: Pergamon, 1973).

MÉNY, Y., *Centralisation et décentralisation dans le débat politique français* (Paris: Librairie Générale de Droit et de Jurisprudence, 1974).

—— 'Financial Transfers and Local Government in France: National Policy Despite 36,000 Communes', in D. E. Ashford (ed.), *Financing Local Government in the Welfare State* (London: Croom Helm, 1980).

—— 'Le Maire ici et ailleurs', *Pouvoirs*, 14 (1983), 19–28.

—— 'France', in E. C. Page and M. Goldsmith (eds.), *Central and Local Government Relations: A Comparative Analysis of West European Unitary States* (London and Beverly Hills, Calif.: Sage, 1987).

MÉNY, Y., 'Radical Reforms and Marginal Change: The French Socialist Experience', in B. Dente and F. Kjellberg (eds.), *The Dynamics of Institutional Change: Local Government Reorganization in Western Democracies* (London and Beverly Hills, Calif.: Sage, 1988).

—— and Wright, V. (eds.), *Centre Periphery Relations in Western Europe* (London: Allen & Unwin, 1985).

MEYERS, G. G., 'Villeneuve: A Communtiy Study in French Political Subculture and Public Policy', Ph.D. thesis, Stanford University, Calif., 1982.

MILLER T., 'The Emergence of Participatory Ideas on Swedish Planning and Local Government', *Scandinavian Political Studies*, 2 (1979), 313–32.

MLADENKA, K., and HILL, K., 'The Distribution of Urban Police Services', *Journal of Politics*, 40 (1978), 112–33.

MOLIN, B., MANSSON, L., and STRÖMBERG, L., *Offentlig förvaltning* (Stockholm: Bonnies, 1975), 178–81.

MONTAGU–HARRIS, G., *Local Government in Many Lands* (London: D. S. King, 1933).

—— *Comparative Local Government* (London and New York: Hutchinson, 1949).

MOURITZEN, P. E., and NIELSEN, K. H., *Handbook of Comparative Urban Fiscal Data* (Odense: Dansk Data Arkiv, 1988).

—— and NARVER, B. J., 'Fiscal Stress in Local Government: The Danish and American Cases', in T. N. Clark (ed.), *Research in Urban Policy* ii: 1986 (Greenwich, Conn.: JAI Press, 1986).

MOUSNIER, R., *État et société en France au XVIIe et XVIIIe siècles: Le gouvernement et le corps.* (Paris: Centre de Documentation Universitaire, 1968).

MUGHAN, A., 'Belgium: All Periphery and No Centre?', in Y. Mény and V. Wright (eds.), *Centre Periphery Relations in Western Europe* (London: Allen & Unwin, 1985).

NAMIER, L. B., *The Structure of Politics at the Accession of George III* (London: Macmillan, 1929).

NANETTI, R. Y., *Growth and Territorial Policies: The Italian Model of Social Capitalism* (London: Frances Pinter, 1988).

National Association of Local Authorities in Denmark, *Economic and Political Trends in Danish Local Government* (Copenhagen: National Association of Local Authorities in Denmark, 1981).

NEVERS, J.-Y., 'Du clientèlisme à la technocratie: cent ans de démocratie dans une grande ville, Toulouse', *Revue française de Science Politique*, 33 (1983), 428–54.

NEWTON, K., *Second City Politics* (Oxford: Oxford University Press, 1976).

—— *Balancing the Books: The Fiscal problems of Local Government in Western Europe* (London and Beverly Hills, Calif.: Sage, 1980).

Organization for Economic Co-operation and Development, *National Accounts for OECD Countries* (Paris: OECD, 1987).

PAGE, E. C., 'The New Gift Relationship: Are Central Government Grants Only Good for the Soul?', *Public Administration Bulletin*, 36 (1981), 37–52.

—— 'Grant Consolidation and the Development of Intergovernmental Relations in the United States and the United Kingdom', *Politics*, 1/1 (1981), 19–24.

—— 'The Value of Local Autonomy', *Local Government Studies*, 8/4 (1982), 21–42.

—— 'Laws and Orders in Central–Local Government Relations' (Glasgow: University of Strathclyde Studies in Public Policy, No. 106, 1983).

—— 'The Marginalisation of Local Political Elites in Britain', *Environment and Planning C: Government and Policy*, 2 (1984), 167–76.

—— *Political Authority and Bureaucratic Power: A Comparative Analysis* (Brighton: Wheatsheaf Books, 1985).

—— 'The Political Origins of Bureaucracy and Self–Government: Otto Hintze's Conceptual Map of Europe', *Political Studies*, 31/1 (1990), 39–55.

—— and GOLDSMITH, M. J., (eds.), *Central and Local Government Relations: A Comparative Analysis of West European Unitary States* (London and Beverly Hills, Calif.: Sage, 1987).

PETERSON, P. E., *City Limits* (Chicago: University of Chicago Press, 1981).

PITT-RIVERS, J. A., *People of the Sierra* (London: Weidenfeld & Nicolson, 1954).

POLA, G., 'Recent Developments of Central–Local Financial Relations in Italy', *Environment and Planning C: Government and Policy*, 4 (1986), 187–98.

RATTSØ, J., 'Local Government Allocation of Labour and the Grant System. An Applied Model Analysis of Local Government Behaviour in Norway', *Environment and Planning: C. Government and Policy*, 7/3 (1989), 273–84.

REISSERT, B., 'Federal and State Transfers to Local Government in the Federal Republic of Germany: A Case of Political Immobility', in D. E. Ashford (ed.), *Financing Local Government in the Welfare State* (London: Croom Helm, 1980).

RHODES, G., *Central–Local Relations: The Experience of the Environmental Health and Trading Standards Services* (London: Royal Institute of Public Administration, 1986).

RHODES R. A. W., *Control and Power in Central–Local Government Relations* (Aldershot: Gower, 1981).

—— *The National World of Local Government* (London: Allen & Unwin, 1986).

RHODES, R. A. W., *Beyond Westminster and Whitehall: The Sub-Central Governments of Britain*: (London: Hyman Unwin, 1988).

—— *et al.*, 'Corporate Bias in Central–Local Relations', SSRC Central–Local Relations Discussion Paper (Colchester: University of Essex Department of Government, 1982).

RIDLEY, F. F., 'Integrated Decentralization: Models of the Prefectoral System', *Political Studies*, 21 (1973), 13–25.

ROBERTS M., 'Sweden' in A. Goodwin (ed.), *The European Nobility in the Eighteenth Century* (London: Adam and Charles Black, 1953).

ROKKAN, S., *Citizens, Electors, Parties* (Oslo: Universitetsforlaget, 1970).

ROSE, R., *Do Parties Make a Difference?* (2nd edn., London: Macmillan, 1984).

—— *et al.*, *Public Employment in Western Nations* (Cambridge: Cambridge University Press, 1985).

ROSÉN, J., 'Scandinavia and the Baltic', in *The New Cambridge Modern History: The Ascendancy of France 1648–1688* (London: Cambridge University Press, 1981).

ROSS, C., *Local Government in the Soviet Union* (London: Croom Helm, 1987).

Royal Commission on Local Government in England, *Report*, Cmnd. 4040 (London: HMSO, 1969).

RUSH, M., *The Selection of Parliamentary Candidates* (London: Nelson, 1969).

SACKS, P. M., *The Donegal Mafia: An Irish Political Machine* (New Haven, Conn.: Yale University Press, 1976).

SANCHO J. R. L. 'The Autonomous Communities: Politics and Economics', *Environment and Planning C: Government and Policy*, 5 (1987), 251–7.

SANTANTONIO, E., 'Italy', in E. C. Page and M. J. Goldsmith (eds.), *Central and Local Government Relations: A Comparative Analysis of West European Unitary States* (London and Beverly Hills, Calif.: Sage, 1987).

SARTORI, G., 'Concept Misformation in Comparative Politics', *American Political Science Review*, 64 (1970), 1033–53.

SAUNDERS, P., 'Rethinking Local Politics', in M. Boddy and C. Fudge (eds.) *Local Socialism* (London: Macmillan, 1984).

SCHATTSCHNEIDER, E. E., *The Semi-Sovereign People* (New York: Holt, Rinehart, and Winston, 1960).

SCHMIDT, V. A., 'Unblocking Society by Decree: The Impact of Governmental Decentralization in France' *Comparative Politics*, 22/4 (1990), 459–81.

SHARPE, L. J., 'Theories and Values of Local Government', *Political Studies*, 18/2 (1970), 153–74.

—— 'Reforming the Grass Roots: An Alternative Analysis', in D. E. Butler and A. H. Halsey (eds.), *Policy and Politics* (London: Macmillan, 1978).

—— (ed.), *The Local Fiscal Crisis in Western Europe* (London and Beverly Hills, Calif.: Sage, 1981).

—— 'Is There a Fiscal Crisis in European Local Government?', in L. J. Sharpe (ed.), *The Local Fiscal Crisis in Western Europe* (London and Beverly Hills, Calif.: Sage, 1981).

—— 'Local Government Reorganisation: General Theory and United Kingdom Practice', in B. Dente and F. Kjellberg (eds.), *The Dynamics of Institutional Change* (London and Beverly Hills, Calif.: Sage, 1988).

SHAW, A., *Municipal Government in Continental Europe* (New York: The Century Co., 1895).

SHEFTER, M. 'Patronage and its Opponents: A Theory and some European Cases', Cornell University Western Societies Program Occasional Papers No. 8 (1977).

SMALLWOOD, F., *Greater London: The Politics of Metropolitan Reform* (Indianapolis, New York, and Kansas City: Bobbs Merrill, 1965).

SMELLIE, K. B., *A History of Local Government* (4th edn., London: Allen & Unwin, 1969).

SMITH, B. C., 'Approaches to the Measurement of Decentralisation', *International Review of Administrative Sciences*, 3 (1979), 214–22.

—— *Decentralisation: The Territorial Dimension of the State* (London: Allen & Unwin, 1985).

SORBETS, C., 'Est–il légitime de parler d'une présidentialisme municipale?', *Pouvoirs*, 24 (1983) 19–28.

STEWART, J. D., *Local Government: The Conditions of Local Choice* (London: Allen & Unwin, 1983).

STRÖMBERG, L., and WESTERSTAHL, J., *The New Swedish Communes: A Survey of Local Government Research* (Lerum: Lerums Boktrykeri AB, 1984).

SULEIMAN, E. N., *Politics Power and Bureaucracy in France: The Administrative Elite* (Princeton, NJ: Princeton University Press,1974).

SWANN, B., 'Local Initiative and Central Control: The Insulin Decision', *Policy and Politics*, 1 (1972), 55–63.

TAAFE, P., and MULHEARN T., *Liverpool: The City that Dared to Fight* (London: Fortress Books, 1988).

TARROW, S., *Peasant Communism in Southern Italy* (New Haven, Conn.: Yale University Press, 1967).

—— *Between Center and Periphery: Grassroots Politicians* in Italy and France (New Haven, Conn.: Yale University Press, 1977).

—— 'Introduction', in S. Tarrow, P. J. Katzenstein, and L. Graziano (eds.), *Territorial Politics in Industrial Nations* (New York: Praeger, 1978).

TERRAZZONI, A., *La Décentralisation à l'epreuve des faits* (Paris: Librairie Générale de Droit et de Jurisprudence, 1987).

THOENIG, J.-C., *L'Ère des technocrates* (Paris: Éditions d'Organisation, 1973).

THOENIG, J.-C. 'State Bureaucracies and Local Government in France', in K. Hanf and F. W. Scharpf (eds.), *Interorganizational Policy Making* (London: Sage, 1978).

—— 'Local Subsidies in the Third Republic', in D. E. Ashford (ed.), *Financing Local Government in the Welfare State* (London: Croom Helm, 1980).

TOCQUEVILLE, A. DE, *The Ancien Regime and the Revolution* (Oxford: Blackwell, 1949).

TUDESQ, A. J., 'De la monarchie à la Republique: le maire petit ou grand notable', *Pouvoirs*, 24 (1983), 5–18.

United States Advisory Commission on Intergovernmental Relations, *State and Local Roles in the Federal System* (A–88) (Washington, DC: Government Printing Office, 1982).

—— *The Question of State Government Capability* (A–98) (Washington, DC: US Government Printing Office, 1985).

VERNEY, D. V., *Parliamentary Reform in Sweden* (Oxford: Clarendon Press, 1957).

VIOLLET, P., *Histoire des Institutions politiques et administratives de la France*, iv: *Le Roi et ses ministres pendant les trois derniers siècles de la monarchie* (Darmstadt: Scientia Verlag, 1966; repr. of 1912 edition).

WATERBURY, J., 'An Attempt to put Patrons and Clients in their Place', in E. Gellner and J. Waterbury (eds.), *Patrons and Clients in Mediterranean Societe*: (London: Duckworth, 1977).

WEBB, S., and WEBB, B., *English Local Government from the Revolution to the Municipal Corporations Act: The Parish and the County* (London: Frank Cass, 1924), 279.

—— —— *The Story of the King's Highway* (London: Frank Cass, 1963).

WEINGROD, A., 'Patronage and Power', in E. Gellner and J. Waterbury (eds.), *Patrons and Clients in Mediterranean Societies* (London: Duckworth, 1977).

WHITE, C., *Patrons and Partisans: A Study of Politics in Two Southern Italian Comuni* (Cambridge: Cambridge University Press, 1980).

WILLIAMS, P. M., *Crisis and Compromise: Politics in the Fourth Republic* (3rd edn., London: Longmans, Green and Co., 1964).

WOLMAN, H., and GOLDSMITH, M. J. 'Local Government Fiscal Behaviour in a Period of Slow National Growth: A Comparative Analysis', *Environment and Planning C: Government and Policy*, 5/2 (1987), 171–82.

—— and PAGE, E. C., 'The Impact of Intergovernmental Grants on Subnational Resource Disparities', *Public Budgeting and Finance*, 7 (1987), 82–98.

WOOD, B., *The Process of Local Government Reform 1966–74* (London: Allen & Unwin, 1976).

WORMS, J.-P., 'Le Prefet et ses notables', *Sociologie du travail*, 3 (1966), 249–75.

WRIGHT, D. S., *Understanding Intergovernmental Relations* (2nd edn., Monterey, Calif: Brooks Cole, 1982).

WYLIE, L., *Village in the Vaucluse: An Account of Life in a French Village* (New York: Harper & Row, 1957).

ZUCKERMAN, A., 'Clientelistic Politics in Italy', in E. Gellner and J. Waterbury (eds.), *Patrons and Clients in Mediterranean Societies* (London: Duckworth, 1977).

—— *The Politics of Faction: Christian Democratic Rule in Italy* (New Haven, Conn., and London: Yale University Press, 1979).

Index